ISBN 978-1-934013-02-1

The Pose Method of Triathlon Techniques

For information, contact: Pose Tech Press™,
1825 Ponce de Leon Blvd., #460, Coral Gables, FL 33134, or e-mail: info@posetech.com.

For info about Certified Pose Coaches and Pose Method® Clinics, call 877-POSE-TEC or visit our website at: www.posetech.com.

Concept: Nicholas Romanov, Ph.D.
Text: Nicholas Romanov, Ph.D. with John Robson
Editing: Svetlana Romanov, Ph.D., Severin Romanov
Cover Design: Lana Romanov
Cover Photography: Kip Grossman, Francisco Guzman, Nicholas Romanov, Ph.D., Graham Fletcher

Book Photography: Kip Grossman
Illustrations: Andrey Pianzin, Ph.D.
Book Design: Severin Romanov

Logo Design: Severin Romanov, Andrey Pianzin, Ph.D., Lana Romanov

Published by Pose Tech Press

Library of Congress Catalog Number   2008925520

Printed in the United States of America

NICHOLAS ROMANOV, PH.D.

THE POSE METHOD® OF TRIATHLON TECHNIQUES

A NEW PARADIGM IN TRIATHLON

To my priceless family: Svetlana, Marianna, Svetlana Jr.,
Severin, Nicholas Jr., and Sophia.

TABLE OF CONTENTS

ACKNOWLEDGEMENTS

It has been a long journey getting here, but nothing worthwhile is ever easy. The book is finally finished! It would have never come together without the efforts of my family, colleagues, and friends who worked around the clock on this project with me. I owe a debt of gratitude to these essential people in my life without whom this would have never resulted in a fruitful finish.

Without the belief and relentless will power of my wife Svetlana, spirit of my daughter Marianna, creativity and passion of my daughter Lana and son Severin, and heart warming support of my son Nicky and granddaughter Sophia, this book would not be in your hands today.

I am pleased that a brilliant journalist and my good friend, John Robson, applied his talent to make this book a light read and a real page–turner while still preserving the science and essence of the Pose Method.

I would like to express my gratitude for the extraordinary illustrations, design, and life–long support of a dear friend of mine, Dr. Andrei Pianzin.

I would like to thank my friend and colleague, Dr. Graham Fletcher, for his tremendous work in organizing and conducting several scientific studies in different countries to provide the Pose Method with valuable scientific backing and his personal long standing support of myself, my ideas, and his loyal friendship.

I am grateful to my friends and colleagues, Lynn McFadden, Connie Sol, and Debbie Savage, for their valuable input into my work on the book as well as their warm friendship.

I would like to extend my appreciation to my student and friend, Arturo Garza, elite triathlete and Mexican National team member, who exemplified responsibility and courage to learn and successfully implement the Pose Method into his training and racing performance.

It is difficult to name everyone who made, in one way or another, contributions to this project, but among those valuable people are Cyle Sage, Pat Manochia, and Jim Woodman who have supported me from the beginning of my career and continue to do so today. Other invaluable individuals include PoseTech® coaches and my friends, Michael Collins, Claudia Rivera, Francisco Guzman, and many others, with whom I shared my ideas.

Many thanks to my students and clinic attendees who had the foresight and courage to make a blind leap of faith to trust my ideas and change their understanding and perception of movement.

Yes, the book is out and you are entering into a different field of movement, which I call the Pose Method. Most importantly, I am grateful to you for your desire to discover this new world of movement with me.

Dr. Romanov

FOREWORD

By: Graham Fletcher, Ph.D. of Sport Biomechanics

Why should you read this book of many written on triathlon? Perhaps Dick Fosbury's words may help. "I was told over and over again that I would never be successful, that I was not going to be competitive and the technique was simply not going to work. All I could do was shrug and say 'We'll just have to see'." Dick Fosbury won an Olympic gold medal at the 1968 Mexico City Games after he invented a revolutionary high-jump technique, the Fosbury–flop.

When I first listened to Dr. Romanov explain Pose running to me, all I could think about was that this made perfect biomechanical sense and why had no one seen it before. I decided there and then to change the topic of my Ph.D. research and take up investigating Pose running. The Ph.D. research identified that all runners fall forwards via gravitational torque, supporting Dr. Romanov's theory.

Further, when I trained eight heel–toe runners in Pose running they improved their 1.5 mile time trial by an average of 25 seconds over one week. As in the case with Dick Fosbury, his method made biomechanical sense and improved his performance, therefore, what Dr. Romanov puts forwards in reference to swim, bike, and run technique should be similarly assessed; that technique should be evaluated according to the laws of physics and not whether it is new or different or does not conform to people's opinions.

The saying goes, "If you train like the rest, you will compete like the rest," however, this book is refreshingly different, giving you an opportunity to think and practice your sport from another perspective. This book may just revolutionise your training! Further, this book is not just about swim, bike and run technique, but about movement in general.

Dr. Romanov has developed these techniques based upon an underlying theoretical principle that one's body weight creates motion by moving from balance to imbalance and how well we do this determines how well we move and perform. I thoroughly recommend this book to you as one who has researched Dr. Romanov's ideas and seen them at work in elite athletes' Olympic preparation. I hope you enjoy reading the brilliant and refreshingly different perspective Dr. Romanov brings to movement as much as I have had over the last ten years.

Graham Fletcher, Ph.D. (Biomechanics)
Lecturer on Biomechanics, University College of Fraser Valley; Vancouver, Canada
Former British Triathlon National Team Coach

PREFACE

To know the movement of a body is to know the series of positions that it has occupied in space in a series of successive moments.

— *E.J. Marey*

The idea of this book has a long history, almost as long as the Pose Method itself. While the original concept of the Pose Method had its roots in the world of track and field, I saw from the beginning that the thoughts being developed had more universal applications.

All movements contain an infinite number of poses of different forms, but the poses that stood out to me also have another purpose; they serve the needs of energy transformation. Nature doesn't produce meaningless things. Everything has a purpose and where there is a beginning and an end there is energy transformation.

On Earth human movement (without the assistance of machines working on non-biological sources of energy) is governed by gravity, oxygen consumption and the mind. Within the context of this powerful trilogy, the Pose respectfully serves to shape and channel the transformation of energy of gravity, oxygen and the mind into a single "minded" system.

So the shape of Pose is a means of utilizing gravity, oxygen and the mind. There is a divine hierarchy derived from gravity, which literally keeps everything on Earth together from the air we breathe and the water we drink, to every last element of our living environment. Even the shape of the human body is designed to fit gravity and accommodate our movement inside the gravitational field. So the design of our muscles, bones and connective tissue has developed to fit these requirements of moving within a gravitational field as well.

In turn, our internal physiology system exists and functions in order to provide muscles with energy by consuming oxygen from the air and other products from the environment.

Our mind, with its main organ — the brain — and an incredible cellular network of a central and peripheral nervous system functions to bring everything together creating a complex creature called the human being.

Humans are capable of performing an incredible array of tasks on land, in the water and now, in space. Not only are we capable of performing these tasks, but we can perform them extremely well or extremely poorly.

The concept of Pose has always been to examine the physical tasks that humans desire to perform, break them down, analyze them and come up with unifying and uniform principles that allow us to get better and better at those tasks using just three things — gravity, oxygen and the mind.

With this book, I present the Pose Method as it applies to running, cycling and swimming. Three elements, three sports. One method. Enjoy.

SECTION I
INTRODUCTION

Drs. Svetlana & Nicholas Romanov.

CHAPTER 1
THE NECESSITY OF TRIATHLON TECHNIQUES

Necessity is the theme and the inventress,
the eternal curb and law of nature.

— *Leonardo da Vinci*

Endurance. Conditioning. Fortitude. Perseverance. Willpower.

When the word 'triathlon' is mentioned in polite conversation, the above qualities are most likely to be associated with the sport. With images of epic struggles on the lava fields of Hawaii seared into the collective subconscious, the popular view of the sport is that it is one prolonged exercise in prevailing against the odds and enduring massive suffering until the finish line is reached.

This is understandable since, with the exception of the avowed non–swimmers among us, almost everyone in the general population can run, ride a bicycle and swim — at some level. Most people see nothing particularly difficult in the disciplines involved; they see the challenge to be getting in good enough 'shape' to complete a triathlon, no matter the distance involved.

And, to be fair, that view is correct, if your only objective is to enter one race and finish it, say as the result of an ill considered bar bet. If your mouth has written a check that your body must now cash, it *is* a relatively simple matter to round up an old bike, invest six weeks or so in a 'training' program and struggle to the finish of a sprint distance triathlon.

To be sure, many are the committed triathletes who have come to the sport through just such a route. A funny thing can happen once you've got that first 'tri' under your belt. You suddenly start thinking about the next one — and how you can do it better. Probably the first thing that comes to mind is getting a better bike. After that, normal thoughts include new running shoes, perhaps joining a masters swim program and, of course, training harder.

Here's something else to add to the list: learn to run, ride and swim!

If that sounds a little counter intuitive — it's meant to be. As mentioned above, just about everyone can run, ride and swim, but relatively few do all three well. However, most people think of these as endurance sports, not skill sports, so the natural inclination is to just go out and start training without regard for improving one's technical abilities in the three sports.

Unless you happen to be unnaturally gifted in all three, this approach is a one way ticket to a dead–end. Certainly, your times will improve and you will get stronger, but by not investing the time and effort to learn the proper technique for each discipline, you'll put a rather low ceiling on exactly how good you can get.

Consider for a moment the fact that newcomers are drawn to triathlon from a variety of backgrounds. Some may already excel in one or two of the sports and have been told by friends that they should give triathlon a try. Others may be looking for a transition from team sports to an individual sport, so that they can participate on their own schedule, instead of having practices and games dictated to them. And still others may have no real sports background at all and are looking for a mid–life challenge and change of direction.

Whatever the motivation, it's obvious that virtually no one comes to the sport of triathlon with a high degree of technical skill in each sport. Now if triathlon were comprised of tennis, golf and archery, the obvious first step would be to seek out lessons to master the techniques of each one. But since most people think they already know how to run, ride and swim and since they don't regard running, cycling and swimming as skill sports, they skip that crucial first stage, even though they obviously aren't technically proficient in all three sports.

The results of jumping right into a triathlon training regimen without first developing the necessary sport–specific skills can range from frustration and stagnation to overuse injuries and complete abandonment of the sport. From a coaching or teaching standpoint, this creates a two–fold challenge. The first is to communicate to new triathletes that there is a distinct need to achieve technical skills in running, cycling and swimming. The second is to present a program for achieving these proficiencies in a way that is accessible, digestible and time–efficient.

While triathlon is regarded as a lifetime sport, it is also true that most new triathletes are in a hurry. They're excited about their new undertaking and probably have already selected their first 'target' event even before lacing up their shoes for their first training run. While it can take years to achieve true mastery in any one of these three sports, these 'newbies' are more concerned about crossing their first finish line than in engaging in any systematic approach to truly mastering the sports.

So, in order to get them to learn first, compete later, the system of instruction has to reduce the normal learning curve from 'years' to 'months' or even 'weeks'. That's a tall order, particularly when you're dealing with three distinctly different sets of movements that must be mastered. We're dealing with true *technique* here, which, as you might imagine comes from the Greek word 'techno' — the skill of doing.

The first step in embarking on a triathlon–learning program is to accept that running, cycling and swimming techniques require the same approach as any other highly technical sport. To get the right mental framework you have to understand the theory, concepts and rules of the related movements and to develop the proper images, perception, mental, psychological and biomechanical structure of those movements in their most efficient execution.

In developing a teaching program for any sport, we first define 'skill' as the ability to use all available resources to reach the desired goal. Achieving these skills requires the athlete to follow a system of drills to build the proper biomechanical movements and to correct errors in those movements against an existing standard. In short, the athlete has to think, feel and act in one logical way or system.

This system is based on the rather simple assumption that all movements in all sports — including running, cycling and swimming — consist of a series of positions or poses through which the athlete moves with every repetition. Essentially, if you are going to do the same thing over and over and over again, it makes sense to be able to do it perfectly.

More importantly, within these frames of repetitive movements, there are a few specific poses that affect the creation and flow of movement. Identifying these specific poses is the critical element in understanding and performing efficient movement. These *Pose* positions have distinctive and specific features (Fig.1.1) that are the key to becoming more skillful in your chosen sport.

is to develop the perception that allows the athlete to apply his body–weight quickly from Pose to Pose, from one support to the next, for each sport. Throughout this book, we will apply this logic to the three sports of triathlon and illustrate how the theory of the Pose Method is applied to achieve skillful movement.

Success in Triathlon = Skill Development

This book is based on the Pose Method, a unifying concept of learning and teaching movement, and is an attempt to provide real, measurable help for all triathletes, from beginners to elite Olympic level competitors. All these athletes are literally starving to improve their performance while avoiding injuries. It is our sincere hope that all will benefit from the techniques explained here and go on to achieve their goals in the sport.

Fig.1.1 Swim, Bike, & Run Poses.

The distinguishing feature and principal advantage of the *Pose* position is that from this position it is easiest to destroy balance and then change support. This is the basic rule that we apply to achieve skillful and efficient movement in all sports. The goal

While it is beyond dispute that the attributes listed at the start of this chapter — endurance, conditioning, fortitude, perseverance, and willpower — are absolute requirements to achieve your goals in triathlon, it is equally clear that they will only take you so far without mastery of the skills in each sport.

Roger Bannister, the first person to run a sub–four minute mile, was once asked what it took to achieve that feat, which had been considered humanly impossible. His answer was revealing (1), "It's the ability to take more out of yourself than you've got." With the skills to do all three sports and the mental toughness to break through your own limitations, you just might be able to take more out of yourself than you've got and succeed at mastering the sport of triathlon.

Reference:

1. Bannister, R. *The First Four Minutes*. Sutton Publishing, 2004.

SECTION II
CONCEPTS AND PRINCIPLES OF MOVEMENT

Dr. Romanov presents the Pose Method theory.

CHAPTER 2
GRAVITY

The starting point of motion is indivisible time, for it originates at the end point of the line of motion created by weight, the cause of thrust.
— Leonardo da Vinci

The constant and unyielding force of gravity has shaped human movement from time immemorial, but it was entered into the realm of scientific fact only about 400 years ago by the English genius Sir Isaac Newton (Fig.2.1). Courtesy of Newton's Earth shattering insights, gravity was recognized as a powerful force of the Universe, artfully moving all planetary bodies in the cosmos at incomprehensible speeds in ideal orbits with the orchestrated precision of a high tech mechanism.

"The earth upon which we are at rest is travelling round on its axis at the speed of 1,000 miles an hour, and revolving round the sun at the speed of 20 miles every second. Nor is this all. The entire solar system is moving within the local star system at the rate of 13 miles a second; the star system within the Milky Way at the rate of 200 miles a second; whilst the Milky Way is moving in relation to the remote external galaxies at the speed of 100 miles a second" (1). And all that impressive movement is powered by gravity.

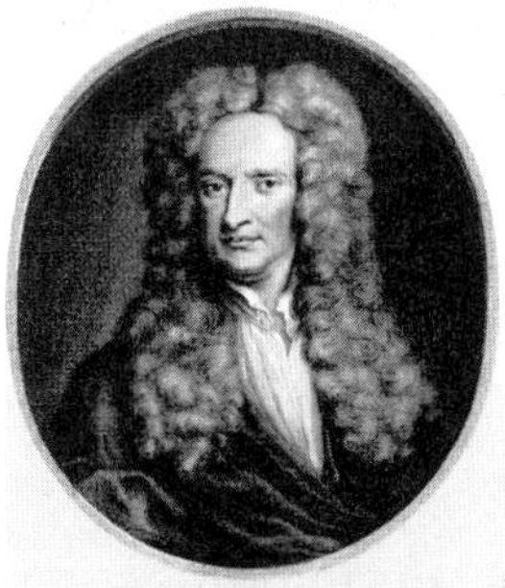

Fig.2.1 Newton's discovery of gravity and its application to human movement in sports has been largely overlooked by sports biomechanists throughout centuries.

Source: Wikipedia.org/Public Domain.

Here at home on Planet Earth, while we seem to be in a state of constant 'energy crisis,' gravity continues to be the most reliable source of power as it works non–stop 24 hours a day, seven days a week, never letting up for even a second. The Russian scientist and academic Peter Anokhin (Fig.2.2) puts it this way: *"The most essential characteristics of all biological systems are defined by the Universal Law of Gravity"* (2).

On Earth, gravity is the most valuable factor of life. Just try imagining life on Earth without gravity. Even abstract thinking would allow seeing undeniable chaos and horror in the absence of gravity.

Fig.2.2 Russian Academic Peter Anokhin made an astute observation about gravity and our relationship with it.

Source: Wikipedia.org/Public Domain.

This abstraction clearly shows that life, as we know it, is impossible without gravity. To start, we wouldn't be able to safely move on the surface of the earth without gravity because the first contact with the ground would send us speeding toward outer space. But that's okay, because without gravity, we wouldn't have an atmosphere... no air to breathe, no water to drink, no functioning biological systems at all.

The influence of gravity shapes and structures all living creatures (3), including human anatomical and physiological structure, size and weight. Human movement is a gravity–dependent function as was graphically demonstrated, when American astronaut Neil Armstrong took his historic 1969 moonwalk. Walking in an environment of diminished gravity is a considerably different activity than it is here on terra firma.

Leonardo da Vinci (Fig.2.3) was the first to recognise gravity as a propulsive force,

Fig.2.3 Leonardo da Vinci, the first to recognise gravity as a propulsive force in movement on Earth.

Source: Wikipedia.org/ Public Domain.

when he wrote that *"motion is created by the destruction of balance, that is, of equality of weight for nothing can move by itself which does not leave its state of balance and that thing moves most rapidly which is furthest from its balance"* (4).

A mere 400 years later Thomas Graham–Brown (Fig.2.4) expanded on da Vinci's thoughts, writing, *"It seems to me that the act of progression itself — whether it be by flight through the air or by such movements as running over the surface of the ground — consists essentially in a movement in which the centre of gravity of the body is allowed to fall forwards and downwards under the action of gravity, and in which the momentum thus gained is used in driving the centre of gravity again upwards and forwards; so that, from one point in the cycle to the corresponding point in the next, no work is done (theoretically), but the mass of the individual is, in effect, moved horizontally through the environment"* (5).

Fig.2.4 Thomas Graham-Brown expanded on da Vinci's observations, defining movement on Earth as essentially allowing the centre of gravity to fall forwards and downwards under the action of gravity.

Source: Wikipedia.org/Public Domain.

With these thoughts in mind, gravity must be considered as the dominant force on Earth, the strongest mechanical force among all the forces of nature, a force so constant and omnipresent that its attractive pull can never be cancelled out. Therefore any movement on Earth is both influenced by, and subordinate to, gravity. In order to study and improve any form of human movement, we must begin by understanding gravity and using its force to develop the most efficient forms of locomotion possible. Thus, gravity will be the unifying theme underpinning all the techniques discussed, as we seek to improve your performance in the three disciplines that constitute the sport of triathlon.

References:

1. Pears Cyclopaedia, A & F. Pears Limited, Isleworth, Middlesex, 1956, p. 163.

2. Anokhin, P. K. Selected works. *Philosophical aspects of the Functional System Theory.* Nauka. M. Publications (In Russian), 1978, pp. 27–48.

3. Bejan, A. *Shape and Structure, from Engineering to Nature.* Cambridge University Press, 2000.

4. Keele, K.D. *Leonardo da Vinci's elements of the science of man.* New York: Academic Press, 1983, p. 173.

5. Graham–Brown, T. *Note upon some dynamic principles involved in progression.* British Medical Journal, 1912, pp. 875–876.

CHAPTER 3
SUPPORT, MOVEMENT, ACTION
THE TRILOGY OF CONCEPTS UNDERLYING TRIATHLON

And you thought triathlon was all about swimming, cycling and running!

Of course, those are the three activities that comprise the sport of triathlon, but the principles that lead to success in triathlon are the same as those that govern all human activity. While it is possible to achieve a measure of success in any sporting endeavor without truly comprehending how humans move their bodies from point 'A' to point 'B', the process of mastering these three sports will be made much easier by taking a small amount of time to consider and understand how we move.

Once you appreciate the fundamentals of movement, you will realize that for all their seeming differences, swimming, cycling and running are very similar means of human locomotion. In turn, you'll be able to transfer your skills from your 'best' sport to your 'worst' sport and become equally adept at all three.

In short, you can consider 'support' as your starting point; the place where you are composed, balanced and ready to translate your desires into action. While many of your peers may consider you *unbalanced* in your desires to become a triathlete, you ignore them and begin to move mentally and physically. The result is action, — the physical manifestation of your thoughts and desires, literally the first steps, pedal

rotations or strokes of your life as a triathlete.

Now, with your support, let's move on to the active life of a triathlete.

SUPPORT

Give me a place to stand and I will move the Earth.

— Archimedes

Fig.3.1 Support can enable a physical feat of unfathomable proportions — moving the Earth.

The concept of support merits special attention because it is critical for understanding the fundamental nature of movement. On the physical plane, the Archimedes quote (at the beginning of this section) accurately describes the relationship: a place to stand — support — can enable a physical feat of unfathomable proportions — moving the Earth (Fig.3.1). Certainly, if Archimedes could use support so effectively, then understanding the support concept could help propel you down the road a little bit more efficiently.

But there is more to support than just the simple balance of a physical object in relation to gravity. Support manifests itself every day and in every way. Like gravity, it is so omnipresent in our lives that we rarely discuss or ponder the subject. Yet, it has deep meanings that govern everything we do.

Support binds everything together. Ideas support ideas. People support people. Physical objects support other physical objects.

Newton's Law of Gravity — an idea about physical objects — was itself supported by Galileo's (Fig.3.2) ideas about Free Falling. Both thinkers faced much skepticism from their contemporaries, but their ideas, which supported each other, proved to be perceptive and enduring.

Fig.3.2 Gilileo Galilei was an Italian physicist and astronomer who proposed that falling bodies, regardless of size or mass would fall at the same rate under the constant pull of gravity.

Source: Wikipedia.org/Public Domain.

Similarly, as I have worked to articulate the ideas of the Pose Method, I have found support in Aristotle's ideas about the origin of movement in biological creatures.

In your daily life, you face a myriad of decisions. The support of friends, loved ones or experienced counselors may help you make the right choices and succeed in your efforts. Many may find your idea of becoming a triathlete to be folly, but you will gravitate toward, and draw strength from, those who support your decision. This is true, whether it is the daily support from your family that allows you the time to train or on race day, when the cheers of the fans lining the course actually help propel you on your way. Support is more than a physical relationship — it operates as well on the mental and spiritual levels, all of which can have a positive impact upon your efforts.

Within the human anatomy, the interdependence of our physiological functions also displays the role of support. The contraction of a muscle is supported by the central nervous system, the cardiovascular system and the respiratory system, but in turn, all three of those systems are stimulated, strengthened and developed by repeated muscular contractions. The result is a beneficial circle of support, where the entire human organism functions more efficiently through this interaction.

This support system allows the human body to move in the desired direction through muscular effort applied to body weight. Whether that weight is applied against another body or the ground itself, the body is transferred in space, relative to that object against which the weight is applied. Aristotle (Fig.3.3) expressed it like this: *"Now every continuous whole, one part of which is moved while the other remains at rest must, in order to be able to move as a whole while one part stands still, have in the place where both parts have opposed movements some common part which connects the moving parts with one another."*

Fig.3.3 Aristotle was a Greek philosopher who proposed that support is drawn from parts of the body that are at rest, as they provide support for those parts in motion.

Source: Wikipedia.org/Public Domain.

So... support is necessary to apply our body weight through which we can direct and apply our muscular effort. The *mass* of our body — that 'thing' that must be moved — only becomes *body weight,* when it is applied to another body, i.e. the ground, a floor or some other object. This other object stops your body's gravity–propelled free–falling downward movement and gives it a condition of relative rest. This is the manifestation of gravity — the force against which, and through which, all movement takes place. Until the human body is attached, however briefly, to another object, muscular efforts cannot be applied and the body's direction of movement cannot be changed.

Simply stated, we can't move unless we have something — support — against which force can be applied.

In running, the most fundamental of human movements, your body weight is applied to the ground through your foot,

which provides support for the body. At the same time, the ground provides support for the foot. Extending this logic, the leg, supported by the foot, in turn supports the trunk. At the same time, your muscles provide support for the "system" of your body as it passes over the support foot on the ground.

This uninterrupted interdependent chain of support continues even in the flight stage of running, when the body itself becomes the support, permitting the foot to be lifted from the ground. As soon as the next foot touches the ground, the cycle starts over again. Running really is nothing more than the rapid, controlled, alternation of support. Whenever this finely calibrated cycle of support is interrupted, running form immediately deteriorates.

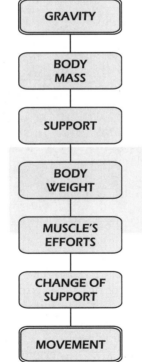

The diagram in the center (Fig.3.4) details how support is channeled in the running motion.

As the diagram shows, the force of gravity is transferred into your *body weight,* when your *body mass* is on support. At exactly that moment your muscular effort should

Fig.3.4 Diagram of gravity application shows that the hierarchy of movement starts with gravity.

be applied. That effort during destruction of balance on support frees your body to accelerate due to the force of gravity.

In other words, gravity creates body weight, when the body receives support from the ground. Only then are your muscles applied to the body. You can experience this relationship in a simple test with a friend (standing in front of you and trying to push your upraised finger with his palm, while you have one or two fingers pushing his chest (Fig.3.5). All his efforts to push your finger back will be useless. Why? Because the

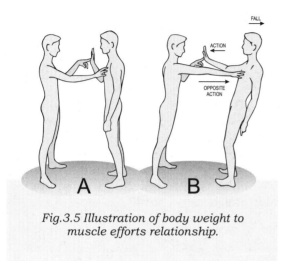

Fig.3.5 Illustration of body weight to muscle efforts relationship.

pressure of your fingers against his chest prevents your friend from destroying his balance and using his body weight/gravity and therefore his muscles, to push your finger. While balanced on support, it is impossible to put muscles to work effectively. This logical scheme helps us understand the interrelations between these elements — gravity, support and balance — as a system, where gravity plays the main role.

Perhaps the most surprising thing about the relation of gravity, body weight and muscular effort is that it applies to cycling and swimming exactly the same way as it does to running. While we tend to think of both of those sports as being low impact and, therefore somewhat gravity–free; in fact the same principles of support, body weight and free–falling come into play, no matter what form of human locomotion is being performed. We'll explore these relationships further in the sections about cycling and swimming.

Movement

Our Nature consists in motion, complete rest is death.

— *Blaise Paskal*

While human knowledge has exploded at an almost incomprehensible rate in the computer age, the underlying principles of movement and life have been well understood since the first philosophers began articulating their thoughts. The concept of 'life' is an energy transformation encompassing everything from the trapped energy of a dense body to the pure free flowing energy of light waves. Ironically, the same four components of life — energy, matter, space, and time (Fig.3.6) — represent both the world's simplicity and its incredible diversity. Our very existence is testament to just how diverse our world has become.

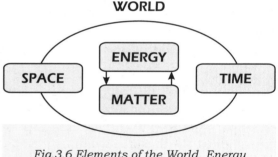

Fig.3.6 Elements of the World. Energy interacts with matter through space and time.

The fundamental law that governs all existence: *"Life is movement, movement is life,"* symbolizes this philosophy. Reality is a constant change, a continual transformation in space and time from one form of energy to another.

In this broad sweep of things, human existence can be artificially divided into five strata: *mechanical, physiological, psycho-*

logical, mental, and spiritual (Fig.3.7). Each represents a different kind of energy we channel in our daily lives. Our skills in life and movement reflect our ability to properly channel the specific energy required for a given situation. As each type of energy flows freely through us, it overlaps with and transforms into one of the other

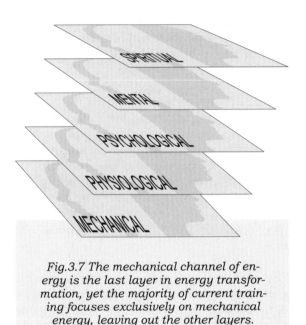

Fig.3.7 The mechanical channel of energy is the last layer in energy transformation, yet the majority of current training focuses exclusively on mechanical energy, leaving out the other layers.

forms of energy as the situation demands. In our development of athletic movement we need to understand and to accept that to approach perfect performance we must achieve perfection in channeling the right type of energy at the right time.

When we approach any physical activity, such as the three disciplines of triathlon, it is the mechanical movements that are the most obvious manifestations of the use of energy. The mechanics of running, cycling and swimming seem to be the obvious focal point for the distribution of our energy, yet this mechanical energy is completely interrelated with all the other types of energy. The actual movements you make in

these — and all other sports — are just the visible representation, the gate, if you will, through which all other forms of energy are channeled.

So when you run, ride or swim, the actual physical movements that the outside world sees are just the result of the other forms of energy set into motion. Lest you think this original thought, be mindful that Aristotle (1) in his work "Movement of Animals" noted: *"it is plainly reasonable that motion in place should be the last of the movements in things that come into being."*

And the great Russian physiologist I.M Sechenov (Fig.3.8) in his book "Reflexsy Golovnogo Mozga" (2) wrote: *"all infinite diversity of external appearance of brain activity can be boiled down to only one phenomenon — muscular movement."* Sechenov stressed that our internal, mental, psychological and physiological activity at the final point ended up in muscular activity producing movement.

Fig.3.8 Sechenov wrote that muscular movement is the culmination of our internal, mental, psychological, and physiological activity.

Source: Wikipedia.org/Public Domain.

Why is this important? Why do we need to understand that the mechanical act of running, riding or swimming is not the first step in the process, but is in fact, the last step in the energy chain that leads to movement?

Because... life is movement, movement is life. Life is energy channeled into physical movement. And, in the great circle of things, in order to stimulate our physiological, psychological and mental state, we must move. In this infinite process of energy transformation, we seek perfection of life and movement.

As the saying goes, anything worth doing is worth doing well. When we seek to improve our abilities in physical activities, we have to understand that those activities start with a deeper understanding of how movement is achieved. Basically, the process of running, riding or swimming better is the process of understanding movement and developing new and higher levels of skill in transforming and channeling energy to perform those movements.

To understand the importance of focusing all levels of energy in the physical acts we perform, it is helpful to understand the limitations we place on ourselves, when we don't channel this energy. Here's a scenario we've all witnessed a time or two: it's six a.m. at a modern health club, filled with all the latest equipment. Already, the stationary cycles are filling up with earnest executives, dutifully cranking the pedals while they read the newspaper propped on the handlebars or, more likely, staring intently at the early morning business news from CNN, MSNBC or Fox News on the nearest monitor.

These execs, however well–intentioned they may be, are not there because they are aspiring Tour de France racers. In all likelihood, they've been ordered into the gym by doctors concerned about any number of maladies — high blood pressure, excessive weight, heart problems, etc. This could be called exercise as prescribed medicine and the only energy these guys are investing in their cycling is the pure mechanical turning of the pedals. Their minds are as far away from the bike as they would like their bodies to be. In essence, they are dutiful robots, turning the pedals as commanded

with not one whit of interest in performing athletically.

We mention this not to make fun or belittle, but just to illustrate that it is possible to perform mechanical acts that resemble athletic performance with minimal investment of non–mechanical energy and still gain some benefit. These earnest exercisers will tone their bodies, they will elevate their heart rates, and they will realize gains that will promote longer, healthier lives. But they won't become athletes.

As much as we would like to think that we, as aspiring athletes, are different than the robots on the health club bikes, the cold truth is that we are just as apt to train robotically as people who have no athletic ambitions whatsoever. Once we've established our training routine, that training almost becomes a second job, something to be checked off the daily list of responsibilities.

Even if we approach this training with great enthusiasm, it's nearly impossible to drive all the other realities of our lives out of our minds during the time we've set aside for training. A big project at work, trouble at home with the kids, an upcoming business trip, an aging parent in decline... these and a million other issues easily intrude on the focus that we really want to put into our running, swimming or cycling.

And there we are, training robotically. Slogging through a 1,000 meters in the pool, sitting in with the peloton for 40 miles or running 10K without ever thinking about it. Sounds great, right? Got the workout out of the way and maybe figured out how to get the taxes paid, the old house sold, the new house closed and maybe what to buy the wife for her birthday in the bargain. What could be better?

It all sounds great until you look in your training log and realize that while you've put in the time, you haven't put in the energy. You're not getting any better. But the real eye opener comes when you line it up to race. At first, things may go well, but as fatigue becomes a factor, you may not understand what is happening. From all the training you've been doing, you think you should be going faster, but instead you lack the control of your energy to keep performing at your desired level.

By training robotically, without involving your psychological, mental and spiritual energies, you have left yourself seriously undertrained, despite the number of miles reflected in your logbook. Now, in the heat of competition, when you need every ounce of energy to flow to your task, you've got nothing. Instead of being calm, focused and intent on success, you find yourself in mental turmoil. When you should be in a zone of spiritual tranquility, you begin falling apart, first mentally, then physically. Why am I so tired? How far do I have to go? Why am I hurting? He/she never beat me before. These and a hundred other questions reflecting doubt invade your untrained mind.

As the cacophony of doubts takes over completely, you may well wind up running, cycling and swimming slower, than even your average practice paces. By training only your mechanical and physiological energy systems, you've only done a small part of the job. You will finish the race, but you won't realize your performance goals.

On the evolutionary scale it is easy to see why any modern athlete would have difficulty training to use all forms of energy. For most of us, racing a triathlon is just a proxy for the real world experiences of our forebears, for whom running may have meant the difference between life and death. When your survival depends on outrunning a hungry beast, it's a relatively simple matter to put every ounce of available energy into survival mode. But when completing a race

or training session is just one more activity to be squeezed into our ever more crowded schedules that complete dedication to task is extremely difficult to achieve.

Essentially, in the course of human development, all levels of energy channeling have been focused, in one form or another, on needs and necessities to maintain life and movement. We can call NEED an immediate physiological or psychological requirement for the well–being of an organism, such as food, clothing and shelter. NECESSITY would be the pressure of the circumstances, where something is lacking, where action must be taken, in order to meet the requirements of life.

Our existence depends on continually satisfying these necessities and needs and prioritizing them according to our circumstances at any given time. We always have a hierarchy of necessities that range from the biological level all the way up to the spiritual level, which create needs we are compelled to satisfy. Driven by these needs, we channel our energies accordingly. Where we channel that energy is driven by choice as we focus our thoughts and desires on specific needs and necessities.

When survival was at stake for primitive man, there was a need to run. It literally was a question of eat or be eaten, so the choice to focus energy on running was an easy one. Now our need to run is less obvious. You don't really need to trot out to the car to jump in the car and head to the drive–through at the local burger stand. And you certainly don't need to train to become a triathlete to enjoy a healthy, happy life.

Yet the luxuries we have developed for ourselves still haven't undone our genetic need to run. Running can now be seen as a form of escape from those luxuries, a necessary means to promote the health and well being of a growing population. And when we choose to compete, running — and other sports — serve as a test bed for our evolving human abilities. The course of human history has had no effect on the fundamental biomechanics and physiology of running, nor has it reduced the need to channel all our forms of energy into the act of running in order to be successful. Whether the goal is to survive or simply to cross the finish line first, nothing has changed. We must learn to transfer all our energies to the task at hand in the most efficient way possible.

Reference:

1. Aristotle. *Movement of Animals. The complete works of Aristotle.* Edited by Jonathan Barnes. Volume one. Princeton University Press, Sixth Printing, 1995, p. 1091.

2. Sechenov I.M. *Reflexsy Golovnogo Mozga (Brain Reflexes).* Selected works, Moscow, 1953, p. 33.

Action

Material motion is born of spiritual motion.

— *Leonardo da Vinci*

How do we move? It should come as no surprise that it was our friend Aristotle who first described the links in the chain that lead to action: *"desire, and thought concerned with action — [are] the movers. All desires also aim at the same goal; for the object of desire is the starting point of intellect concerned with action, and the last stage (of our reasoning) is the starting point of action"* (Fig.3.9).

Let's break this down a little further. Even the simplest movement we make is the final step in a logical thought process common to all living creatures. The structure of this chain is always the same: thoughts, desires, action. To badly paraphrase Descartes: we think — and desire — therefore we move.

Further, for movement to take place, the entire chain must be complete. Aristotle pointed out that thoughts and ideas could be expressed without leading to action. Similarly, those thoughts and ideas could exist independent of desires. For example, take the statement 'my thoughts about running as a form of exercise are a subject of scientific research'. In this case, there is no desire expressed to either run or do research. There is simply of statement of facts about research and running.

Even adding the component of desire to the formula doesn't guarantee action. With the statement changed to 'I want to start a running routine', there can be action implied, but not taken. (And don't we all know many people who have boldly proclaimed a desire to start running, to lose weight or to do a better job at work without ever following through on their stated desires?)

Thoughts and ideas may lead to desires and desires may lead to action. Thoughts and ideas mainly reflect the intellectual and spiritual level of our existence; it is our way of seeking knowledge about the world. Desires are initially based on our material needs for food, water, clothes and shelter.

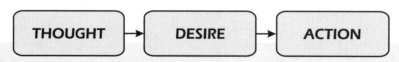

Fig.3.9 Our thoughts must be aligned with our desires in order to execute the correct action.

When our primary material needs are satisfied, then our desires are free to move on to our ideas and thoughts, our mental and spiritual development. Desires may be defined as our feelings towards something we want.

Action is something that we do: talking, screaming, breathing, writing, walking, sleeping, watching, throwing, running, etc. Actions can be instantaneous or prolonged. An entire lifetime is a process, a chain of actions fulfilling our thoughts and desires.

Actions, for our convenience, could be categorized according to time frames into short (kick, punch, swing) and long (study, training). We can also categorize by the level of brain involvement: voluntary (jumping, running) and involuntary (yawning); conscious (reading) and sub–conscious (breathing). Conscious actions usually derive from our thoughts, sub–conscious actions stem from the desire to satisfy our primary needs for existence. Actions can be reactions, if they are taken to oppose or avoid some other action.

Clearly, actions are initiated by thoughts and desires, but the same thoughts and desires do not necessarily lead to the same actions. Actions from our thoughts can be completely opposite to actions from our desires. For example, I think about doing some work on a computer, but at the same time I have a desire to sleep. So I have to resolve this situation by making a choice as to what action I prefer to do at that specific moment — work or sleep. From this point of view, we can define 'action' as **movement finalizing a decision!**

Our thoughts and desires lead us to the necessity of making a decision as to which action to prefer and to take? The action "to move" always has a specific relationship with our dominating thoughts and desires. The movement comes from our needs through which we realize our thoughts and desires.

As humans we have a quite diverse set of needs and necessities. On the spiritual and mental levels we deal with ideas, concepts and thoughts. Emotional (I feel good! I feel bad!), to biological survival (reproduction, seeking sustenance), which finalize in movement as the last element of the life reproduction cycle. Multiple choice of decision–making depends on priority of our needs at the moment of taking an action in order to satisfy our most critical or compelling need. This choice gives us the direction to channel our energy to the appropriate action.

The ultimate choice made could conflict with our other needs and could be the result of a poor decision based on the wrong understanding, perception, or feeling, or just by sacrificing other needs. For example, concerned parents may sacrifice their own desires in order to provide for the needs of their children.

In sport, conflicting needs are commonplace. On the most basic level, there is the ever–present conflict between growing fatigue and the necessity to continue optimum performance during a race. In this case, our thoughts could direct us to hold the same pace, but our desires could scream just the opposite — slow down right now! Our thoughts about winning the race are at constant odds with our desires to avoid the pain and suffering of maximum effort, which can not only be uncomfortable, but can actually be physically dangerous.

How we react to this inherent conflict determines in large part our results. If we continue to be directed by our thoughts, we hold pace and continue the race. If desires rule, we stop or slow down with the objective of 'saving' our living, breathing organism.

In order to perform at our best, we must keep all our thoughts–desires–actions in a strict hierarchical order. If we really want to continue our racing performance, both in a given race, as well as over time, then our thoughts should lead our desires and action in one direction, which will support and enhance our racing performance. Therefore, our thoughts as a mental focus should lead our desires to do the specific action (or actions) leading to successful performance.

All roads lead to Rome...

Our thoughts, feelings, and actions can co–exist only *now*, in the present tense. They can exist separately as just thoughts, or feelings, or actions, but only when taken together do they lead to a complete performance.

We can think about running without actually running. We can even visualize a perfect running stride, but still not move. We can also run without any thoughts or feelings of running by talking to a friend or listening to music on an iPod. In either case, by not forging all our thoughts, feelings and actions into a focused effort, we change our effort and diminish our ultimate performance.

When we do focus our thoughts, feelings, and actions, we are *in the moment*. The enhanced skill of performance reflects an organism that is functioning on all cylinders. There is no past or future, there is only the present.

When this happens, our thoughts of how to perform a particular action, our perception of how we are performing and the actual physical, biomechanical performance are all synchronized in a seamless whole. The highest level of performance demonstrates that all your thoughts, feelings, and actions belong exactly to this moment.

To illustrate, if you are half way through a 10 kilometer running race your thoughts shouldn't be focused on the finish line. This very common mistake divorces the current action — the running stride — from your thoughts, which are now 5 kilometers down the road. This inattention to the task at hand brings about a loss of physical precision. Instead of directing the current effort, your thoughts are looking at the finish line clock or toweling off. The desire to have the effort ended is overwhelming the action needed to bring it to an end. Now, undirected by your thoughts, your muscle work and the closely choreographed movement of your various body parts lose precision in their space and time cycles. Basically, the well–oiled machine that was your body quickly loses its coordinated movement and your performance suffers.

If our thoughts don't stay in the present, with proper attention to the action being performed, the result is improper use of energy resources, reduced neuromuscular coordination, increased muscular tension, etc. At the end, instead of a personal best we can wind up with a disaster.

The ability to achieve and maintain a reliable chain of *thought–desire–action* function as one logical unit happening in the same space–time frame is a learnable and necessary component of training for success in any sport. Each space–time frame unit must be filled up with its own chain unit of *thought–desire–action* and form one complete and logical circle. From this perspective we need to perfect our focus on our thoughts always directing our actions to produce a successful athletic performance.

In the following chapters of the book we'll analyze the specifics of using our thoughts to direct our actions in all three disciplines of triathlon.

Reference:

1.   Aristotle. Selections. *De Anima*. Book III, Chapter 4. [Desire and Action], [The Role of Thought and Desire in Producing Action]. Hackett Publishing Company, Inc. Indianapolis, Cambridge, 1995, p. 202.

CHAPTER 4
THE PERCEPTION CONCEPT

The world is nothing but change.
Our life is only Perception.
— *Marcus Aurelius*

Human history is a continuing story of accommodation and adaptation to change. How humans perceived and reacted to change guided the development of societies and shaped the world in which we now live. Perception itself — the ability to recognize and analyze change — became the fundamental tool in human relations with the forces of nature, upon which mankind's survival depended.

As human history progressed and the development of modern creature comforts like secure housing and continuous food supply insulated us from the day–to–day vagaries of life in the wild, the need for the highest levels of perception have eroded away bit by bit. The average human could get through a day, a month, a year, yes — even a lifetime — without the need for high levels of perception and split–second decision–making.

The comfort zone that humans created for themselves led inevitably to an erosion of the very survival skills that allowed them to thrive in the first place. However, select fields of human endeavor still depended on higher states of perception. With life or death on the line, those in the military, firefighters, policemen, mountain climbers, deep sea divers and the like retained the need to be ever–vigilant; to perceive and react to constantly changing situations.

At the same time, those who chose to pursue higher planes of activity in the arts and athletics were compelled to nurture their perceptive abilities. Just as a master wine taster can tell you the grape, the vintage, the country of origin and the type of soil — blindfolded — an accomplished ballerina or pianist can recognize and shape the finest nuance of a performance, making corrections to flaws most of us would never notice.

In sports, as well, the most accomplished athletes are guided by an elevated level of perception, understanding intuitively each deviation from perfect form and constantly working to correct flaws that detract from their performances. By contrast, most weekend warriors and mediocre athletes concern themselves very little with perception and are content just to put in time at their favored activity.

The many definitions of perception underscore its vital role in human activity:

- "awareness of the elements of environment through physical sensation" (1);

- "a single unified awareness derived from sensory process while a stimulus is present";
- "the act or faculty of apprehending by means of senses or of the mind; cognition; understanding";
- "immediate or intuitive recognition, as a moral or aesthetic qualities; an artist of rare perception" (2);
- "a complex process of receiving and interpreting of information, providing for the organism ability to reflect the existing reality and orientation in surrounding world" (3).

These definitions demonstrate that perception incorporates all senses, feelings and mental activity during human interaction with surrounding nature. In other words, without acutely developed perceptive abilities, we're unlikely to do anything truly well.

The main organ of perception is the brain. How the brain functions was beautifully described in Lawrence Gonzales' *"Deep Survival"* (4): *"[The brain] receives images from receptors in the body and from the sense organs that take in the outside world. (The images can be smells, sights, sounds, or feelings (Fig.4.1)). At the same time, the brain provides a stream of outputs that shape the body's reactions to the environment and it-self, from adjusting blood pressure to mating. So the brain reads the state of the body and makes fine adjustments, even while it reads the environment and directs the body in reacting to it. In addition, that process continually reshapes the brain by making new connections. All of this is aimed at one thing only: adaptation, which is another word for survival."*

Another aspect of survival is how quickly we learn to do everything that we need to survive. Gregory Bateson (Fig.4.2), a great American scientist, wrote (5) that learning, and *"science is a way of perceiving... But perception operates only upon difference. All receipt of information is necessar-*

Fig.4.2 American biologist and anthropologist, Gregory Bateson pointed out that perception operates upon differences and that structure of input must be reflected somewhat in the structure of output.

Source: Wikipedia.org/Public Domain.

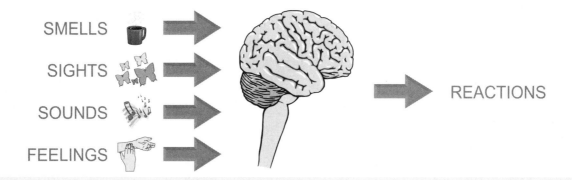

Fig.4.1 Our perception is derived from our senses, the more we tune our senses, the more precise our reactions become.

ily the receipt of news of difference (Fig.4.3), and all perception of difference is limited by threshold. Differences that are too slight or too slowly presented are not perceivable. They are not food for perception. Knowledge at any given moment will be a function of the thresholds of our available means of perception."

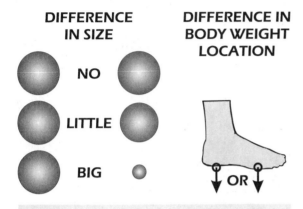

DIFFERENCE IN SIZE   NO   LITTLE   BIG

DIFFERENCE IN BODY WEIGHT LOCATION   OR

Fig.4.3 The threshold of difference gives depth to your perception. In essence, the more in tune your perception, the more you will be able to perceive minor differences in your technique, training, etc.

This important part of learning has an intrinsic relationship with the development of our biomechanical abilities and skill development in sports training and performance. Our progress will only be as good as our ability to differentiate one movement from another, one effort from another. Our success in taking in and processing all the signals, all the information about our body position in space, the timing of our movements and the level of efforts exerted will determine our success in the given sport.

Examples of highly developed perceptive abilities abound in sport. World–class high jumpers are reputed to be able to "feel" the difference when one support for the bar is a mere half–centimeter higher than the other

support. Olympic weight lifters can recognize the difference when the weights on one side of the bar are but a few ounces heavier than those on the other side. Professional basketball players have been known to stop a game to point out that the back of the rim is a half–inch lower than the front.

While this list could go on indefinitely, the essence of it is that perception is the cornerstone of skill development. Assuming that skill is the ability to use all available sources of information and feedback to reach the desired goal, then it follows that those sources are only available through the highest levels of perception. With acute perceptive abilities, we recognize signals, evaluate deviations from the desired standard, and make the necessary corrections. Everything is based on perception: the guideline for our development in technique, mental and psychological condition or the physical attributes of strength, speed, endurance and flexibility.

In order to raise our athletic performance to a higher level, we must develop the ability to perceive and shape all the movements and variables in our chosen sport. Just as a ballerina's virtuoso performance is refined by the development of high levels of perception, so should be the efforts of runners, swimmers and cyclists.

Take, for example, running, arguably the most basic human athletic endeavor and certainly the one most closely associated with human survival. While we tend to think of "a run" as an activity lasting anywhere from fifteen minutes to three or more hours, the actuality is that the basic running cycle is a process that is repeated over and over, more than a hundred times per minute.

While seemingly simple, that one single cycle of changing support from one foot to the next involves complex interaction of all your muscles and connective tissue, your entire cardiovascular system and the focused attention of your complete mental faculties. Further, that action must be repeated in the presence of nature, with varying terrain, changing atmospheric conditions and all manner of obstructions — cars, dogs, other runners, etc. Factor in fatigue, emotions, and distractions and it's no wonder that your perception may begin to deteriorate and with it, your performance.

To an outside observer — indeed to the athlete himself — a declining performance might be attributed to fatigue, a failure to eat enough or the weather conditions, but the real culprit is a diminished capability for perception. During an intense athletic performance, our perception of own movements begins to fall apart. And when we lose the ability to monitor our own actions, our performance begins to suffer as well. Old survival instincts kick in and begin to convince the brain that this hard activity — running — presents a clear and present danger to the body.

As we lose the belief that we can continue running at this pace, our focus shifts from action to protection. It's better for survival, the brain now believes, to throttle back and slow down the activity. In turn, the finely–tuned interaction of brain and body is compromised, coordination is lost and the running machine may quickly shut down completely.

It's all because at the highest levels of brain activity, we lose belief in our own capabilities. We haven't been able to perceive that we can perform at the level we desire.

While all of us have our personal 'walls', none has been more famous than running's four–minute mile. It wasn't just that athletes believed man couldn't run a mile in less than four minutes — the whole world believed it was impossible. With no scientific basis whatsoever, it became common

knowledge that no one could achieve the feat.

Thus, as he closed in on the barrier, England's Roger Bannister (Fig.4.4) (6) not only had to change his own perception, he had to change that of the world. When he ac-

Fig.4.4 Roger Bannister on the final leg of his historic and record breaking sub–four minute mile run.

Source: Ralph Morse/Time & Life Pictures

complished his goal, the psychological floodgates opened. What once was not possible is now commonplace — over 20,000 humans have now run under the previously–unassailable four–minute barrier.

While Bannister proved to the world what is possible, as athletes our biggest challenge remains proving to ourselves what we can accomplish on our own. The difficulty of perception development is part–and–parcel of everything we do. We face this reality again and again on a daily basis as one of the enduring realities in our lives. Developing our perception is about developing our belief in what we can do. When we develop the mind beyond what it was able to perceive, the body will soon arrive in the tracks of the mind's discovery.

References:

1. Merriam Webster's Collegiate Dictionary, Tenth Edition, 1993, p. 861.

2. Webster's Encyclopedic Unabridged Dictionary of the English Language, Gramercy Books, 1989, p. 1069.

3. Soviet Encyclopedic Dictionary. Moscow, 1988, p. 248.

4. Gonzales, L. *Deep Survival*. W. W. Norton & Company, 2003, p. 33.

5. Bateson, G. *Mind and Nature: a Necessary Unity*. Bantam New Age Books, 1980, p. 30.

6. Bannister, R. *The First Four Minutes*. Sutton Publishing, 2004.

SECTION III
FRAME OF LEARNING AND TEACHING

Dr. Romanov instructs clinic participants.

CHAPTER 5
HOW DO WE LEARN AND TEACH?

*We need a method if we are to
investigate the truth of things.*

— *René Descartes*

The question *"how do we learn and teach?"* is as old as humankind. The word 'cognition' (taken from the Latin *cognoscere* "to know"), literally defines the human ability to process information and pass along knowledge from one person to another, from one generation to the next. Learning and teaching are the essential characteristics that led to survival and development of humanity. The march from surviving to thriving was directly dependent on the quality of teaching and learning. Human society always required teachers and has always depended on students to learn from its teachers.

No matter how complex or scientific the topic at hand, successful teaching has always been more art than science. Still, even considering the artistry inherent in dynamic teaching, the greatest teachers in history have always attempted to develop specific ways of imparting wisdom and truth. Most historically significant teachers were great philosophers and thinkers capable of observing, accumulating, analyzing and delivering knowledge to their disciples. These teachers developed both the means to discover truth and knowledge, and the structure for teaching it, which we call a *method* (1).

René Descartes (Fig.5.1) in Rule IV of his work, *Rules for the Direction of our Native Intelligence* (2) wrote "We need a method if we are to investigate the truth of things... By 'a method' I mean reliable rules which are easy to apply, and such that if one follows them exactly, one will never take what is false to be true or fruitlessly expend one's mental efforts, but will gradually and constantly increase one's knowledge 'till one arrives at a true understanding of everything within one's capacity..."

Source: Wikipedia.
org/Public Domain.

Fig.5.1 René Descartes championed a "method" to investigate the truth of things.

Helvétius C. A. (Fig.5.2), one of the 18th century French legendary thinkers, considered method to be the resource used to achieve the goal (3). This way of thinking has carried forward to modern dictionaries (1) which define method as the "way of doing something, especially according to a defined plan;" Greek *methodos* (met – **meta** + hodós) (4) meaning "way, a going, a traveling."

Source: Wikipedia. org/Public Domain.

Fig.5.2 Helvétius C.A. *considered method a way of doing something.*

Everything in teaching and learning points to the necessity of defining the frame of what is to be studied, how we study it, and what major resources we can bring to the table to make the process more productive, efficient, and successful. This list should always include our senses and perceptions, the images used to illustrate the concepts, the ideas to be applied, the thoughts we must process, and the actions we take *and* correct as our specific method.

Inside this process, which can be called the 'frame of teaching', we develop our knowledge, formalize it, and transfer it to students. The teaching process never culminates on some kind of apex of perfection. On this matter it helps to quote the genius painter, Salvador Dalí, who powerfully illuminated the essence of teaching and learning when, a student asked him what he was supposed to do if he got everything perfect. Dalí answered, "Do not be afraid to be perfect, you'll never reach it!"

Human learning is an endless developmental process, where ideas, thoughts and perception progress from one plateau to the next, where each new achievement is not an end, but the beginning of a new cycle of discovery. With each new level reached, we learn more of the truth and more of ourselves, reflecting the ancient Greek philosophy of life — "Know thyself" (5).

While the human quest for perfection covers a bewildering complex and far–reaching array of topics, the challenge to "Know thyself" continues to be as challenging as it has been throughout the course of human history. In the physical realm of the science of movement — running, cycling, and swimming represent some of the most elemental human endeavors, yet we still don't know how to use our bodies to perfect these movements. It is to come closer to this elusive goal that I have developed the *Pose Method* as a system for learning and teaching these and other sports.

References:

1. Thorndike–Barnhart. *Student Dictionary*. Harper Collins Publishes, 1992, p. 703.

2. Descartes, René. *Rules for the Direction of our Native Intelligence. Descartes Selected Philosophical Writings*. Translated by J. Cottingham, R. Stoothoff, D. Murdoch, Cambridge University Press, 2006, p. 4.

3. Helvétius, C. A. *Oeuvres completes d'Helvétius*. Nouvelle edition, t.III. Paris, 1818.

4. Webster's Encyclopedic Unabridged Dictionary of the English Language. Gramercy Books, New York, p. 902.

5. Bartlett, J. *Inscription at the Delphic Oracle*. From Plutarch, Morals. Bartlett's Familiar Quotations. Little, Brown and Company, 1992, p. 55.

CHAPTER 6
SENSES AND PERCEPTION

*Man's desires are limited by his Perceptions;
none can desire what he has not perceived.*

— *William Blake*

*O for a life of sensation rather
than of thoughts.*

— *John Keats*

Life is an endless complex mixture of sensations (Fig.6.1). Everything that a human being experiences comes in the form of a specific sensation (1, 2). Surprisingly, this part of our existence is nearly always overlooked and misunderstood in the training process, in learning and teaching of movement. Why?

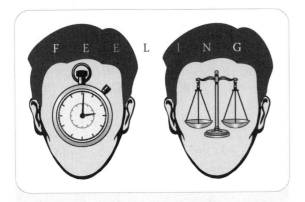

Fig.6.1 Important feelings in movement include the heightened perception of time and balance, which allows an athlete to perform at the peak of his abilities.

Generally speaking, coaches tend to move past less tangible or quantifiable characteristics like sensations and thoughts and instead concentrate on visible traits like specific muscular movements. Understanding the value of sensations is considered less important in the teaching and learning of sports, which are typically regarded as physical, not cerebral, activities.

Certainly, coaches talk about traditional proprioception as feedback from muscles, ligaments and tendons in order to teach and correct our movement and there are some terms frequently used to describe our senses — such as "effortless," "light," "flow" or "heavy," "flat," "stiff," etc. But mostly these terms are tossed off as general descriptions, without understanding what they represent or how to use them to take corrective measures.

Athletes are often surprised when you talk about sensations as being key to the learning process, as if the feelings experienced in our muscles and connective tissue were somehow divorced from the actual activity being mastered. We have to understand that senses and perception are more than just the feelings in our muscles and contain the keys to mastery of movement.

Senses and perception are closely related but are by no means the same thing. For an analogy, you could look to the sprawling intelligence agencies like the FBI and the CIA. The senses are like field agents, intercepting, retrieving and reporting raw data back to the central office. As human beings, we have a special physiological and anatomical apparatus, replete with receptors delivering very specific information from outside and inside of our body to our brain. It's all raw data, unconnected and uninterpreted.

Perception is a much more complex process, more along the lines of the analysis that takes place back at headquarters. In an intelligence agency, all the raw data from the field agents has to be analyzed, correlated and evaluated before recommendations are made and actions are taken.

The same thing goes for the perceptive process in the human brain. All the information that floods in from nerve endings and receptors throughout the body has to be processed. All this data has to be memorized, interpreted and analyzed on an ongoing basis, with instant decisions being made that result in immediate choices and actions.

Senses and perceptions are vital to the learning process. Learning is much deeper than just sensing something. Learning means achieving a specific outcome from what you've sensed and your reaction after certain sensations (Fig.6.2). Perception is the ability to sort through the sensations, focus on those that are important and meaningful, and choose the correct actions.

YOU FEEL

1 OR 2 FINGERS ON HAND

BODY WEIGHT ON HEEL OR ON BOF

Fig.6.2 Test yourself and those around you: place two fingers on a friend's wrist and ask how many fingers they feel with their eyes closed. Depending on how far apart you place your fingers, the answer will probably be "one." Sometimes your own perception can be misleading.

To return to the intelligence agency analogy, before every major 'event' in recent American history, whether it was the bombing of Pearl Harbor or the 9/11 hijackings, there has been raw data to suggest something momentous was about to take place. At the same time, however, there was such a flood of data about other risks and other possibilities that intelligence agencies were not able to pinpoint and prevent the specific situations that ultimately led to disaster. Gathering information is relatively easy, processing it is a much more difficult task.

So it is after we gather all of the information our senses provide us, when we engage in any physical activity. We must recognize what is valuable and pertinent for learning. From this point of view, we do not train according to apparatus of our senses. Instead we train our attention to these senses, because that's what perception is.

Here's just one simple example. How skilled are we at sensing our body weight?

For most athletes, the real answer is that we have essentially zero ability to sense our own body weight. Even though every single athletic function involves body weight, athletes basically never consider it, never perceive it, until the moment it becomes a source of pain or pleasure. Body weight generally never enters the mental conversation, yet it is an unavoidable and essential component of the athletic experience.

Perception is not just a complex process; it is also a deliberate process, a learned ability to pay attention to sensations and selectively feel each one separately from the others. This is the essence of perception. You have to select from the rush of signals, information or "noise" those specific sensations that are valuable to you and learn how to deliberately focus on those that matter. This is the most important part of learning.

Senses and perception comprise an integrated system, where senses play an important role, but are subordinate to perception. Senses are an anatomical and physiological apparatus of sensing temperature, color, size, smell, pressure, time, acceleration, etc. Perception operates with all this information arriving at the cerebral cortex and central nervous system to be processed, accumulated, memorized and evaluated. Then it's decision time. What do we do next?

We cannot even get valuable information from our senses, if we do not understand how the system works. Perception development comes from a deliberate focus on specific information, which we have to select out of the vast quantity of signals we receive. This is a decision making process, which leads to the ultimate action taken.

It is critical in learning, to know which senses to monitor and consistently separate, differentiate and focus our attention on those select sensations. For example, in the development of athletic movement, the sense of smell has little or nothing to do with the learning process. Conversely, acute hearing can be an extremely important component of learning movement.

The first step in developing perceptive ability is to select the specific information we need for a given endeavor. This requires tremendous mental effort and the expenditure of energy because this part of the learning process is not 'free'. We have to work and work on developing higher levels of perception; the outcome of this work will be enhanced skill development.

A top gourmet chef has an innate ability to infer from a given recipe and the exact taste of the dish it will yield the recipes related to the specific taste. A skilled painter has a tremendous perception of how different colors, forms and sizes bring to your attention the concepts or feelings he wants to express. A ballet dancer expresses through movement his or her deepest feelings. Musicians perceive unique melodies, sounds, tones and rhythms, which they combine in sonata or jazz, rock or hip hop, evidencing their skill in the perception of music.

How do we teach and learn the same high level of perception to athletes? We focus the athlete's attention on very specific information. In running, swimming and cycling, for example, these are specific senses and perceptions related to the biomechanics and form of these movements. And this is what we'll discuss in all following chapters, the senses and perceptions that are the basis of the Pose Method.

References:

1. Гельвеций К.А. Об уме самом по себе. Том 1. Академия Наук СССР. "Мысль," Москва, 1974, стр. 148.

2. Helvetius, C. A. *Oeuvres completes d'Helvetius.* Nouvelle edition, t. III. Paris, 1818.

CHAPTER 7
VISUAL IMAGES OF MOVEMENT

We see what we understand.
— *Ray Bradbury*

It is true to say that we perceive the world mostly through our vision. The eyes are our most effective receptors of sensations, delivering full color, three–dimensional images to our brain at a frighteningly high rate of delivery. This information is used ceaselessly in life, especially in learning and teaching. Visual images create very powerful standards that influence our ideas, our thoughts and our desires (Fig.7.1). No matter the endeavor, we attempt to learn by copying someone or something. We imitate celebrities from Hollywood; top athletes from baseball, football or tennis; rappers or singers, politicians or preachers. The list goes on. In our media saturated world, there is a hero on every corner and an accompanying visual image, available for immediate copying.

The world is an amalgamation of images that come together to form our personal world vision. So the world is how we see it, isn't it? Yes and no. Yes, because at a given moment, it's true, but ultimately no, because our vision of everything changes all the time. As Marcus Aurelius said, "The world is nothing but change. Our life is only perception" (1).

Do you remember the town where you grew up? Do you still see it now as it was in your childhood? Is that the image you carry with you or have you updated it to reflect the changes brought on by time? Have you returned again and again to a museum to see your favorite painting? The painting hasn't changed, so what is it that you are looking for? Isn't it the same picture? You know that it is not.

Images govern and rule our lives. Society creates a massive amount of images to move your mind and direct your actions in the desired direction. We live under this "image attack" mostly without even noticing.

Fig.7.1 Seeing is believing, but not necessarily doing. Our perception of our actions can be far from what we are actually doing.

The same is true for our image of running. Is running what we see on the cover of "Runner's World" magazine? Is this how elite athletes run? Not really. You just need to watch best runners, in the biggest races, to get a clear understanding that the magazine images are wrong.

But why are these images reproduced millions of times? Because they somehow suit an accepted image of "proper" running form, lacking validity from science and commonsense. One could go as far as to say that imagining running as depicted on countless magazine covers is a mild form of insanity, accepted without question by the majority of the worldwide running community.

A regular feature of the Pose Method running clinics is to ask all participants to draw a stick figure of a runner. The results never fail to astonish. Most recreational, competitive and elite runners and their coaches have no clear picture or vision of running form. Despite devoting a large percentage of their time to running and despite being inundated with visual images of running in print and on television, almost no one delivers an accurate depiction of running. The best illustration ever created in a Pose clinic came from a student in Quito, Ecuador, Monica Crespo (Fig.7.2). Monica is a multi–talented person, a professional coach and trainer with a university degree, yet her image of a runner was based on her artistic vision, which is far from the biomechanical reality, mostly hidden from our eyes. Monica's type of image reflects more of our feelings, rather than specific knowledge about running and how to learn it.

Images of great athletes such as Tiger Woods, Michael Jordan, Michael Johnson, Lance Armstrong and many others, are copied by millions of followers without even understanding of how this or that movement is happening. In the absence of other available instruction, learning by imita-

Fig.7.2. Image of running (courtesy of Monica Crespo).

tion of visual images is not all bad. Even some leading sports scientists have been known to counsel this approach. Dr. Ernie Maglischo (2) has said, "I think you look at the stroke patterns that most world class swimmers are using, and then that is what you teach."

This sounds fairly logical, if you ignore the conventional folk wisdom that the best copy is never as good as the real thing. Nevertheless, a proper image presented at the beginning stage of the learning process provides good guidance, a map to move in the right direction. That being said, though, a copy is still a copy, the very nature of which presents its own limitations and restrictions.

To illustrate this, consider an actor in a sports movie. A skilled actor could easily watch film of talented athletes and imitate fairly closely the form of the movements, but something would be missing. The inner side of the movement would be empty. Even viewers with no experience in the sport being portrayed could easily sense fakery in the action.

That's why any serious actor called upon to play a renowned athlete insists on going through real sports training with a high level professional in the field. There is very specific appearance of the inner side of correct movement evidenced through external expression and there is a unique interrelationship between the internal and external aspects of movement. We constantly look for these signs in order to use them in learning and teaching of sports activities. We call them Poses of the movement.

Our muscles serve to achieve these poses. Muscles are not designed to express our feelings per se; their functions are to serve the movement, connect the different parts of the body and link them into one system of movement and action. The great Russian theoretician of theater K. Stanislavsky (Fig.7.3) (3) taught his actors not to play on stage, but to *act*. His thought was that an *action* expresses real feeling and real life. Therefore, the role of the visual image of movement we use is to help us reflect, express and prepare for the action we have to take. This is what we'll discuss in the following chapters.

Fig.7.3. K. Stanislavsky taught his actors that actions evoke real feelings, the same as actions recruit the necessary muscular contractions to achieve a goal, not vice–versa.

Source: Wikipedia.org/Public Domain.

References:

1. Aurelius, Marcus. *Meditations.* Translation by Gregory Hays. Phoenix, 2003.

2. Maglischo, E. *Newton to Bernoulli and Back again. Modern History of Articles In Freestyle From Past ASCA World Clinic's and Related Sources.* American Swimming Coaches Association Advanced Freestyle School. Ft. Lauderdale, FL, 1995, p. 29.

3. Stanislavsky, K. *Creating a role.* Theatre Arts Books, New York, 1961.

CHAPTER 8
THOUGHTS AND IDEAS

It is not enough to have a good mind.
The main thing is to use it well.

— *René Descartes*

Knowledge is power.

— *Francis Bacon*

The difference between a bee and the worst architect (builder) is that the former relies on instinct and heredity to build a hive, while the latter has a design in his mind and on paper before starting construction of a house. If we apply this analogy to running, then, as humans, we have to have an idea of how to run correctly (Fig.8.1), which we can use as a model of what to teach. We need a plan to learn and teach running technique.

When we first decide to take up the sport of running as a personal project, what do we do first? Do we 'just run?' Yes, this is what most people do! They just run, assuming that they know how to run. They just run, without any drawing in mind or plan on paper. They may buy new shoes, shorts and shirts and they may read magazines for advice on how far or fast to run, but they almost never consider the technical aspects of running itself. This is a major conflict in running. We run without a clear idea of how to run. Nothing like this happens in any other sport.

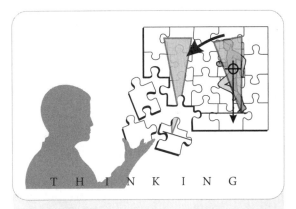

THINKING

Fig.8.1 Putting together the elements of running technique to create a clear picture in our minds of what we need to achieve and a standard to refer to.

The bee has an innate instinct to build the beehive with perfect construction. At this point the bee's "creativity" is ended, illustrating that instincts are very restricted, if we want them to be the guiding force in our lives. Human progress starts, where instincts end and goes beyond this point. This is the function of the mind. Mankind's superiority has always related to the mind, but as René Descartes said *"It is not enough to have a good mind. The main thing is to use it well"* (1).

Yes, effective use of the mind is the problem. Humans mostly rely on their own minds in the development of certain ideas, one of which, lamentably, is the concept of running. Somehow, the idea has taken hold that running is a natural human movement and that how we run is how we run. To paraphrase a quote from the American Vice President, Dick Cheney, running technique is an unknown; we don't know that we don't know how to run.

By assuming that our running style is preordained at birth, we emphatically eliminate any improvement we could make through technique, leaving only training as a means to improve performance. It's a tough step for many people to take, admitting that they don't know how to run.

Over the years, in the course of developing the Pose Method, I questioned many coaches, athletes and recreational runners on the simplest concepts. "What does it mean to run?" "How do we run?"

Again and again, the hesitancy and the insecurity reflected in the answers brought me no satisfaction. Dealing with these questions surprised people and made them anxious and angry. But once past the initial reaction, they became curious and reflective. Indeed, how do we do what we do?

What at first seemed a simple question was anything but simple, when these veteran runners began considering the answer. We're not bees. We don't have a hereditary code in our DNA that makes us perfect runners the way that bees are born to build the perfect hive.

So if running isn't governed by nature, it must be something we do according to thoughts and ideas. We need guidance, a map, a plan to provide the direction for developing a running technique that approaches perfection.

This guidance can only come from knowing what to teach and how to teach it. Once we know that we don't know how to run, we have to develop a standard for running. The process of developing a standard is set in motion by the thoughts and ideas that are fueled by our perceptions. We have minds, and now as Descartes reminded us, the job is to use them well.

So the standards of doing, of running as it were, have to be guided by the standards of effective thinking. The first thinking standard is determining what to teach. This is an objective in itself, the challenge of defining the exact model of running technique. The second standard is determining the method of teaching, which is necessarily based on the first standard. This logic is universal and has an application to anything that we teach and do, which will be demonstrated later in the chapters for running, cycling and swimming.

No matter what physical act we perform, the highest level of performance attainable results from using the mind to construct a method and then having the body follow the mind's plan.

Reference:

1. Descartes, R. *Discourse on the Method. Descartes Selected Philosophical Writings*. Translated by Cottingham, Stoothoff, and Murdoch, Cambridge University Press, 2006, p. 20.

CHAPTER 9
WHAT TO DO:
THE CIRCLE OF TRANSFORMATION

The way to do is to be.

— *Lao-tzu*

Developing perception doesn't mean anything, if the end result is not the desired action. Action is the culminating point in the complex process of perception and thoughts. Correct action leads us to the specific change we would like to make, based on our existing level of perception and the desire to progress to an even higher, unknown level of perception. Perception, thoughts and ideas all come together through action and *into* the action. We could call this coalescing of perception, thoughts and ideas the Circle of Transformation. In this circle, the body and mind perceive a wide range of information as a signal to change the relationship with the environment. The action then taken, both finalizes this circle of change and brings us to the starting point of the next circle of change.

We always act based on our current perception, but as soon as the action is taken we need to perceive on a still higher level and initiate the next action. This repetitive cycle incorporates everything: our physiological, anatomical, and perception systems. And while the anatomical and physiological components have limitations, perception is an endless process. The Circle of Transformation has its own inner circle of interrelationships among outside signals, our senses, our perceptions and our actions.

The essence of this Circle is to develop a more and more perfect system of interaction with the environment and with energy transformation in and out of our bodies. Action plays a critical role in this chain because a proper action is an extension of a proper perception and a proper reflection of that perception. A correctly performed action leads to the next level of possible perception. However, if our perceptions are flawed, the resulting action is incorrect and we cannot move on to the proper perception on a higher level. Energy from outside will be channeled not in an efficient way as it should be. Development of the system of channeling energy will be stifled and so the goal is not reached.

Action is the harmonic manifestation of our perception, the implementation and expression of perception. The Pose Method of Running offers a simple example of the correlation between perception and action. In Pose Running there is one very simple rule called the action of pulling. This rule says that in running, you must pull your foot from the ground directly under the hip (Fig.9.1). The rule is very clear and unambiguous.

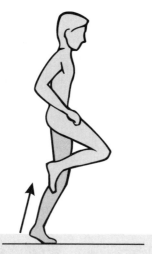

Fig.9.1 Regardless of speed, you must invariably pull your foot under your hips. Pulling the foot under the hips is a directional command, not to be confused with the vertical height of pulling, which varies depending on your speed.

But when attempting to learn Pose Running, most students fail to perceive the second part of the rule. They can pull the foot from the ground, but not under the hip. This is a true failure in perception, for these students will insist that they are in fact pulling their feet up under their hips. Only when confronted with video evidence to the contrary do they understand their mistake, both in action *and* in perception.

This deceptive perception is a frequent occurrence in the learning of any movement and is probably the biggest challenge in learning new skills. Until we can perceive accurately, what we are doing, we cannot progress to the next level. All our action should be very precise and coincide with accurate perception to lead us toward more perfect movement.

The correct action is the one that expresses proper perception of movement and proper application of force, proper timing, proper efforts, and proper direction. It all yields one single action, an idealized model of movement, resulting in the minimum expenditure of energy with maximum efficiency.

This ideal action starts the movement and finishes the movement, in effect making the movement cyclical and allowing us to continue moving. In running, swimming and cycling and in virtually all movement, this action is integrally related with the repetitive application of body weight and the change of support. Each movement leads to the next and the next, and the next... This is the Circle of Transformation.

CHAPTER 10
THE POSE STANDARD AND
THE CORRECTION OF ERRORS

*It is the true nature of mankind to learn
from mistakes, not from examples.*

— Fred Hoyle

Akey element of learning and teaching is the correction of errors. This process includes defining errors and correcting them through a variety of approaches. As pointed out by the quote from Fred Hoyle (above), it helps to understand that making errors is an integral part of the learning and teaching process. We all make errors all the time. Those who improve the most are the ones who are the most skilled at recognizing and correcting their errors.

The general definition of an error is very simple. It is a deviation from the standard, the standard being anything taken as a basis of comparison, model, rule, test, or requirement (1) (Fig.10.1). Without a standard, there is nothing to look for, no way to determine what is right and what is wrong and no way to correct the mistakes.

No matter what kind of sport and movement you may be attempting to learn, errors can be classified into groups according to the following table (Fig.10.2).

Closely related with the above group of movement errors are errors in perception

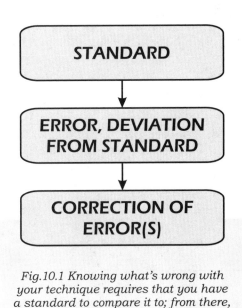

Fig.10.1 Knowing what's wrong with your technique requires that you have a standard to compare it to; from there, any deviation can be considered an error.

and errors in thinking and understanding. Errors in perception come in many hues. At the end of the previous chapter, we discussed runners who mistakenly believed they were bringing the feet up directly under their hips. Other perception errors might include underestimating your level of exertion or misjudging the distance to the finish line. Errors in perception involve any internal or external feedback.

Mistakes in thinking come from misguided concepts and incorrect ideas. A good example of an error in ideas comes from "Basic Track and Field Biomechanics" by Tom Ecker, where the author presents the relationship between body lean and running acceleration as follows: *"An illusion of forward lean may be observed at the completion of the driving phase, when the runner is in more classic running position"* (2).

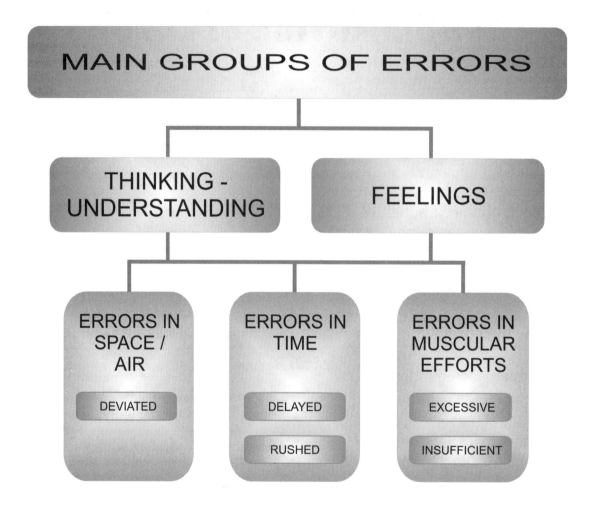

Fig.10.2 As the table of errors demonstrates, errors can be traced to your understanding of movement and your perception of that movement. From there, errors relate to the precise execution of only what's necessary to complete the movement, because if you don't do enough — or you do too much — it's probably an error. Spacial errors can be summed up as any unnecessary effort while you are changing support. Errors in time could be delays or rushing to perform an action. Finally, errors in muscular efforts could be excessive use, or insufficient use of muscles, which puts an unnecessary strain on tendons, ligaments, and joints.

If you read this statement carefully, you'll see that he implies that forward lean comes from acceleration, and not vice versa. From this point of view, leaning is the result of acceleration. Therefore acceleration is the cause and lean is the effect, not the opposite.

But from the point of view of the Pose Method, the cause and effect are opposite. How can you perform the first step? Is it more logical to use muscular effort to propel the body forward or to simply lean forward and *allow* the body to begin moving? Placing the focus on muscular effort is an example of a wrong idea leading immediately to incorrect technique and teaching.

Why is this a wrong perception and a wrong action? Because it leads to a hierarchical structure of the forces involved in running, where muscular efforts assume the primary role. Possible consequences could (and frequently do) include excessive muscular tension and overuse injuries. How do we correct this error? We need the proper thought, the proper idea and the proper perception, all of which lead to the proper action.

To get there, we first have to examine how we relate to the environment in which we operate? If we try to fight against the environment, we limit our efficiency. The essence of nature is to cooperate, not conflict. We have to cooperate as part of nature. Our actions should be directed to using nature as a support mechanism and thereby minimize our own efforts. Nikolai Bernstein defined it like this, *"The movement is more economical and therefore more efficient, when the organism utilizes more reactive, [gratuitous forces] for its performance and adds less active [muscular] work"* (3).

We should interpret our movement errors by the degree of deviation from the standard. In this case, the optimal indication of the standard would be movement that minimizes our work against the environment (nature) and maximizes the use of nature's forces. So we have to look for errors in our relationship with the environment.

The force of gravity is the most dominant feature of the environment for us here on Earth So our best results would come — naturally — from minimizing our work against gravity and instead using as much of the force of gravity as possible to propel us forward.

Fighting gravity puts a tremendous load on our muscles, bones and connective tissue. So to correct the error of fighting gravity by an excessive use of muscular effort, we create a standard based on the environment provided by nature. Following nature's lead, we develop proper ideas, proper perception and proper actions. With the standard in place, we can then identify errors and correct them through specific drills.

Taken together, our thoughts, desires and actions comprise a system (an integrated whole) of interacting with the environment most efficiently. Throughout this book, standards will be developed according to the environment in which we run, ride and swim and measures to correct the inevitable errors will be prescribed for each sport.

References:

1. Thorndike–Barnhart. *Student Dictionary*. Harper Collins Publishers, 1992, p. 1074.

2. Ecker, T. *Basic Track and Field Biomechanics*. Tafnews Press, Los Altos, California, 2002 p. 62.

3. Bernstein, N. *On constructing movement*. Medgiz, Moscow, 1947, p. 31.

SECTION IV
RUNNING TECHNIQUE

Dr. Romanov corrects running technique.

CHAPTER 11
DO WE NEED TO KNOW HOW TO RUN?

The people may be made to follow a course of action, but they may not be made to understand it.

— *Confucius*

There's a popular saying in golf that goes "You drive for show and putt for dough." In triathlon, it wouldn't be a stretch to rework the axiom ever so slightly: "You swim and ride for show and run for dough." Coming at the end of this three–sport event, running is key to your overall success in a race, and the longer the run is, the bigger a factor it plays.

The irony is that most sports experts maintain that there is no proper one–size–fits–all technique for running. While virtually everyone agrees that proper swimming technique must be taught and theories abound about the most efficient means to pedal a bicycle, when it comes to running technique, there is a great void. Somehow the notion that running is a "natural" (Fig.11.1) innate human capability has taken hold.

Over and over the same point is made: each human has his or her own running style. There is no need — or even possibility — of teaching proper running technique. In the absence of focus on technique, great volumes have been written about training to run and a huge industry has developed

We don't need to teach how to run, because it's natural. As human beings we were born knowing how to run.

RUNNING IS NATURAL

Fig.11.1 With respect to art and artists, you'll find that there are different styles and opinions based on individual preferences. However, the same is not true for running. We have physical limitations on our interactions with our environment. Thus working within the boundaries of our physical framework makes us more efficient and keeps us injury free.

to service runners with all their needs, not least of which are running shoes designed to correct — or prevent — running injuries.

The voices against teaching proper running technique are loud and persistent. Many of the most successful athletes in the sport vigorously deny the existence and necessity of correct running technique. None other than Kenya's Paul Tergat (1), former holder of the fastest marathon performance in history (2:04:55) told *Runner's World* magazine, "Kenya's success is not depending on form. No runner's is." Further along, he added, "Kenyans do not learn or even discuss form. That's the way their coach wants to be."

In the same *Runner's World* story, Dr. Gabriele Rosa, the Italian coach who founded Kenya's training camps program and has been credited for much of Kenya's distance running success, carried on the same theme, saying "you can't run thinking about how to move your feet, your body, your hands — it's too distracting. It's all training, nothing else."

Still another Kenyan voice, that of the country's first globally successful champion, Kipchoge Keino, ascribes running ability to the Creator. Keino, who scored a stunning victory in the 1500m at the Mexico City Olympics in 1968 and now serves as the head of Kenya's National Olympic Committee, puts it very simply: *"There is no correct running form, so you can't learn it. Form is God–given. If you systematize it, you destroy it."*

While the prevailing opinion among scientists, athletes and coaches has always held that there is no one proper way to run, there have always been schools of thought as to how to run better. Chief among them was to copy the style of a successful runner. In the case of Kenya, it was Kipchoge Keino himself who became the archetype for the Kenyan style of running. You can clearly see echoes of Keino's style in virtually every top Kenyan athlete, right up to today's Paul Tergat. The same could be said

for the great runners of Ethiopia, where the likes of Mirus Yifter and Haile Gebrselassie call to mind the 1960 barefoot Olympic marathon champion, Abebe Bikele. Copy the greats though certain athletes might, the verdict from the scientific community was final: "there is no scientifically founded ideal technique that suits everyone" (2).

Wow! Against this backdrop of some of history's greatest runners maintaining that there is no such thing as teachable, proper running technique, it almost seems heretical to argue the opposite point; that there is in fact a teachable, proper way to run — and that's what we're about to show you.

First, though, let's look at an athlete who falls somewhere between the "natural" school and the "proper technique" school. Michael Johnson (Fig.11.2), unquestionably has been history's most successful runner over 200m and 400m, still holding the world records in each event long after his retirement following the Sydney Olympic Games in 2000.

Johnson was largely self–taught in his running style, which he developed through the willingness to experiment and a gift to recognize and perceive effective technique. Combined with a coach with the insight not to change his style (3) and, of course, rigorous training, Johnson ran his way to five Olympic gold medals with a style that clearly was different from his competitors.

According to the online Wikipedia (4), Johnson was once asked by a reporter, "If you had a usual running technique like other runners, do you think you would go faster?" His response was, *"If I ran like other runners, I would be back there with them."*

Interestingly, the same Wikipedia entry describes Johnson's unique style, but still can't decide what it all means: "Johnson was noted for his unique running style. His upright stance and very short steps defied the perceived wisdom that a high knee lift was essential for maximum speed. Whether this affects his speed is still a mystery."

Ponder that for a second... history's greatest runner employs a completely different technique to all his competitors and the (non) conclusion is "whether this affects his speed is still a mystery." That's something like observing the switch from steel to fiberglass equipment for pole vaulting and making the conjecture: "whether this affects the height is still a mystery."

Is there any other human activity, where there is similar resistance to finding a 'best way'? Nothing could be more 'natural' than childbirth, but there are many theories on the best way to achieve safe birth. Chewing food is a 'natural' activity, but again there are experts out there counseling the 'best way' to chew. Various theories abound even for proper breathing and use of meditation to control heart rate.

But when it comes to running, we are told that it is a natural human movement. We are human; therefore we know how to run. Of course, to give lie to this concept all you have to do is go to any local 5km race and observe the wide variety of running styles on display. Obviously, some techniques are better than others. Does it make any sense to conclude that those with poor techniques are forever consigned to inferiority? Is it

Fig.11.2 Michael Johnson in action on his way to winning the 200 metres gold medal in a new world record time of 19.32 in the Olympic Stadium at the 1996 Centennial Olympic Games in Atlanta, Georgia.

Source: Gary M. Prior/Getty Images

unthinkable to believe that by learning a better way to run those runners could significantly improve their performances?

In addition to running faster, there's another consideration to weigh in the matter of learning improved running technique — injury prevention. In the late 1970's, when Runner's World first published a survey of injury rates among runners, they found that a startling two–thirds of all recreational runners reported sustaining a running injury *every year*. Now this was at the end of the first decade of the so–called "Running Boom," when the fashion was to run long, slow distance and the available running shoes were relatively crude.

The most recent survey presented at the American College of Sports Medicine's annual conference in Nashville, TN in 2005 reveals an astonishing fact: the number of athletes reporting running injuries increased substantially to a full 85% of all respondents. Despite over two decades of theoretical improvements in running shoe technology and countless articles and books on training, more people than ever are getting hurt by running.

Still, if you read the available literature (5, 6, 7, 8) on running injuries, you'll find virtually no mention of running technique as a contributing factor. When you think about it, it's almost spooky; this aversion to recognizing what is so patently obvious: running with poor technique leads to running injuries.

Just as obvious is this: the further and faster you run with poor technique, the more likely you are to suffer running injuries. A twice–a–week runner who coasts through a leisurely 12–minute mile simply doesn't put enough stress on the body to bring on injury, but as the mileage and the intensity ratchet up, the margin for error diminishes. With enhanced volume or speed, there is a premium put on perfect form. Even the slightest errors in technique are magnified; vastly increasing the odds of injury.

Now let's go back to the widely–held notion that running is a natural, simple human activity. If that were the case, then what is the explanation for the almost universal incidence of injury among its practitioners? If all humans were genetically programmed to run with a natural gait, as unique for each human as each snowflake is from all others, wouldn't it make sense that running injuries were rare indeed?

The more logical conclusion is that running is a skill: a teachable, learnable skill. That being the case, the next questions are: what is the proper technique for running and how can it be taught? It's worth noting that many of the talented runners cited above, who argue against the teaching of running, are in fact genetically gifted with efficient running styles.

Just as others may have a natural talent for art or music — or throwing a football, for that matter — greats from Bikele and Keino through to Gebrselassie and Tergat have been blessed with superb natural running styles. It only makes sense that those to whom excellent running technique comes easily would be the most persistent in arguing against the need for teaching running as a skill. But, just as the rest of us can markedly improve our abilities in painting or playing an instrument, so too can we benefit from instruction in running.

With the perpetual insistence of the running community that running is a natural trait, what's been missed is that natural factors hold the key to developing — and teaching — proper running technique. As living beings existing in nature, humans are no different from other land–based animals. When we run, we are co–existing and interacting with natural forces and our progress is completely determined by how well we use our body movements to take advantage of those natural forces.

We run best when we work with nature, not against it. The predominant mechanical factor found in nature that shapes and governs all our movements is gravity. If we perceive gravity to be a force against which we have to work, then there are profound limits on our ability to run as far or as fast as we desire. Any time we hear such common running terminology as 'push off' or 'pound the pavement', we know we are hearing the words of someone who (subconsciously) believes we have to work against gravity in order to run.

When we hear a runner described as having a 'light, fluid stride', then we know the observer recognizes (again subconsciously, no doubt) that the runner is working with gravity. The very term 'light' contrasts nicely with the image of 'pounding'; the first indicates harmony with nature, the other a struggle against nature.

These contrasting images reinforce the central thesis that there must be a skill to running. If there is a choice between working with nature (harnessing the power of gravity), or working against nature (trying to overcome gravity's pull), then it must require skill to do one instead of the other.

Which brings us to the salient question: how do we run in order to make the best use of the energy nature presents us with in the form of gravity? Clearly, we have to examine and understand the interaction between a human, transferring his body horizontally through space (running) and time; where the pull of gravity is commonly perceived as only 'down', i.e. directed toward the center of the Earth. The skill required then, is to efficiently redirect gravity's 'free' energy into the horizontal plane. We call that skill the Pose Method of Running and that will be the focus of the ensuing chapters as we begin the process of molding an integrated

approach to success in all three disciplines of triathlon.

References:

1. Wallack, Roy M. *I will learn to run better.* Runner's World, October, 2004, p. 68–73, 109.

2. Nitro, A. *What is Correct Technique?* Track Technique, Vol. 100, 1987, pp. 3195–3205.

3. Wischnia, Bob. *Point to Point.* Runner's World, Vol. 31, No. 10, October, 1996, p. 16.

4. <http://en.wikipedia.org/wiki/Michael_Johnson>

5. Guten, N.G., Editor. *Running Injuries.* Philadelphia, W.B. Saunders Company, 1997, pp. 61–65.

6. Krissof, W.B. and W.D. Ferris. *Runner's Injuries.* Physician Sports Medicine, Vol. 7, 1979, pp. 55–64.

7. MacIntyre, S.G. *Running Injuries: a clinical study of 4173 cases.* Clinical Journal of Sport Medicine, New York, 1(2), 1991, pp. 81–87.

8. James, Stanly L. and Donald C. Jones. *Biomechanical Aspects of Distance Running Injuries, Biomechanics of Distance Running.* Champaign, IL, Human Kinetics, 1990, pp. 249–269.

CHAPTER 12
FORCES IN RUNNING

*Motion is caused by force and applied to
bodies that are removed from their places.*

— *Leonardo da Vinci*

Few people ever stop to think about the forces that are in play when we run. In general, we view running as something we do, a 100% human powered effort. Where does the force come from? Well, it would have to come from within the human body, wouldn't it? Not really. To run well, it helps to have a complete understanding of force and how it affects human movement.

In classical mechanics the term "force" is understood as a magnitude of interaction between material bodies. The outcome of this interaction is a change in movement, manifesting in the change in direction and speed or acceleration of the material body.

Mathematically, force was expressed by Sir Isaac Newton in the equation **F=ma** (Force equals mass times acceleration). Following from this equation, acceleration of a material body could be expressed as **a=F/m** or as a product directly proportional to the force or net forces applied to a material body and inversely proportional to its mass. No other meaning can be derived from this term in mechanics.

In running, there are several major working forces recognized and accepted by the scientific community, including muscular contraction, muscular–tendon elasticity (also known as stretch–shortening) that produces a recoil effect, ground reaction force and gravity. Each one of these forces has its own meaning, function, place and logic of application.

Some of these are called external or outside forces and the others are internal or inside forces. Gravity and ground reaction force, which are generated outside the body, are external forces and muscle–tendon elasticity and muscular contraction are internal forces.

Another way to classify force is to call it either gratuitous or non–gratuitous. A gratuitous force does its work without the consumption of adenosine triphosphate (ATP, the main energy source for our body), while non–gratuitous force consumes ATP energy through muscular contraction.

ATP can be considered a universal currency traded for movement in all living creatures. It's the true 'cost of living' and just like the U.S. is the world's biggest consumer of oil, your muscle activity burns through the lion's share of your available ATP. In order for the body to replenish its stores of ATP that have been used for muscular work either carbohydrates, fats or proteins have to be processed in the presence of oxygen.

We huff and puff during strenuous movement because we need to bring more oxygen into our bodies to stoke the furnace that is processing our available nutrients. Therefore, the harder our muscles work in movement, the higher our energy bill will be. Conversely, the more use we make of gratuitous forces, the more efficient and economical we will be, thereby lowering our cost of movement.

While this seems pretty self–evident, the current paradigm of running pretty much ignores the essence of the relationship between gratuitous and non–gratuitous force. It has never really been explained, how these forces interact as a system to provide forward movement. The esteemed Russian scientist, Nikolai Bernstein, once suggested that as a general rule, *"The movement is more economical and therefore more efficient, when the organism utilizes more reactive, [gratuitous forces] for its performance and adds less active [muscular] work"* (1). This rule is good guidance and easy to accept, but it still fails to explain exactly how these forces work together as a system.

Over the last 100 years or so, a number of scientists and exercise physiologists have made attempts to explain how these forces work in running (2, 3, 4 5, 6, 7), but what they all had in common was a failure to see these forces as an integrated system. To this day, there still is no recognition in the running community that these forces work in a hierarchical system with very specific roles for each type of force.

The current paradigm of running is based on the notion that the primary sources of force are the muscular–tendon elastic component (5, 6), muscular efforts and ground reaction force (7). Even so, no one has articulated the relationships among these forces and how they contribute to forward propulsion.

In this paradigm, consideration of gravity is limited to its role in returning the body from an airborne condition to the ground. In other words, gravity is thought to bring the body down — not forward — and is therefore thought to be a neutral force in regards to forward propulsion.

Fortunately, that happens not to be the case. Rather than acting as a neutral force, gravity is a dominating and regulating force that establishes relationships among all other forces applied to the body. This leads to the Pose Method's paradigm of forces in running.

Under this paradigm, gravity is the governing force defining the most efficient application of forces to movement in running. All other forces involved in running are subordinate to gravity and gravity determines what the other forces contribute to the specific action of running.

Through the upcoming chapters, we'll discuss each type of force, how they relate to gravity and how we, as runners, can learn to maximize the use of gratuitous forces and minimize our energy expenditures on non–gratuitous forces, such as muscular contraction.

And once we've got the entire concept of how gravity applies to movement in running, we'll start all over again and demonstrate the applications to cycling and swimming, showing that the same forces and logic apply in all movement related activity.

References:

1. Bernstein, N. *On constructing movement*. Medgiz, Moscow, 1947, p.31.

2. Marey, E.J. *Movement*. Arno Press and The New York Times, New York, 1972.

3. Fenn, W.O. *Work against gravity and work due to velocity changes in running*. American Journal of Physiology, Vol. 92, 1930, pp. 433–462.

4. Bernstein N. *Some biodynamic data of running of outstanding athletes*. Theory and Practice of Physical Culture, no. 4. Moscow, 1937, pp. 328–341.

5. Cavagna, G.A., Saibene, F.P. and Margaria, P. *Mechanical work in running*. Journal of Applied Physiology, Vol. 18, 1964, pp. 1–9.

6. Alexander, R. McN. *The human machine*. London: Natural History Museum Publications, 1992, pp. 74–78.

7. Weyand, P.G., Sternlight, D.B., Belizzi, M.J. and Wright, S. *Faster top running speeds are achieved with greater ground forces, not more rapid leg movements*. Journal of Applied Physiology, Vol. 89, 1991–1999, 2000.

CHAPTER 13
MUSCULAR ACTIVITY IN RUNNING

Things are not always what they seem.
— Phaedrus

Now more than ever, the idea that muscular strength is the key to athletic success has taken hold. Strangely, the focus on steroids and other prohibited substances has reinforced the view that muscles do all the athletic work and that bigger and stronger muscles do the work better and faster. And while it is certainly true that muscular strength contributes to athletic achievement, how that contribution is made is widely misunderstood.

"All sporting movement is the consequence of muscle action" writes M.C. Siff in the "Biomechanical Foundations of Strength and Power Training" (1) and it would seem to be a little bit crazy to argue with this seemingly obvious statement. Whenever we see movement around us, it appears to be the result of muscular activity. We flex, therefore we move, you might say. Everything that life experience has shown us, seems to mesh very neatly with the world of science in this simple statement.

So it would be just a bit off kilter to argue that athletic movement was a consequence of anything but muscular activity, right? Perhaps, perhaps not. The best way to put it is to say that muscular strength supports athletic movement, but does not create it.

Let's begin with the notion that muscular activity is only a *function* of transmitting the energy of gravity into the movement of the athlete's body weight in a desired direction. You're probably shaking your head at this point and that's understandable. It certainly is difficult to give up what is so strongly ingrained in our minds and what for so long has seemed as undeniable logic.

But if we hold on to the idea that only muscular activity creates movement, we place severe limits on the powerful role of the force of gravity to create movement, instead relegating it merely to something that holds us to the surface of this planet. Keeping us where we are on Earth is undeniably a major role of gravity, but it's hardly its only function. As good as it is at keeping us where we are, gravity is just as good at getting us where we want to go.

Since we all accept the role of gravity keeping us safely rooted to the Earth, it's not a huge leap to see the work of our muscles as "transmitters" of this force. This brings up the question of what is called the "extensors paradox" (2). Extensors are the muscles involved in opening the various joints in the body, which leads to extension of the limb involved.

The very name "extensor" would lead to obvious conclusion that a given extensor muscle would be working its hardest when its assigned joint was being opened. Thus, the "extensors paradox." Instead of showing hard work being performed, when a runner's leg is rapidly extending as it leaves support from mid–stance on the ground, EMG (Electromyography) data reveals an electrical silence on the part of those muscles (Fig.13.1).

when it appears that the most work should be taking place? It's not that they're shirking their duties; they're just fulfilling their role in a very intelligent, integrated system, a system that conventional movement theory has failed to regard as an integrated whole.

At this point we have to step back a bit and look at our assumption that the mind is the command center for muscular activity and consider that there is another force in play. That force is gravity.

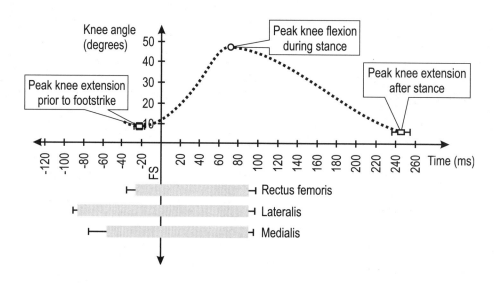

Fig.13.1 Results of phasic quadriceps EMG and knee angle for typical subject averaged over six footstrikes (adapted from McClay et al (2)).

This 'electrical silence' simply means that the extensor muscles of the legs are not active during extension. This finding does not support the conventional view of muscle activity, hence it has been called a paradox.

How could these extensor muscles 'turn off' at what has been considered the most important point of forward propulsion in running? How could they shut down just

At the moment when gravity is propelling a runner's general center of mass in horizontal movement during the forward lean (fall), the muscles are taking their cue from gravity and remaining silent. Data confirming this relationship between gravity and muscle activity at support time in running has been around since the early 1970's and continues to be confirmed up to the present day.

Why would the extensor muscles stop working when the leg is extending? The better question is to ask why they would work, when the force of gravity is going to pull the body forward automatically and without energy expenditure. The muscles turn off simply because they don't need to work to accomplish the task of moving the body down the road.

Many studies have confirmed that the runner's quadriceps work their hardest just when the knee is being flexed (bent) the most and immediately before extension begins. This point coincides with the maximum vertical ground reaction force (3, 4). After this, knee extensor muscle activity drops and ends completely just as leg extension begins (5).

What this means is that our muscles work hardest, when they work against gravity (during landing and mid–stance), under the maximum magnitude of the vertical component of ground reaction force. Then, when gravity takes over to move the body forward, these muscles are off the job. A certain degree of muscular activity is always needed to hold the body together and maintain an effective running posture for efficient falling, but this maintenance work doesn't provide forward propulsion.

In other stages of running, there is muscle activation to serve vital needs of the body during landing. Just before foot–strike the muscles kick back in, so to speak, to cushion the impact on the body as it returns to support on the ground. In order to stabilize the runner at the knee and hip, the quadriceps and hamstrings both contract as the foot touches the ground and the knee begins to flex. All of this general activity of leg and hip muscles has been confirmed through EMG research data (5, 6, 7, 8, 9, 10, 11, 12).

Reviewing all that we know today about muscle activity, it is possible to draw a close approximate model of a single running stride of one leg with peak activity occurring at specific points — the *defining points* or points of changing direction. It is this model which forms the basis of the Pose–Fall–Pull structure of the Pose Method of Running.

These defining points show that our muscles are not completely *off* at any point during the running motion. It's a relative thing; there is no such thing during activity as complete relaxation of your muscles. It's just that some are working less than others at any given point in time. Relaxation during running means that a specific muscle group does not work in opposition to the efforts of another muscle group; it doesn't mean that muscles that are supposed to be working simply switch off.

Considering the running motion, we already know that maximum quadriceps muscle activity occurs at the transition between knee flexion and extension and coincides with maximum vertical ground reaction force. After this, knee extensor muscle activity starts to diminish and ends almost entirely just as leg extension begins (4, 5). So as the leg is rapidly extending, the leg extensor muscles are silent. This is the 'extensor paradox' we mentioned earlier.

What this tells us is that the concept of running as a push–off movement, which at first glance would seem quite "logical," is shown in these studies to be obviously wrong. But let's not call it a "paradox." It's really just a misunderstanding. As science has shown, the exact muscles that are thought to be working during this supposed "push–off" are in fact silent.

The Real Paradox

The first reaction about this misunderstanding might be a yawning "so what?" After all, what difference could it possibly make, whether or not certain muscles are working or whether or not a runner actually initiates the running movement by attempting to push–off?

The problem stems from this misguided thinking. If a runner even thinks about pushing off, much less tries to do it, not only is he wasting energy in the attempt to flex muscles that are not in a position to be flexed, but more importantly, he postpones the work of the muscles that are supposed to be working in a coordinated fashion. Specifically, the push off attempt will delay the work of the hamstrings to pull the foot from the ground at a very specific time.

The lack of understanding about what is really happening in the running stride means that the runner ends up wasting time — and time is the ultimate measure of success in competition. Trying to push off instead of focusing on simply pulling the foot from the ground, literally amounts to working against oneself. It may seem a small thing, but it is precisely the small things that are the basis of perfect running technique.

As an example, when you are on a bicycle going down a very steep hill and you try to pedal, your efforts are absolutely empty — and wasted. The power of gravity is overwhelmingly higher than the power of your muscles to drive the pedals. The same thing is true when you try to contract muscles that are supposed to be "off" in a specific point in the running stride. It is a complete waste to try and work muscles that don't need to be worked.

It is necessary to understand that we have two distinguished types of muscular activity — voluntary and involuntary — and that

there is a big difference between the two. Involuntary muscle activity takes place as a reaction to gravity, to changing direction of the body, to losing balance, etc. All involuntary muscle activity is reactive; you don't need to control it at all. Landing activity is also involuntary.

On the other hand, voluntary muscle activity is mostly related with specific goal–oriented movements, such as touching, bending, swinging, etc. These movements occur as a result of a conscious decision, in the case of running, the decision to pull the foot from the ground. Of course even here we'd like to transition these conscious movements to the sub–conscious. The goal would be to perfect these specific movements so that it becomes second nature to do them properly, without active thought.

You could equate this to the advanced state of performance of a martial arts fighter, a "Zen–like" state, where we are able to perform conscious movement unconsciously. In such a state the mind is not disturbed by anything — you think nothing, but are ready to do anything. In running we have only one point where we need to perform conscious activity — pulling the foot from the ground.

The problem is that most runners constantly confuse the distinction between the types of muscle activity and attempt voluntary activity where involuntary activity is already taking place. This confusion substantially increases the workload of the muscles resulting in an excess of muscle tension. This is the real paradox of running. If you earnestly try to do something, but it happens to be the wrong thing, you are both wasting energy and working against the technique that would give you the best results.

We must be absolutely clear as to how to perform a voluntary movement, but not create pointless voluntary muscle activity.

Voluntary movement does not equal voluntary contraction. You can command your body to perform a specific action, but you can't tell it which specific muscles it needs to use in the action. Your muscles will work it out.

You shouldn't even attempt to tell your muscles how fast or how forcefully to contract. The intricate communication between the brain and the muscle groups handle these decisions. We can command which movements to produce and only this, nothing more. The actual recruitment of muscles to perform the desired action is done according to the present state of the body and its ongoing movements.

Which kind of simplifies things nicely doesn't it? As an athlete, the only thing you need to know is *which* movements to produce, not *how* to produce them. You need to know that you must pull your foot from the ground, but need not concern yourself with what muscles. Just that it needs to be done and done right–on–time. The drills in the later chapters will help you refine this skill of using your body correctly during running.

References:

1. Siff, M. *Biomechanical Foundations of Strength and Power Training.* In Biomechanics in Sport London. V. Zatsiorsky Editor. Blackwell Scientific Ltd., 2000, pp. 103–142.

2. McClay, I.S., Lake, M.J. and Cavanagh, P.R. *Muscle Activity in Running. Biomechanics of Distance Running.* P.R. Cavanagh, Editor. Champaign: Human Kinetics, 1990, pp. 165–185.

3. Brandell, B.R. *An Analysis of Muscle Coordination in Walking and Running Gaits.* Medicine and Sport: Biomechanics 111 S. Cerquiglini, A. Venerando and J. Wartenweiler. Basel, Editors. Switzerland: Karger, 1973, pp. 278–287.

4. Nilsson, J. and Thorstensson, A. *Adaptability in Frequency and Amplitude of Leg Movements During Locomotion at Different Speeds.* 10th International Congress of Biomechanics Abstract Book, 20. Solna, Sweden: Arbetar–Skydd Sverket, 1985, p. 194.

5. Mann, R.A. and Hagy, J. *Biomechanics of Walking, Running and Sprinting.* American Journal Sports Medicine, Vol. 8, 1980, pp. 345–9.

6. Paré, E.B., Stern, J.T. and Schwartz, J.M. *Functional Differentiation with the Tensor Fasciae Latae.* Journal of Bone and Joint Surgery, Vol. 63, 1981, pp. 1457–1471.

7. Schwab, G.H., Moynes, D.R., Jobe, F.W. and Perry, J. *Lower Extremity Electromyographic Analysis of Running Gait.* Clinical Orthopaedics, Vol. 176, 1983, pp. 166–170.

8. Montgomery, W.H., Pink, M. and Perry, J. *Electromyographic Analysis of Hip and Knee Musculature During Running.* American Journal of Sports Medicine, Vol. 22, 1994, pp. 272–278.

9. Wank, V., Frick, U. and Schmidtbliecher, D. *Kinematics and Electromyography of Lower Limb Muscles in Overground and Treadmill Running.* International Journal of Sports Medicine, Vol. 19, 1998, pp. 455–461.

10. Elliot, B.C. and Blanksby, B.A. *The Synchronisation of Muscle Activity and Body Segment Movements During a Running Cycle.* Medicine and Science in Sports, Vol. 11, 1979, pp. 322–327.

11. Mann, R.A., Moran, G.T. and Dougherty, S. *Comparative Electromyography of the Lower Extremity in Jogging, Running and Sprinting.* American Journal Sports Medicine, Vol. 14, 1986, pp. 501–510.

12. Heise, G.D., Morgan, D.W., Hough, H. and Craib, M. *Relationships between Running Economy and Temporal EMG Characteristics of Bi–articular Leg Muscles.* International Journal of Sports Medicine, Vol. 17, 1996, pp. 128–133.

CHAPTER 14
MUSCLE–TENDON ELASTICITY IN RUNNING

Nature does nothing uselessly.

— *Aristotle*

Muscle–tendon elasticity sounds like something best left to the sports scientists, doesn't it? The truth is that it's a critical element in your development as a successful, injury–free runner.

Muscle–tendon elasticity occurs during your interaction with the ground (or support) through the use of the stretching–shortening elastic component of the muscular–tendon complex (Fig.14.1). Simply put, it is your body's ability to store energy during support and then to apply that energy, when support is removed. It's a little like the snap–back after a rubber has been stretched.

This elasticity is integral to your body's natural efficiency and economy in movement. If you recall back in Chapter 12, elasticity was listed as a gratuitous force right alongside with gravity and ground reaction force. Muscle–tendon elasticity allows us to consume energy more efficiently, as opposed to using only muscular contraction. When muscle–tendon elasticity is effectively used, oxygen consumption and muscular effort are reduced, which in turn reduces the overall use of your available energy reserves.

Fig.14.1 A rubber ball's recoil is immediate. Animals like cats and dogs use their elasticity innately to leap great distances vertically. The same should be developed in your stride, using gravity to pull your foot down and muscle–tendon elasticity to provide a jump–start to your leg pull.

As early as in 1964 this was confirmed by Giorgio Cavagna *et al* (1). In a study that measured the oxygen consumption during running, it was estimated that metabolic cost is 50% less by the contributions from elastic storage and return of strain energy. Giorgio Cavagna and various colleagues (2,

3) continued to build on this concept with a number of studies, one (2) of which indicated that mechanical efficiency of running exceeds the efficiency of the conversion of chemical energy to muscular kinetic energy (the ability of the body to do work by the virtue of its motion). Further, elastic strain energy stored during eccentric contractions during early stance subsequently releases during concentric contractions (1, 2, 3, 4, 5, 6).

While this may seem like relatively dense science, what it all adds up to is relatively simple. If you run efficiently with correct technique, you will use less energy and perform better than if you work your muscles too hard.

Relax and Release

The important thing to understand is that the 'relax and release' action that optimizes your use of muscle–tendon elasticity happens in a very specific body position and time frame. If the body position isn't precise or if the time frame is too long or short, then the beneficial effects of muscle–tendon elasticity are compromised.

To effectively use stored elastic energy in your muscle mechanisms, time spent on support must be short (7, 8). While there is currently no exact method of quantifying storage of elastic energy (9), there is a consensus that this phenomenon contributes to both efficiency and economy of movement (3, 5, 10, 11, 12, 13).

The runner's body has minimum kinetic energy at maximum vertical ground reaction force, while the stretch–shortening cycle of the muscle–tendon unit contains maximal potential strain energy at this point. This potential strain energy results from gravity's work during impact (1), however, an 'ideal' body geometry that maximizes potential strain energy and the ability to reduce stance time was not clearly documented through these studies.

What this all points to is that running is a precise and technical skill sport. In the first instance, gravity is the primary source of force and efficiency. As a gratuitous force, it is 'free' and makes the fewest demands on the body's energy stores. But in the hierarchy of forces, it's clear that muscle–tendon elasticity is preferable to muscular contraction, because it is more efficient. But as pointed out above, it has to be applied precisely — at the right time, when the body is in the right position.

Given the lack of documentation from the studies referenced above, how can you make the most efficient use of this muscle–tendon elasticity? Easy. The Pose Method of Running is designed to give you the exact body geometry to maximize this energy — the Pose stance.

Making the Most of Your Elasticity

Muscle–tendon elasticity occurs during muscular activity both separately, as well as together with muscular contraction, as a component of involuntary activity activated by voluntary activity. This yields a complex system based on a puzzling relationship of entities that at first glance do not appear to be related. While muscular activity is voluntary, elasticity is completely reactive. Muscles and tendons work in relation to the loading and unloading of these tissues.

So how is this accomplished most efficiently in the Pose Method?

It's as simple as Pose–Fall–Pull, which we'll discuss in chapter 19. In the Pose stance, gravity serves as the loading external force during support. When the runner falls forward and pulls the foot from the ground in one single movement, the potential strain of muscle–tendon energy is automatically released — at precisely the right place and at precisely the right time. There is no need to actively (voluntarily) load or unload your muscles; the loading and unloading actions are simply by–products of performing the overall actions of pulling and falling.

In Pose Running, use of the elastic component comes down to using the Pose–Fall–Pull as one complex system and the elastic component is the automatic outcome of these actions. You just have to relax and let it happen!

To develop and optimize your muscle–tendon elasticity, we have formulated a series of very specific Pose drills that include change of support, hopping in the Pose, Pose drills with jump rope and a very wide range of elasticity exercises (jumps). These drills can be found in chapters 24 & 25.

Patience is a key virtue in your development as a new Pose runner. The development and nurturing of your muscle–tendon elasticity takes time. Work on these drills without rushing and give your body plenty of time to adapt. Progress from one level of performance to the next will not happen overnight. Over time you'll find you can effectively use your muscles' elasticity over longer and longer distances as you learn the Pose technique. Enhancing the elastic component of your body is an essential element in developing your capacity as an endurance athlete, as well as a sprinter.

References

1. Cavagna, G.A., Saibene, F.P. and Margaria, R. *Mechanical work in running*. Journal of Applied Physiology, Vol. 18, 1964, pp. 1–9.

2. Cavagna, G.A. and Kaneko, M. *Mechanical work and efficiency in level walking and running*. Journal of Physiology, 1977, pp. 268, 467–481.

3. Cavanagh, P.R. and Kram, R. *The efficiency of human movement — a statement of the problem*. Medicine and Science in Sports and Exercise 17, 1985, pp. 304–308.

4. Alexander, R. M. *The human machine*. London: Natural History Museum Publications, 1992, pp. 74–78.

5. Taylor, C.R. *Relating mechanics and energetics during exercise*. Advanced Veterinary Science, Vol. 38A, 1994, pp. 181–215.

6. Jung, A.P. *The impact of resistance training on distance running performance*. Sports Medicine, Vol. 33, 2003, pp. 539–552.

7. Zatsiorsky, V. M. *Science and Practice of Strength Training*. Champaign: Human Kinetics, 1995.

8. Paavolainen, L., Hakkinen, K., Hamalainen, A.N. and Rusko, H. *Explosive–strength training improves 5–km run time by improving running economy and muscle power*. Journal of Applied Physiology, Vol. 86(5), 1999, pp. 1527–1533.

9. Fukunaga, T.Y., Kawakami, S., Funato, K. and Fukashiro, S. *Muscle architecture and function in humans*. Journal of Biomechanics, Vol. 30, 1997, pp. 457–463.

10. Cavagna, G. A. and Citterio, G. *Effect of stretching on the elastic characteristics and the contractile component of frog striated muscle*. Journal of Physiology, Vol. 239, 1974, pp. 1–14.

11. Winter, D.A. *Moments of force and mechanical power in jogging*. Journal of Biomechanics, Vol. 16, 1983, pp. 91–97.

12. Luhtanen, P. and Komi, P.V. *Force–power and elasticity–velocity relationships in walking, running and jumping*. European Journal of Applied Physiology, Vol. 44, 1980, pp. 270–289.

13. Komi, P.V. *Stretch–shortening cycle: a powerful model to study normal and fatigued muscle*. Journal of Biomechanics, Vol. 33, 2000, pp. 1197–1206.

CHAPTER 15
GROUND REACTION FORCE

It is important to recognize what GRF data can and cannot tell us about the biomechanical basis of running.

— *Doris I. Miller*

"Ground Reaction Force?"

If the term brings to mind the deployment of troops to fight insurgents in some distant land, don't worry. Your confusion is an understandable reflection of the times in which we live. On the other hand, if you immediately think of the shock you feel when your foot hits the ground during a run, you're on the right track, but probably still a bit confused.

As it happens, ground reaction force is one of those wonderful little concepts that causes scientists to endlessly bicker with each other in scholarly journals, while running shoe companies gleefully exploit the confusion with ever–thicker shoe soles that they promise will cushion your joints from overuse injuries.

All in all, it adds up to the notion that ground reaction force (GRF) is a negative side effect of running and is something that needs to be minimized. That being the case, ground reaction force merits a closer look.

In order to understand how ground reaction force impacts running, we have to first understand what it is. Ground reaction force is force that the ground (or any other external surface) exerts in response to any force that you exert on the ground (1). Put simply, if you stomp on the ground, GRF is the impact you feel back up your leg and body, through all your joints and muscles.

It's the famous Third Law of Sir Isaac Newton: for every action, there is an equal and opposite reaction. Who knew? Newton knew. You stomp; the ground stomps back. Ouch!

Since during the course of a run of any length your feet will come in contact with the ground, oh, thousands of times, it seems a sound idea to understand how this ground reaction force impacts (pun intended) your running.

Ground reaction force is a non–propulsive force (2), not an active force that would drive your body forward. It arrests the downward movement of your body and reacts to all the force that you apply to the ground, including that of your body mass, as well as your muscular efforts.

As Newton so neatly summarized, ground reaction force adds up all the force you apply and sends it right back in three directions: horizontally, vertically and medial-laterally (side–to–side) (Fig.15.1).

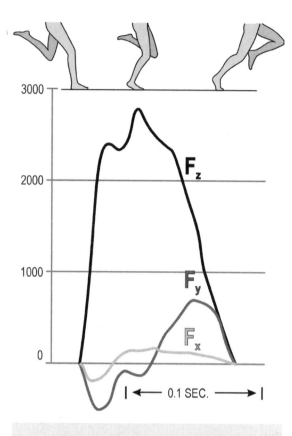

Fig.15.1 Three components of ground reaction force in running during the support phase.

F_z – vertical
F_x – medial–lateral components
F_y – horizontal anterior–posterior GRF

You can see right away how ground reaction force could cause problems. If, for example, you have a tendency to land unevenly on the ground, then too much of the ground reaction force will be distributed side–to–side and you will eventually suffer injuries in your ankles, knees, hips or even right in the many bones of your feet. You

would recognize the terms over–pronation or over–supination to describe these types of errors. The running shoe companies prescribe specially built (and pricey) shoes to correct these errors; the Pose Method of Running suggests that you learn proper running technique... but we digress.

The Conflicting Views of the Scientists

While everyone agrees that ground reaction force exists, that seems to be about the end of any consensus on how it affects running. Doris Miller (3) described the contribution of the individual components of the body to acceleration of the body as a whole as about 80%, concluding, "It is incorrect to attribute the entire GRF–time history to the action of the foot–ankle–leg of the support limb. The support limb simply transmits the force to the ground and, theoretically, need not make any contribution to the push." Got that?

Countering Miller, Peter Weyand (4) insisted that: "At any speed, applying greater forces in opposition to gravity would increase a runner's vertical velocity on take-off, thereby increasing both the aerial time and forward distance traveled between steps." He also concluded that "achieving longer strides would be applying greater forces to the ground."

Additionally, Weyand (4) negated horizontal GRF data, claiming that they "couldn't explain differences in the top speeds attained." Mr. Weyand seems to be implying that the higher you fly, the faster you run. This is quite a different approach from mainstream biomechanics (3), in which horizontal ground reaction force is called a forward propulsive force.

If we take Weyand's (4) approach to explain increases in sprinting speed, then we would have to reject the conclusions of Joseph Hunter (5) with his findings that "faster athletes tended to produce only moderate magnitudes of relative vertical impulse." In the same way, Hunter's findings that the magnitude of the relative vertical impulse correlated with a "flight time just long enough to allow repositioning of the lower limbs," clashes with the hypothesis that propulsion can be maximized through extra extension of the stance limb (6). Whew!

It's a lot to absorb, isn't it? What all of this research into ground reaction force seems to have overlooked is the concept of forces working in a hierarchical system. This oversight has resulted in a lack of clear focus on the relationship between the forces and their functions. In sum, the existing ground reaction force data in running has created more uncertainty than understanding and lacks a "sensitive measure" (3) for getting a true picture of interaction of forces.

A Thought Provoking Example

To see how the forces interact, let's compare the ground reaction force data in long jumping (7, 8) with running. Among the questions raised is the obvious, "when do we push forward?" Good question. The accompanying graph (Fig.15.2) shows that in long jumping there is basically *no such thing* as pushing forward (7). There is only one dominant action, that of lifting the body up (related to the magnitude of the vertical component of ground reaction force). The horizontal "propulsive" component appears only at the end of support for a mere 100th of a second (8).

It is clear that there is a horizontal component of body movement in both long jumping and running. In the long jump, this horizontal movement occurs *entirely* through momentum with essentially zero horizontal component of ground reaction force. In running, particularly in sprinting, the horizontal velocity of body movement is close to or higher than in long jumping, but the "propulsive" horizontal component of

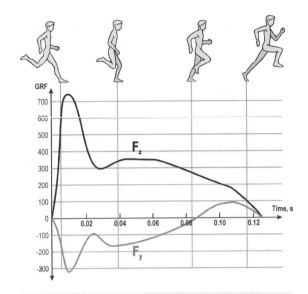

Fig.15.2 Ground reaction force graphs in the long jump.

F_z – vertical GRF F_y – horizontal GRF

ground reaction force has a larger magnitude than in long jumping.

This begs the question of why the long jump, with its vastly longer forward flight, has almost no horizontal component of GRF, but running seems to be just the opposite? Why there is no need for forward propulsion in the long jump, but there is in running? These interesting questions lead to the biggie: what's the real meaning of the horizontal component of ground reaction in running?

Obviously we can guess that in both running and long jump, momentum can move the body forward. Why not? But if so, what is the extra propulsive force in running that is absent in the long jump? The only explanation is that in long jump we don't fall forward to recover the speed lost during the support phase (takeoff).

And why is this important? Because, without the fall, you lose speed and slowly decelerate with every step.

Picture This

Think of the movement of your leg as it moves through the running motion. As a unit it moves both horizontally (forward) and rotationally around your foot on support. The horizontal component of the force on your leg is greater than the gravitational torque (rotating) component. As torque peaks at the point when your foot is about to leave the ground, your foot must accelerate forward, because your body and upper leg are already moving ahead.

Your foot is stuck on the ground and needs to move in order to go up under the hip. Without horizontal propulsion, your foot is in danger of being left behind. The movement of your general center of mass and the effort of your muscles to pull your foot from the ground bring about this propulsion.

Ground reaction force only reflects the force being applied to the ground and any incorrect application of effort. If, for example, you land with a heel strike, or with the so called, "paw back" foot motion (9), the first spike (vertical peak) on a graph of ground reaction force will be much higher than the second spike (Fig.15.3). When you realize that the first spike represents 'impact' and the second peak is 'propulsion', you see the implications right away. Heel striking results in greater impact and lesser propulsion. Who wants that?

Obviously no one, but now a picture is beginning to emerge of how knowledge of ground reaction force can impact our running technique. If heel striking is inherently a bad running technique, doesn't it make more sense to change your technique, than to accommodate it by wearing shoes with thicker heel cushioning? Of course it does. But instead many runners buy the thicker

heeled shoes, which in turn make it even harder to land properly on the ball of the foot. The key to avoiding impact injuries to your heels (and to run faster) is not to cushion the impact, but eliminate it entirely by landing on the ball of your foot.

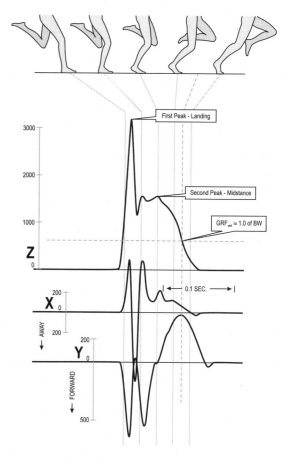

Force-time recording of a heel-toe runner (mass 63 kg, velocity 9.5 ms-1)

Fig.15.3 Ground reaction forces graph. Adapted from Payne, 1983 (12).

Z — vertical component of ground reaction force
X — lateral component of ground reaction
Y — anterior–posterior ground reaction force.

The first peak of vertical ground reaction is a "paw back" motion.

The Real Meaning of Ground Reaction Force

The real meaning of ground reaction force is a reflection of body weight, the force applied to the ground to keep the body in a falling position, as well as to reflect that force so that it was possible to quickly remove the support foot off the ground. All of these forces appear as body weight fluctuates from zero, before touch down of the foot and at the end of support, to the maximum (up to 3 times your body weight) at peak vertical ground reaction force during mid–stance (3).

Your muscular efforts should be limited to equaling the force necessary to maintain support during this fluctuation. Anything more is unnecessary and wasted effort. If you hit the ground harder than is necessary, what you get is impact — not propulsion — plus a lot of wasted energy. If you try to push the body forward by pushing with your support leg on the ground, you can increase your efforts only in a vertical direction, moving your body up. Why waste energy and move your body vertically only to fall down again on your next support?

You can also see the same effect in cycling, when riders try to apply their muscular efforts more than necessary, attempting to apply more force to the pedals, instead of changing gears to allow for easier pedaling and application of body weight. If the pedal doesn't move downward, the vertical component of ground reaction force from the pedal will exert more force than you are able to apply, thus you will move yourself upwards, not increase your pedaling output. That's right, instead of going faster, the rider will bounce up and down on the saddle. You can call it a directional change on the vertical line if you want, but it's really just wasted effort that moves the body up and down, instead of moving the bicycle — and rider — forward.

Now ponder this: faster running with application of body weight requires less muscular effort, not to mention it exerts less ground reaction force on your body. Think about it again: the faster your cadence, the more gratuitous forces you use. In turn, less force is felt by your muscles, your bones, your joints and your connective tissue. On a very basic level, this makes a lot of sense. If you plod your way down the road, your body will feel the full impact of your weight on every foot strike. But as your cadence increases and you spend less time on support, the impact is minimized.

All this confirms one thing: with speed we start to consume gravity (in the form of body weight) more and more. The magnitude of the push–off is not directly related to forward speed, which is a phenomenon related to body movement. What we find is that the fastest runners move with smaller vertical oscillation (10, 11, 12), while less talented distance runners run with much larger vertical oscillation, up to twice as much!

Bouncing on the ground or bouncing on the saddle — it's all the same thing. Unnecessary efforts are reflected through ground reaction force as bouncing up and down, not moving forward faster.

Using Knowledge of Ground Reaction Force to Perfect Running Technique

Since we know that additional muscular efforts are not rewarded and that ground reaction force itself does not create horizontal propulsion, how can we use our knowledge of GRF to perfect running technique? It comes down to perfecting your interaction with the ground at the moment of support. Good interaction is quick interaction. Consciously focus on having 'quick feet' and limit your efforts against gravity to only the actions that allow you to alternate support.

Any time you bounce, you know you're making an error in technique and wasting energy. When you run properly, the graph of your personal GRF will reflect gravitational torque from your efforts to pull your foot from the ground. All the sensations related to ground reaction force appear right at the moment of take–off, thus they can be difficult to discern. That's why perception is so critical. You won't be looking at a bar graph as you run; you have to learn what it feels like to run smoothly and eliminate bouncing or incorrect foot strike.

The key to this is the concept of "one body weight" — your weight under the influence of gravity. When you are falling, your body weight is less than one. In running, this means that you have lost support and must find a new support. To find it, you have to break contact with the ground and prepare for your next fall, which happens on your next support.

This isn't just 'coaching'; this is biological law. Every movement we do revolves around the concept of one body weight. When you no longer have one body weight on support, you have lost support and, by definition, you are falling. All your muscles, tendons, etc. are instinctively attuned to this feeling of one body weight and react accordingly.

You reach one body weight at different angles of falling, depending on the speed at which you are running. Fast runners reach one body weight (and then have to change support) at around 16° degrees whereas recreational runners reach one body weight at eight degrees. This is called the decay rate of ground reaction force. The faster the decay, the faster you fall.

The one body weight principle explains every movement we perform. Not coincidentally, it's also the reason why we lose our ability to run on the Moon (13); we don't have the same body weight there, which is 1/6 of Earth's magnitude. Even though you might think we would be faster runners on the Moon, without gravity slowing us down, quite the opposite is true. On the lunar surface, we can expect to set world high jumping records, but on the other hand that bounce–bounce–bounce is going to slow our 100 meter times significantly.

The bottom line is that when you lose support you have to change support. Doing so as quickly and efficiently as possible, with the minimum of vertical oscillation, will make you a faster and less injury prone runner. Later on in the book, we'll take you through a series of specific drills to help develop your perception around this feeling of running smoothly on the horizontal plane, in blissful harmony with ground reaction force.

References:

1. Bartlett R. *Linear and angular kinetics.* Introduction to Sports Biomechanics. F & FN Spon, 2001, p. 84.

2. Zatsiorsky, V. M. *Kinetics of human motion.* Champaign: Human Kinetics, 2002.

3. Miller, I.D. *Ground Reaction Forces in Distance Running.* In Biomechanics of Distance Running. P.R. Cavanagh, Editor. Human Kinetics Books, 1990, p. 203.

4. Weyand, P.G., Sternlight, D.B., Belizzi, M.J. and Wright, S. *Faster top running speeds are achieved with greater ground forces not more rapid leg movements.* Journal of Applied Physiology, Vol. 89, 2000, pp. 1991–1999.

5. Hunter, J.P., Marshall, R.N. and McNair, P.J. *Relationships between ground reaction force impulse and kinematics of sprint–running acceleration.* Journal of Applied Biomechanics, Vol. 21, 2005, pp. 31–43.

6. Легкая атлетика: Учеб. Для институтов физ.культ./Под ред. Н.Г. Озолина, В.И. Воронкина, Ю.Н.

Примакова.-Изд.4-е, доп., перераб.М.: Физкультура и спорт, 1989, стр. 45.

7. Уткин В.Л. Прыжки в длину с разбега. Биомеханика физических упражнений. М.: Просвещение, 1989, стр. 171.

8. Донской Д.Д., Зациорский В.М. Биомеханика: М.: Физкультура и спорт, 1979, стр. 185.

9. Payne, A.H. *Foot to ground contact forces in elite runners*. In Biomechanics Vol. 8B, H. Matsui and K. Kobayashi, Editors. Champaign: Human Kinetics, 1983, pp. 19–41.

10. Cavanagh, P.R. *Biomechanics of Distance Running*. Human Kinetics Books, 1990, p. 117.

11. Williams, K.R. *Biomechanics of running*. Exercise Sport Science Review, Vol. 13, 1985, pp. 389–441.

12. Miura, M., Kobayashi, K., Miyashita, M., Matsui, H. and Sodeyama, H. *Experimental studies on biomechanics on long distance runners*. In review of our researches, H. Matsui, Editor. Dept. of Physical Education, University of Nagoya, Japan, 1970–1973, pp. 45–46.

13. Margaria. R. *Biomechanics and Energetics of Muscular Exercise*. Oxford University Press, Oxford, 1976, p. 128.

CHAPTER 16
CORIOLIS FORCE

*The cause is hidden, but
the result is well–known.*

— *Ovid*

Coriolis force is a fictitious force, a force that appears in rotational movement as a result of the changing radius and mass of a rotational body (Fig.16.1).

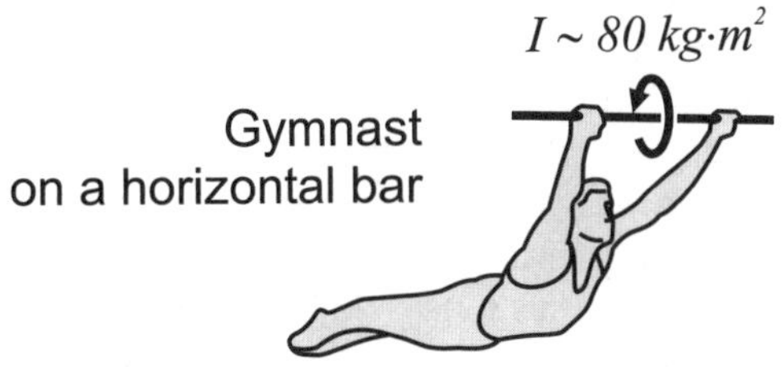

$$I \sim 80 \ kg \cdot m^2$$

Gymnast
on a horizontal bar

Fig.16.1 A gymnast on a horizontal bar is a good example of Coriolis force.

Coriolis force is named after the French physicist, Gaspard–Gustave de Coriolis (Fig.16.2) (1), who lived from 1792 to 1843 and first described this force. While he wasn't the first to work out

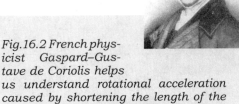

Fig.16.2 French physicist Gaspard–Gustave de Coriolis helps us understand rotational acceleration caused by shortening the length of the swing radius with the force that bears his name — Coriolis Force.

Source: Wikipedia.org/Public Domain.

We devote this chapter of the book to the interesting nuances of Coriolis force to give you a little insight into how a commonly held belief can be misinterpreted and affect the way running technique is taught. We do this because Coriolis force is often mentioned as a propulsive component in running, but the way that force is generated is widely misunderstood.

the math behind the force, and describing it may not even have been his greatest achievement, it nonetheless carries his name. May the Force be with Coriolis.

The underlying principles were later applied to mechanics, where increasing and decreasing rotation occurs. Coriolis force is related to the increasing and decreasing moment of inertia, and can be expressed by the formula $I = \sum m_i r_i^2$.

In the human body, most movement stems from rotation around axes, and so Coriolis force appears in every single movement. Because our body mass itself doesn't change, Coriolis force manifests itself through the functional change in the length of our arms or legs caused by straightening or bending.

Where Current Thinking Misses the Point

In running, this occurs particularly with the so–called swing of the leg, particularly when the leg trails behind the body (Fig.16.3). In the prevailing paradigm of

Running

$$r_1 > r_2 \implies$$
$$I_1 > I_2$$

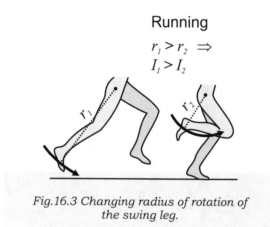

Fig.16.3 Changing radius of rotation of the swing leg.

running, this is called the swing or recovery phase. Theoretically, this swing phase is powered by the effort of the hips and leg muscles to drive the leg from behind the body to the front, helping to propel the runner forward. It's a fine theory except for one little thing: from the standpoint of basic physics, it is completely absurd.

The first and main part of this so–called "propulsion" occurs in the air. Coaches and sports scientists believe that there is a powerful propulsive swing. But it is only the action of pulling the foot from the ground.

Because the length of the runner's leg has been decreased around the axis of the hip, due to bending, as the foot is lifted from the ground, the Coriolis force comes into play and swings the leg forward reducing to minimum possible muscular effort. There is no need at all to move the swing leg forcefully forward; all the runner needs to do at this point is to continue to fall forward.

In this current coaching/teaching paradigm, swinging the knee up and forward is given priority and called the "driving" phase. This would then be combined with a push–off to become the "propulsive" phase. At first glance, this sounds plausible, yet from a biomechanical point of view this concept is just nonsense. Basic physics is very clear about this. There is a simple Aristotelian relationship between the mover and the moved (2). If something is to be moved, then the mover must be still.

So in order to move one part of the body, another part must not be moved. If you actively move your leg forward, then you need to keep your body still. Thus, the active effort to swing the leg forward reduces the forward movement of the runner's general center of mass. It is a fallacy to think that we move the body forward by driving the knee. We may feel and think we are moving ourselves forward by actively driving the leg forward, but this is nothing but an illusion.

The forward movement of the leg is the result of decreased radius of the leg and is related to the necessity of bringing the general center of the leg's mass to the general center of the body's mass. Their vertical alignment at the Pose stance is a starting point of the body falling forward. This is the main reason why we need to get the foot under the hip.

When the foot is pulled from the ground, it goes under the hip. Why do the rear and front leg fall down? Because as a pendulum, the rear leg at the terminal stance at the end of support and front leg in the Pose position is in the highest point of the pendulum swing, so the next movement can only be powered by the downward pull of gravity. So the rear leg is "swinging" downward forward to the lowest position and align with GCM. The same thing is happening to the front leg, which moves downward backward in order to "catch–up" alignment with GCM on support as well

Additionally, there is an elastic component of the thigh and hip muscles acting on the leg helping to bring it back under the body. The final work is done through the runner's interaction with gravity. It is completely natural to want to find the next point of support, so the foot goes quickly under the hip. You don't have to think about putting the leg under the body — only pulling the foot from the ground under the hip.

A Little Bit of Science

It might help to give you a little bit of scientific background. As mentioned above, Coriolis force can be stated as $I = \sum m_i r_i^2$, where I is the moment of inertia, m is mass of the body and r is the radius of rotation of the body.

In movement, where the body mass is constant, there is only one variable — the radius of rotation. This is the only thing that can be changed. In running, this refers to leg length, where the pivot of rotation is the axis of the hip. When you want to increase rotation of the leg, you need to reduce the radius of rotation, because the mass cannot change. You can use this knowledge to your benefit in three aspects of the Pose running movement:

1) On support: when the entire body is rotating around the support foot. Quickly bending the knee and holding this position gives you the ability to increase rotation. Gravity also plays its part, but this quick bend of the knee allows you to recover quickly during landing;

2) The swing leg: to increase the speed with which your foot is moving from the ground under the hips. Simply pull your foot from the ground and allow your knee to bend, and in so doing, you'll reduce the radius of rotation of the leg. Because your leg is bending at the knee and the axis of rotation (your leg) is shortened, it therefore ends up moving with acceleration "by itself" with little or no conscious muscular effort;

3) Your arms: by keeping them bent you reduce their axis of rotation and thereby the moment of inertia. Keeping arms bent and close to the body creates an easier pendulum rotation. However, be sure not to hold them tense and rigid at the elbows.

An Exercise in Visualization

Finally, here's a little piece of visual imagery that may help you understand how Coriolis force affects your running. We have all seen ice skaters work their way into spins (Fig.16.4). While there are many vari-

Axel in figure skating

Fig.16.4 Alternating the swing leg from extended to compact facilitates rotational acceleration.

ations of spins, they generally all start out with arms — and sometimes legs — outstretched away from the body. As the spin progresses, the skater gradually draws the limbs in closer to the body, thereby shortening the radius of rotation. The impact of this is instantly visible as the speed of the spin increases dramatically. This is a classic application of Coriolis force.

To see how this works in running, imagine a situation where you deliberately overextend both your arms and legs. In your mind, picture a running technique, where the arms swing broad arcs back and forth and the legs reach far ahead of the body and then subsequently trail the body by an equal measure. All this extension vastly increases the frame in which the 'run' takes place. It should be clear that all this long reach takes both time and excess energy.

Now, continue your visualization and begin to shorten the swing length of the arms and legs incrementally, thus decreasing the frame in which the run happens. Just as the skater fits into a smaller physical space by bringing the arms and legs in, so too does the runner. Now all the movements are much quicker and more forceful. Speed increases dramatically, while energy use actually drops. Coriolis force has been applied properly to minimize muscular activity while helping your mental runner go faster... and isn't that the objective?

This little bit of science can go a long way to helping you to your next PR. Realizing that by shortening your axes of rotation you will reduce the internal friction of your body can go a long way to reducing your energy consumption and increasing your overall running efficiency.

References:

1. *The New Webster's International Encyclopedia*. Trident Press International, 1994, p. 265.

2. Aristotle. *Movement of Animals*. The Complete Works of Aristotle, Vol. 1, Princeton University press, 1995, p. 1990.

CHAPTER 17
GRAVITY IN RUNNING

*For we conceive ourselves to know about
a thing when we are acquainted with
its ultimate causes and first principles,
and have got down to its elements.*

— *Aristotle*

What makes us 'go' when we run? Sounds like it should be a pretty easy question to answer, doesn't it? After all, humans have been running since... forever. You would think someone would have sorted out something that basic to human existence by now, wouldn't you?

Strangely, there has never been any scientifically definitive judgment on the propulsive forces in running, leaving the average person to assume that the legs provide the power that moves us down the road. In turn, all running instruction has been based on getting the most out of the legs.

If you've read any popular running literature, you've undoubtedly been drawn into the entire school of running thought based solely on the concept of the legs providing the power in running. Knee lift. Leg drive. Heel–toe action. Toeing off.

Not only has the instruction been based on leg power, but a whole industry of providing running shoes for specific stride flaws has flourished. Are you a pronator or a supinator? Do you need more support or lighter shoes? And don't forget the injuries. Sports physicians worldwide have enjoyed steady business from the wounded legs of frustrated runners.

Still — it all makes sense, if the legs do provide the power for running. But what if they don't? Wouldn't that change everything?

What if there was a source of power that was omnipresent, limitless and free for the taking? A source that everyone knows about, but no one ever thinks about? A source that the intelligent well–schooled athlete could channel into increased forward running speed, while minimizing the chance of injury?

Sound interesting?

Good, because there exists just such a magic, renewable source of power and it will change the way you run. It's called 'gravity'.

Gravity Provides the Power

Gravity, you ask, I thought gravity made it hard to run, not easy? Therein lies the rub. When you attempt to use your legs to power your running, you do work against gravity and the result is that commonly known description of running — pounding the pavement. But if instead of fighting against gravity, you flow with it, everything about your running technique will change.

Heretofore, the common perception of gravity's effect on running is that it is neutral, and that it is really only a consideration during flight. When both feet are off the ground, it was assumed that gravity pulled the body straight down, acting against the body in the vertical plane, not providing momentum along the horizontal vector.

Fortunately, that happens not to be the case. The following explanation of how gravity works to propel running is deliberately short and simplistic. If you prefer to immerse yourself in the complete, unabridged version of the explanation, you will find the complete text in chapter 53 at the end of this book.

We all recognize that the acceleration due to gravity is measured at 9.8 meters per second, per second. That is some serious acceleration, more than you could ever wrest from your legs operating on their own power. The challenge is to harness that acceleration and apply it to your body along the horizontal axis.

Da Vinci Understood The Lean

While we mentioned above that there was no scientifically definitive judgment on the forces involved in running, there was one individual, who figured it out a long time ago. Leonardo Da Vinci said it like this, *"Therefore a man will always present more of his weight towards that point to which he desires to move than to any other place. The faster a man runs the more he leans towards the place to which he runs and gives more of his weight in front of his axis of balance than behind"* (1).

When you are standing at rest, some form of acceleration is required to begin movement. The two obvious sources of acceleration are your legs or gravity. To use your legs, you must engage a whole process of muscle contraction, pushing off, driving your legs, all that stuff. To use gravity, you just... lean forward (Fig.17.1).

Fig.17.1 Fall forward using gravity from your point of support on the ground.

Try it yourself. Stand still and begin leaning forward. Don't bend at the waist or look down by bending your neck. Just make like the Tower of Pisa (Fig.17.2) and start falling forward. Rather abruptly you'll have a very good sense of exactly how fast 9.8 meters per second, per second really is. Very soon you'll have a choice to make. You'll either continue your fall and make a very nasty face plant on the ground or you'll put one foot out in front of you in an attempt to arrest the fall.

If you, like most people, opt for option two, you will be taking your first step toward a running style powered by gravity. The idea is not to arrest the fall, but to *continue* the fall, using the alternating placement of your feet under your body to keep you from hitting the ground, while you fall and fall, and fall, all the way to the finish line.

Fig.17.2 World famous Leaning Tower of Pisa in Italy leans at 5.5° degrees.

Source: Wikipedia. org/Public Domain.

have to work very hard to achieve your best times, but at least you'll be running smart. You will learn how to minimize wasted energy and stay mentally focused on doing only what is necessary to keep moving forward. Ultimately, you'll find that run at the end of a hard triathlon to be something to look forward to, a place to pass many of your competitors, instead of a dreaded finish to a mercilessly hard race.

Reference:

1. Keele, K.D. *Leonardo da Vinci's Elements of the Science of Man*. Academic Press, 1983, p. 175.

Throughout this process, the forward lean of your body acts as the accelerator pedal for your body. One of the world's greatest runners, Haile Gebrselassie, maintains a forward lean (or angle of deviation) of about 16° degrees. A mid–packer running a 50–minute 10K leans about 10° degrees, while the maximum sustainable lean for a world–class sprinter tops out at about 20.5° degrees.

Accepting that gravity provides the acceleration in your running does in fact change everything. Instead of using your legs to drive you forward, you'll learn how to use them literally to prevent a fall. Even shoe choice gets simpler. You won't need heel cushioning or additional support. You'll land softly on the ball of your foot and simply lift that foot as soon as possible to continue the fall.

Using gravity to propel your running doesn't mean that it will suddenly become very easy to run fast. Don't worry, you'll still

CHAPTER 18
LEARNING RUNNING TECHNIQUE

It is only the ignorant who despise education.

— *Publius Syrus*

How do we learn? How do we learn to move? How do we learn to move properly? More importantly, for the purposes of this book, how do we learn run properly?

When you boil things down, we have two major questions: how do we run and how do we *learn* to run?

In any other sport, these are moot points. If we want to learn a sport, for example, golf or tennis, we carefully consider our options and seek out qualified professional instructors and then augment that guidance with advice gleaned from books and videos. Throughout the process of learning a new sport, we are constantly open to advice about what movements we should make and how we should make them. We read each new bit of advice in magazines and eagerly put it to the test, hoping that the latest refinement in technique will be the one that raises our game to the next level.

But when it comes to running, it's a different story entirely. Out the window goes the careful approach and all the attention paid to technique. Instead of focusing our energy on learning *how* to run, we instead seek out advice on how much to run, how far to run, how fast to run. For whatever reason, we take it for granted that we already know how to run, indeed that running is a natural human endeavor. Running, we believe, is simple and natural, not something to be taught, but something that is ingrained in our DNA. But is it so?

The fact is that most people never really learn *how* to run because in the running community, with no real justification, the prevailing opinion is that running is simply second nature to human beings. In the aforementioned sports of golf or tennis, almost anyone will be happy to share their opinion on how you can improve your performance. But in running, people just throw up their hands. *The way you run is the way you run* is the sentiment, as if there is nothing that can be done to improve your technique.

But if running is natural, ask people to define "natural running" and see if you get a satisfactory answer. It just won't happen. The fact is that there *are* people who are naturally gifted runners; there is no disputing that. But because some people have the natural ability, doesn't mean the rest of us can't significantly improve our technique.

If you delve into the literature of traditional running technique (1), you'll find visual images of running and detailed description of running movement indicating what our muscles should do (2), the effort we should apply and the actions we should produce (push off, drive the knee, rapid foot landing on the ground, etc.) This general guidance tends to focus on the direction of movement, range of motion and level of effort (more–less, big–small, slow–quick). Among the choice adjectives used to describe running movement are *smooth, flowing* and *effortless*. Frequently cited images typically come from nature: cheetahs, smaller cats, and deer being among the most popular. All of these images are very familiar to us, yet our efforts to replicate them generally meet with very little success.

It is true that elite runners can be described as *effortless, flowing* and *smooth,* yet that is hardly how you would refer to a huge field of recreational runners. Are we talking about two different entities here? Do elite runners and the rest of us exist in two different worlds? As completely crazy as this sounds, this pretty much represents exactly what people believe about running, to the point that some simply accept running talent as being "God–given" (3).

If you believe that there is divine intervention at work here, then it's going to be a tall order to convince you otherwise, but that's exactly the point of the Pose Method. Our vision is that running, just like any other movement, has a specific theory and rules of performance that we have to understand in order to perform better. Further, once we understand those rules, then we should be able to develop specific drills and exercises in order to execute this proper running technique in the most efficient way possible.

In other words, we have to understand *how* to run and then we have to understand how we *learn* to run.

The sport scientist, Dr. Ernie Maglischo (4), once proposed that learning the swimming stroke is best done by copying the technique of the world's best swimmers *without* consideration of any theories of the propulsive forces supporting their techniques. Based on this proposition, we theoretically should copy the technique of elite runners.

While that is an appealing proposition, it leads to the question of which runner and which element of his or her technique is really the key to superior performance. When you look at it like that, it really doesn't make a lot of sense.

A far better and more consistent approach is to understand the fundamentals of running technique and develop a curriculum that permits anyone to learn how to run. That is what we have done with the Pose Method of Running. We explain the fundamental science underlying running technique and then give you a series of drills that will make this technique truly second nature to you.

References:

1. Doherty, J.K. *Modern Track and Field*. Englewood Cliffs, N.J. Prentice–Hall, Inc. 1953, pp. 166–177.

2. Bosch, F. and Klomp, R. *Running. Biomechanics and exercise physiology in practice*. Elsivier Churchill Livingstone, 2005.

3. Wallack, Roy. *I will learn to run better*. Runner's World, Oct 2004, pp. 68–73, 109.

4. Maglischo, E. *Newton to Bernoulli and Back again. Modern History of Articles In Freestyle From Past ASCA World Clinic's and Related Sources. American Swimming Coaches Association*. Advanced Freestyle School. Ft. Lauderdale, FL, 1995, p. 29.

CHAPTER 19
MAJOR COMPONENTS OF THE POSE METHOD OF RUNNING

Things are entirely what they appear to be and behind them... there is nothing.

— Sartre

The main objective of the Pose Method of Running is to harness the power of gravity as the principle source of energy and the main force propelling forward movement. We do this by a simple progression Pose–Fall–Pull (PFP) (Fig.19.1). The Pose is the key body position on support, the Fall is the body's gravity driven tendency to fall forward and the Pull is the removal of the foot from its support on the ground.

If you imagine stop–action footage of a runner in full gait, the Pose is the frame that shows the runner in mid–stance with the ball of one foot on the ground and the other foot at just about knee level. The body of the runner appears to be S–shaped with the knee of the support foot bent and the body weight centered over the support foot (Fig.19.2). At this point, the runner's body is in a pose stance of balance, ready to fall forward. The slightest force, either external (gravity) or internal (releasing muscular tension) will destroy the runner's balance and

Fig.19.1 Pose–Fall–Pull, the main elements of Pose running are meant to be the primary focus while running, everything else happens as a resultant of these three elements, i.e. arm movement, range of motion, etc.

Fig.19.2 The Pose stance at a brisk pace. Please note that the height of the pull is regulated by the speed of your run.

cause the forward fall that we call running (Fig.19.3).

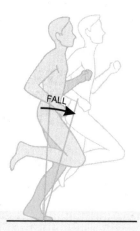

FALL

Fig.19.3 Allowing yourself to be pulled by gravity allows you to "fall" in a desired direction from a point of support.

To run, we allow our bodies to fall forward, with the emphasis on "allow" because we can't force falling, we can only allow it to happen. As a result of the fall, gravity accelerates the body weight forward and down. This acceleration, if repeated with the same angle of deviation and a minimum of braking due to landing on support, *creates* the horizontal velocity of the body.

The final key component of Pose running is the Pull. Pulling the support foot from the ground, as the body weight passes the point of support, allows you to disengage with support (Fig.19.4), reestablish the body's balance in the air, and prepare for the next support and subsequently, the fall. When the body weight is no longer centered over support, there is no reason for the foot to remain on the ground. During the falling phase, it is critical not to make any physical effort in an attempt to increase the speed of the fall. No matter how hard you try, there is nothing to gain by trying to force more speed out of your body.

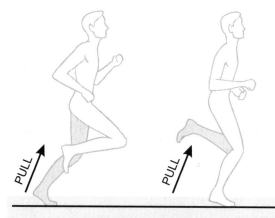

PULL

PULL

Fig.19.4 In the pull phase of running, it is important to focus solely on pulling, releasing the airborne leg to fall by the force of gravity. Don't actively force your landing foot down, just pull!

If you refer to the falling rod model in the chapter "How Gravity Works in Running," which is the final chapter of this book, the horizontal component of the falling rod depends only on the angle of deviation from the vertical position on support — nothing else. To emulate the falling rod, the runner's body needs to maintain a firm posture in a whole, compact line.

Any effort to "push off" the ground with the leg would only result in moving the body in a vertical direction, thereby introducing a *vertical* oscillation, which has a negative influence on *horizontal* velocity. The idea that the extension of the leg joints could help you run faster, as would happen in an attempt to "push off," simply isn't supported by logic.

To put this in deadly scientific terminology, the smallest angle of the ground reaction force vector relative to the horizontal plane at the end of support in running according to R. Margaria's (1) research data is roughly 63.5° degrees. Simultaneously, the vertical oscillation of the body is about 4 to 6 centimeters in the best runners, which produces about two to three degrees of body movement relative to the horizontal direction (Fig.19.5).

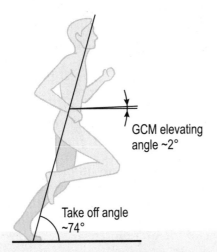

GCM elevating angle ~2°

Take off angle ~74°

Fig.19.5 The angle of deviation at the end of support in running. To attain faster speeds, the runner must fall at a greater angle and be able to maintain this extreme incline with faster cadence; "pushing off" only extends your support time and hinders cadence.

Thus efforts to "push off" would result in a much bigger angle than required for optimum horizontal trajectory of the body. This ratio doesn't support the concept of pushing off. Additional scientific data, such as the extensor paradox (2), demonstrates diminishing electrical activity of the quadriceps during the "push off" phase, again indicating that there is nothing to be gained by trying to force acceleration by pushing off.

Conversely, pulling the foot up off the ground is what we really need to do in running. In the Pose Method model of running, we consider the pull as the vertical displacement of the support foot from the ground under the hip. Here we have to consider the difference between what we feel (or perceive) and what an outside observer would see as the mechanics of our running.

Psychologically, we perceive that we are lifting our foot straight off the ground. The foot hits support, the general center of mass of our body moves past support and the foot is lifted straight up.

Mechanically, however, what an outside observer would see is a circular motion of the foot, which is the true biomechanical structure of this movement. This biomechanical structure is the result of momentum (inertia) and reactive forces as the foot is displaced from, and replaced on, support — yielding a circular trajectory of the foot.

One of the benefits of this structure of running is that we don't really need to know which muscles to use, and by which trajectory to move the foot. All we have to know is what part of the body we have to move (and when) and the brain takes over, recruiting the proper muscles by request to get the job done. When we send the signal "lift the foot," the brain enlists the hamstrings to do the job and the optimum trajectory results.

Even though we happen to know that it is the hamstrings at work, we don't need to know it as long as we simply pull the foot. We can create problems by sending out incorrect signals, such as "lift the knee" or "drive the leg forward." These bad instructions can lead to poor mechanics and potential injury.

So, done properly, the Pose Method of Running really is a simple progression — Pose, Fall, Pull. However, the seeming simplicity of this three–part progression doesn't mean that pure Pose running is easy to learn. It is not!

The challenge between understanding intellectually how simple Pose running is and actually learning to do it is quite a difficult barrier — our perception. In chapter 4 we already discussed the implications of perception and its role in learning. Perception is the job of the brain, a complex process of receiving, memorizing, analyzing and estimating information from our sensors and memories. In order to perform even the most simple task, the brain runs through a progression, weighing thoughts and desires, factoring in memories of past action with anticipation of the future, measuring our fears and hesitations, constantly making comparisons and conclusions, and eventually (in microseconds) coming up with a state–of–the–body evaluation and making a final decision on what action to take. This process of perception involves sorting out a continuous blizzard of information to produce an immediate outcome — action.

The massive amount of signals from both the external environment and inside our bodies bombards our sensors, but the vast majority are not recognized and perceived. Call it the threshold of perception; we can only process and react to so much information at any given moment.

How these signals are prioritized and processed is a very good question. Over the millennia of human development, the mind has evolved to single out and prioritize certain data as being crucial to the health and survival of the organism. The mind weighs all the incoming information and makes decisions to take actions based on current situations.

To put it in an overly–simplistic picture, consider the matter of a routine training run for an upcoming sprint triathlon. It's been a rough week and your motivation is low. The mind takes this into consideration and yields to your desire to just take it easy. But just at that moment, as the decision is made to slow down, a large dog breaks free and begins to chase you. All the other thoughts that have been cluttering your mind and pointing to reduce performance loose priority. You immediately have the clarity of survival in your mind and make

an instantaneous decision to run very, very fast.

And, at this point, it is easy to run very fast. The instinct to survive is much more basic and powerful, than the desire to do a good race at some point in the future. And therein lies the challenge of running well. Winning races is not crucial to our organism. The thought of winning or doing well is a desire, and fulfilling desires depends on the focus and determination of the mind.

As an athlete, you alone make the decisions every second, to do or not do a specific action. In running, those actions are very simple — Pose, Fall, Pull — but the focus required to do them over and over and over again is quite intense.

In running, the process of perceiving our body weight falling forward and pulling the foot from the ground at just the right moment is a mental process resulting in physical action, and it's quite challenging to learn. As we head into the next few chapters our objective will be to learn how to focus the mind and perform the physical act of running at the highest level of efficiency.

References:

1. Margaria, R. *Biomechanics and Energetics of Muscular Exercise.* Oxford University Press, 1976, pp. 127–128.

2. McClay, I.S., Lake, M.B. and Cavanagh, P.R. *The Extensor Paradox Experiment.* In Biomechanics of Distance Running. Human Kinetics, 1990, pp. 129–186.

CHAPTER 20
PERCEPTION OF BODY WEIGHT

Weight, force, and a blow resemble
each other as regards pressure.
— Leonardo da Vinci

When all is said and done, the idea in running is to transport the sack of skin and bones that is your body from point 'A' to point 'B'. Viewed in terms of pure work, running is the application of energy and technique to a fixed number of pounds — your body weight — to get them to where you want them.

Without gravity, of course, you have no weight, only mass. Gravity is the force that creates weight. And that ties in neatly with the main premise of the Pose Method of Running, which is to use the force that creates the weight — gravity — to move the weight.

While we are aware that our bodies have weight, we only perceive that weight when we are on support. The progression of our awareness of body weight in movement goes like this: Gravity — Body Mass — Support — Body Weight — Muscular Effort — Change of Support — Movement (Fig.20.1).

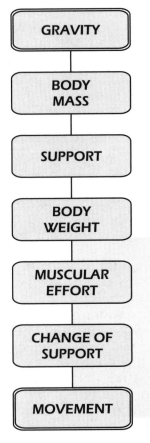

If you follow that progression, you quickly realize that we only perceive gravity when we are on support. We don't perceive gravity directly and we don't perceive it as body mass. We are only confronted with the reality of gravity as a force when we feel the pressure on the support foot and the subsequent resulting muscular tension. The foot touches the ground, body mass transforms into body weight and we have the "a–ha" moment — there's gravity at work.

Fig.20.1 Transformation: Gravity to Movement. Contrary to conventional thought, movement is not governed by our muscles, but by a rather complex chain of energy transformation. Movement begins with gravity, is enabled when the body is on support, and finally results in movement through change of support.

Body weight is the centerpiece (Fig.20.2) in

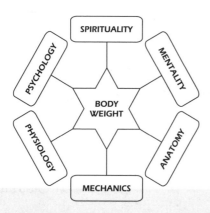

Fig.20.2 Our relationship with gravity is greater than we think. Simply because this divine force is always present, we overlook its effects on everything we do. Our body weight is our connection to this world, it's our direct interaction with gravity. Since everything we do is governed by this ever present force, our body weight represents this connection in ways we are not yet able to define.

this progression or chain of movement connecting all elements of the chain together in one integrated system. We actually perceive the body weight as pressure on the ball of the foot where it contacts the ground, as well as in the resulting sensations of tension in certain muscle groups, the lengthening of tendons and even bone load — all related to being on support (Fig.20.3).

Perception of the body weight is important because it represents gravity, which the process of evolution has ingrained in us on a cellular level as a survival mechanism. All living creatures inherently operate with the perception of body weight in order to move. While physically connected to our bones, the work of our muscles is really attached to our body weight. The function of our muscles is to move our body weight from one point to the next.

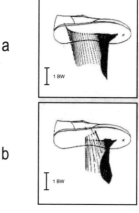

Fig.20.3 Body weight as pressure on the Ball of the Foot.

Vector representations of the ground reaction force in running for two participants (a) a heel-toe runner, (b) a forefoot runner. The view is of the right shoe from the lateral aspect with the shoe tilted 30° upward (adapted from Cavanagh and Lafortune, 1980).

Animals, as we know, have no academic knowledge of anatomy, biomechanics, etc., yet they move with fluidity and grace. How is this possible? They simply seem to have an innate perception of their body weight and its relationship to support and muscular effort. If you watch a slow motion film of a big cat — say a puma or a panther — moving at full speed, you'll notice that they seem to be completely and utterly relaxed while in flight. But the moment that they touch support on the ground there is an instantaneous muscular explosion to lift their legs back–off from support. Ultimately big cats run so fast because they spend so little time on support and expend energy in the form of muscular movement only at the exact moment it is needed to continue their forward fall.

As we develop our perception of our own body weight, it is a key to comprehend the concept of **one body weight,** which is your weight when standing in a stationary position (Fig.20.4). Your brain, as the main organ of perception, perceives the pressure of **one body weight** as reliable support, a signal of where the body is located and balanced at this particular place and moment in time.

This perception of **one body weight** carries with it a whole system of support, involving neuromuscular coordination and

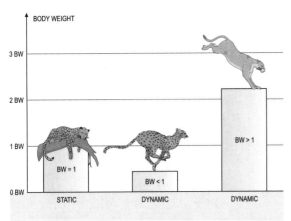

Fig.20.4 One body weight. Static body weight = 1. Dynamic body weight is less than one, when you leave support, and greater than one as you are landing.

of our bodies coming in contact with the ground, right?

BODY WEIGHT ON HEEL OR ON BOF

Fig.20.5 It's a very subtle perception to be able to perceive the difference between body weight on the heel or the ball of the foot.

careful positioning of your skeletal structure and connective tissue. As soon as there is a perception that the body weight is "disappearing," the signal is given from the brain to change support for the body and immediately "dismiss" all the previous efforts of the system to remain at rest. Even though the body at a condition of **one body weight** is at rest, all elements of the system that supported the body at rest were working to stay there. Now, with the introduction of movement, they have new functions to perform to permit your body to keep moving.

Generally speaking, you can say that all functional systems are attached to your body weight when it is on support and detached from it when the perception of the body weight/support disappears. This is directly related to the body falling forward and pulling your support foot from the ground.

Theoretically, it should be a very simple matter to have an ongoing perception of one's own body weight (Fig.20.5). What could be easier than feeling the effects

Just this... most of us have no perception whatsoever of our own body weight because of louder and more urgent signals being broadcast by our cardio–respiratory system. Who can focus on things like support, body weight and falling forward when the lungs are screaming for more air and the heart is warning that if it goes a few beats higher, a complete shutdown is not out of the question.

These are the kind of signals that evolution has assigned the highest priority, signals of survival. Your conscious mind may be trying to operate in a coldly efficient manner — giving out calm signals to keep falling forward and picking the foot up from support — but the subconscious mind is in overdrive, drowning out the conscious mind with vitally important warnings of imminent failure.

While the battle between the conscious and subconscious minds is waged, the inevitable result is the loss of focus on the basics of running technique, which begins to deteriorate. In a cruel blow, the deterioration of technique makes the cardio–respiratory system work even harder and eventually go into overload, which is followed quickly by a slow–down in pace.

Returning to the initial concept of running being a means to transport your body weight from one point to the next, we can now view training in an entirely new context. It is by no means a purely physical act, unrelated to thoughts. Instead, it is a process by which we develop the conscious mind to continue giving orders and screen out the signals of impending doom. The more effective we become at maintaining focus on the simple act of perceiving and transferring our body weight, the better we will become at running.

CHAPTER 21
PERCEPTION OF THE BODY LEANING FORWARD

You're walking.
And you don't always realize it,
but you're always falling.
With each step you fall forward slightly.
And then catch yourself from falling.
Over and over, you're falling. And then
catching yourself from falling.
And this is how you can be walk-
ing and falling at the same time.

— Laurie Anderson

It is a pretty easy task to perceive one's own body weight as described in the previous chapter. Bounce lightly on the balls of your feet and you can say to yourself: "yep, that's my body weight." As discussed, it does become substantially harder to stay focused on body weight as your physical efforts increase, but at least you know what that weight feels like at rest.

Learning to perceive the forward lean of the body is a little bit trickier. To begin, the forward lean, by definition, involves movement. With your feet moving, your arms lightly swinging, your heart rate increasing and your breathing growing more labored, it takes real concentration to feel the lean of your body.

There is an intrinsic relationship between the perception of your body weight and the perception of the forward lean. The lean frees your body weight to fall forward, which starts the process we call running.

A very simple drill demonstrates the relationship. Begin by running very softly in place. Don't make any strong efforts; just barely lift your feet off the ground, as you remain perfectly erect and look toward the horizon. After establishing your rhythm, do nothing more than lean slightly forward from your hips or belly button (the point of your General Center of Mass). Having made no other effort, no push–off with the feet and with no thought of running in mind... you are running. Your feet are automatically alternating support in order to keep you from falling from even the slightest lean.

Play with this drill a little more. Think of your GCM as your accelerator pedal. Lean forward a little more and your feet move faster in order to keep up. Pull back on the GCM and you slow down. You're not bending forward from the waist. Instead what you are doing is keeping your upper body in line, staying rigid, but not tense, and just pressing forward.

The relationship of the body weight and the forward lean moves your body forward as the resulting fall requires you to alternate support to keep from landing on your face. Despite this integral relationship between body weight and the forward lean, we have to consider falling/leaning as a separate element of Pose Method in the sense of the body's deviation from balance on support. There are several specific elements of the forward lean that need to be addressed independent of body weight. These include the angle of the lean, the angular velocity of deviation from support and the body and trunk position during the lean.

With all this discussion of forward lean, you might be conjuring up a mental image of a runner at a 45° degree angle, sort of a human Leaning Tower of Pisa, scooting down the road. Wrong image. As would be the image of a runner bent over from the waist; that is the image of a struggling runner, not one moving perfectly.

In fact, with an effective body lean, a runner appears to be curiously upright. At least, that's what they used to say about Michael Johnson, the Olympic champion and world record holder at 200 and 400 meters. When you have the proper lean, the straight line extending from the ball of your foot on support through your general center of mass and up to your shoulder doesn't vary. Johnson was the classic example of this: he always looked like he was upright, but closer analysis revealed the rather extreme angle of his hips ahead of his point of support (Fig.21.1).

That's the tricky part about perceiving your angle of lean. There is no dashboard in front of you with digital displays of your angle of lean or your angular velocity; devel-

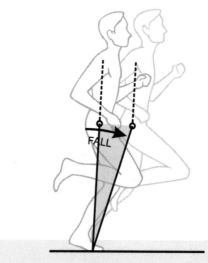

Fig.21.1 Leaning from the hips (GCM).

oping the proper lean is entirely a matter of perception. Just as your forward lean has a relationship with your body weight, on the one hand, it is equally related to your stride length, cadence and speed of running, on the other. It is the key link in the chain of moving your body forward.

No matter what speed or distance you intend to run, the governor of your performance is the body lean. It all fits in with the Pose Method theory, as it will be discussed in chapter 53 "How Gravity Works in Running." In the little demonstration at the beginning of this chapter, you saw for yourself how just a slight lean could take you from running in place to starting to run down the road.

When you are running a reasonable distance at a pace you consider too fast, the first mental command you will give yourself to slow down is "straighten up a little." You don't tell yourself to shorten your stride or slow your turnover, you simply straighten up. This has the effect of decreasing the angle by which your hips are leaving the point of support; the rest of it — the shortening of the stride and the slowing of the cadence

— happens as a consequence of your body weight remaining closer to support.

Learning to control your body lean is the definitive skill in refining your running technique. As we saw above, when you keep your body weight directly above support you can move your feet all you want and you won't go anywhere at all. Conversely, if you lean (fall) too far forward, your feet will not be able to keep up with you and the result will be a fall on the face. Your ideal running lean, for any speed and distance, falls somewhere in–between these two extremes, and it is only through perception that you will find it.

In essence, by controlling the angle of your body lean you are regulating your gravity–propelled fall forward and determining how fast you will run at any given moment. The first step in this process is to develop a feel for what it means to lean. You have to develop a physical awareness of your body operating as a single, coordinated unit. While your upper body should remain relaxed during running, it should be held in a consistent posture, maintaining that straight line from support, through the general center of mass and up into the shoulders.

There should be no rolling forward of the shoulders, no wild swinging of the arms, no bending at the waist (Fig.21.2). You could say your body is relaxed and supple, but held in a rigid posture. When your body leans, it doesn't bend; it tilts. As you progress through each cycle of leg turnover, the orientation of your body doesn't change. The feet and legs move under the body, while the body remains relatively motionless.

What does determine the angle of lean, as mentioned above, is your hip deviation from the vertical line which begins at the point of support on the ball of the foot. As the hips move forward in front of support, a variety of signals bombard your brain with the information that your body is no longer

Fig.21.2 Bending at the waist is not the same as leaning from the hips. It is incorrectly placing your upper body ahead of your lower body, forcing your legs to play "catch–up" instead of being synchronous with your GCM movement.

where it was just a fraction of a second ago. The absence of pressure on the support foot, the feeling of your body being suspended in the air (Fig.21.3), the desire or need to re-

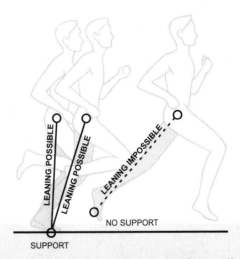

Fig.21.3 Leaving your support foot well behind your GCM makes leaning impossible, due to a complete lack of support.

turn the body to support on the next foot, all provide information to the brain as it (literally) calculates the next steps.

These are all pieces of perceived information, not hard data. Even if you knew that you needed to maintain a certain angle of deviation to maintain a 5:30 mile pace, there would be no way to measure this and — while being interesting from an intellectual standpoint — it would still be useless information.

So it comes back to perception, which you develop through repetition and training. That simple concept of the GCM as your accelerator pedal can be refined into a very accurate reflection of exactly how fast you are running at any given moment. Through practice, you can become skilled at ignoring the distress signals of physical effort — the higher heart rate, the heavier breathing — and focus instead on the more clinical details of your run — the forward lean and the cadence — which are the actual determining factors in your speed.

By running varying tempos in your training, you can teach yourself what the lean feels like to run that 5:30 (or 7:30 or even 9:30) pace. You'll learn that acceleration comes from leaning further forward and deceleration from the opposite action. Over time, you will automatically be able to tell from your posture and lean, just how fast you're running.

And the key really is the angle of the lean and not the rate at which you change support — your cadence. As we have noted, you can move your feet with extreme quickness, but as long as there is no forward lean, you don't move an inch. Until you let yourself fall, that is lean forward, the rate at which your feet move is irrelevant. Cadence, while very important to your overall success, only works to serve the rate at which you fall — your forward lean.

CHAPTER 22
PULLING YOUR FOOT FROM THE GROUND

What we think, or what we know, or what we believe is, in the end, of little consequence. The only consequence is what we do.

— *John Ruskin*

When the average person defines running, the definition would invariably contain references to leg movement and stride, with the basic idea being that running is an act performed by the legs. Pressed further, most would go on to mention knee lift or leg drive or pushing off, all of which infer that the force and speed of running comes from the effort of the legs. Even the prevalence of running injuries reinforces this image. There aren't too many people who break their collarbones or sprain their wrists through running (unless they happen to trip and fall). No, what you get from running are leg and foot injuries — plantar fasciitis, stress fractures, sore hips and knees, that kind of thing.

Further, the mental image of what the legs actually do in running is focused in front of the body, on the leg that comes in contact with the ground. People believe that the leg reaches out ahead of the body, lands on the ground, accepts the magnified weight of the body and then makes a heroic effort to push off and propel the body further down the road.

And, in fact, this is what most people do, which explains the high rate of running injuries quoted a few chapters back. You remember, don't you? Back in the 1970's 2 out of every 3 runners reported suffering running injuries every year and in 2005, in spite of over 30 years of supposedly improved running shoes and training techniques, that number had shot up to 85%. Those are pretty startling statistics, particularly when we are talking about an activity that is theoretically fundamental to all humans.

Now let's look at running as redefined by the Pose Method: running is a controlled fall wherein the body weight of the runner is propelled forward under the force of gravity and the alternation of support by the legs keeps the runner moving forward instead of landing on his or her face.

Since running is falling and it is the lead foot that arrests the fall, it is quite understandable that people focus on the role of the front foot. From a biological, evolutionary perspective that front foot is performing a vital survival role by keeping the body from going SPLAT! But that is all it really does. Since we know that our speed and acceleration comes from gravity attracting our body weight, it is obvious that the leg is not providing the power that drives us down the road.

It would only be possible for the leg to provide power, if it stayed planted on the ground until the body weight caught up with the place where the foot is planted on the ground and then managed to deliver some propulsive thrust... which of course would be upward and not forward, as the body weight at that point would be directly over the foot.

So the key to running in the Pose Method is to rethink the fundamental role of the legs, specifically as regards to which leg is actually working at a given moment.

In running, the leg does its work by pulling the foot off the ground.

It is not the job of the 'plant' foot to wait for the body weight to catch up to the foot, but for the 'plant' foot to catch up to the body weight in time to prevent a fall. The focus should not be on the act of landing, but on the act of removing the foot from the ground. Landing is going to happen — gravity ensures that a foot will quickly contact the ground while making no effort whatsoever.

What does require effort is the removal of the foot from the ground, i.e. working against gravity. It may seem like a simple matter, lifting your foot from the ground, and indeed it is. But lifting that foot upwards of 90 times a minute gets to be a challenge when you're running anywhere from 100 meters to more than a marathon.

Here's how to look at it from the Pose perspective. The least amount of time that your foot stays in contact with the ground at a given spot will result in the fastest run-

ning time. If your foot lands out in front of your body weight and waits for the body weight to catch–up, then it is destined to stay rooted to that spot for quite some time, absorbing all the punishment from supporting your weight and slowing down the run at the same time.

However, if your foot lands directly under the body weight (the general center of mass, if you will) and not in front of it, there is no wait time. The foot can then instantly be lifted back off the ground in an effort to catch up to the weight that is already out in front of support. In manufacturing, they call this 'just in time' delivery. In running, it's the same thing. Get the foot under the body just in time to momentarily support the body and then get it ready to support the body again as quickly as possible.

This way of thinking about running also clarifies two common concerns in running: stride length and cadence. Both of these concepts are rooted in the notion of running being a leg–driven activity. But, in fact, neither determines how fast you go; they are determined by how fast you are going.

Go back to your first experiment in the previous chapter, the one where you progressed from running in place to a very slow forward movement, achieved when you moved your GCM or hips just slightly forward and found yourself forced to put one foot in front of the other. At a very slow speed like this, your stride length is quite short and your turnover is very slow; you're basically just shuffling along.

As you increase the degree of lean, however, gravity pulls harder and harder as it accelerates your body toward the ground. In order not to fall, you have to move your feet faster and the distance they will travel between footfalls increases. By leaning more (running faster), your cadence increases and your stride lengthens, automatically.

This brings us to the point where your organism determines just how much of this activity it can support — and for how long. Your mental focus has to be on lifting the foot from the ground, not on landing it on the ground. As was said earlier, lifting the foot from the ground seems like a simple matter, but as your forward speed increases and all those physiological warning signs or our survival instincts — heart rate, respiration, perspiration, etc. — kick in and our focus changes to looking for a new support (focus on landing) rather than staying focused on getting rid of current support, it becomes extremely challenging to stay focused and keep lifting your feet off the ground.

The movement of the foot is very basic. The hamstrings contract and pull the foot straight up under the hips, positioning it to drop down right under the body weight. There is no forward movement, no reaching, and no driving. It is a simple, precise lift — straight up. The timing of the pulling action to lift the foot from the ground is crucial. If you are late in lifting your foot, then you postpone your next 'fall' and slow down your run (Fig.22.1).

This brings us back, inevitably, to the concept of perception. The first element of perception is to focus on the pulling action itself. One quick contraction of the hamstrings gets the job done. You have to concentrate to make sure that is all you are doing — you don't want to lift the knee or use your thigh muscles and hip flexors to drive the thigh forward. One quick pull of the foot — that's it.

And it has to be a 'pull', not a 'push'. The idea is to lift the foot under the body, not lift the body. There should be almost zero vertical oscillation; your head, shoulders, even your belly button should be traveling in a straight line parallel to the ground, not bobbing up and down.

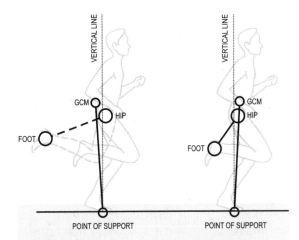

Fig.22.1 The first graphic illustrates "late" pulling a.k.a. leaving the support foot on the ground too long. This places the GCM far behind your point of support forcing you to expend more energy to recover to the Pose position and get ready for your next change of support. The second graphic demonstrates the benefits of pulling immediately upon loss of balance, allowing you to be in position for your next change of support with no additional effort.

Next is what we might call the chain of perceptions, the timing and effort of the pull and the intricate interrelationships among the fall, the Pose stance and your body weight. You perceive the body weight as pressure on the ball of your foot, you feel the pressure lessen as the body weight leaves the foot and begins to shift to the next foot, and you sense the forward lean of the body. All of these elements are connected and define the moment when you take action and pull your foot from the ground.

It all boils down to developing a perception of where your foot is and what it is doing. Our experience shows that most runners pay very little attention to the foot itself and concentrate instead on the knee lift or thigh drive or, even more likely, the physiological warning signals. Most tend to let the legs go on autopilot and measure their efforts solely by how tired they are and how far they still have to go. Sound familiar?

But developing an acute perception of your foot puts a whole new spin on running. When it first touches ground, the sensation of pressure must come from the ball of the foot, not the heel or the toes. You have to feel the foot and make sure you're not rolling across it or attempting to push off. The ball of the foot touches the ground; body weight passes through the support and unweighs the foot as it moves forward, the hamstrings, already engaged in movement, contract and lift the foot up under the hip.

At its essence, running can be characterized as leaning forward and lifting your foot. While it seems — and is — very simple, it also takes great mental focus to continue lifting the foot in precisely the same way, mile after mile. Learning to run the Pose Method is very much an exercise in mental discipline. If you narrow your focus to concentrate on lifting your foot quickly and with precise timing, your body will come along for the ride every step of the way.

CHAPTER 23
TO DRILL OR NOT TO DRILL

There is no royal road to geometry.

— *Euclid*

Oh, boy ... drills.

Don't you just cringe at the thought of 'doing drills?' Whether it conjures up images of 7th grade gym class, piano lessons or, perish the thought, military boot camp with its drill sergeants, very few of us have warm and fuzzy thoughts when the word "drill" is mentioned.

'Running' brings to mind thoughts of freedom. We run away from it all, breaking the bonds of our daily responsibilities, setting aside the time to 'just run' and escape mundane reality for some unstructured alone time.

'Drills', on the other hand, connote authority, the very thing we run to escape. Whether it's the gym teacher, the iron–willed piano teacher or the Napoleon–complexed drill instructor, there's usually someone on the other end of the word 'drill' making you do something you don't want to do.

So why on Earth would we voluntarily sacrifice the wonderful freedom of a long run for the structure of a set of drills? It's quite a paradox, isn't it? If what we really want to do is 'just run', why go to all the trouble to take the fun out of it and turn it into a big production?

Here are a few possible answers: 1) to reduce running induced injuries; 2) to make running easier; 3) to run faster.

Okay, okay. That all sounds pretty good... so how does it work?

First, let's all accept the fact that anything worth doing is worth doing well. If you look at commonly accepted 'skill' sports like swimming, golf, and tennis, you'll find that all are taught by a series of drills. Master the individual movements and eventually you will master the sport. The same can be said for activities at the intersection of art and sport, as in ballet, or in things that are completely in the realm of art, like playing a musical instrument.

Each activity has fundamental components that must be learned in order to play the game, dance the dance or perform the composition. And for every component, there's a drill attached. The drills may be boring and at times they may seem to stifle creativity, but in the end they give free reign to creativity, allowing the free expression that can only be facilitated by knowing the building blocks of your chosen endeavor.

But do we really need to go to all this 'trouble' for running? In running, don't we just run? What is the point of this new concept — Pose drills? And if we have to do them, what's the minimum we can get away with?

Over the last several chapters, we've gone through a comprehensive redefinition of exactly what running is… and it's not at all what you thought it was. Running is not the work of your legs providing the power to propel you down the road. Instead, it's gravity that provides the power; your legs just keep you from falling straight onto the ground.

Given this new way of thinking about running, it seems logical to acquire a new skill set to take full advantage of what we now know to be the essence of running. To acquire the skills, we need to do the drills.

That's right — skills. Contrary to what most people believe, running requires as much specific skill as tennis and golf… or ballet and piano, for that matter. You might be willing to accept the first two — the sports — but ballet, c'mon? That's an art, not a sport.

Here's where you have to invest a little time and effort and open your mind to a new way of looking at running. Again, it is a matter of our perception allowing us to see things as we thought they were, and then see them again, as they really are.

While the art of ballet is that it permits non–verbal expressions of human emotion through movement, that art is made possible only by precisely — repeated movements. You can't exactly stumble around the stage and communicate deep and meaningful emotion, can you?

Similarly, you can't stumble your way through a 5K and record a personal best time either. While the point of running is seemingly not to create art, you can certainly look at the actions of a supremely talented runner and describe them as artful. Everybody can run, but only a few run artfully and it is skill that separates the few from the many. Fortunately, these skills can be learned and that is the point of doing the drills.

Drills simplify and dissect the learning process into smaller parts that we can see, feel, perceive and perform. The goal is to develop our perception of fundamental movements that we couldn't perceive in any other way. It is not about muscle strength, endurance, speed, agility or flexibility. It is all about perception.

What are the things we need to perceive in running? Just our body weight, its location and its transfer or movement from one point to another. All three elements of the Pose Method: Pose–Fall–Pull, are part of this perception. The body weight manifests itself when we have a support on the ground and are in the Running Pose, with the body weight centered on the ball of the foot. The perception of the body weight at this position is extremely important because it is only from this position that we can start falling (leaning) forward.

Doing Pose drills develops the perception of holding and transferring the body weight from one foot to the other. This means we have to feel precisely both, where the body weight is located, and what it feels like to transfer it as well. So when we do the Pony drill, for example, our focus must stay fixed consistently and strongly on these things — the location and transfer of the body weight. The Pony drill should be developed to the level of being a skill, just as if it were a key movement in dancing.

As you ponder the long list of Pose drills, you will no doubt ask, how many of these things do you need to do, how often and how good do you have to get at them. At a minimum, you should do a quick set of drills to reawaken your perception of Pose–Fall–Pull both before and after each training session or run. Before the session, it really helps to refresh your perception just before putting in hard efforts. After a particularly hard session or long run, the drills can help to bring back that perception that may have been lost despite all your best efforts to stay focused during the run.

A quick run through of drills can be particularly helpful between each repeat of an interval session. Intervals put your running in bite size morsels; reinforcing your perception before you set out on each repeat is invaluable in mixing the concepts of drilling and training.

How many drills should you do? That depends on the circumstances... and your perception. As soon as you have developed or re–acquainted yourself with a specific perception that you've been targeting, go ahead and start running while the perception is fresh in your mind.

It is important to remember that perception, once acquired, is not something you can bottle up, put on the shelf and keep forever. Like physical fitness, perception is something of a fluid state of being. It can be developed and then lost, or it can be consistently maintained. Just as you have to do a certain quantity of cardiovascular work and strength training to maintain a viable level of fitness, you must continually integrate perception drills into your overall plan.

You wouldn't run for six weeks and then expect to be in good condition to run for the rest of your life. Similarly, you can't just do six–week program of drills and figure you've got them ingrained for life. If the idea of doing drills really puts you off, at the very least try to figure out the most difficult perception for you to master and focus on doing the drills that help you deal with that concept, while doing minimum maintenance on the others.

An even better way of approaching the drills is to try to change your perception of drills themselves. Instead of treating them as something dull and obligatory, consider these drills as a secret personal voyage of discovery, a key that unlocks the door to a hidden chamber of knowledge and wisdom. Through your mastery of these drills you can learn truths about 'simple running' that few will ever comprehend. That's kind of a cool advantage to take to the starting line, isn't it?

CHAPTER 24
INTRODUCTORY DRILLS FOR RUNNERS

One world at a time.

— *Thoreau*

While most people have the urge to turn and run the other direction at the prospect of doing something perceived as boring, tedious or challenging as drills, fear not. Most of the drills that follow are very simple and you can go through an entire set in a matter of minutes. These are not junior high calisthenics with endless sit–ups, push–ups, pull–ups and squat thrusts (though there's nothing wrong with incorporating those in your overall fitness plan).

Instead, the first Pose Running drills are very carefully constructed to heighten your awareness of your body weight and give you the resources to hone your skill of running. In fact, some of these drills are so subtle that you may think you're doing nothing at all and be tempted to skip right over them. That's a mistake you *should not* make. If you start at the beginning and really think your way through these drills, you'll build the foundation of perception that will make it easy for you to pick upon the intricacies of the Pose Method of Running.

Even better, once you've broken the code, so to speak, it will be even easier for you to progress through the similar drills for cycling and swimming and apply the Pose principles to all your sporting endeavors.

Why Body Weight Perception Drills?

The Running Pose is related directly to body weight perception. In the Running Pose, you hold your body weight on support and then fall forward. How do you feel your body weight? The most obvious sensation is the pressure on the ball of the foot where it contacts the ground. The pressure should be centered right on the ball of the foot, not the toes, not the heel.

To foster your transition to the Pose Method I propose the following structure of lessons to enhance your perception and skill of movement.

Introduction to Drill Lessons: Lesson Structure

Education, learning and teaching — no matter if it is an individual or group process — is traditionally structured in a specific form called a lesson. The length and educational structure (lecture, presentation, exercise, etc.) could vary, but as we move through the lessons you can be assured that you will learn through trial and error.

Studies have been conducted to determine the optimal duration of a lesson, which ranges from 45 minutes to 2 hours. Two major factors account for this specific time frame. On the one hand, if the lesson is shorter than 45 minutes, the minimum length of most college courses, then there is not enough time in the lesson for sufficient learning to take place. On the other hand, if the lesson is longer than 2 hours, the maximum attention span of most college students — and probably everyone else, it overloads the brain, negatively impacting the retention of the course material. Thus, we've come up with an optimal lesson time frame — so let's use it!

Now that you have an idea of how long an optimal training session should be, you'll be glad to know that the following lessons are structured in just such a manner. By following these simple lessons, you'll be able to vary your workouts, while constantly being able to tune–up your skill and perception of movement. After learning these drills you will have all the tools necessary to train and maintain your technique — not getting distracted and keeping focus while drilling — well, that's your job!

Certainly learning is not and should not be restricted to the length of a given lesson, however having a set time to perform your drills will aid you in being more constructive with your time. In our ever evolving world, we are constantly learning and heightening our perception — in essence becoming more aware of what we are doing and how we are doing it. Think about it, everything we have ever learned or discovered has always been there, simply our perception of it changed when we became aware of it. We have to be ready to perceive, accept and digest new information, allowing us to become better in our interaction with the outside world — our environment.

If a race distance and course was ambiguous, no one would win or lose, because no one would know where to start or finish. The same is true about learning a desired skill. Just jumping in the pool, or hopping on a bike, or even lacing up the shoes is not going to make you great at any of these sports. In order to improve, we must first know exactly what it is we're trying to improve, and why. Unfortunately, conventional training methods have focused primarily on *quantity* over *quality*, while in reality, for most intents and purposes, just the opposite is true.

Of course you need to train, but training with poor technique is like doing test laps in NASCAR with a flat tire. You're not going to reach your potential, training that way. With the Pose Method, you now have a standard to guide you throughout your training. But just knowing a method or technique will not make you any better — in fact, things may be more complicated at first, as you adjust to the new technique. However look at the bright side, you are now changing trains from an unknown destination, to a known destination — all that's left is to get there through practice.

The lesson structure below applies to any sport and fitness, including the events of triathlon in this book. Therefore we will follow a general structure of lessons for each event (Fig.24.1).

Traditionally a lesson consists of three major parts: a warm–up (introduction) lasting about 10–15 minutes, the core workout lasting about 30 minutes within a 45 minute lesson and twice as much during a two hour lesson, and finally a cool down (finalizing) which takes about 5–10 minutes.

The warm–up includes the setting of goal(s) and/or orientation and practice (warm up exercises to prepare the body and mind for specific tasks). The core workout consists of selected exercises and drills; as well as their analysis and corrections, according to the Pose Method standard.

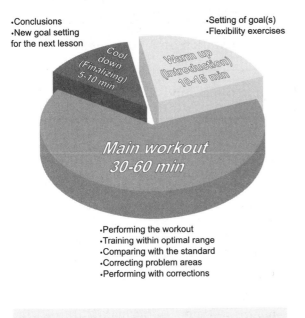

•Conclusions
•New goal setting for the next lesson

•Setting of goal(s)
•Flexibility exercises

Cool down (Finalizing) 5-10 min

Warm up (Introduction) 10-15 min

Main workout 30-60 min

•Performing the workout
•Training within optimal range
•Comparing with the standard
•Correcting problem areas
•Performing with corrections

Fig.24.1 Lesson Time Frame.

You will finish with a cool down: finalizing your session with findings and conclusions of what was and was not achieved/accomplished, allowing you to set new goals for the next lesson.

Goals in the Pose Method

It's important to note the strategic differences in the Pose Method philosophy: regardless of the length of time in the lesson, deliberate attention must be paid to specific fundamental goals in the learning of the movement, which are different from traditional schools of thought. For instance, in the Pose Method we are not concerned about teaching our muscles to do the work per se — instead, we are focused on executing the correct movement through psychological commands to our body, such as

pulling the foot under the body, instead of deliberately trying to "fire the hamstring."

In general, we are not actively engaging our muscular system for learning and teaching. Instead the Pose Method focuses your attention to perform the action of running, allowing your body to recruit the necessary muscle groups to perform the movement far more efficiently. We do not teach the body to produce efforts via specific muscle groups as proposed by the conventional running paradigm, which uses terms like "push–off," "knee drive," "pump the arms," etc.

If not our muscles, what do we have to develop to improve our technique? In the Pose Method, learning and teaching is based on the development of our perception (chapter 4) of movement and producing a specific action, based on that perception. As a result, that action provides the execution of the main task — movement. That movement can be running, cycling or swimming — or all three.

In running, as in any other movement, the main goal is to employ gravity through using our own body weight (chapter 3) in the most efficient way, at the highest rate possible. Certainly, application of gravity differs for every event, but the essence and fundamentals remain the same.

Therefore, efficient running would utilize more body–weight than muscular efforts to move forward. The most efficient forward propulsion is achieved by the proficient execution of the three elements of running (chapter 19): Pose–Fall–Pull. **Developing our perception of performing these elements in running is our major goal.**

The whole process of learning and teaching running technique follows the development of perception of the following elements (each element is followed by its associated perception(s)):

Elements of Running Technique and Their Perception
1. Body Weight — Support — The pressure on the ball of the foot.
1. Pose — The balanced position which we are falling (leaning) from.
1. Falling — Leaning forward, magnitude of deviation of the GCM of the body from the balance point on the support.
1. Pulling — Removing the support foot from the ground and bringing it under the hip or the GCM of the body.

No matter how fast or how long your run will be, this structure will never vary. It's not about an elite or recreational runner, sprinter or long distance runner — the presence of gravity remains the same. It's an invariable condition of our existence on Earth. As long as we move within this environment, our running technique and any other movements will be governed by this external power of nature.

Perception, as I've already mentioned in chapter four, is very alien for most people. From my perspective this is because perception is left to the pros, some talents have it naturally like, Michael Phelps, Lance Armstrong, or Michael Johnson — some heighten it through years of experience and practice. However by and large, perception development is not taught in sports — instead we swim laps, ride in groups, and run miles — all without putting much thought or concentration towards the skill of our movement. Our technique development depends almost entirely on our ability to perceive even the most minute of details, thus making us more skillful athletes; so developing our perception will be the main focus of our lessons. By and large, strength conditioning will be a factor of our perception work — not the foundation; although some supplemental strength work is beneficial.

When we learn a new skill, we do so through our perception. Things that were not apparent before, all of a sudden become second nature. But did you ever stop to think of how or where you acquired all the knowledge you possess today? Probably not. Our ability to perform an action mostly comes from our level of perception. Despite the fact that we'll go through different drills and perceptions that single out and improve specific skills, we have to keep in mind that we learn running as a system, where these different elements are interrelated and depend on each other.

So from this brief introduction to our lessons we are going to discover new perceptions of running, cycling and swimming. Exercises and drills are our tools to develop our perception. While we progress through these new and alien perceptions, our muscles will develop entirely new interrelations between themselves, body weight, and movement.

You will learn that thoughts and desires don't necessarily make you a better athlete, but heightening your perception of body-weight will. This is quite a new concept for most of you and it will take some getting used to, but don't worry, it will not take very long. Your improvement will speak for itself.

Let's move on and get into the lessons, where we'll start from the most important aspect or our training — perception of the body weight.

Lesson One: Learning Major Elements of the Pose Method.

Learning objectives: develop perception of the body weight, running Pose, falling (leaning) from the Pose and pulling the foot from the ground under the hip.

Beginning level "body weight" Perception Drills.

The running Pose is related directly to *body weight perception.* In the running Pose, you hold your body weight on support and then fall forward. How do you feel your body weight? The most obvious sensation is the pressure on the ball of the foot where it contacts the ground. The pressure should be centered right on the ball of the foot, not toes, not the heel.

After you feel the pressure on your foot, there are other sensations to explore, such as specific sensations of muscular tension, tendons lengthening and bone load related

with support. All of these senses are called proprioceptions and they are key to truly understanding what you are doing in any athletic movement.

Take a moment to simply stand on both feet and identify where the pressure is located (Fig.24.2). If you feel a pressure on your heels, then your weight is located there. If your sense of the pressure is on the balls of the feet, then your weight is there.

Once you have a sense of the pressure, move it around a little bit. You can put your body weight on the sides of the feet (Fig.24.3) to get a feel of the body weight loading on different areas of the feet and see how comfortable you feel being at this position. How would it feel to fall forward from this position with your weight out on the periphery of your feet?

After few of these simple perception drills it becomes very obvious that the only position that makes it easy to fall forward and

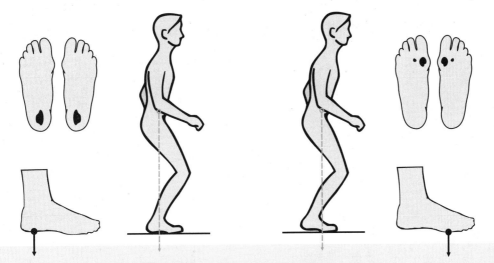

Fig.24.2 Standing on both feet, looking straight ahead with knees slightly bent, lean backwards until you feel your body weight on your heels. Then transfer your body weight to your forefoot, or the balls of your feet. This subtle difference in your perception will take your running to new heights.

change support is when the body weight is located on the balls of the feet.

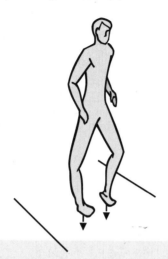

Fig.24.3 Supinating while moving forward will help you familiarize yourself with incorrect landing.

To further your sense of how easy it is to shift and detect your body weight, try lifting your toes and notice how the weight shifts to the heels (Fig 24.4). Then do the reverse

Fig.24.4 Toes up, body weight shifts to the heels.

Fig.24.5 Heels up, body weight shifts to the balls of the feet.

and lift your heels and feel the weight shift to the balls of the feet (Fig.24.5).

This demonstrates how even minute adjustments can dramatically alter the placement of body weight on support and shows how skillful you have to become to insure that you always land with your body weight located on the balls of your feet.

To extend these perception drills have a partner hold you by the shoulders and rock you gently back and forth as you note the shifting location of your body weight (Fig.24.6).

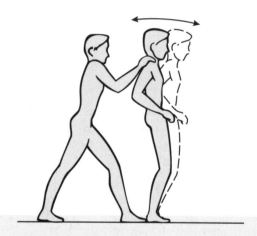

Fig.24.6 Body weight location shifting with a partner's help.

Then ask your partner to move you in a circular motion (Fig.24.7).

In each of these drills it is important to focus your attention on the shifting pressure on your feet indicating the movement of your body weight location from one part of the foot to another.

After each drill take a 15–20 meter run at comfortable pace and focus on landing with your body weight on the balls of your feet.

Fig.24.7 Moving the body in a circular motion with a partner's help.

Don't worry about anything else, just put your body weight on the balls of your feet.

At this point, you should be ready to transition to a more complex perception of your body weight location in the Pose Running stance (Fig.24.8).

Fig.24.8 Body weight location on the ball of the foot, while in the Pose stance.

After being introduced to body weight perception, it's logical to move to the Running Pose to further expand your perception.

Beginning level "Pose" perception drills

The first Pose is called the Springiness Pose (Fig.24.9). Stand with both feet on the ground, knees bent, your body weight on the balls of the feet, arms and elbows slightly bent, hips very slightly bent as well.

Fig.24.9 With knees slightly bent lightly bounce on the balls of the feet.

In this position bounce lightly on the balls of the feet (without leaving the ground) and see how comfortable you feel. If you lack either strength or balance, you may feel very uncomfortable doing this simple drill. By bouncing up and down you can distinguish which angles of bending the knees are the most comfortable. It is very important to keep your heels low, even brushing the ground as you lightly bounce. If possible, have a partner shoot some digital photos, so you can immediately see how you look in this stance and relate that to the sensations you felt as you did the drill.

For your first experience with the actual Running Pose, it helps to either steady yourself with one hand on a wall, or have a partner support you (Fig.24.10). The Running Pose is always balanced on one leg in mid–stance. The body is erect with the leg on support slightly bent at the knee, with the heel held low. The airborne foot is close to the knee of the support leg. As seen from the side, the legs should appear to resemble the numeral '4', which should help you visualize the Pose better.

Fig.24.11 We're back to the Pose. This time try to do as little as possible to maintain the position again and again.

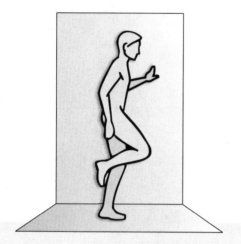

Fig.24.10 Leaning against a wall will help you maintain balance while you're experimenting with your perception.

After you feel comfortable in the Running Pose, try maintaining the same position without outside support (Fig.24.11). The objective is to feel the perception of balance, with no excessive muscular tension. If your quadriceps are overly tensed, your knees are bent too much. No matter what the conditions are when you are running, if you feel too much tension in the quads, you are bending your knees too much.

Also pay close attention to any tension around the knee of the support leg. If you feel tension, that's an indication that the lateral or medial muscles of your thigh are working too hard in maintaining your balance. The tension on the knee means that you are unbalanced on the side, where you

feel tension. The same thing holds true about ankle tension.

Focus your attention on the position of your hips directly above the ball of the foot. This is what you control — and it doesn't require a lot of effort. The rest of your joints are only moderately loaded. This is what it's all about: keeping your balance by keeping your hips above the ball of your foot. This rule remains constant as you go further into Pose Running so we'll say it again: keep your hips above the ball of the foot.

Alternate each drill with a 15–20 meter run at a comfortable pace with the primary focus of reproducing the Pose with minimal effort every step of your run.

Beginning level "Falling" perception drills

Falling may be the element of Pose Running that is the hardest to grasp. It's hard to dispense with the notion that athletic movement is the result of muscular activity, but the fall is just the opposite. No strength is required to fall; you just have to let yourself fall, so these drills have been designed to build the confidence that will let you fall without fear.

Remember, in Pose Running muscular strength is required to maintain the Pose stance, but plays no role in falling. There is nothing you can do to make the fall faster. All you have to do is let yourself fall freely.

Assume the Springiness Pose on two legs while standing close enough to a wall so that you can support yourself with your hands (Fig.24.12). Relax your hands so that you fall gently toward the wall, then use your hands to push yourself back to the Springiness Pose. Do this several times to get the feeling of falling.

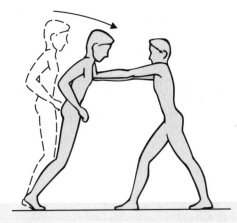

Fig.24.13 The next step is to test your trust in your partner. Having a dynamic reaction to your falling will further enhance your perception of falling freely.

Fig.24.12 Start out closer to the wall, then work your way further back as you get more comfortable with it.

Fall in the Springiness Pose with a partner (Fig.24.13). Your partner stands in front of you with hands lightly on your chest or shoulders. Fall freely forward and let your partner catch you, then push you back to the starting position. As you gain confidence, your partner can let you fall farther each time.

As you fall, make sure that you hold your body in the rigid Pose. Don't 'do' anything; just maintain the Pose and fall forward and let your partner return you to the starting position. When you 'land' on your partner, your hips should remain stable and should not continue moving forward. When the upper body stops falling forward, the hips must stop too. Keep your knees in the same position and don't have any activity in your ankles; just hold the Pose. Repeat this several times. The main thing is to keep the Pose unchanged.

Fall in the Running Pose in front of the wall (Fig.24.14). Start out by standing close to the wall, which will limit the angle of your fall. As you become comfortable, move farther away from the wall and continue to maintain the Pose as your fall lengthens.

Fall in the Running Pose as before, but this time do it with your partner who can easily return you to the starting position (Fig.24.15).

Start out in the Springiness Pose on two legs, leaning slightly forward toward your partner, who provides support on your chest or shoulders. Pull one foot from the ground and assume the Running Pose. As you do this, your partner releases the support from your chest, which allows you to drop airborne leg to the ground and arrest your fall. Don't actively force your foot down, just release it and let gravity pull it down.

Fig.24.14 Falling against the wall in the Pose position will help you grasp the free acceleration you've been missing all along.

Fig.24.15 Having a partner's help is instrumental in expanding the depth of your perception. Fall in the Pose position, this time with a partner.

Alternate each drill with a 15–20 meter run at a comfortable pace allowing your body to fall (lean) forwards expending just enough effort to maintain the Pose.

The last element, which we have to learn in order to complete the running cycle is the pulling action:

Beginning level "pulling" perception drills

Pulling the foot from support on the ground is the only specific action we do in running. Period.

When you pull your foot from the ground, you do it deliberately and consciously, thinking about nothing but pulling your foot from the ground directly under your hip. Don't think about how high or low you pull your foot, because that is a function of how fast you are going and not the reverse. The motion of pulling the foot under the hip should have no thought given to which muscles are being used.

Your psychological perception of the pull is a vertical movement of the foot off the ground under the hip. There is no knee or thigh lifting. Any lift of the knee or thigh is a consequence of rotational movement

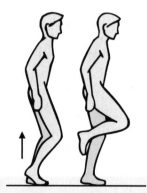

Fig.24.16 Pull your foot directly under the hip. Vary the height of the Pull.

of your leg around the hip axis. More than anything else, focus on pulling the foot up UNDER THE HIP. If you pull your foot up behind the hip instead of under it, this is an error and must be corrected.

Start out in the Springiness Pose on two legs (Fig.24.16). Pull one foot from the ground directly under the hip while holding the springiness position with no other movement. Just pull your foot vertically under the hip.

Stay in the Springiness Pose on one leg, with one hand on a wall and simply tap your foot on the ground (Fig.24.17). The key is to actively pull your foot from the ground and passively let it fall back to the ground. Your foot moves up and down — nothing else.

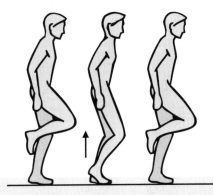

Fig.24.18 Now give it a try without extra support. Just pull! Let your foot fall back down with the force of gravity. It will take time to disengage your muscles from actively lowering your foot. Keep that in mind, pull and release.

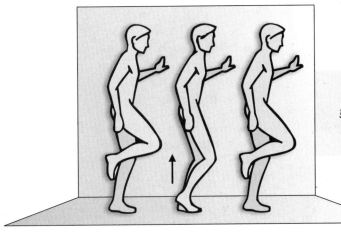

Fig.24.17 Stay relaxed and lightly tap your foot on the ground. Use your hand to keep balance while you experiment.

While standing with one leg on support in the Running Pose (Fig.24.18), repeat the tapping drill with your airborne leg. Always let your foot drop to the ground; don't force it.

Front lunge (Fig.24.19). This is not the same position as a lunge in the health club. With your rear leg as a counterbalance providing support, pull your front foot from the

ground under your hip and then let it drop back down again. Do several pulls with one leg and then switch to the other and repeat. Don't do anything other than pull your foot up from the ground.

Using either the wall or your partner for support, assume the Running Pose and change support from one leg to the other (Fig.24.20). The action is initiated by lifting the foot on support from the ground under

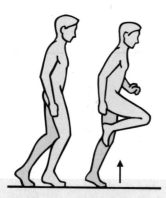

Fig.24.19 The front lunge is meant to guide your pull while your GCM is in front of your support, make sure support stays on the pulling foot.

the hip; the airborne leg will automatically drop to the ground. Don't run in place, just do this one foot at a time, and concentrate on centering your body weight on the ball of the foot.

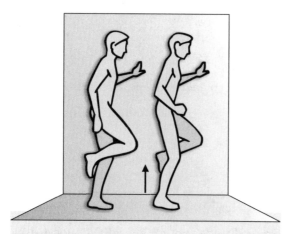

Fig.24.20 Putting it together in sequence. Use the wall or a partner to maintain balance and change support by focusing only on the pull of each leg in succession.

Repeat the drill from above without outside support (Fig.24.21). The objective is to land on the new support foot with the mini-

mum of effort while maintaining complete balance at all times. If you waver as you change support, try bending your knees a little more until you can comfortably change support and stay balanced.

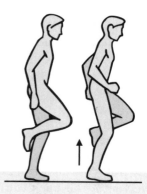

Fig.24.21 Changing support without an external source of balance. Focus on the pull; allow your other foot to fall.

Again after each drill take a 15–20 meter run at a comfortable pace and focus on pulling your support foot from the ground without worrying about anything else.

After mastering the first six pulling drills that are done in place, you can move on to the next drills where forward movement is introduced.

Lesson Two: Learning Major Elements of the Pose Method.

Learning objectives: continue to develop perception of the body weight, the running Pose, falling (leaning) from the Pose and pulling the foot from the ground under the hip. There are no direct drills for body weight perception, but this focus continues through the rest of the drills, because it is the fundamental principle which we need to exploit and employ in running. To reinforce the perception of body weight you can come back to the same drills we went through in the first lesson, as you feel necessary.

Beginning level "Pose perception" drills

For your next trick, try the Running Pose with your support foot on a brick or a section of standard pine 2" x 4", just slightly above the ground (Fig.24.22). From a mental standpoint, this makes it harder to maintain your balance. Everything else is the same. Just stand on the brick on the ball of the foot with the knees slightly bent, hip above the ball of the foot, ankle/knee tension minimal.

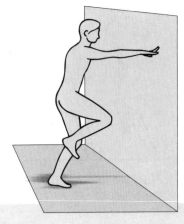

Fig.24.23 Get into the "Pose" position and begin to lean against the wall. Pay close attention to your "Pose" and the location of your airborne foot, regardless of height, it should always be directly under the hips.

Fig.24.22 Holding the "Pose" position on a slightly elevated object such as a block of wood or a brick will help you focus your body weight on the balls of your feet.

Get in the Running Pose, and then lean slightly forward and support yourself with one hand on a wall (Fig.24.23). This stationary position is a necessary step in developing your perception of falling forward. Keep one leg on support in the Pose, with the slight knee and hip bends as above and just maintain the Pose stance in the leaning position. Raise your foot to different heights to get a better feel of your comfort zone while performing the drill. As always, don't forget to take a short run after you do this drill.

To wrap up this series of drills, get back in the springiness position, but this time with your eyes closed (Fig.24.24). This should reveal how far you've already come in perceiving where your body weight is located... and how far you still have to go.

Fig.24.24 Springiness position with your eyes closed. Your perception should be climbing to new heights as your awareness of the body weight increases.

Beginning level "Falling perception" Drills

Run sideways with criss–cross steps (Fig.24.25). Start out with your knees slightly bent and your hands held in close and your elbows pointed in the direction of movement to create stability. The trailing

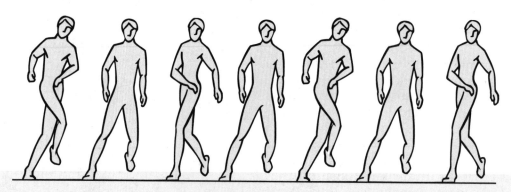

Fig.24.25 While running in criss–cross steps the trailing foot does the majority of the work. Running sideways permits you greater control over your lean. Try different angles to see how much faster you can get.

foot first crosses in front of the leading foot and then crosses behind. The trailing foot is always the one making the major movements. Alternate cross in front, and then cross behind. Start out with a very small angle of sideways lean until you master the footwork, then increase the lean and move faster on successive attempts.

It's a good idea at this point to remind you to do a short 'regular' run after each criss–cross run.

The drill below (Fig.24.26) is similar to the first criss–cross drill, but this time extend your arms sideways in the direction of travel.

Face your partner and hold his or her hands. Repeat the criss–cross run together, be sure to synchronize your steps. Just like in dancing, one partner leads and the other follows. Take turns leading and following, until you both feel comfortable.

Beginning level "Pulling perception" drills

Starting in the Running Pose (Fig.24.27), shuffle forward by pulling up the support foot without dropping the airborne foot. Lean only slightly forward and just barely pull the support foot from the ground.

Fig.24.26 Extending your arms allows you greater control of your balance while running side-ways with criss–cross steps.

Fig.24.27 This drill takes a significant amount of control and focus. You must pull quickly and moderately, while staying airborne.

The Pony is a very subtle drill emphasizing change of support (Fig.24.28). Start out in the Running Pose with your airborne leg barely off the ground. Change support by lifting the support foot and shifting the weight to the airborne foot. The total movement is really just about an inch and the purpose is to do this with virtually no muscular effort.

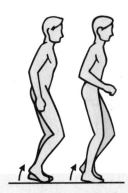

Fig.24.28 The Pony drill is all about subtly changing support, enough so that you feel the pressure on the ball of the foot during each support phase.

Pulling foot from the "ground" on parallel bars into the Running Pose (Fig.24.29).

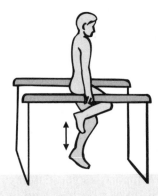

Fig.24.29 Holding on to parallel bars will allow you to focus on your pull and foot release in place.

Pull the same way as you did on the parallel bars, but this time lean toward the wall as you change support in the Running pose (Fig.24.30).

Fig.24.30 Leaning on the wall will help you perceive your maximum falling angle where you feel comfortable consistently landing in the same place with little effort to keep balance.

Lesson Three: Integration of Pose Elements into the System.

Learning objectives: Put all elements of the Pose Method of running together as one single system and continuous motion. Develop a holistic perception of running as a system of efficient use of the body weight.

Beginning level integration drills

Start in the Running pose on one leg, facing a wall (Fig.24.31). Fall forward and pull your support foot from the ground. Do one change of support, as you catch yourself on the wall with your hands. End in the Running Pose on the opposite leg.

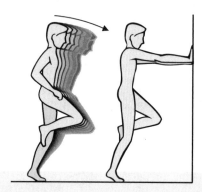

Fig.24.31 Putting the Pose, Fall, and Pull together. Start in the Pose, begin falling and quickly change support by pulling your support foot and get into the Pose position with the opposite leg. Use a wall for support to catch yourself.

Stand in the Running Pose on one leg and lean forward in the falling position with the hand of your partner supporting you on your chest (Fig.24.32). Your partner then releases you to fall and you do one change of support and end up in the Running Pose on the opposite leg having moved forward one stride. At the exact moment your body starts falling, you have to pull your support foot from the ground. Developing your per-

ception of the fall and the pull being simultaneous is the key to this exercise.

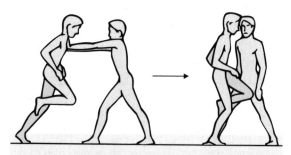

Fig.24.32 Instead of starting out upright, your beginning position will be at full lean. Your partner will remove his hands from your chest. As soon as you feel the absence of his support, you must pull your foot directly under the hips.

Forward change of support (Fig.24.33). Lean slightly so that you move forward from one Running Pose to the other. Pay attention to the position of the airborne foot near the support knee, making sure the legs resemble the numeral '4'. Be careful to stay in the Running Pose and keep your body weight on the ball of the foot. This perception must be kept throughout the entire exercise.

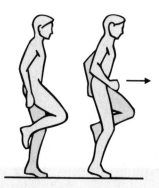

Fig.24.33 Change support from one foot to the other, while moving forward.

Forward pony (Fig.24.34). Keep your feet low to the ground and close to each other in space and time. Do not separate the feet; they should be along a vertical line compared to your general center of mass, all the time. After you've got the concept, put it in motion by leaning forward and continuing the exact same movements.

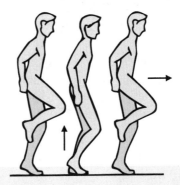

Fig.24.35 Forward tapping in motion, do not allow your feet to extend in front of the GCM.

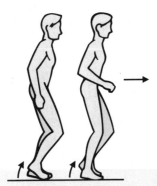

Fig.24.34 Forward pony in motion, do not allow your feet to extend in front of the GCM.

Forward tapping (Fig.24.35). This drill is a little trickier as you integrate the Pose concepts. The airborne foot taps up and down along the vertical line, as you did in previous pulling drills (24.18) and (24.19), where your body weight remains on the support foot. This time, however, you hop on the support foot throughout the entire exercise. Pull your support foot up from the ground under the hip. The downward return to the ground is done by gravity and requires no muscular effort on your part. It's helpful to perform the tapping drill to a specific rhythm of pulling, by counting 1,2,3,4 as in a music score, counting only the foot moving up, not down.

When your foot goes down you have to reduce the impact on the ground by decelerating it. You accomplish this by giving pull command to yourself before the foot actually touches the ground. Literally say to yourself, "Pull!" before the foot touches the ground.

Doing so decelerates the foot from the pull of gravity, allowing it to touch the ground with almost zero speed. This is what makes our landing and running silent and soft — reducing impact during the landing phase.

This reinforces a very key concept: on the subconscious level landing should be pulling. There is a natural conflict between having your foot in the air and having it on the ground.

In Pose running, as soon as you have pulled one foot from the ground, your attention must immediately shift to the other foot, you don't want to be thinking: 'land', you want to be thinking 'pull'. Your priority is not to land; it is always to pull, otherwise you introduce an extra element into the cycle, which throws your technique out of rhythm. Instead of Pose–Fall–Pull, you'll complicate the process and begin to Pose–Fall–Land–Pull, and so on. This is where mistakes can be made. By the time you reach the ground with your descending foot, the other foot is already in position under your hip, which gives you the ability to fall immediately. You don't have to wait for it while you land, because it's already there, so your thought is always to pull, never to land.

Psychologically and mentally you must execute one action at a time, by shifting the focus to pulling your airborne foot (decelerating it) before it lands, when you have pulled your support foot from the ground.

As you work through this drill, you will experience a discrepancy between your level of perception and the level of your body's strength and flexibility. Your muscles have a gravitational reflex, so they know how to react to gravity; they react to body weight. This doesn't need to be 'taught' to your muscles. What you have to do instead is develop perception of the body weight on support.

Don't get frustrated with the tapping drill and merely rush through it. At first, you may feel very uncoordinated and you may find yourself slamming you airborne foot to the ground, instead of merely letting it tap. That's an indication that you are trying to do too much.

Take a break, think through the drill and then try it again. While lightly hopping on the support leg, tap the airborne foot. Easy right? Good.

Forward front lunge (Fig.24.36). Pull the foot from the ground, just like you did previously in the forward pony drill. Emphasize giving yourself the 'pull' command before you land. Landing is actually an extension of pulling.

Double lunge in place (Fig.24.37). Pull both feet (first in front and then in rear) from the ground under the hip.

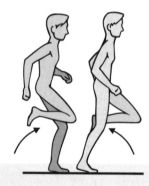

Fig.24.37 Double lunge in place is designed to take you through an entire sequence of Pose–Fall–Pull focusing on one leg at a time.

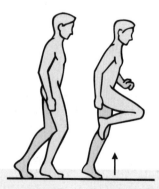

Fig.24.36 Shifting your GCM forward, keep your body weight on the lunge foot.

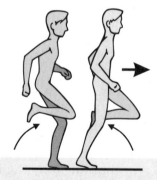

Fig.24.38 Double lunge while moving forward further enhances your perception each time you land and switch around the lunge foot while progressing forward.

Forward double lunge (Fig.24.38). Pull both feet (first in front and then in rear) from the ground under the hip, while leaning slightly so that you move forward as you pull.

Lesson Four: Integration of Pose Elements into the System.

Learning objectives: Integrate perceptions into continuous motion.

The drills below continue to expand your perception as you start to run from a variety of positions. Carefully note what you feel as you start running from each position and let those perceptions guide your next stage of development.

Forward pony and run is the drill with forward body movement via the slight leaning of the body (Fig.24.39). Your feet stay close to the vertical line (together) and the unloaded foot is just off the ground with the forefoot still touching the ground. The specific perception of this drill should be incorporated into your running.

Start with forward change of support and transition that into a run (Fig.24.40). Forward movement in this drill happens by the body leaning forward.

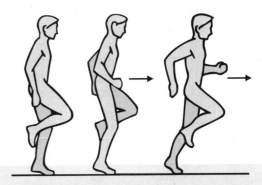

Fig.24.40 Forward change of support transitioned into a run.

From the running Pose, fall forward and start to run (Fig.24.41). If you maintain falling at the same angle your acceleration will continue. In order to stop you have to bring your body into a vertical position by decreasing the body's lean forward.

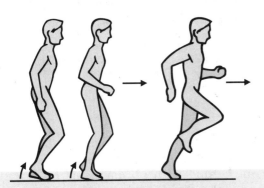

Fig.24.39 Start off doing the forward pony drill and then slowly transition into a run, while incorporating the new sensations you have just experienced.

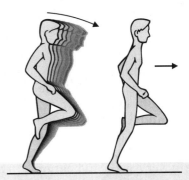

Fig.24.41 Begin with the running Pose and lean forward until you are forced to land for support. Continue with this angle for as long as you can, throughout your acceleration.

Place your middle and index fingers on your belly button and run (Fig.24.42). This very simple perception of the pressure of your fingers on the belly button is a sign that you are falling forward. It's a delicate process, try not to push your fingers. Instead lightly place your fingers on your belly button, and try to catch up to them as you run. If there is no pressure, then you not falling. It is easy to check this sensation by running backwards, where there is no leaning forward, and your fingers are not pressing on your belly button, either.

Fig.24.43 Run with your hand on the glutes to test if you are bending at the waist, instead of falling with the entire body.

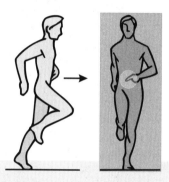

Fig.24.42 Try running with your fingers on your belly button to test your lean.

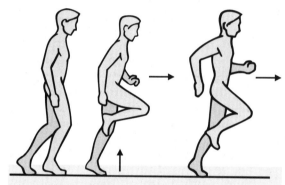

Fig.24.44 Forward lunge, followed by a run. The pulling action is emphasized and is designed to give you very good feedback on how well you've performed the pulling.

With one hand on the same side gluteus, fall forward and start to run (Fig.24.43). This arm placement is a good checking point for position of the trunk (bending at the waist) and hips (left behind or above the ball of the foot). Geometry of the body — shoulders and hips connected by the arm will be a very good indication of the hip/trunk positions.

Start with the forward lunge and transition into a run (Fig.24.44). The pulling action in the front lunge is very deliberate and designed to provide you with the perception of how well you performed the pull, while running.

Perform the running lunge with one leg at a time (Fig.24.45). The other leg is going to trail behind with no emphasis on pulling under the hip. Switch the lunge foot after each pull, while lightly skipping forward. This drill is an excellent way to enhance your perception of falling.

Clasp your hands together in front of you and run (Fig.24.46). The arms' position provides a good reference point for feedback about possible over–striding (if hands

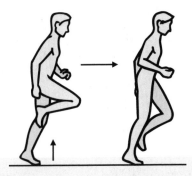

Fig.24.45 Perform the running lunge by lunging, while lightly skipping forward. The trailing leg should be actively kept behind, placing all of the emphasis on the leg lunging forward and the pulling perception it provides.

are moving side to side), and late pulling of your foot (if arms are moving up and down). This is because as you run, your hands and arms shift your GCM forward, and your arms become isolated points of balance, which clearly indicate any abnormalities in your stride. When you can comfortably run with your hands in front of you, without any additional movement to the sides or up and down, you can be fairly certain that your legs look just as smooth to a bystander.

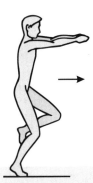

Fig.24.46 Run with your hands clasped in front of you. This is a great self analysis of your technique.

Run with your hands clasped behind you (Fig.24.47). This exercise is also a good indicator of over–striding and bending at the waist. It also provides almost instant feedback about mistakes in your running.

Fig.24.47 Running with your hands clasped behind you.

Your progression from lesson one to lesson four should not be a linear process. You could actually spend more time on some lessons by repeating the drills again and again to be certain that your execution is spot on. Being on lesson three or four doesn't mean that you can't go back to lesson one for partial or full refreshment of your new perceptions.

It is never a bad idea to come back to the previous lessons, and, as a matter of fact, it is very helpful to refresh and refine your perception development.

Now that we'll be moving to the advanced drill lessons, the logic we discussed previously will remain the same — perception is the main avenue of development of your skill.

CHAPTER 25
ADVANCED DRILLS FOR RUNNERS

Act without doing; Work without effort.
— *Tao Te Ching*

If Pose Running were a martial art — which it really is, in a way — then the drills in this chapter would be the ones designed to attain black belt status. Like most runners, you probably have always been conditioned to think that the path to running better times is to train more, train harder and train faster. The alternative is to become a runner with highly developed skills that will make your running seem to flow effortlessly.

In general, the following drills will fine–tune your perceptions of falling and pulling to levels you wouldn't have previously imagined, ultimately opening your personal doors of perception and helping you become a much better runner.

While you certainly won't do all of these drills all the time, work your way through the full set a few times with a training partner and then remember to incorporate a varied selection of the drills into your weekly training routine.

In order to guide you through the drills they have been logically compiled in the form of lessons, just like those that you've already gone through in the beginner level drills. Any combination of drills in a given lesson is conditional to your needs. Selec-

tion of drills should be based on your needs and necessities at that specific moment. These sample lessons of drills will give you guidance for further development of your skills, coordination and perception.

Lesson One: Enhance your perception.

Learning objectives: enhance the perception of balance and the "Running Pose."

Advanced level "Pose" drills

Fig.25.1 Pose stance on the medicine ball. Adding the extra element of insta-bility to your Pose stance takes your skill and coordination to another level.

Running Pose stance balancing on a medicine ball (Fig.25.1). This is a very challenging drill with many benefits. Since the position on the medicine ball is relatively high and unstable, you will want to look down as you assume the Running Pose. Don't! If you look down, you will take your body out of correct alignment. Instead, look out toward the horizon and let your proprioceptions tell you when you're balanced. Because the ball is unstable, you'll recruit more muscles and connective tissue to help you maintain your balance, making this a strength development exercise, as well as a balance drill. Once you are comfortable on the ball, you can do shallow one–legged squats from the Running Pose, again strengthening your vital connections while enhancing your balance.

Running Pose stance on an IndoFlo™ Balance Stimulator (Fig.25.2). Though not as high as a medicine ball, this inflatable cushion is specifically designed for balance exercises. Start out with the cushion at low inflation and work through the same drills as you did on the medicine ball. Then gradually increase the inflation as you get better and better.

Place an Indoboard™ deck on the Indo-Flo™ cushion and work through the same drills (Fig.25.3). Once you have mastered the basics, you can add many of the beginners drills like the Pony, various hops, and change of support to your balance stimulator routine.

Fig.25.3 Pose stance on the IndoFlo™ cushion and Indo™ Board. Standing on a firm surface like the board isolates your ankle to provide balance for your body.

Fig.25.2 Pose stance on the IndoFlo™ cushion. Standing on the cushion creates a very unstable surface which demands more control from the lower parts of your leg.

Fig.25.4 Pose stance on the Indo™ Board roller. Performing the "Pose" on the roller is extremely challenging.

If you want to get very advanced, replace the IndoFlo™ cushion with an Indoboard™ roller (Fig.25.4). Doing the running Pose on this set–up is very challenging, but it is possible (and, yes, there is a risk of falling. Try it in a doorway or have your partner support you, when you first try it).

Advanced level "falling" drills

Run with your partner's hand resting lightly on your upper back (Fig.25.5). Your partner just holds the hand there, but does not push. This gives you the constant perception of being in leaning position. After a short distance, the partner should remove the hand and you should keep going another 10 meters or so.

Fig.25.5 Falling: forward leaning perception. Run with a partner's hand on your back for a consistent angle of falling.

Fig.25.6 Falling: forward leaning perception. Chase your partner's hand with your chest.

Now run with your partner's hand on your chest (Fig.25.6), catching you as you fall onto his or her hand. Focus on leaning forward to stay in contact with the hand.

In the Springiness Pose on two legs, have your partner push on your back (Fig.25.7). Resist against the push while remaining centered on the balls of your feet. The concept here is to develop your perception of resistance on the balls of the feet.

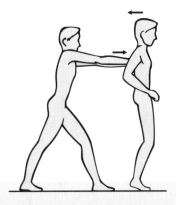

Fig.25.7 Falling: resisting the fall. As your partner pushes you forward, resist with your entire body. As a result, your support should be pin–pointed on the balls of the feet.

Springiness Pose as in the previous drill, but don't resist against your partner's push (Fig.25.8). When your partner pushes, you release your support. Pay very close attention to the fact that when you offer no resistance to falling, there is NO pressure on the balls of your feet. It is very important to feel the lack of pressure as you fall, because it means that you are not resisting gravity, rather allowing your body weight to fall forward.

Repeat the resisting the fall drill, but this time assume your stance in the running Pose, first on one leg, then the other (Fig.25.9).

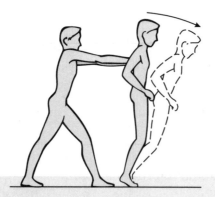

Fig.25.8 Falling: allowing the fall. Now that you've resisted, the next step is to allow yourself to fall.

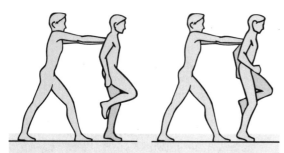

Fig.25.9 Falling: single leg resisting the fall.

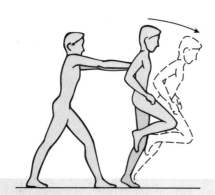

Fig.25.10 Falling: single leg allowing the fall.

As before on two feet, don't resist your partner's push, instead fall freely from the running Pose (Fig.25.10).

Advanced Level "pulling" drills

With the following advanced level drills, you not only develop advanced perception of the pull, but you also begin the process of developing neuromuscular coordination and neuromuscular strength. This muscular strength is very specific to the action of running.

Knee flexion with weights on the bench lying face down (Fig.25.11).

Fig.25.11 Pulling: hamstring curl on the weight bench.

Fig.25.12 Pulling: hamstring pull into the "Pose" position with free weights.

Stand on an elevated platform or a box with the body weight placed on the ball of the foot and free weights strapped on your airborne ankle (Fig.25.12), pull your foot up under the hip (the knee flexes as a result of the pull, do not use the quads to lift the knee, pull the foot up instead).

Pull the foot under the hip with an ankle weight on the ankle while supporting yourself with your arms on the parallel bars (Fig.25.13).

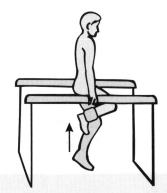

Fig.25.13 Pulling: hamstring pull on parallel bars.

Pull the foot up with the stretch cord attached to the ankle, while supporting yourself with your arms on parallel bars for support (Fig.25.14).

Fig.25.14 Pulling: hamstring pull with stretch cords on parallel bars.

Integration drill

Run with your partner's hands on your shoulders (Fig.25.15).

Fig.25.15 Running with your partner's hands on your shoulders will make you more aware of your vertical oscillation as you run.

Lesson Two: Enhance your perception.

Learning objectives: Fine tuning the Pose stance, falling, and pulling.

Maintain the running Pose in a stationary position, but have a partner or use a stretch cord to disrupt your balance (Fig.25.16). A

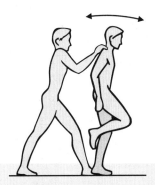

Fig.25.16 Pose stance: challenge your balance. Your partner should guide you as your point of support moves up and down your foot.

stretch cord should be applied to the chest level of the body to disturb balance. A partner can also disturb your balance by slightly pushing on the front, side or the back. Maintain position against the external efforts to disrupt your balance.

Hop in the running Pose. Keeping the Pose stance, perform small jumps forward and sideways (Fig.25.17). This reinforces your sense of body weight on the ball of the foot, as you maintain balance.

Fig.25.17 Pose stance: body weight perception jumps.

Stand in the running Pose with your eyes closed (Fig.25.18). This is a very effective proprioceptive drill. Once you feel comfort-

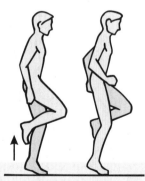

Fig.25.18 Pose stance: change of support with your eyes closed.

able, go ahead and switch support from one leg to the next, while keeping your eyes closed.

Advanced level "falling" drills

Assume your stance in the springiness position (Fig.25.19). Loop a stretch cord around your waist. Your partner should pull on the stretch cord in different directions, while you resist and maintain your stance in the springiness Pose.

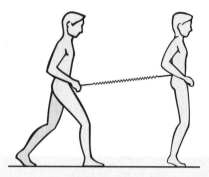

Fig.25.19 Resisting the fall: using the stretch cords and a partner.

In the same position as the previous drill, don't resist your partner's pull on the stretch cord, but instead fall freely forward (Fig.25.20).

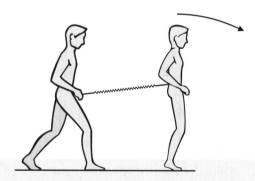

Fig.25.20 Allowing the fall: using the stretch cords and a partner.

Run with your partner pushing lightly on your back in a situation similar to the previous drill (Fig.25.21). Resist your partner's push as you run and notice the pressure on the ball of your foot. Be careful that both your partner's push and your resistance are very light, just enough that you get the correct proprioceptive feeling of resistance and pressure.

Fig.25.21 Running with your partner pushing you from behind.

Now reverse the situation when your partner was pushing you and you had to resist (Fig.25.22). Instead of resisting your part-

Fig.25.22 Allow your partner to keep his hand on you, but mentally try to escape the pressure of your partner's hand by leaning forward as you accelerate.

ner's push, move away from the pushing hand by leaning forward as you run. This will help develop your sense of how leaning leads to acceleration.

Advanced level "pulling" drills

Flex your knee, while pulling the foot with a stretch cord (attached to your ankle) for dynamic resistance, while lying face down on the floor (Fig.25.23).

Fig.25.23 Hamstring pull facedown with stretch cord resistance. It's very important to isolate your hamstring when performing this drill. Using an elastic band, as opposed to weights, provides dynamic resistance for your muscles, further enhancing your perception.

In push up position with stretch cords attached to your ankles, pull each foot in succession toward the hips (Fig.25.24).

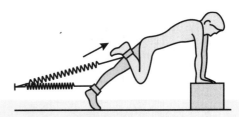

Fig.25.24 Hamstring pull with stretch cords attached to both ankles. Change support, while being pulled out of position by the stretch cords.

With the support on the elbows and hips on a floor, face up, with stretch cord attached to ankle, pull the foot towards the hip (Fig.25.25).

Fig.25.25 Hamstring pull facing up. Having the stretch cord pull from an angle above, forces you to consciously pull in a straight line along the side of your opposite foot.

Face up with support on the arms, hips in the air, the stretch cord attached to the ankle, pull the foot under the hip (Fig.25.26).

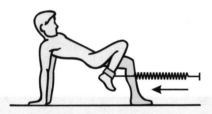

Fig.25.26 Hamstring pull facing up. The combination of angles — which you pull from, and the dynamic resistance from the stretch cord prepare you to run at any speed.

Integration drill

Run on one leg (Fig.25.27). This drill can be best described as the "phantom landing." In reality, you're trying to run like normal, but skipping the landing phase of one foot entirely. This reinforces the speed of your pull and also strengthens your foot simultaneously.

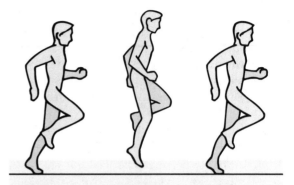

Fig.25.27 Running on one leg. This may take some time to perfect as it requires a lot of coordination to accomplish correctly. Land on one foot only; follow it with a "phantom landing" of the other foot, as you move forward.

Lesson Three: Enhance your perception.

Learning objectives: Fine tune your falling and pulling perception.

Advanced level "falling" drills

Stretch cord resistance (Fig.25.28). With the stretch cord looped around your waist, your partner provides resistance from be-

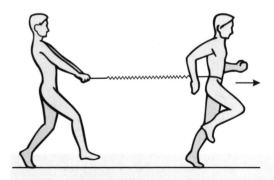

Fig.25.28 Forward falling: with partner and stretch cords. With your partner pulling you back, this drill forces you to actively lean forward to accelerate.

hind. To continue running, you have to lean forward applying your body weight to the rubber band.

Here your partner holds the stretch cord from the front and pulls you forward, while you slightly resist the pull (Fig.25.29).

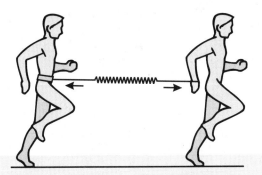

Fig.25.29 Resisting forward falling. As your partner pulls via a stretch cord attached to your waist, you must run by actively resisting the fall.

Continuing on the previous drill, this time stop resisting the pull, instead lean and fall forward (Fig.25.30).

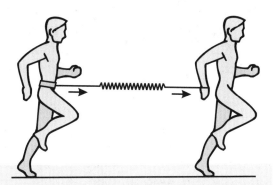

Fig.25.30 Falling forward while being pulled by your partner with a stretch cord. Instead of resisting, you should experiment with releasing your falling.

Run downhill on a very shallow slope of 2–3° degrees (Fig.25.31). The perception of falling is so easy that you don't need to DO anything; you just fall very freely.

Fig.25.31 Run downhill to put it all together. Focus especially on your falling and quick turnover to minimize impact.

Advanced level "pulling" drills

Change of support with the stretch cord strapped on the ankles and resistance from behind (Fig.25.32); remain in place with no forward movement, focus on the pull.

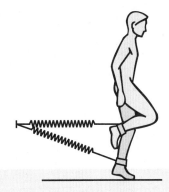

Fig.25.32 Pulling: the change of support with posterior stretch cord resistance.

Repeat the same drill as above, but attach the stretch cords for resistance from the front (Fig.25.33).

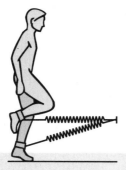

Fig.25.33 Pulling: the change of support with anterior stretch cord resistance.

From the front lunge position, with a stretch cord attached from the back, pull the foot under the hip (Fig.25.34).

Fig.25.34 Pulling: the front lunge with stretch cord resistance from the posterior.

In the same position as the previous drill, but now the stretch cord is attached from the front, pulling the ankle forward. Execute the same pull under the hip (Fig.25.35).

Change of support with resistance of the stretch cords attached to the ankles, while leaning into the wall (Fig.25.36).

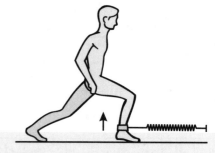

Fig.25.35 Pulling: the front lunge with stretch cord resistance from the anterior.

Fig.25.36 Pulling: the change of support with stretch cord resistance, while leaning against the wall to simulate falling.

Foot tapping, with the stretch cord attached to your ankle assisting your pull (Fig.25.37). The stretch cord will pull your

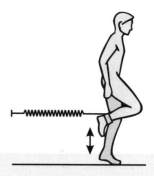

Fig.25.37 Pulling: the foot tapping with a stretch cord attached to the ankle.

foot backwards to simulate the position of a "late pull." Be sure to keep your tapping foot in line with your support foot as you tap up and down.

Integration drill

Run with your eyes closed (Fig.25.38). This should help reinforce many of the drills you've done, by allowing you to focus your perception on landing on the balls of the feet, falling immediately upon landing, and pulling quickly each and every stride.

Fig.25.39 Pulling: with a partner's resistance on the heel.

Fig.25.38 Running with your eyes closed being, guided by your partner.

Stay in the running Pose while your partner pushes your heel down, until the foot drops to the ground (Fig.25.40). This drill is meant to reinforce the "muscle memory" of your hamstring, as you go from the Pose stance to the springiness stance and back again.

Lesson Four: Enhance your perception of the pull.

Learning objectives: quickly and accurately pulling your feet from the ground with minimal effort.

Advanced level "pulling" drills

Staying on one leg pull the other foot from the ground under the hip with the partner's resistance, applied to the heel (concentric) (Fig.25.39). Your partner's role is to gauge the proper amount of resistance necessary, while you perform the drill.

Fig.25.40 Pulling: the partner resistance is directed downward, while you maintain the Pose.

This drill is similar to Fig.25.39 with the partner's resistance, but this time your support is on your hands, as you face up (Fig.25.41). This specific angle and partner's resistance expands your perception and skill of the pull. Take a short run after these drills to reinforce your new perceptions.

Fig.25.41 Pulling: partner resistance as you pull the foot under the hips.

Get into the same body position as in the previous drill with the foot near the hip (Fig.25.42): your partner pulls your foot against your resistance, until your foot leaves from the initial position (eccentric).

Fig.25.42 Pulling: your partner pulls your ankle, as you resist to remain in the Pose position.

Front hop on a box. Face the box with one leg on the box and pull your foot from the ground under your hip (Fig.25.43).

Fig.25.43 Pulling: the front hop on an elevated platform or box.

This is the same as the previous drill, but now face away with your rear foot on the box and pull your foot from the ground under the hip (Fig.25.44).

Fig.25.44 Pulling: the back hop on an elevated platform or box.

Integration drills

Forward single skip and run. The skip requires you to jump starting from the springiness position on both feet (Fig.25.45). Jump and pull your foot into the Pose position, land in the springiness position, and do it again with the same leg.

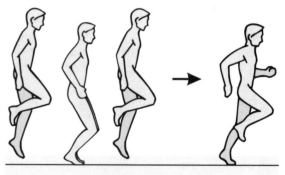

Fig.25.45 Forward single skip followed by a run.

Forward double skip and run (Fig.25.46). This time around you will switch legs each time you land. Start by jumping and doing the Pose with one leg, land, then follow with the other leg. This reinforces your pulling, change of support and muscle elasticity all at once.

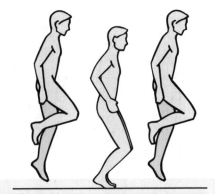

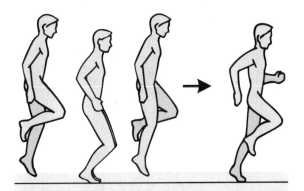

Fig.25.46 Forward double skip followed by a run.

Fig.25.47 Single skip in place. Start and land from the springiness position.

Lesson Five: Enhance your perception of the pull.

Learning objectives: increase muscle elasticity along with new pulling perceptions.

Advanced level "pulling" drills

Single skip in place (Fig.25.47). Pull your foot from the ground under the hip. The drill starts from the hop on two feet, and an almost simultaneous pull of one foot under the hip. Landing happens on both feet, and continues to the hop and pull of the foot under the hip.

Single skip forward (Fig.25.48). This is the same as the previous drill, only with the forward movement by the body leaning forward. Instead of landing in the springiness position directly beneath you, continue to jump in the forward direction, while pulling.

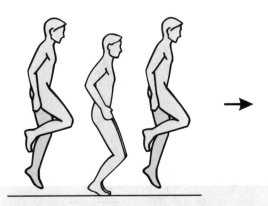

Fig.25.48 Single skip while moving forward. Perform with one leg at a time.

Double skip in place (Fig.25.49). It is the same drill as the single skip in place drill with alternation of the pulling foot after the hop. Notice that after you land back in the springiness position, you skip with the alternate leg and so on. Try to achieve a rhythmic–like comfort with this drill as it will greatly improve your muscle elasticity.

Double skip forward (Fig.25.50). You guessed it... It is the same drill as the double skip in place drill, only with forward movement to simulate running.

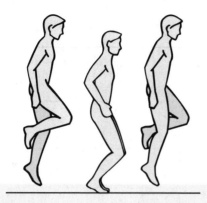

Fig.25.49 Double skip in place. Instead of one leg at a time, now alternate.

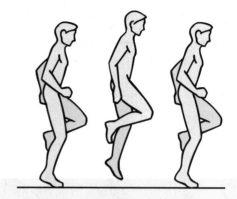

Fig.25.51 Hop in the running Pose on one leg.

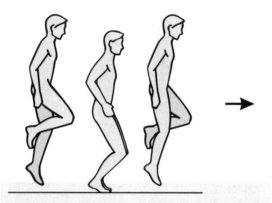

Fig.25.50 Double skip forward as you alternate your change of support.

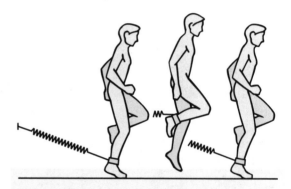

Fig.25.52 Hop in the running Pose on one leg with a stretch cord attached to the ankle.

Hop in the running Pose on one leg (Fig.25.51). It is a quick bounce with a simultaneous pull of the foot at a low height from the ground.

Hop in the running Pose with the resistance from the stretch cord strapped to the ankle of the support foot (Fig.25.52). This will continuously throw you off balance and force you to land very precisely on your support foot.

Hop in the running Pose with an ankle weight (Fig.25.53). Pull your foot under the hip. This should further enhance your pulling perception and strengthen your hamstrings at the same time.

Integration drills

Elastic forward change of support (Fig.25.54). Your partner holds the stretch cords attached to your ankles, pulling your feet up, as you run. This provides valuable feedback, letting you know to pull your foot quickly if your support is too long.

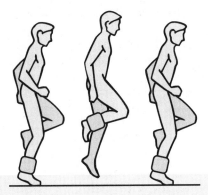

Fig.25.53 Hop in the running Pose on one leg with an ankle weight attached to the ankle.

Fig.25.55 Run with stretch cords held overhead to reinforce quick pulling.

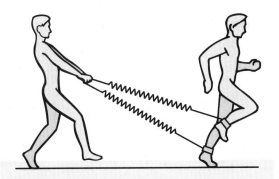

Fig.25.54 Forward change of support with stretch cords to provide pulling resistance.

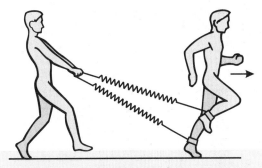

Fig.25.56 Run with your partner's resistance from behind, holding the stretch cords attached to the ankles.

Run with the stretch cord held overhead behind your back and attached to your ankles (Fig.25.55).

Run with a partner providing resistance from behind by holding the stretch cords strapped to your ankles (Fig.25.56).

Run with the partner in front and the stretch cords strapped to your ankles (Fig.25.57). Your partner pulls you forward. This simulates "landing ahead" of the GCM and forces you to focus on landing truly underneath your GCM.

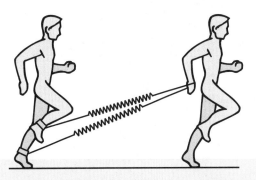

Fig.25.57 Run behind your partner who should run ahead and pull your feet.

Run with the EZ Run Belt® attached to your waist and ankles (Fig.25.58). This should provide some immediate feedback regarding the length of your support time.

Fig.25.58 Run with the EZ Run Belt® attached to your waist and ankles.

Run side–by–side with your partner with the stretch cords attached to your left ankle and your partner's right ankle (Fig.25.59). This may remind some of you of the potato-sack races you competed in as a kid, however this can be a powerful tool to evaluate your overall form. Don't have too much fun!

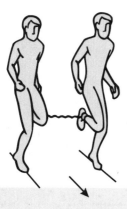

Fig.25.59 Running side–by–side with your partner can point out potential discrepancies in your form as well as increase your overall coordination.

Lesson Six: Put it all together.

Learning objectives: combine the Pose, Fall and Pull perceptions you've gained and apply them to your running.

Integration drills: Pose–Fall–Pull

Integration is the combination of several elements into a single system. In these drills the three elements, Pose–Fall–Pull are integrated into a single system of performance.

Advanced level "integration" drills

In place, hop on your two legs with the stretch cords stretched above your head pulling your feet up to your hips as you jump (Fig.25.60).

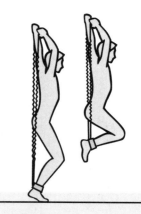

Fig.25.60 Hop from the springiness position with the stretch cords attached to the ankles.

Elastic forward hop on one leg with the stretch cord attached to your ankle and your partner behind you pulling the stretch cord up (Fig.25.61).

Run with the stretch cord around your waist, controlled by your partner, who creates resistance from behind and then re-

Fig.25.61 Forward hop on one leg with the stretch cord attached to your ankle and your partner pulling up as you hop.

leases you to run freely (Fig.25.62). This will allow you to experiment with leaning more or less, depending on how quickly you want to accelerate. Again this ties in the elements of Pose, Fall, and Pull as you're released by your partner to run freely.

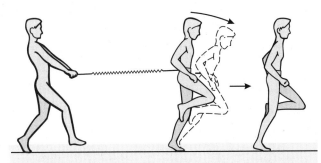

Fig.25.62 Run with a stretch cord around your waist and a partner's resistance before you are let go to run freely.

Run uphill (Fig.25.63). It's as simple as that. But is it really? If you've ever run a marathon — or watched one, you're probably familiar with the term "heart–break hill." Why is running uphill such an up-hill battle (pun intended)? Many of us exert too much energy running uphill (normally a short distance), which throws you out of

rhythm during a long run. Be sure to go up a hill at the same pace as you would run on level ground. The only adjustment you need to make is to pick up your cadence and take shorter strides depending on the incline of the hill. The steeper the slope, the shorter the steps!

Fig.25.63 Run uphill with your new perceptions. Be sure to increase your cadence as you conquer the hill.

Run downhill (Fig.25.64). Now that you've run up that hill, you need to run down. Be careful not to make the mistake of overstriding, while you're quickly accelerating down the hill. Instead, try this: keep your cadence as is and limit your range of motion, but vary

Fig.25.64 Run downhill and avoid over-striding as you make your descent.

your lean to test the acceleration power of gravity that can take you down the hill with effortless ease.

Run upstairs (Fig.25.65). To conclude your advanced drills of putting it all together, try running up a flight of stairs like Rocky, but with less effort. Given your new perceptions and body weight awareness, you should be able to apply these concepts to run effortlessly on any terrain. Remember, the GCM leads, and your legs follow.

Fig.25.65 Run up a flight of stairs making sure that your GCM is ahead of your feet. Remember, its not your legs ascending up the stairs, but rather your entire body. Lead with your GCM and experience how much easier it is to run up the stairs!

CHAPTER 26
ERRORS IN RUNNING AND THEIR CORRECTION

*Anyone who has never made a mistake
has never tried anything new.*

— *Albert Einstein*

It goes without saying that as you learn this new method of running you're going to get some things wrong. Mistakes are an unavoidable — and very useful — part of learning any new skill. Old habits creep back into your running every so often, your perception takes time to develop and what you feel or think you are doing will not always be what you really are doing.

The value of any error is that by recognizing and correcting it you can learn and continue to move forward in developing your new technique. Conversely, small errors left unchecked will lead to ever–larger errors, decreasing your efficiency as a runner and in all likelihood leading to soreness and eventual injury.

The first part of the equation is to recognize your error, which the dictionary defines as a deviation from the accepted or developed standard. Taking the Pose Method as our "developed standard," an error will be any movement that doesn't fit within the Pose system of movement.

To fix errors, we need to identify them and their origins. All too often when problems arise, the tendency is to treat the symptoms and not the cause. A runner with a sore leg may go for a massage, skip a couple of runs and then hope for the best in the next workout. The better plan is to ask, "What is causing this pain?" Of course, it's even better to identify errors before they manifest themselves as injuries, and some errors may never lead to injury but could still limit your performance.

With the Pose Method as our standard, we have the framework for identifying and correcting these problems. The major components of the Pose Method — Pose–Fall–Pull — are the starting point in the search to pinpoint the errors. In this regard, a little pain is actually a good thing. It's nature's way of telling you, "you're doing something wrong." The errors that don't lead to pain are even harder to identify; they'll require your highest level of perception to find and fix.

In the course of a training run, you might experience cramping in your calves, a sharp pain in the ankle or numbness in your hip. Absent any traumatic event, like stumbling on a rock or having a bad fall, you know that your pain or injury must stem from a flaw in your technique. You're doing something wrong, but you're not sure what. What do you do?

Because of all the possible factors involved it's important to take a very logical approach as you play "error detective" and work to correct your problem. There might even be several errors mixed up in your pain, making it even more important to identify the biggest factor and correct it first.

It's safe to say that most errors occur during the time of interaction with support (the ground) and are therefore a result of the way in which we interact with gravity. Simply put, it often boils down to how much we work with — or against — gravity.

If gravity is the main external factor when considering errors, then the mind is our main internal factor. The way in which we think and perceive our running has a tremendous impact on our relations with gravity, our focus and our psycho–emotional condition. So keep this in mind as we move ahead.

All of the error categories outlined in this chapter are strongly related to our understanding of gravity. And considering that the Pose Method has been developed as a way of utilizing gravity, anything reducing or preventing us from getting the most out of nature's free ride is viewed — to a greater or lesser extent — as an error. It is with this approach that we will go on to examine the various aspects of running technique.

Errors in the Running Pose

Errors in the Running Pose are almost always related to one of two things: the location of your body weight on support or allowing body parts to deviate from the vertical line running through your general center of mass on support. Put simply:

1. If your body weight is not on the ball of your foot (Fig.26.1); or,
2. If any part of your body deviates from the vertical line going through your GCM while on support; resulting in a less–than–optimal position for neuromuscular coordination and excess muscular tension (Fig.26.2).

Fig.26.1 Landing on the heel well in front of your GCM.

Fig.26.2 Swing leg left behind the GCM while the other foot lands on the ground.

What's the fix?

1. Location of the body weight: The following exercise is extremely useful in developing the correct perception of your body weight on the ball of your foot.

(Exercise: holding the Pose barefoot). Place a small object on the ground, such as a brick (Fig.26.3) or — for more of a challenge — a medicine ball (Fig.26.4), and stand on the object practicing the Pose stance. Make sure your support is only on the bottom of the foot and your heel is not on support. The exercise heightens your sensitivity to your body weight's location.

eral center of mass: A visual image is best used to correct this problem. Get a friend to take a photo of you standing in the Pose stance (Fig.26.5). Now compare this picture with the Pose standard (Fig.26.6). Make any necessary corrections by moving your shoulders, hips, knees, arms or head in alignment with the rest of your body. If you can't get a photo taken, check yourself in a mirror. Even better, have your partner talk you into the proper position.

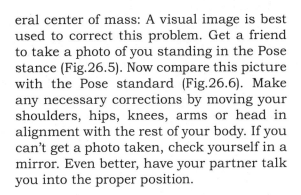

Fig.26.3 Maintain the Pose stance while balancing on a brick or other stable, slightly elevated object.

Fig.26.5 Incorrect Pose stance.

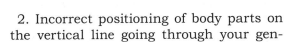

Fig.26.4 Pose stance on a medicine ball.

Fig.26.6 The Pose ideal. Pay close attention to the low heel placement, body alignment, and support on the ball of the foot while slightly leaning forward.

2. Incorrect positioning of body parts on the vertical line going through your gen-

Remember that the standard in the Pose Method is about replication — reproducing the Pose each and every time when you land. The Pose by itself is all about your perception of this very compact position — the most compact position possible. All parts of your body should be located very closely to the vertical line going through support and your general center of mass.

Many runners misunderstand this perception but replication is easy once you develop a feeling for having your hips directly above the ball of the foot. When it is no longer difficult to hold the hips above the ball of the foot, you will find that you have a greater perception of the Running Pose. If your upper body (such as the shoulders) deviates from this vertical line, you will feel an uncomfortable tension in the hip area — making it difficult to keep the hips above the ball of the foot. This is a useful test for identifying and correcting this type of error because the proper Pose position is a relaxed position, involving minimal effort and tension.

Don't forget that the Pose position is the body position from which we fall. If you are able to fall forward without any effort, you're in the Running Pose. But be honest with yourself: if you have too much tension in your ankle when you fall forward, for example, then it's a fair bet that you're holding your shoulders back.

If you can't get anyone to check your Pose, it's a little tougher to make corrections and you'll have to become acutely aware of internal signs. Muscular tension is the first sign that you are not properly settled into the Pose. If you feel any tension, use that as a guide to work your way into the relaxed, balanced position of the Pose.

Errors in the Fall

Falling is the essence of running. This can't be stressed enough: the Fall is an effortless action which uses gravity to generate forward momentum.

Try as you might, you can't increase your falling speed through enhanced muscular effort. You can only "allow" gravity to play its part.

You might catch yourself thinking: "But I can put my leg down quicker than falling," or "When something is falling from the table I can catch up with it." But you would be forgetting that you are only moving one part of the body once. It's true that the body can act as a support for the arm to move quickly to catch something, for example. But for the whole body to move repeatedly (as in running), you need some form of external support.

When it comes to centering your body weight on your general center of mass, there is no internal mover; we're totally reliant on our friend gravity. And there's no way to fall faster than gravity pulls you. Remember that falling is your body's rotation as one piece around the pivot point of the ball of your foot on the ground. The only work your muscles need to do is to hold your body in the best position to lean and fall.

So all mistakes in falling come from a misunderstanding of how to increase your fall. Take bending at the waist (Fig.26.7), for example. Many runners try to use the trunk as leverage to increase their fall, but in reality, their GCM doesn't actually leave the support point. Once again, the fall has to be done with the whole body. On top of this, by bending at the waist you have unbalanced the whole system and in order to find a new balance you will need to counteract this position by leaving your rear leg behind. Newton's Third Law never relaxes — the action of bending from the waist has to be countered somehow, and the trailing leg is that counter. This snowballs into yet another mistake: late pulling, because bending at the waist means you will no longer be pulling your foot from the ground under the hip, but well behind the hip.

Fig.26.7 Bending at the waist. Some of our coaches lovingly call this beginner error "the Special K" because the form resembles the letter "K." Leaning happens from your GCM and is measured in degrees from your point of support.

rotation can you maintain transition. Correspondingly, if you want to have transition you have to rotate. Obvious, isn't it?

Fig.26.8 Knee extension error while attempting to "push–off."

Another seemingly obvious, but common, error is to not allow your body to fall at all. If you hold your upper body (shoulders and chest) very rigid and prevent your torso from moving forward, you're effectively putting on the brakes. This usually is the result of your inability to handle your present running speed and is closely related to your ability (or inability) to pull your foot from the ground. In order to buy more time or to slow down you tense your muscles and brace your upper body against the fall. Very often this stems from a subconscious desire to slow down and ease the pain of your effort.

Another falling mistake is the desire to push off. Instead of just rotating around the pivotal point (falling), you extend the knee (Fig.26.8) thinking that it will propel your body. This action immediately impedes the forward rotation of your body. Biomechanically speaking, Pose running is about transition (horizontal movement) and rotation. When we fall, both movements take place: you go forward and you rotate. When you stop rotating, you stop transitioning, or moving forward. Only by maintaining your

Then there's the million–dollar question: how do we correct all these falling errors? They're particularly troublesome because falling is not a muscular effort — it's a "non–action." It is only a psychological and mental freedom, when you can allow something to happen without your active participation.

So let's go through our problems one–by–one:

1) Bending at the waist: this is easily overcome by using a visual image (photo or video) to show the alignment of the body and trunk position and then correcting this manually. It can also help to over–exaggerate the bend. Once you're bent over at a comical angle, you should feel your spine and shoulders come into alignment as you straighten back up.

Another way to develop your feeling for a good body position is to hop on two legs (Fig.26.9) and one leg (Fig.26.10) in the Pose position, which prevents bending at the waist.

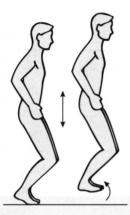

Fig.26.9 Hops on two legs. Focus on keeping the knees bent at the same angle while resiliently hopping.

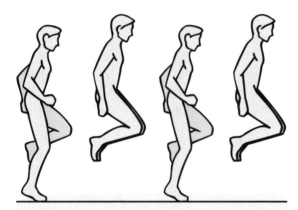

Fig.26.10 Hops from the Pose stance. Be certain that you are not compromising your body position when jumping.

If you don't have any rubber bands handy, try running downhill which also helps to correct your body position.

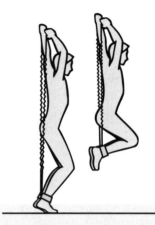

Fig.26.11 Hops with stretch cords attached to your ankles. The cords should promote a quick pull from support.

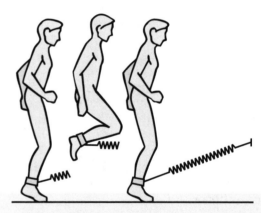

Fig.26.12 Hops with stretch cords attached to the ankles in front of the body. This should provide some instability when you try to land — forcing you to keep the correct body position landing beneath your GCM.

From there you can progress to performing the hops with rubber bands on the ankles (Fig.26.11). A more difficult exercise is to use the rubber bands on the ankles in front of you (Fig.26.12) and getting a friend to pull you forward. This will really work your ability to keep your body in a straight line. Running with rubber bands on the ankles and holding them above the head (Fig.26.13) is another exercise that will make bending at the waist impossible.

2) Holding your upper body rigid and not allowing the fall. This error is almost 100 percent related with the skill of pulling the foot from the ground. You become afraid of

Fig.26.13 Running with stretch cords held above the head.

The first fall helps us gain speed (velocity). To maintain this speed and momentum we continue to fall at the same angle again and again, merely changing support from one foot to the next.

Errors in Pulling

Pulling is where all the real physical action of running takes place.

Pulling is the change of support. Pulling the foot from the ground is the action that allows you to produce the next fall and gain or maintain speed by changing support from one foot to another.

The "standard" of pulling is the ability to pull your foot from the ground at any speed and bring it directly under your hip. The height of foot in the air is unimportant; the critical factor of the pull is that it is under the hip.

In slow running, the foot pull is quite low (but still under the hip), whereas in fast running it is much higher and closer to your hips. This height is only a by–product of your speed — not of your effort.

The main errors in pulling are to pull your foot from the ground so that it is not under your hip, but behind (Fig.26.1, Fig.26.2) or to the side. These errors are caused by mistiming or completely forgetting about the pull.

Having analyzed hundreds of participants in Pose Running clinics we have found that many people fully believe they are pulling their foot from the ground correctly until video analysis reveals the true story that most beginners don't perform the pull so that the foot comes up directly under the hips. Quite often this is the result of underdeveloped hamstrings. While at certain speeds you can get away with this by falling late with a late pull, but at faster speeds it becomes a real problem.

your running speed only when you are unable to change support in time. You can't pull your foot off the ground in time so you increase the time you spend on support by holding the upper body back. In order to get rid of this error you must improve your skill of pulling your foot from the ground.

Falling forward in faster running is closely related with the skill of pulling your foot from the ground directly under the hip. In the instant that your angle of falling becomes too great (and correspondingly, so too your speed) your ability to pull your foot from the ground straight under your hip is diminished and your falling stops.

You cannot run faster by trying to use muscular effort to increase your speed of falling. It is imperative to mentally release yourself from this notion that muscular work increases speed. Falling is only about allowing your body to fall without any kind of voluntary action or muscular effort. So this error is very much about shifting your mental process and accepting that falling is an involuntary thing.

A common question is how falling increases speed. The answer is that we use gravity to accelerate the body during the fall.

Corrections to pulling errors are based on one simple thought: pull your foot from the ground under your hip. We can't stress this too much and you have to develop your perception of this feeling to a very high level.

Watch any video of top–level runners and you will see that their foot traces an oval (Fig.26.14) pattern. But this is not what we "do;" it's an illusion and simply a result of pulling the foot from the ground. To achieve this perfect pull, you have to develop a mental image of what it feels like to pull your foot from the ground under the hip in the air. All the pulling exercises are centered around developing this perception, because it is only from this position that we are able to fall forward.

Fig.26.14 An oval pattern of airborne foot traces. The line represents body position and lean. It's an important concept to understand, what you see from top sprinters or runners when they have a large range–of–motion is not the cause but a factor of their technique. In other words, they are not intentionally making large strides, the strides are large as a factor of their speed and technique, which is actually comprised of up and down commands to the legs.

The second most common error in pulling is to use the knee or thigh to pull the leg up

(Fig.26.15). Notice that at no time have we mentioned pulling your leg, thigh or knee — we want to focus on the foot, and only on the foot. That's why we use rubber band exercises tied to the ankles, (Fig.26.16.) not on the knees. By doing these drills and controlling the movements with the rubber bands, you can practice purposefully and forcefully pulling your feet from the ground.

Fig.26.15 Incorrect pulling with the active work of the quads. This error is commonly related to incorrect practice of "high–knees" drills.

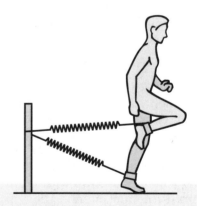

Fig.26.16 Drills with strech cords attached to the ankles.

To develop the action of pulling you can use numerous strength conditioning exercises with ankle weights (Fig.26.17), rubber bands (Fig.26.18), weight machines

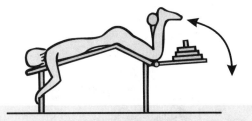

Fig.26.19 Pulling exercise on a workout bench.

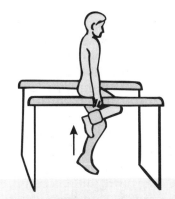

Fig.26.17 Strength conditioning exercises with ankle weights.

Fig.26.20 Pulling drill with a partner's resistance. The resistance should be dynamic and focused on the ankle.

Fig.26.18 Pulling drill with stretch cords. Support rests on forward leg.

(Fig.26.19) or your partner's resistance (Fig.26.20). You want to simultaneously develop your perception of pulling your foot (and again, only your foot) and strengthen the muscles that do the work of the pull — your hamstrings. Many recreational runners have poorly developed hamstrings and very low to non–existent perception of what it feels like to pull the feet from the ground.

Errors in landing

Errors in landing? What possible errors could occur when all you have to do is land, you might ask? For starters, one of the most common and damaging errors is landing on the heel (Fig.26.21), which generally also involves a large or small amount of dorsiflexion (how high the toes are raised). Other errors include landing on the lateral side of the forefoot — supination (Fig.26.22) or landing ahead of the body on the rear inside on the foot — over pronation (Fig.26.23).

Fig.26.21 Error of landing ahead of the GCM on the heel.

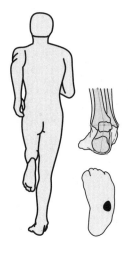

Fig.26.22 Landing on the lateral side of the forefoot — supination.

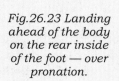

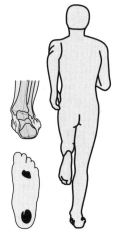

Fig.26.23 Landing ahead of the body on the rear inside of the foot — over pronation.

To revisit the Pose Method, the standard is to land on the ball of the foot under the body.

Again playing the error detective, the first issue in correcting these problems is to determine why they occur. Generally, it is about incorrect thinking — not comprehending how to land under the body on the ball of the foot and run correctly.

Also affecting this error is the deeply ingrained desire to create a safe support. This could be on a conscious or subconscious level but the need for safety is always a compelling issue. This often shows up in a runner actively landing — actually forcing the foot to the ground instead of just letting it fall. Even if this doesn't cause pain, which it ultimately will, as it vastly increases impact on the whole body, it is something you can perceive simply by listening to your footfall. In Pose running, you should run very quietly. If you hear the slap–slap–slap of your feet on the ground, you're working when you should be relaxing.

Finally there is often a lack of skill in falling or in changing support. Landing anywhere other than directly on the ball of the foot is related to "buying time" to re–adjust your body position while preparing to fall again. You are preventing the fall from it happening, in effect adding effort in a bid to slow down.

Why would you want to add effort to slow yourself down? Surely we all want to speed up! For most people, slowing down seems more comfortable even though it takes extra effort to achieve those slower speeds. But this perception of comfort comes at a tremendous cost — a huge waste of energy and an incredible overloading of their body. Think of it like driving a car: if you give a poorly–skilled driver an F1 racing machine, it won't be long before they have a nasty accident. They are out of their comfort zone in such a powerful machine.

It's the same with runners; if someone tells you that they feel more comfortable running inefficiently, then it's a fair bet that they don't want — or are afraid — to go to the next skill level. On the other hand, if they want to achieve a personal best then they have to improve their skill level. Fate favors the brave.

So what's the bottom line — how do you correct these mistakes if you catch yourself doing them?

You have to understand that you pull in order to be ready for the next fall, not the other way around. The whole essence of the pull is to change your support and bring your foot under your hip to get into the next fall. It is all about your body position.

So we have to learn the skill of pulling and falling, pulling and falling. This sequence of pull and fall produces a very specific feeling of the body weight on the ball of the foot. In this case, all Pose Running drills are helpful. Start by simply hopping on two feet, then progress to jumping in place with a jump rope to help develop the perception of landing on the ball of the foot.

Then try running with rubber bands with a partner (Fig.26.24) — you can't land ahead of your body, so your perception of landing under your body on the ball of the foot is developed. Also using the bands (with or without a partner), practice pulling your feet up and producing a good pull. Once you can do this repeatedly with a band, you will be able to produce this perfect pull in normal running. In fact, always intersperse your stretch band drills with short 30–40 yard runs — you always want to reinforce the drill with actual running so that there is immediate translation of the perception of the proper foot pull to the act of running.

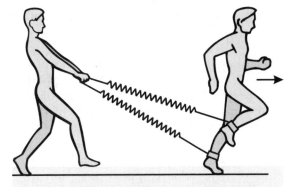

Fig.26.24 Running with stretch cords being pulled by a partner.

Another good foot pull drill is to run with your training partner holding his or her hands on your shoulders (Fig.26.25). It sounds a little awkward, but this keeps your feet from getting ahead of your body. At the same time, it also prevents you from delaying your foot pull. Do that and you will be kicking your partner.

Fig.26.25 Running with your training partner holding his or her hands on your shoulders to prevent vertical oscillation as well as keeping you in frame.

All of these drills help you frame your running action into the Running Pose. Once in the Pose frame, you simply repeat the Pose pull and fall, step after step, from the start line to the finish line.

Whether you have discovered the errors in your application of the Pose Method of running technique through the unwelcome intervention of pain and injury or by developing higher perception that has alerted you to inefficiencies in your running, you should now understand all errors are ultimately the same thing — deviation from the Pose standard. Whether the deviation is small or large, it must be corrected or it will grow and lead to even greater errors. Everything in movement is connected and errors tend to build upon themselves one after the other.

Each error entails a psychological component, either a degree of misunderstanding or an incorrect perception. Devoting the time to truly understand the logic of the Pose and then developing higher levels of perception will give you the background to run in the Pose Method. Then it is simply a matter of working to achieve the necessary skill and strength to ensure that you are able to run farther, faster and pain free for life.

CHAPTER 27
THE ROLE OF TECHNIQUE IN THE TRAINING PROCESS

We are what we repeatedly do; excellence, then, is not an act, but a habit.

— *Aristotle*

It's time to create another mental movie. Close your eyes and picture a diver preparing to dive from a three–meter springboard. This particular diver is serious, dedicated and determined — but he happens to be a pretty poor diver. The dive he is attempting is a forward 2 ½ somersault, tuck position, degree of difficulty 2.2, in other words, a very basic, simple dive.

But because our diver lacks good technique, he doesn't wrap tightly into his tuck. This limits the Coriolis force and slows his rotation so that when he comes out of this tuck — splat! — he lands face–first. That's gotta hurt, you think and marvel as the diver remounts the board and repeats the dive exactly, once again splatting face first. Again and again, the face plants come one after the other. While his consistency is remarkable, his results are disastrous.

After awhile, you develop a grudging admiration for your imaginary diver's tenacity, but mainly you think he's an idiot for not learning to do the dive properly. If he'd just learn to do it right, you think to yourself, he'd save himself a lot of pain and get a lot better. But, unfortunately, your diver has other ideas. He's thinking that if he just keeps working, he'll get a lot stronger, a lot fitter and eventually, through sheer perseverance, he'll become a good diver.

Of course, you know better. It's perfectly obvious to you, the observer of this little film, that repeating the same mistakes does not make him a better diver. It makes him a guy with a stinging red face who will NEVER get better.

Sound familiar? If you're one of the millions of runners that diligently rack up the miles, regularly wear a heart rate monitor, enter road races and triathlons, but never bother to work on technique, you're just like the hapless diver. Despite your earnest tenacity, you'll probably endure a lot of pain while never reaching your true potential.

There's a reason that over 80% of regular runners sustain at least one significant injury per year and it's not because running is inherently bad for you. It's because the vast majority of runners don't know how to run properly and constantly repeat mistakes that are destined to bring them pain and injury.

The Mystery of the Missing Technique

In the overwhelming literature of training advice, which is full of marathon programs, interval workouts, heart rate monitor guidance and on and on, the one thing that is almost universally left out is technique. So what happens is that runners dutifully follow their chosen program until the inevitable injury forces them to rest until they recover — and then they go back and do the same things all over again. Pretty crazy, isn't it?

It's as if the running community has divorced conditioning from technique. Training the heart–lungs–legs is treated as an entirely separate concept from learning — and practicing — the skill of running.

Here's the Pose solution: training is only effective when it serves the ability of the body to maintain the best possible running technique from start to finish. You see examples of this all the time in world–class marathons, where the winner is always the one who holds his or her form all the way to the finish line. TV commentators always search for signs in the competitors, looking for loss of form and trying to divine which runner looks best as the lead pack gets whittled down.

Form matters more than any other aspect of training and perfect form matters most of all. Knowing this, it becomes a relatively simple matter to reorient your world view of training and try a new approach that places technique at the priority position, with everything else — strength training, intervals, distance and heart rate, even nutrition and rest — supporting your ability to hold your technique at higher speeds and longer distances.

It all goes back to the central fact that running is a skill sport, just like diving, skating, pole vaulting or anything else.

There is no point in training anything but the best possible form — all the time. In reality, the name of this chapter is backwards. It should be The Role of Training in the Technique Process, because that's really the correct priority.

Once you view training as a means to support your technique, instead of vice versa, your entire concept of the training process should — and will — change. In the real world of running and triathlon training, most athletes, whether they are elite world class or age group mid–packers, are self–trained and more importantly, self–coached.

Even those athletes who sustain some form of relationship with a coach spend the majority of the physical training time either alone or in the company of other runners, not under the direct supervision of their coach. Thanks to the wonders of the Internet, lots of people now train through the services of a coach who may be a continent away. Closer to home they may see their coach once a week. These intermittent coach/athlete relationships are ideal for data analysis (the download of all kinds of workout telemetry), but woefully inadequate for the teaching and reinforcing of skills.

The end result is that these coaches and athletes, even if they do understand correct technique, focus on numbers, charts and graphs, because that fits the mold of their relationship. To appreciate the hopelessness of this situation, imagine the conversation of your imaginary diver with his coach, who happens to be 10 states away... How'd it go today... not bad, coach, I did three sets of ten two and a halves, with thirty seconds rest. My face is a little sore, but other than that I felt pretty good... okay, let's go easy tomorrow and then on Friday, lets do five sets and cut the rest back to 20 seconds.

Of course, that's absurd, but so is a running program that doesn't have technique as its core value. But that's just what happens from beginners all the way up to the elite levels.

Putting Technique at the Center of Training

To understand how to reverse this situation and put technique at the center of all training activities, it helps to understand the role of technique. Instead of thinking of technique as an adjunct to training, a thing to be developed (or ignored) while the business of cardiovascular fitness is conducted, it helps to think of technique as a 'gate', through which all training efforts must pass.

If you want to train for speed, your efforts must pass through the gate of technique. If you want to train for endurance, it's the same gate. Load, volume, intensity, VO$_2$ max... whatever you want to call it, all efforts must be channeled through, and focused on, the technique gate.

It's really very simple when you think about it: there is no point in practicing and reinforcing bad technique. Or, to drag out an old bromide, anything worth doing is worth doing well. And if you're going to bother to go out and run, you might as well run as perfectly as possible, no matter how fast or far you plan on going.

Here's the key fact: technique is the pivotal point of energy transformation. And movement is all about channeling energy into forward progress. The more perfectly you move, the more efficient you will be at using your available energy resources.

From this perspective you can see how important a role technique should play in your training. Your ability to run for a given length of time or at a given speed is determined by the quality (stability and perfection) of your technique.

In any given workout, you should only run for as long as you maintain proper technique, if you want to progress soundly in your development. To run longer (or faster), you have to focus on maintaining your good technique for a greater length of time. Certain physiological factors can limit your abilities, but eventually you'll achieve your best results through technique.

The Hierarchy of Pose Running

To demonstrate the relationship between technique and training, the hierarchical model of The Pose Method of Running (Fig.27.1) places skill at the top (directly related to performance) and aerobic capacity on the bottom. It doesn't mean that aerobic capacity is insignificant, not at all. What it means is that aerobic capacity logically only serves to enable the proper execution of technique.

Technique is the regulator of the training process. It is a measurement of our ability to run at a given talent level. Technique is the major contributor in the training process and should take the highest role in a hierarchical system of training.

Eventually everything comes down to technique. Technique in the Pose Method of running is falling from the Pose and pulling your foot from the ground in Pose and repeatedly recycling this triangle.

No matter what kind of aerobic capacity you have, if you can't pull your foot from the ground in a certain space and time frame, you will fail to fulfill your personal potential. Your aerobic capacity will not be efficiently transferred to your running movement and whatever physiological capabilities you have will be squandered.

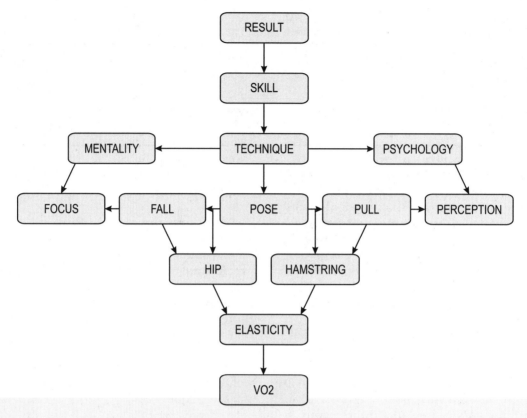

Fig.27.1 Hierarchical model of training in running.

Consuming Gravity and Oxygen

As living, moving creatures we consume two principle items: gravity and oxygen. Technique, the skill of performing movement, is the conduit for transforming the energy of gravity and oxygen into the desired movement. As runners, we are the channels by which the energy from gravity and oxygen results in movement.

Historically, the thinking was that runners produced the running movement, rather than utilized and channeled an outside force. It's a little like the geocentric view of the Universe Ptolemy articulated before Copernicus came along and pointed out that the Earth revolved around the sun and not the opposite.

As runners, we are not at the center of movement creation. In movement there is no such thing as a center; there is only a non–stop transformation of energy. In order to be a transformer, you must be a consumer. If you don't consume energy, you cannot transfer it.

Take this simple example: with respect to running, if you are not falling, you are neither consuming gravity, nor oxygen. You are simply staying in one place and keeping everything together in your body. The hierarchy is that you must first consume gravity and then oxygen. You cannot consume oxygen without gravity — gravity is the absolute governor and everything else is a subordinate factor.

So technique boils down to our ability to consume gravity and oxygen efficiently. And this depends on two things: how we perceive the process of consuming gravity and oxygen and how we perceive our body weight and support, the manifestations of gravity for us as humans.

The Major Goal in Training

Training then, is about developing our perception of body weight and transferring that body weight through any given distance or speed of running. This is the major training goal and we have to understand it very clearly and deliberately. There is nothing more important than developing this perception.

Unfortunately, in practice, as mentioned earlier in this chapter, the whole training process usually slides into simply training the physiological system. As with everything else however, our physiological system is also a consumer of gravity and it can't be developed without consuming gravity. This requirement repeatedly forms the frame of our training process. And how much and how well we use our physiological system depends on our technique.

There is a theoretical relationship here: if runner 'A' has the greatest physiological abilities, but the poorest technique, then all the physiological abilities are trapped and never revealed. The gate through which those abilities must pass is essentially locked.

We see this regularly in the training methods of elite runners. They finish their careers on a very low level, never realizing that they have incredible potential that was not revealed because of a lack of technique development.

Runner 'B', on the other hand, has a low VO_2 max, but because of her very good technique, she can be developed to much higher levels of performance, the result of her ability to effectively use every last bit of her aerobic capacity.

The Role of the Mind in Training

Hand in hand with technique and the consumption of gravity and oxygen, there is one other critical factor: the human mind. As part of an integrated running 'system', the mind directs us to better utilize everything at hand. A strong, focused mind can help the transformation process become more effective and efficient.

Technique doesn't just materialize out of whole cloth; it is the result of a mental model that executes the running movements through a voluntary process of initiating the action. The action is the final point at which everything comes together. Consumption of gravity and oxygen and our mental processes all culminate as a system in one simple action — pulling the foot from the ground and beginning to run.

With that in mind, we return to the central issue at hand, the matter of reorienting your run training to put technique at the top of the pyramid. Technique is nothing more than your rate of falling and your rate of pulling your foot from the ground: angle of deviation from the vertical and cadence. At the most fundamental level, it is these two aspects that need to be trained in order for you to reach your potential.

In the past you probably thought of your training in terms of physiological factors such as breathing, heart rate and perceived effort. But these elements only reflect how well you are implementing your technique.

If, on a given distance, your heart rate and breathing are easy, you can easily tell that you are not falling enough and not pulling quickly enough for this distance. The primary goal is not development of your physiological systems though — it is to improve your rate of falling and pulling. The physiological development occurs as a consequence of good technique practiced at a high level. Conversely, if your technique is poor and you become injured on a regular basis, then you will never be able to train enough for your physiological systems to develop to peak levels.

Incorporating Technique in Your Training Routine

On a practical basis, here are a few examples that can help you implement a focus on technique in your training routine:

In your overall approach to training, subordinate your thoughts of weekly mileage totals and think instead of how many quality efforts you make each week. Quality in this case doesn't equate to speed; it means training sessions where you really concentrate on technique and make every step count.

In interval workouts, worry less about your time for each repeat and more about holding your form all the way through to the end of each interval. Nearly all runners begin struggling in the last 50–100 meters of an interval in an effort to make a certain time. Instead of swinging your arms in a wider arc or trying to take longer strides, make an extra effort to stay in your form; you'll actually finish faster that way.

Break up your run on long days. There is an almost universal habit among runners to simply run one given distance non–stop unless they are specifically on an interval workout. There is no physiological basis for this and from a technique standpoint it can actually be a drawback. There is a tendency on non–stop runs to 'zone out' and drift along, sacrificing all concentration in the interest of just getting it over with. Instead,

go ahead and stop when you feel your concentration waning. Walk a little, do a couple of Pose drills, and, once you feel mentally refreshed, start running again with a renewed focus on technique.

During intense sessions, resist the urge to slow down when your breathing and heart rate 'warning' signals you to back off. Try recovering your form instead. What often happens in intensity is increased is that you will inadvertently stretch out of your running frame. Instead of keeping your knees bent, you start extending them straight out. You rise up and run 'taller' than you should and extend your stride length. All of this makes you work harder without any increase in speed. So don't slow down; settle back in your form and see if you can recover sufficiently to maintain your pace.

At least once, and probably twice a week, leave the stopwatch or the GPS at home and focus 100% of your session on technique and nothing but technique. Don't worry how far or how fast you run; an incredibly beneficial session may total less than a mile or two. In the session, really work on developing the full range of perception. Listen to your footfall and make sure you're not slapping or pounding on the pavement. Concentrate on keeping your legs bent at all times and feel the ball of your foot make contact with the ground.

A 'perception session' is not necessarily easy and in fact can be quite taxing. One effective exercise is to establish your best Pose technique at a modest sustainable pace and then begin ratcheting up the speed until you are unable to hold your form at the increased pace. Figure out right then and there, what caused you to lose form. Recover briefly and try it again. Test the outer limits of your ability to hold form. By extending your top end, you'll hone the form that will enable you to hold slightly slower paces for much longer distances.

Always monitor your body in the days following workouts for any signs of muscle soreness or pain in bone or connective tissue. These are certain signs that there is a flaw (or flaws) in your technique. Left uncorrected, these flaws will eventually lead to injuries that will result in time away from training.

Realizing Your Potential

By following this logic of focusing on technique in your normal training program you can run any distance or speed you like, limited only by your rate of falling, your rate of pulling and lastly, your physiological system. Your mind works to bring all these things together as one system: it's the glue that binds it all.

So for how long can you run? Simply for as long as you can pull your foot from the ground under your hip. How fast can you run? The answer is the same — at whatever speed you are able to continue to pull your foot from the ground under your hip. Corrections are made by using the signals from your physiological systems telling you whether or not your body has enough energy to support this falling and pulling.

Obviously, you need to develop a very specific level of strength to allow for efficient falling and pulling. As is illustrated in the hierarchy of figure 27.1, there are subordinate relationships between these elements and strength exercises. Falling is related to strength in the hips, and pulling with the strength of the hamstrings. Change of support is related with muscle–tendon elasticity, as well as hip and hamstring strength. So the training process for running includes these types of exercises, so you can continue to perfect the individual elements of running.

It should be clear by now that Pose Method training requires a categorically different approach to the conventional paradigm of training. The basis of the training program is to focus on technique — the skill of doing. This skill development becomes and remains the most important element of training. By optimizing your skill in consuming gravity and oxygen you will minimize pain and injury and be able to run farther and faster, ultimately reaching your peak performance.

SECTION V
CYCLING TECHNIQUE

Dr. Romanov instructs Pose cycling drills.

CHAPTER 28
INTRO TO BICYCLE SECTION

The map is not a territory.

— *Alfred Korzbyski*

It's one of humanity's most universal rites of passage, acted out in every language in parking lots, on paved driveways, in rutted dirt roads and on manicured lawns, in every country on Earth. A parent, a child, two wheels, a saddle and a set of handlebars (Fig.28.1).

Fig.28.1 Dr. Romanov standing next to an old cycle at the bicycle museum.

With few variations, the drill is always the same: the parent is the eager teacher; the child the apprehensive student. The pusher and the pushee. The one who understands momentum and the one whom momentum terrifies.

Sometimes it happens in that first lesson, sometimes it becomes a long, drawn–out affair of despair and bodily damage, but eventually the apprentice grasps the concept: keep pedaling and the bike will keep moving. And, of course, the converse: stop pedaling and eventually the bike will fall over.

At the point of epiphany there are smiles around. The proud parent glows, secure in the reaffirmed knowledge that "my kid does too have the necessary motor skills and brains to ride a bicycle." As for the child, now radiating exuberance, it'll be at least another decade before he or she experiences a comparable thrill to the freedom and sheer joy that comes from riding a bicycle. Horizons have expanded, vistas are open; the world has just become comfortably smaller.

In the afterglow of that first success, there are some peremptory instructions: ride on the right (or left, if it's in England, Australia, South Africa...) side of the road, obey all traffic signs, watch out for cars, and get home before dark. Triumph. The kid knows how to ride a bike.

And that's pretty much it. For the vast majority of people, there is never another word of instruction on the technique of riding a bicycle, because everybody knows, you never forget how to ride a bike.

So, when the beginner first latches onto the notion of becoming a bike racer or doing a triathlon, there's never a thought given to learning how to ride. It's all about gear, gears and training. Get a trick bike, super light with the best components, the newest tri–bars and the most aero wheels and then start training like a pro, putting the time in and racking up the miles.

Crazy, isn't it? Cycling newbies will start riding 100, 200, 300 or more miles a week and never give a thought to the technique of riding a bicycle. In fact, most will think there is no room for technique. After all, your legs move in a fixed circle, right? What else can you do except move them faster and faster and ride bigger and bigger gears?

For those who do enter the strange realm of trying to improve performance by improving technique, there are enough theories and strategies to confuse even the most lucid thinker. Apply force evenly throughout all 360° degrees of the pedaling stroke, goes one theory. You can get the feel by acting like you're scraping mud off of the bottom of your shoe. Another variation of the same theory encourages single–leg pedaling during training, until you get to the point where you can feel the pull on your leg all the way through the upstroke. Feel that pull and you know you're applying power... or so you would be asked to believe.

Another plan suggests riding cadences of 90 rpm for group riding, but pushing much bigger gears at cadences of 75–80 rpm for time trialing and triathlon. Ride huge miles, pedal low cadences for fast speeds and you'll be winning your age group in no time. Right.

Or you could wind up with serious saddle sores, dead legs, limited family life and an ongoing frustration with your chronic inability to improve.

Which brings us back to the central question that lingers in the shadows of all human locomotion sports: is there a single, definable, BEST WAY to ride a bicycle? In a word, yes.

Not only is there a best way, but the relatively small amount of time you will devote to mastering proper cycling skills will pay off with benefits far in excess of simply grinding out the miles with no adjustments to your riding technique.

CHAPTER 29
THE COMPLEX NATURE OF A SIMPLE SYSTEM

*You can only find truth with logic
if you have already found truth without it.*

— *G.K. Chesterton*

It's a bit of enduring folk wisdom that the bicycle is the most efficient form of human transportation ever developed. Indeed, when compared with the other tri–sports, the efficiencies are obvious: with roughly the same expenditure of effort, a cyclist moves roughly three times as fast as a runner and ten times as fast as a swimmer.

In the larger scheme of human movement, the humble bicycle will never equal cars, trains or planes for speed, but in terms of moving vast quantities of people throughout a metropolitan area, the bicycle remains unmatched for minimal expenditure of non–renewable energy sources and the ability to get its passengers as close as possible to their ultimate destination.

The bicycle is quite simply a marvel of human engineering (Fig.29.1). And the combination of a rider and a bike creates an elegant system for human movement. Riding is not something you do to a bike, it is something you do with a bike. In a sense, the marriage of cyclist to bicycle created the first cyborg, the original man/machine combination. No matter how fast a bike looks or feels, its average land speed with-

out a human aboard remains resolutely stuck at zero miles per hour.

Fig.29.1 A generic bicycle.

As for a human without a bike, figure about eight, maybe ten miles per hour for anything beyond an all–out sprint. So, when we talk about cycling technique, what we're really talking about is systems engineering — devising the optimum means for a human to interact with a bicycle for the most efficient forward progress.

This means we have to figure out strictly mechanical efficiencies as well as balancing anatomic and aerodynamic considerations, not to mention keeping the all–important psychological considerations at the top of the list.

Whew! For such a seemingly simple device, the art (or science) of riding a bicycle can be stunningly complex. Perhaps that explains the paradox that no matter how many studies of cycling technique we have from a mechanical or psychological viewpoint, the question of pedaling technique itself as a human movement remains unresolved.

If you study the technical literature of cycling, you'll find reams of information and conjecture about one cycle of a pedaling stroke, but virtually nothing about the whole picture of pedaling as an interaction between the athlete and the bicycle as a means of improving overall cycling performance.

So, that's what we want to start with here: a discussion of pedaling technique as an integral system of interaction of the athlete/machine with the external environment. In this discussion, we will focus on gravity, balance and the optimum application of body weight as the primary consideration in developing proper pedaling technique.

No doubt you're now thinking, *hold on, what do gravity, balance and body weight have to do with riding a bicycle fast?*

Only this — everything!

Look at it this way. The pull of gravity leads to appearance of the body weight. Unless some action is taken to reassign the force of gravity, it will keep any given object rooted to its spot. In other words, any body will stay where it is, on its current support, until that body is released from its balance on that support.

Fig.29.2 The cycling Pose.

Now picture this particular pose (Fig.29.2). As a cyclist, you are standing on your pedals, clipped in, with your feet in the three and nine o'clock positions, perfectly motionless, in what is commonly called a track stand. In most cases, what will happen next is that you will lose your balance and gravity will cause you to fall to one side or the other. Let's face it, most of us just aren't that good at track stands and we'll fall over just like that guy on the tricycle in the old *Laugh–In* re–runs (Fig.29.3).

But you don't want to fall; you want to move this integrated unit of you and your bicycle in a forward direction. How do you do this? Most people would answer that you do this by pushing down on the pedal in the three o'clock position, reasoning that this active push moves the pedal downward, which rotates the chain, which engages the rear derailleur that powers the rear wheel and ultimately propels the integrated unit of you and your bicycle down the road.

But here's the catch: you can't simply push down on the three o'clock pedal. Why not? Remember, you're perfectly balanced on the support of the two pedals, with exactly half of your body weight on each pedal. No matter how strong you think you are, there is no pushing movement you can perform that will overcome the perfect balance you have established.

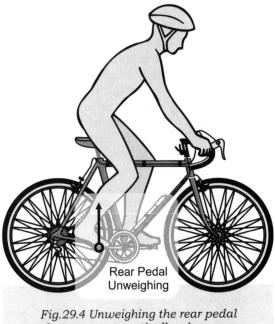

Rear Pedal Unweighing

Fig.29.4 Unweighing the rear pedal happens automatically when you change support from one foot to the other. No extra effort is needed to "pull through" with your foot, the 180 degree separation of the pedals makes it possible to focus on just changing support on the pedals, nothing more.

Fig.29.3 A sketch of a tricycle.

In order to achieve forward motion, you will have to lose that perfect balance and transfer a greater percentage of your body weight from the nine o'clock pedal to the three o'clock pedal. To do this, you *unweigh* on the rear pedal (Fig.29.4), causing more of your weight to be transferred to the front pedal, which sets off the desired chain of events resulting in forward motion. This forward motion was not caused by pushing on the pedal; in fact, you didn't push at all.

And there you have it. With one simple movement, shifting the body weight on support, you have not only started the bicycle moving in the proper direction, but you have fundamentally altered both your psychological and biomechanical concepts of what riding a bike really is.

Your prior psychological understanding of cycling was that it was an arduous push–pull task by which the human body propelled a mechanical conveyance, the bicycle, forward. Now you can view cycling as a process by which an integrated unit moves forward through time and space by rapid repetition of the loss and gain of balance on support.

Biomechanically, your previous concept of cycling involved an attempt to apply uniform force to a pedal and crank arm through 360° degrees of rotational movement. In this view, the human legs do all the push/pull work and the mechanical elements of the bike transfer that leg–generated force into forward motion. Your new biomechanical picture of cycling is that the legs are the transmitters of your shifting body weight, which, amplified by gravity, is the true source of the power that drives you forward.

Just like all human movement, riding a bicycle can be reduced to a very fundamental equation. From a stationary position, where the body is balanced on support, movement results from a loss of balance on support, followed by an alternation to balance on new support.

In running, support is clearly found when the feet touch the ground. In cycling, just as clearly, support is realized when body weight balances on the pedals.

These fundamental psychological and biomechanical views of cycling will form the basis for all the techniques that will allow you to develop a more efficient pedaling technique and ride a bicycle further and faster.

The key is to now look at the athlete/machine system that differentiates cycling from running and structures the most favorable conditions possible for rapidly and repetitively changing support from one pedal to the next, as balance is continually lost and regained.

For the moment, and only for the moment, we're going to set aside two very important factors: the technical construction of the bicycle itself and the aerodynamic positioning of the body on the bicycle. What remains, and what determines cycling efficiency, is pedaling skill, the art of performing a full 360° degree rotation of the pedal over and over again.

Not surprisingly, the most important element of pedaling skill is the precise application of power. Ah, power. How we lust for power. Whether we seek it through hill climbing, weight training or the injudicious ingestion of banned substances, cyclists are gluttons for power. But to be used to full effect, power first must be understood.

Power, in purely technical terms, is the amount of work performed over a certain unit of time. The formula is simple: power (P) equals to work (W) divided by unit of time (t) or to force (F) multiplied by speed (v):

$$P=W/t=Fv$$

In rotational movement, such as pedaling a bicycle, power is determined by the *force moment* (Fd) multiplied by *angular velocity* (ω–omega):

$$P=Fd\ \omega$$

where the angular velocity is expressed as the number of rotations per unit of time (aka cadence). The force moment is determined as the product of the force module (F) and its arm (d):

$$M(F)=Fd.$$

Cadence (what we would call rpm in our cars) is the number of rotations of the pedal per unit of time (T=n/t), where **n** is the number of rotations and **t** is the time unit.

Hence, and somewhat obviously, the greater the force moment and cadence are, the higher the power output and velocity. So it stands to reason that improving your pedaling technique is intrinsically connected to both higher power output and faster pedaling speed.

Finally, and to answer the question before you ask it, the tandem imperatives of pedaling efficiency and aerodynamic positioning serve to determine the optimal position of the rider on the bike. In other words, your best position will be the one that **optimizes your ability to use gravity to transfer your body weight to the pedals.**

How do we determine that optimal position? In the next two chapters, we'll discuss separately the concepts of force moment and cadence and then see how they combine to guide you to the perfect position on the bike.

CHAPTER 30
THE FORCE MOMENT
IN PHYSICS, IT'S A MOMENT OF THE SYSTEM OF FORCES PRODUCING ROTATION

If knowledge can create problems, it is not through ignorance that we can solve them.

— *Isaac Asimov*

Okay, here's where we do a little myth busting. If you've read anything about pedaling technique in current cycling literature, you've no doubt come across the sage advice to pull up on the pedals, thus generating power to the pedals throughout 360° degrees of the pedaling rotation. "Of course," you think, "that would be very efficient. I'll be a much better cyclist if I can just apply power all the way around."

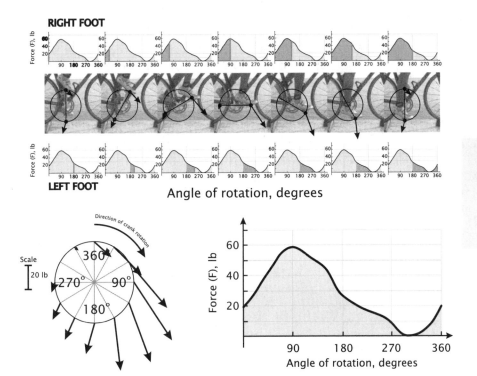

Fig.30.1 Force moment data graph through one 360° degree pedaling stroke.

You might have even tried it, investing training time in single leg pedaling, concentrating on applying force from the dead spot at 6 o'clock right up and over the top. You might have even convinced yourself that you have mastered the art and that you really are a better cyclist because you really do apply power all the way around.

Would that you could. Heaven knows, lots of cyclists will maintain that they are efficient pedalers, applying force all the way around, right until the moment when they stare at a graph (Fig.30.1) of their pedaling power and see that there is absolutely no power whatsoever being applied to the pedal on the rise. Even then, lots of cyclists will insist that they know they are applying power on the upstroke because they 'feel' it. Here's a little clue: what they feel is not force or power, but resistance.

And when you think about it, common sense tells you that there's just no way, you can be applying force on the upstroke, if you also happen to be applying force on the downstroke. Why? Well, it's the work of our friend: gravity.

Let's say you're a 150–pound cyclist, efficiently transferring the majority of your weight to the pedal in the one o'clock position. Acceleration due to gravity is what... 9.8 m/s, acting with the majority of that 150 pounds to drive the one o'clock pedal toward Mother Earth? With all that action going on, with your weight accelerating down (Fig.30.2), what force could you possibly bring to bear to generate power on the seven o'clock pedal? You think your precious hamstring is built out of some superhero stuff that will rocket the pedal upwards with enough force that it could add measurably to what is going on the downstroke?

Sorry, it just isn't going to happen.

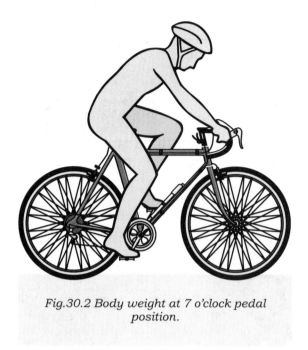

Fig.30.2 Body weight at 7 o'clock pedal position.

What we're talking here is basic physics. We're talking about the force moment.

Most people understand that a rider puts the greatest amount of force on the pedals in the portion of the 360° degree stroke from 30° to 120° degrees or from one o'clock to four o'clock. This is somewhat intuitive, yet it helps to understand why it happens to be right. In only 90° degrees of a 360° degree movement, we're really putting the pedal to the metal ("the metal to the pedal"), so to speak (Fig.30.3).

Why? Going back to physics, we determine that at the 90° degree angle, the lever of the pedal has its greatest effective arm length. A longer lever means greater power. Thus, the 90° degree position affords the highest force moment. We can describe this as:

$$M(F)=Fd$$

where F is the force of gravity applied as body weight — mg, and d is the arm length of the force.

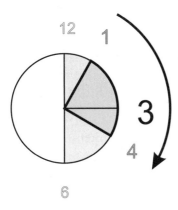

Fig.30.3 90° degree sector of the highest torque in a single pedaling stroke.

Fig.30.4 Lance Armstrong on a bike.
Source: Joel Saget/AFP

So, force is greatest from 30° to 120° degrees, and peaks at 90° degrees. The question is, how do we use this knowledge both to determine the best position on the bike and to become a better cyclist?

Well, first we have to look for a way to get all the force we can out of the place where force is most readily available, i.e. the sweet spot from one o'clock to four o'clock. In turn, this brings up the concept of precision in pedaling. It's one thing to comprehend on an intellectual level that the greatest effort must be applied between one and four o'clock, but quite another to translate that knowledge into practice, particularly when the challenges of fatigue and increased cadence, not to mention tactics and terrain all crowd the racer's mind.

Precise pedaling will be facilitated by first moving the saddle further forward in the horizontal plane than traditional set ups, thus making it easier to hold the rider's weight directly over the pedals. A simple confirmation of this concept can be found by analyzing the position of Lance Armstrong on the bike (Fig.30.4). The now seven–time winner of the Tour de France is clearly farther forward on the bike than the vast majority of his competitors, a position that enables him to spin faster cadences on all types of terrain, whether on his traditional road frame or on his highly specialized time trial set–up. In the book "High–Tech Cycling" (1, p. 115) it was described as: "Interestingly, Armstrong's position on the seat is more toward the front than the position usually adopted."

As noted in the above quote, this forward–shifted position of the saddle decreases negative interaction between the hip and the chest during pedaling. The clearest evidence of this can be seen by watching the riders' positions during the race. During any moment where maximum effort is needed, either to match an attack or to ride hard up a climb, you'll see all the riders shift their bodies forward, subconsciously putting more of their body weight in position to be applied to the pedals.

It's more than a little ironic that while under stress during critical competitive moments, riders adopt a position that they otherwise reject, preferring instead to position themselves in a more "relaxed" position. Doesn't it make sense to be in the perfect position all the time, instead of just when maximum effort is required?

So, to precisely apply power at the point where the most power can be applied, we want to position the saddle so that the leg is in perfect "working" position when the pedal is at three o'clock. The height of the saddle should allow the leg to have a good angle of attack for straightening as it passes through three o'clock. Too bent or too straight at three o'clock and the leg will be an inefficient transmitter of weight at that position, thus robbing the muscles of their ability to deliver maximum force at the most critical point. Further, a too straight leg at three o'clock will result in a "reach" at six o'clock, which will dramatically slow pedal cadence.

Having properly situated the saddle for both height and fore/aft position, the final adjustments are made with stem length, and bar height. The objective here is to place the bars so that an optimal aerodynamic position can be achieved without putting excess strain on the arms and shoulders, while still keeping the body properly balanced on the saddle and pedals. This part will be discussed in details later in chapter 38.

Now that we're properly and comfortably positioned on the bike, we need to return to the concept of what we actually do to put the mettle to the pedal, so to speak.
In other words, where does the force come from that we apply to the pedal?

Watching a cyclist from the side, it seems quite obvious that the rider powers the bike by unbending the leg, using a muscular burst to push the pedal toward the ground. That being the case, it would be a simple matter to conclude that the harder you push in a given gear, the faster you will go.

But are looks really deceiving? Is it possible that pushing down on the pedal is not what makes a bike go forward?

For a hint at the answer, we turn to the noted modern thinker, Aristotle (2), who outlined one of the basic principles of physics when he noted that "For one part of animal must be moved, and another be at rest, and again this one part which is moved will support itself and be moved."

To apply this principle to the act of pedaling a bicycle, we realize that the body must be supported by something in order to apply force to the pedal. Since force is applied only through the pedals, it follows that it can only be applied if our body weight is concentrated on the pedals and that the amount of force we can apply is maximized when the greatest percentage of that weight is on top of the pedal in the one o'clock/four o'clock sweet spot. In other words, the support required to pedal a bicycle is our own body weight.

Okay, now we're getting somewhere. Let's move from Aristotle to Newton and his much-beloved Third Law of Motion for our next clue. According to that Law, when we push down on the pedal, the pedal pushes back with exactly the same force (Fig. 30.5).

So what decides the winner in this apparent stalemate? Support, of course. Body weight. As long as there is no resistance on the pedal greater that the amount of body weight the rider can transfer to the active pedal, the pedal will move down and ultimately rotate the wheel, propelling the rider forward.

To make this concept a little easier to digest, let's consider a real world situation when the resistance on the pedal is greater

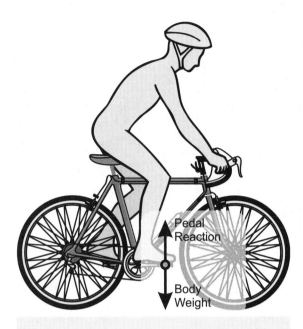

Fig.30.5 Application of Newton's Third law to pedaling.

than the rider's body weight. Riding in a large gear, you round a corner and are suddenly confronted with a steep climb. What happens? The combined resistance of the steepness of the climb and your huge gear means that the pedal no longer easily goes down. Instead, you pop up off the saddle.

At first glance, this move off the saddle might appear to be a conscious decision to apply more force to the pedals. Not so. The reality is that the resistance was so great that your body was lifted off the saddle as your attempted to unbend your leg. In turn, your new position — off the saddle — may just allow you to transfer a sufficiently greater percentage of your weight to the pedals and continue your upward progress, albeit at a greatly reduced pace.

More likely, though, you will probably engage in a frantic downshift of several gears as you search for a gear you can handle while returning to the saddle. Now the

challenge will be to recover a higher rate of cadence and possibly accelerate up the hill.

What this little scenario illustrates is that the legs function as transmitters of your body weight to the pedals, not as "pushers" that create force through muscular contraction and extension. Rounding that corner into the hill, the resistance force of gravity and gear was greater than your transmitted weight as applied to the pedals through your legs. You came out of the saddle not because your legs were too weak, but because the laws of physics were aligned against you.

To restore your progress and get those laws working for you, you had two choices: either transmit a greater percentage of your weight (which is enabled by standing out of the saddle) or reduce resistance (by choosing an "easier" gear). In neither case did you actually work harder with the muscles in your legs.

Further, as you struggled to make your way up the hill, it became clear that your most effective efforts came when the active pedal was in the one o'clock to four o'clock position. This is where we create the highest rotational force moment... where the work gets done.

Which brings us to the question of how the work gets done. While you are firmly planted on the saddle, your weight can only be transferred to the pedals by a shifting of your weight from side to side. A bobbing action, which indicates an attempt to shift weight up and down, only indicates that there is too much resistance created by the gear or the terrain. If your body bounces up and down on the saddle, it doesn't mean you're working hard, it means you're riding inefficiently and wasting energy. Attempts to shift body weight forward and back are even less fruitful (Fig.30.6).

Fig.30.6 Two incorrect bike positions: Over arching the back, and leaning too far forward.

To become an efficient cyclist, you must learn how to precisely shift your weight from side to side (Fig.30.7), with no wasted effort. Whether you are a road racer, a triathlete or a long distance tourist, the vast majority of your riding will take place in the saddle. Your greatest efficiency will come from quick, almost imperceptible, movements that transfer your weight back

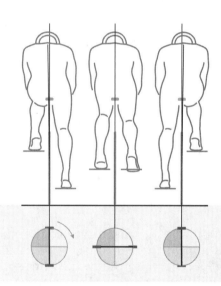

Fig.30.7 The subtle side to side body weight shift when riding a bicycle.

and forth across the saddle with virtually no visible exertion.

In specific situations, the weight transfer becomes more obvious, such as an out of the saddle sprint (Fig.30.8) or a hard effort up a steep incline. In both these cases, the bike is swung back and forth, effectively placing a greater percentage of the body weight over the active pedal. Here, both side

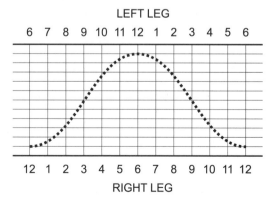

to side and up and down movement is employed for maximum power to the pedals.

Fig.30.8 Correct position of body weight shifting, when riding out–of–saddle.

These out of the saddle efforts also provide a clear demonstration of the need to back off the pedals as you pass the four o'clock position. If you don't quickly shift your weight off the active pedal, you'll be drilling your foot toward the ground, creating a very out–of–synch movement that will be awkward and inefficient.

To see a clear demonstration of how out of the saddle uphill attacks are executed, review any DVD of the Tour de France and look for the sections where Lance Armstrong makes a winning attack. It's not Armstrong's power that impresses; it's the absolute precision of his cycling style. There is no one else in the world who can stay out of the saddle and maintain such a high cadence as the perpetual Tour victor.

Less obvious are the situations referred to earlier in the chapter where a rider will

shift his body weight forward to place it more directly over the active pedal. This usually happens when the pace in the peloton is absolutely full blast and riders are in danger of being dropped from the group.

In this period of maximum effort, a rider will subconsciously slide forward while tucking his head ever closer to the handlebars. Racers call this position being "on the rivet," referring to the brass rivets that used to affix the leather saddle cover to the front point of the saddle. A rider on the rivet knows he's in for a hard push, desperately hoping that whoever is pushing the pace will finally "sit up" and bring the pace back to a more tolerable level.

Looking variously at all the above situations brings into focus that there is a difference, between applying force and applying effort. Force on the pedal is pretty much a mathematical equation, where gravity acts on the body weight to drive the pedal down. Effort, on the other hand, is a muscular action wherein the rider tries to direct the weight to the pedals. Force, in other words, is a net result, but effort can be either efficient or inefficient.

The greatest force that can be applied is ultimately limited by your body weight while tremendous efforts can be made with no net gain in speed or performance. That's why precision in pedaling technique is so important. Pedaling on the flat ground, a quiet upper body with subtle shifts in body weight is the key to efficiency. For an out of the saddle sprint or climb (Fig.30.9), it's not wild flailing that gets the job done, but very efficient and controlled movement on the bike, putting a greater percentage of your body weight on the active pedal at exactly the right point in the pedal rotation. And in a protracted maximum effort, a streamlined position with the body moved forward is the answer.

Fig.30.9 Front view of out–of–saddle body weight shifting, while pedaling.

In all these cases, there is no room for empty effort. The effort must be precisely applied for it to be effective. By way of illustration, think about an unskilled heavyweight boxer who uses nothing but his arm to throw a punch. He may be trying very hard (i.e. making a huge effort), but the result is likely to be no more damaging than a fly swatter to his opponent. By contrast, a skilled middleweight can flick out a quick punch that will focus all his body weight in the punch's delivery and result in serious damage.

Finally, combine the power of a heavyweight with the skill and timing of a middleweight and you get the "phantom punch" that a young Mohammed Ali used to K.O. Sonny Liston in the first round of their title rematch in Lewiston, Maine back in 1963. While many ringside observers claimed no punch was ever thrown, it was Ali's un-

canny ability, speed and quickness that allowed him to focus all his weight at the end of that punch, crumpling poor Sonny to the ground.

While Ali may or may not have known what made him such a great boxer, he had an intrinsic understanding of his gift. The man truly did "float like a butterfly, sting like a bee." In the ring, he was all fluid motion, almost effortlessly staying out of range of his opponent, yet continuing to be very light on his feet. Yet when it came time to deliver a blow, he was nothing but focused energy, beautifully and with astonishing quickness transferring all his body weight into his punching hand. By contrast, his wooden opponents were often left flailing back with great muscular tension, but little effective force.

Returning to cycling, you can easily picture an inexperienced cyclist bobbing up and down and making a great show of putting in a full effort, yet getting dropped by a smoothly moving peloton. The peloton is all poetry in motion, the new rider, no matter how strong, appears heavy, clumsy and out of his element. Hammering away at a giant gear, the newbie can't hold a high cadence and is ultimately left behind.

As we delve further into cycling efficiency, we'll talk more about gears, cadence and precise pedaling, but for now a quick review of the essential points is worth considering:

- Body weight is the dominant force and support for the legs in rotating the pedals.
- The amount of force applied to the pedals is limited by the weight of the rider.
- The maximum rotational force moment comes when the body weight is perpendicular to the pedal at the three o'clock position (90° degree angle).

- The legs transmit body weight to the pedals.
- The maximum force moment to each pedal comes when the body weight is shifted from one side to the other.
- As pedaling cadence increases, it becomes increasingly difficult to shift body weight from one pedal to the next while also decreasing the rotational force moment.
- The difference between "force" and "effort" lies in the fact that the force is a percentage of body weight, while effort is muscular tension providing the application of body weight to pedals.
- Muscular efforts must reflect the percentage of the body weight applied to pedals.
- The position (Pose) of the cyclist is dictated by the necessity of applying the maximum rotational force movement and decreasing the resistance of air in pedaling.
- The cyclist's body weight should be proportionally distributed between the saddle and the pedals according to riding conditions.

References:

1. Lucia, A., Earnest, C., Hoyos, J. and Chicherro, J.L. *Optimizing the Crank Cycle and Pedaling Cadence*. High–Tech Cycling. Human Kinetics, 2003, pp. 93–118.

2. Aristotle. *Movement of Animals*. The Complete Works of Aristotle, Vol. 1. Princeton University Press, 1995, p. 1090.

CHAPTER 31
CADENCE OF PEDALING

You don't fall off unless you stop pedaling.
— *Claude Pepper*

Cadence in Biomechanics is defined as the number of movements occurring during a unit of time (1).

In theory, the most efficient pedaling technique produces the greatest power, which in turn results in the fastest speed for a given distance. Obviously, if you could pedal your biggest gear at your highest cadence for whatever the prescribed distance, you would post your fastest time. Strong cyclists can spin the pedals at 120 to 130 rotations per minute (rpm) for substantial distances and can exceed 300 rpms in track sprints. By contrast, many coaches recommend 90 rpm for normal flat surface riding and even lower cadences for time trialing and climbing.

Not surprising, neither the scientific community, nor the coaching community have reached consensus as to an optimum cadence for cycling. In fact, many would argue that there is no optimum cadence and that both riding conditions and the given rider's physiological capabilities would have to be taken into consideration to determine the optimum cadence for a specific situation (2). While many scientific studies have concluded that low cadence cycling is more economical, the fact remains that most successful cyclists prefer higher, "non–economical" cadences.

The question of optimal cadence and efficiency can get tricky. While at first glance it seems like a simple numbers game, there are many factors to consider beyond external variables like wind, hills and group dynamics. While strict numbers may tell you that the low cadence/big gear scenario is the most economical, researchers like Takaishe et al (3) show that at a relatively low cadence, like 50 rpm, with reasonably high power (+ or - 200 watts), the blood flow and its saturation with oxygen in the cyclists' quads is significantly restricted during the first 1/3 of the cycle of the stroke (from 12 to 3 o'clock), when these muscles are most involved in work. The blood flow is restored after tension ceases and the muscles relax.

In other words, pedal at a slow cadence in a big gear and your blood flow actually stops temporarily right when you need it most, the result of an overlong muscular contraction. The numbers might tell you the low cadence/big gear combination is a winner, but your body supplies a different answer.

Conversely, it is quite possible that pedaling significantly higher cadences, in the range of 110 rpm, actually pushes the blood throughout the body more efficiently.

Instead of the blood flow being interrupted, as in the slow cadence model, the fast cadence creates a faster rate of contractions, in effect turning the leg muscles into an additional pump, thus helping the heart to re-oxygenate the circulation (3). Could it really be true, that high cadence is as effective as EPO in carrying more oxygen throughout the body?

Which brings us, as these things usually do, back to the case of now seven–time Tour de France champion, Lance Armstrong. Armstrong has been dogged by rumors of substance abuse ever since he emerged from the throes of his near–death brush with cancer to become history's greatest Tour champion.

In trying to explain Armstrong's success (assuming that the rumors are false and that he is indeed as clean as he claims) researchers (4, 5) point out his unusually high cadences, even on the most daunting climbs of the Alps and the Pyrenees. For example (2), when Armstrong sealed the 2004 Tour by blasting up the 21 switchbacks of L'Alpe d'Huez in the individual time trial, he raced the 13.8 kilometer climb with an average gradient of 7.9% in roughly 38 minutes. The raw numbers tell the story: he developed consistent power of 475–500 watts and maintained a speed of 22 kilometers per hour, all while pedaling a cadence in the vicinity of 100 rpm. Go to the DVD and you can count it for yourself.

While it is safe to say that Lance Armstrong is in fact a freak of nature, it is also safe to point out that those high cadences are a conscious decision of Lance, his coach Chris Carmichael and his cycling director Johann Bruyneel. While the pre-cancer Lance was a powerful climber, he used lower cadences and his effectiveness was limited to shorter, more intense climbs.

After adopting his new style of higher cadences (and, it must be added, building one of history's greatest support teams) he blossomed into possibly the best climber the sport has ever seen. So, the argument can be reasonably made that at the highest level of the sport, higher cadences have been demonstrated to be a key to success.

Even if you discount Lance (on account of that 'freak of nature' bit) look behind him and you'll see further proof. His only real challenger on the day–to–day climbs of the 2004 Tour was the Italian, Ivan Basso, who also climbed at higher, clearly higher cadences than the rest of the Tour's elite riders. By contrast, the German, Jan Ullrich, who Lance has perpetually dubbed the most talented cyclist in the sport, has resolutely refused to rework his pedaling style and consequently gets dropped when the attacks come in the high mountains.

Looking further at the Basso/Ullrich comparison also shows how tough these things are to parse out. In the normal climbing stages, Basso, with his higher cadence, was able to easily react to attacks and match speed with speed, staying with Armstrong at points where few other riders had ever been able to hold his wheel. Ullrich, with his slower cadence, was never able to react to the change of tempo and would always be dropped. However, by staying to his own style and grinding away, he was always able to limit his losses and remain competitive while other riders who attempted to go with the key attacks eventually blew up and lost significant time.

Look at the Alpe D'Huez climb, though, and you'll see that it was Ullrich placing second while Basso lost considerably more time. Is it possible that pedaling tempo isn't all that important? Well, it's certainly true that a time trial doesn't require the need to react that a road race does, but there's probably more to it than that. A Tour winner as far back as 1997, Ullrich has a vast well of experience to draw from, while Basso was essentially a rookie as far as being a bona fide Tour contender. Add to that the fact that Basso was coming off two heroic performances, where he was the sole survivor in a pair of two–up breakaways with Armstrong and you can see that his performance on Alpe d'Huez can be explained by factors other than pedaling style.

Empirical evidence such as the tales of Armstrong, Basso and Ullrich suggest the value of high cadence pedaling and this is backed by a number of studies (2, 5), which indicate professional cyclists spontaneously pedal faster than 90 rpm on flat surfaces, even when using big gears like 53/13. The explanation offered for this is that quick pedaling, while arguably less economical, physiologically offers the benefit of causing less muscular tension, thus minimizing pain and reducing the risk of damaged muscular and connective tissue.

For a quick mental confirmation of this, visualize the forces at work in your knee as you pedal your bike up an incline of 10% or more. If you attempt to push a massive gear like 53/13, the pressure on your knee joint is going to be tremendous as you grind the pedals ever so slowly. Drop the gear down to a 39/21, however, and the resulting quicker cadence reduces all the tension and potential for damage. In this case, quicker is clearly better.

Now, turn and head back down that hill and we gain understanding of another key element of cadence in cycling. To wit, cadence without the simultaneous application of appropriate force has no effect in increasing the speed of the bicycle. As gravity takes over in hurrying your bike down the hill, you get that "empty" feeling in your pedaling. No matter how fast you seem to turn the pedals, you're not applying additional force to that which gravity has provided for free.

Instead of applying force (i.e. transferring your body weight from one pedal to the oth-

er), you're merely chasing the pedal. While we all intuitively understand this situation, it's still very valuable in showing that making big efforts is a waste of time if you're not actually placing your body weight on the pedals.

In most typical riding situations, especially while on flat surfaces, the relation between body weight and physical effort is usually camouflaged. When you get the bicycle up to reasonable speed and achieve something of a critical value of pedaling cadence, it's tough to distinguish between transferring weight from one pedal to the next from increasing your muscular effort. The natural reaction to wanting to go faster is to "try harder."

This usually means you attempt to push harder with your legs, increasing muscular tension. However, if these efforts don't have the net effect of transferring a greater percentage of your body weight from one pedal to the next, this is all empty effort, with no increase in the force moment, and no increase in pedaling power. So you're working harder (and wasting energy), but you're not going any faster.

Obviously, the next question is simply "what do I have to do to apply more body weight to the pedals as I increase my pedaling cadence?" After all, that is the key to improved performance: transferring more body weight and achieving a greater force moment.

One study, conducted by Faria (4) observed that highly experienced cyclists are visibly more effective than amateurs in applying force to the pedal when it is in the critical three o'clock position. Faria sees this directed power as key to cycling success as it has clear biomechanical advantages and allows cyclists to pedal at high cadences without any loss of efficiency.

Later in the book, we'll delve further into the question of precisely directed power and the correlation between cadence and gears, leg strength and power production. To sum up the cadence discussion thus far, we should review the key factors regarding pedal cadence and transfer of body weight.

- The ability to apply a minimal weight, sufficient for rotating the pedal with the given cadence, to the pedal in the position of 1–4 o'clock.
- The ability to shift the sufficient weight from one pedal to other.
- The ability of legs to **perfectly** transfer the body weight to pedals.
- Muscular system able to quickly transfer the necessary body weight to pedals.
- High level of neuromuscular coordination of the legs, allowing one to complete the process of body weight transfer to the pedals.

References:

1. Donskoy, D.D. and Zatsiorsky, V.M. *Biomechanics*. Moscow, Physical Culture & Sport, 1979, p. 97.

2. Lucia, A., Hoyos, J. and Chicherro, J.L. *Preferred Pedaling Cadence in Professional Cycling*. MedSciSports, Vol. 33, 2001, pp. 1361–1366.

3. Takaishi, T., Sugiura, T., Katayama, K., Sato, Y., Shima, N., Yamamoto, T. and Moritani, T. *Changes in Blood Volume and Oxygen Level in Working Muscle During a Crank Cycle*. MesSciSports, Vol. 34, 2002, pp. 520–528.

4. Faria, I.E. *Energy Expenditure, Aerodynamics and Medical Problems in Cycling: An Update*. SportsMed, Vol. 14, 1992, pp. 43–63.

5. Lucia, A., Earnest, C., Hoyos, J. and Chicherro, J.L. *Optimizing the Crank Cycle and Pedaling Cadence*. High-Tech Cycling. Human Kinetics, 2003, pp. 93–118.

CHAPTER 32
THE PSYCHOLOGICAL FOUNDATION OF PEDALING

To be conscious that we are perceiving or thinking is to be conscious of our own existence.

— Aristotle

One of the most enduring truths about cycling is that the best cyclists are the ones who have learned to suffer the most. Odd, isn't it, that success in a sport would be equated to human misery and that dealing with such misery is indeed an acquired skill? When you start to think about cycling in terms of levels of suffering, golf, tennis and bowling begin to sound like much more desirable alternatives.

Okay, the idea isn't to sell you on the concept of suffering on the bike — at least, not right now — but to demonstrate the profound role that psychology plays in cycling, or any other endurance sport, for that matter. Our arms and legs may be equipped with nerve endings that send out signals of pain, but it's the brain that actually feels the pain and has to deal with it. And a well–conditioned brain calls the shots, informing the extremities to keep on working, pain or no pain.

As important as that is, the brain plays a much more fundamental role in cycling technique. A properly focused and aware brain controls the application of force on the pedals in a very precise manner, maxi-mizing power and minimizing wasted energy. This is a really important concept to accept and understand: you have to think all the time when you ride a bike!

This concept runs contrary to the thought held by a tremendous number of cyclists, who are of the opinion that the best way to ride at maximum effort is to just turn off the brain and hammer away. That school of thought embraces the notion that there is no skill to pedaling a bicycle; all you do is turn circles and pedal until you can't pedal any more.

It's easy to understand why so many cyclists make this fundamental mistake. When you watch someone else pedal a bicycle, what the eye observes appears to be a simple biomechanical process: the legs turn circles, the bicycle moves forward. However, when you actually pedal the bicycle yourself, you quickly realize that there is a psychological component to pedaling that the outside observer would never see.

The ability of humans to imitate observed actions is enabled by what are called mirror neurons. These mirror neurons allow us to replicate an activity by close observation and to a certain extent even give us an idea of what sensations and feelings we should experience as we copy the activity. But there are a couple of catches.

First, is the "to a certain extent" part of the equation? With such a complex, yet seemingly simple activity as pedaling a bike, it is virtually impossible for the body to deduce the proper sensations from mere observation alone. Second, since so few cyclists actually pedal a bicycle properly, we simply can't tell which cyclist to imitate and which to ignore.

So what happens is that cyclists tend to confuse the biomechanical structure of what they think they see when they watch someone else pedal a bicycle, with the psychological structure of what they should be doing, when actually pedaling themselves. It is an absolutely natural reaction to try and copy the physical actions of another person, particularly when that person seems to be having success in the chosen activity.

So, when we watch a cyclist turning the pedals with what we think — and believe — is equal force throughout the entire 360° degree revolution of the pedal stroke, we attempt to do the same things ourselves. Then, when we read, as we often do, advice that says to drag your foot through the six o'clock dead zone as if you were wiping something off your cleats or pull up with your hamstrings through nine o'clock to generate more power, we add further confusion to our efforts.

It's really very simple. The actions we make with our legs and body are the biomechanical structure of cycling, the kinematics and dynamic manifestations of physical effort. The psychological structure of cycling is the progression of commands the brain gives to the body — the directives of what to do and when to do it. Inherent in that

psychological structure are our feelings, perceptions and sensations of our body, all being analyzed, interpreted and reacted to in a constantly changing stream.

Are you hungry to win? Do you feel a cramp coming on? Do you have the confidence to attack on the next big climb? Are you concerned about a possible mechanical failure? While you're riding, an infinite number of thoughts enter your psychological structure, even as you try to give clear and concise set of commands to your legs and body.

What the legs and body actually do — the biomechanical structure of cycling — is a governed or guided activity. In essence, they do what you — the brain — tell them to do. Essentially, the biomechanical structure is a structure of forces applied to the pedals, as was previously discussed in the chapter on "The Force Moment." Somewhat incongruously, the biomechanical structure of cycling is almost a passive activity. There's no thinking that goes on in the legs; they just happily do what they're told.

By contrast, the psychological structure of cycling is where all the real work gets done. It's the hard part. On the most basic level, it's the set of commands we give to our body, regulating and directing the application of force: unweigh here, shift weight now, relax, unweigh here... and so on. These commands come at a dizzying rate throughout the entirety of a ride. Say you're pedaling at 100 rpm and giving as many as four or five direct commands with every pedal stroke. That's something like 500 commands per minute — just for the pedal stroke. Add to that commands for steering and braking and moving around in the pack and avoiding cars, skirting potholes, etc. and you realize your brain is on overload just riding the bike.

And heaven forbid you should even think about your real life... the job, the kids, the taxes that need to be paid, the car that needs to go to the shop. No wonder you want to just turn off your brain and just hammer away. But of course you can't, at least not if you want to be any good on the bike.

So to develop a proper psychological structure for pedaling the bike, you have to truly understand what you're doing as you pedal. When first starting to ride, it appears, from the point of observation, that the primary thing we do is push down on the pedal. That's what we think, we see other people do and it seems to make sense: push down on the pedal, and the bike goes forward.

But is that really what happens? No.

The first movement is the transfer of body weight to the pedal in the one o'clock position. And that only happens if there is a conscious decision to unweigh the body weight from the other pedal. What we see is one thing, the apparent push down on the pedal; what we do is something else entirely, which is to remove weight from the non–working pedal.

And why do we do that? Without weight on the working pedal, it is essentially empty. What is there to push down, if there is no weight on the pedal? To create force, we must load the pedal with our weight, which is then drawn toward the ground by the force of gravity. The legs do not create the force; they transmit the force.

So, in the sequence of commands the brain passes along to the body, the first is simply to unweigh the non–working pedal, remove its weight from support on the pedal. As soon as that happens, there is a natural reaction of the organism (the cyclist's brains and body) to seek another point of support. Thus, there is rapid movement to load the other pedal by transferring the body weight as quickly as possible. The faster the cyclist unloads the pedal, the faster the weight is transferred and — voila — the faster the bike moves.

The key in this ever–repeating sequence is the role of the brain in determining exactly when that unloading and transfer takes place. Your first thought might be that you would keep the weight on the working pedal right through the bottom of the stroke at six o'clock, but it doesn't quite work that way.

The first problem with mashing the pedal all the way to the ground is the matter of ground reaction force. If you keep your weight on the working pedal straight into six o'clock, you'll be in for one bumpy ride. The ground reaction force will have you bouncing up and down in the saddle like you're on a saddled bronco holding on for dear life, instead of riding on a marvel of engineering, a super–light carbon bike.

Second, if your weight stays on the downward pedal too long, you simply won't be able to shift it to the next pedal in time to start the next downward thrust. It takes a measurable amount of time to transfer your weight from one side to the next.

To visualize this, it's helpful to think of the centerline of your saddle as a fulcrum. When your right leg is on the downward stroke, the majority of your weight is to the right side of the fulcrum, supported on the right pedal. In order to load the left pedal, there has to be a tipping of your weight from one side to the next, passing across the saddle's centerline. Even if you're only putting 51% of your weight on the working pedal, that critical balance point has to be passed.

At that brief moment when your weight crosses the centerline, the point of support is the saddle and not either pedal. Obviously, you want a quick transfer with an absolute minimum amount of time spent supported on the saddle. Directing this rapid–fire transfer is the brain's job.

With this image in mind, it's easier to determine where the unloading of the working pedal is initiated. We know that the bulk of force is generated from one o'clock through four o'clock and logic dictates that momentum will carry the foot and pedal on through to six o'clock, so the answer is that effective unweighing begins as soon as the work is complete at three–four o'clock.

Past four o'clock, the Force Moment rapidly diminishes and there is no further reason for your weight to be supported on that pedal. Working efficiently, the brain sends the signal for the beginning of the weight transfer and the process of unloading, shifting and reloading begins, smoothly and rapidly.

As you consider this process of continually loading and unloading the pedals with your body weight, it's important not to confuse unloading the pedal with pulling up on it. There is no need to actively pull the pedal upwards. Being connected as a part of the same lever to the working (downward) pedal, it has no choice but to go up. Attempting to wring some additional momentum out of the pedal rotation by actively contracting the hamstrings does nothing but waste energy and create additional muscular tension. The hamstrings should be relaxed on the upstroke, not actively working.

Further, by not "working" the leg on the upstroke, you can then focus your complete effort on the weight transfer across the saddle, which is what propels the bike in the first place.

Throughout this entire process, the brain has to be acutely attuned to what is transpiring with the body. It has to know where the body weight is supported and what level of muscular effort is being generated, along with monitoring all the normal sensations and feelings.

An important role in our psychological structure is played by feelings and sensations, particularly, sensation of muscular tension, pressure of the foot to the pedal, some pushing efforts, etc. in the process of pedaling. If the body weight is positioned over the pedal, the leg is simply transferring its impact action, and the muscular tension is reflecting that part of the body, which is applied to the pedal. In this case, the force of muscular tension is equal to the part of the body weight, applied to the pedal, and the cyclist doesn't feel overloading, due to an excessive tension.

If the athlete doesn't shift the body weight in time, the muscular tension increases without any real help to the movement of the pedal down, and is accompanied by the "real sensations" of a great amount of efforts, which are not providing for the application of the adequate force moment to the pedal.

Another important sensation in the psychological structure is the sensation of pressing the foot on the pedal, in terms of its amount and its duration in the working part of the cycle from 1 to 4 o'clock. If the foot, according to sensations, is pressing on the pedal more than it's necessary for retaining the balance of the body, positioned off the saddle and balancing on the pedals, in the 3 and 9 o'clock positions, which we accept as the standard, it means that we are applying excessive efforts. In addition to this, it means that the application of efforts is taking too long, the resistance of the pedal is too high (the gear is too hard), but this doesn't affect too much the force moment rotating the pedal.

Thus an effective psychological structure, containing commands and actions, leading to effective sequence of events, may be described in the following way:

- Psychological structure is the structure for governing the forces, participating in pedaling, on the basis of sensations, perceptions, and commands.
- The primary attention in this psychological structure is devoted to the necessity of applying body weight to pedals in the zone of 1–4 o'clock.
- The body weight should be transferred from one pedal to the other.
- The transfer of the body weight depends on taking the foot off the pedal (unloading the body weight) in the zone of 3–4 o'clock.
- The sensation of pressure of the foot on the pedal in the zone of 1–4 o'clock is the signal for taking the foot off the support.

The cadence of pedaling depends on the frequency of taking the body weight (foot) off the pedal.

CHAPTER 33
GEARS AND CADENCE OF PEDALING

Nothing can be created from nothing.
— Lucretius

Go to just about any American state or county fair and there's always one ride where the carnival barker continually shouts to his riders, "Do you wanna go fast? Do you wanna go real, real fast?"

Of course, the patrons always wanna go real, real, real fast and the barker fulfills their requests by pushing down on the throttle which revs up the speed of the engine, blasts more power through the gears and sends the chain of cars careening around the track.

Sounds a lot like cycling, doesn't it? If you're reading this book, chances are you want to go real, real fast when you're on the bike. And to do that, you're talking about finding just the right combination of force, pedal speed and gearing for the conditions at any given time.

At first glance, it sounds like pure mathematics. Multiply the number of pedal rotations by the number of gear inches and you'll have the distance traveled over a given time, i.e. your speed. By that reasoning, quite obviously, you put the front derailleur on the biggest chain ring, the rear derailleur on the smallest cog and you pedal at a speed approaching infinity. Do this and you will go real, real fast.

Just as obviously, this is not a practical solution to the challenge of going fast on a bicycle. Real world conditions of headwinds, gravity, and friction interact with the rider's own physical constitution to define the parameters within which performance takes place. All these factors have to be taken into consideration when searching for the right combination of gearing and cadence.

But there's another less obvious, but more important principle at work here. The simple equation of multiplying the number of rotations of the pedal (cadence) by the number of gear inches traveled does not transfer in fact automatically to the equal speed. The reality is that two riders of equal size, properly fitted on comparable bicycles, can't pedal the same gear at the same cadence because of their different level of skill of application of the body weight to the pedals and therefore they travel at different speeds.

Understanding how this is possible holds the secret to how you can improve your cycling and go real, real fast, achieving greater improvement in your cycling, than any strength training, banned substances or improved nutrition could possibly give you.

Experienced, successful cyclists 'manage' their pedaling action to produce greater power at the same cadence as inexperienced or unsuccessful cyclists. This was pointed out by cycling researchers G. Town and T. Kearney, who noted in their study (1) that the best cyclists consistently produced substantially greater force of vertical pressure on the pedal at its downward motion, than at any other point of its rotation, without any attempts at pulling the pedal on its way upward.

What image does that bring to mind? Greater force of pressure on the pedal on its downward motion? The first image that comes to mind is that of a piston, firing downward, creating the pressure that drives a car forward. And with that in mind, what cyclist immediately comes to mind? Lance Armstrong, of course.

Pull out any DVD of a climbing stage of any recent Tour de France and you'll immediately notice the difference in pedaling between Armstrong and any of his theoretical rivals. And, quite likely, you'll hear the commentator describe that action as being like two giant pistons firing.

People talk about the fact that Armstrong pedals at a higher cadence than other elite cyclists and, while true, that misses the point. He also pedals with visibly different mechanics, clearly directing more energy straight down. His knees seem to rise higher and track straight up and down while other riders seem to pedal in circles with lower knee action and a lack of focus in the application of power.

Want a model for your mirror neurons to emulate? Try Lance and make your pedals dance.

Okay, so we know that the best cyclist focuses his power in the vertical direction and that power results from the application of force in the one o'clock to four o'clock zone of rotation. How do we use that knowledge to become better cyclists and ultimately

and intuitively make the correct gear and cadence selections for any given situation?

It's still an interesting dilemma.

The factors to be considered in improving your cycling ability are still fundamentally infinite, but they can be categorized under the "nature versus nurture" litmus. Going back to the multi–Tour de France champion, many articles have written about him being the perfect cycling machine. **Mentioned in the articles is everything from the length of his thighbones and his incredible ability to process oxygen to even the arch of his back, which apparently affords him an aerodynamic advantage.**

So, from the nature standpoint, each of us has limitations. No matter how hard we work, there are going to be limitations on how much raw energy we can produce. Try as we might, nature has given us certain definable restrictions.

On the other hand, nurture presents greater opportunities for improvement. Physical strength and flexibility can be greatly improved. Living habits like sufficient sleep, improved nutrition, reduced (or eliminated) consumption of alcohol and/or recreational drugs and reduction of stress can all improve your cycling performance.

But even greater potential lies in developing your pedaling technique and learning how to get more power out of the same cadence, becoming a more efficient cyclist. Simply put, practicing and refining your technique can do more to enhance your performance than simply going out the door and piling on the miles. Crazy, but true.

Later in the book, we'll present specific drills to hone your ability to target your application of force, but for now, we'll go back to the matter of gear and cadence selection.

How do we determine the optimal combinations of gears and cadence? What is the interaction between the two and what are the limiting factors in that interaction? With so many variables at play, it helps to go back and look at the fundamental laws of mechanics to put all these questions into context.

Any good student of physics knows the Golden Rule of Mechanics, the essence of which is that the gain in distance is directly proportional to the loss in force, and vice versa.

Application of the golden rule to pedaling a bicycle manifests itself in the specific correlation of pedaling cadence and the amount of force moment. As it has been previously discussed in this book (2), the increase in cadence reduces the amount of force applied to the pedal accordingly (Fig.33.1).

The practical application of this rule is simple: when we lack the strength or ability to apply sufficient effort to rotate the pedals with the given gear, but want to maintain the same power of pedaling, we have to switch to an easier gear and increase the cadence of pedaling.

The corollary of this is that we can increase our pedaling power by applying greater efforts at the same cadence. How do we do this? How do we apply greater effort at the same pedaling rate? Simply put, we

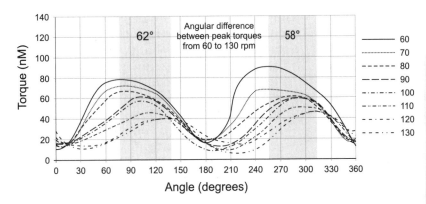

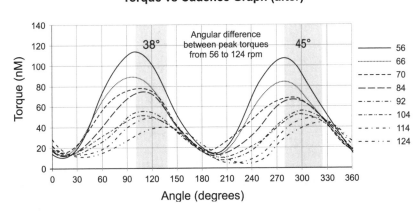

*Fig.33.1 Cadence-torque graphs before and after teaching pedaling technique. Angle in degrees measures the Crank–Pedal position through one full rotation. Pay close attention to the dramatic change in increased torque at lower cadences as well as increased precision of the application of body weight to the pedals. **Conclusion: same work, more output;** the numbers speak for themselves.*

transfer a greater percentage of our body weight and support that increased weight shift with corresponding muscular effort, while maintaining the same cadence.

So what is more important, the weight transfer or the increased muscular effort... or is there a difference? Put another way, does the application of greater muscular force, on the one hand, or greater body weight, on the other, guarantee the desired result of a greater force moment in pedaling?

To get the answer, we need to return to the nurture issue, discussed above. We know that both physical strength and pedaling technique can be improved with practice and training.

We know that to be effective, muscular force must be "entered" into the mechanics of the pedaling movement at a precisely coordinated and specific point in the pedal rotation. In other words, the piston must "fire" at the correct time, every time. This is a highly technical skill, as artful in its execution as are the movements of a ballerina or a figure skater.

The most important features of this movement are the ability to use the body weight to create a high force moment and the corresponding ability to quickly shift the body weight from one pedal to the other. It is a dance, albeit one of very subtle movements, substantially only noticed by the dancer/cyclist.

Following that line of thought, the purpose of working on enhanced strength development is to both facilitate and support this highly technical movement. Without the technical skill to rapidly shift and apply the weight, enhanced strength is a waste. Without the strength to sustain those technical gains, the rider's ability to get the most out of his or her enhanced skills will be short-lived.

Which brings us to the next question: why do we change gears? Is it because we want to have a higher cadence or easier pedaling?

Well... yes, both. We generally change to an easier gear when we either lack the strength to support our shifting body weight or the technical skill and neuromuscular coordination to get the most out of our strength.

To make the bike go faster, we need a very specific combination of gearing and cadence, ultimately producing a high power output. But gearing and cadence are just "instruments" which we choose to use to apply body weight to the pedals and create power.

For many readers, it may be difficult to visualize how the many aspects of the pedaling motion can be changed to direct force most efficiently. Particularly hard to understand is the notion that two riders of equal size can pedal the same gear of matching bikes at the same cadence, yet one can go much faster.

A very simple test can help you put all these factors in place in your mind. Take your bike and grasp it by the stem (Fig.33.2), lifting the front wheel slightly off the ground so that it can rotate freely. Then, using your free hand, tap on the wheel to start it rotating, the way you would if you were checking to see if your front brakes were rubbing or your cycle computer's sensor was working.

You'll notice that it takes very little pressure from your hand to start the wheel turning and that your hand only stays in contact with the tire surface for a short time... roughly from one o'clock to three o'clock. After a few seconds, you'll note that you fall into a rhythm, and that you can maintain the same wheel speed by applying the same amount of pressure every couple of seconds.

Fig.33.2 The wheel rotation model of pedaling.

The first test is to maintain the same rhythm, striking the wheel with exactly the same frequency, but applying more force each time you tap the wheel. Your cadence doesn't change and you don't stay in contact with the tire surface for a greater percentage of the rotation, but the forward speed of the wheel increases dramatically.

Now, try and keep your hand in contact with the tire surface for a greater percentage of the rotation. As your hand stays in contact with the tire past four o'clock, your motion becomes awkward and your hand begins acting as a brake, actually slowing the wheel instead of accelerating it. Further, you're actually working harder as you attempt to stay in contact with the tire, but you're getting worse results. You are now wasting energy, even though you are struggling to make the wheel go faster.

While this is a very simplified analogy, it puts into context all the elements of the pedaling dynamic. Cadence alone doesn't determine forward speed and applying force throughout the entire pedal stroke not only doesn't increase speed but actually is a waste of energy. Efficient pedaling demands that you direct your force at exactly the right time and — equally important — that you remove that force at exactly the right time. Do this and you will become a much more efficient cyclist.

Determining the Proper Gears and Cadence

Okay, this is sort of a trick. If you've skipped forward to this section looking for a "magic bullet" omnibus answer to all your questions about what gears to ride and how fast to turn the pedals, you're sure to walk away disappointed. The objective here is not to tell you the answers to those questions, but to help you understand the factors at work so that in any given situation you can make the most educated decision possible. Only you can determine what gears and cadence you should be riding, and that decision may change from moment to moment.

With so many variables at play in the apparently simple art of riding a bicycle, we have to realize that the variables are interdependent. We can't just change one variable without there being notable changes in several other variables. As with all things in nature, nothing comes for free. Every change exacts a price.

Increase the force applied to the pedals and the energy stores are used up faster. Get the bike moving faster and the wind resistance ratchets up. Select a bigger gear and the muscular demands increase. Any time we do something to improve our performance, there is a corresponding payment we have to make. The key is to understand how to obtain optimum performance in all conditions, for all occasions.

In cycling, this interdependence generally exists among cadence, gears, muscular effort, body weight, neuromuscular coordination and power production, with the uncontrollable variables of terrain, wind, heat, humidity and competition thrown in for good measure.

Eliminating environmental factors, the table below lists the principle variables involved in gear selection.

up to about a 110 cadence and blast down the road.

But of course all cyclists have their own limitations, and not just those imposed by the course and conditions. In fact, in the real, imperfect world, you won't find yourself in the 53/12 all that often.

Gear Selection

Rear / Front	11	12	13	14	15	16	17	18	19	20	21	22	23	24	25
53	130.09	119.25	110.08	102.21	95.4	89.44	84.18	79.5	75.32	71.55	68.14	65.05	62.22	59.63	57.24
50	122.73	112.5	103.85	96.43	90	84.38	79.41	75	71.05	67.5	64.29	61.36	58.7	56.25	54
39	95.73	87.75	81	75.21	70.2	65.81	61.94	58.5	55.42	52.65	50.14	47.86	45.78	43.88	42.12
34	83.45	76.5	70.62	65.57	61.2	57.38	54	51	48.32	45.9	43.71	41.73	39.91	38.25	36.72

Limitations for the use of gears and cadence:

1. Pose of the cyclist: body weight location & aerodynamics

2. Skill of body weight transfer from one pedal to the other

3. Strength of leg muscles

4. Neuromuscular coordination, perception

5. Power production capabilities (VO_2 capacity) of the cyclist

Given standard gearing, the theoretical "fastest" gear would be the greatest number of teeth in the front — 53 and the fewest in the back — 12, which we will refer to as 53/12. In a perfect world, a fit cyclist would simply put his bike in the 53/12, crank it

Some of these limitations have wide latitude for improvement, while others can be changed only marginally. What makes this of particular interest is that many cyclists expend the vast majority of their efforts on the things that have relatively little opportunity for positive change and ignore the areas where vast improvements can be made. As we discuss the areas where improvement can be made, we're going to drift away from the central discussion of gearing and cadence, but we'll make a quick return. Remember, all these factors are interdependent, so we have to get a lot of other things right before we can even worry about gearing and cadence.

References:

1. Town, G. and Kearney, T. *Swim, Bike, Run*. Human Kinetics Publishers, 1994, pp. 73–77.

2. Burke, E.R., Editor. *High–Tech Cycling*. Human Kinetics, 2003, pp. 147–174.

CHAPTER 34
PEDALING SKILL

*Change is a challenge and
an opportunity; not a threat.*
— *Prince Phillip of England*

The ultimate goal in racing a bicycle is to pedal efficiently. This holds true no matter what the competition is, be it on the road, the trail, the velodrome or the cyclocross circuit. If you're racing a triathlon, a mountain stage or a flat four–corners criterium, the objective is always the same: pedal as efficiently as possible at all times.

Given the wide diversity of conditions you can expect to face on your bicycle, it is clear that there is no one–size–fits–all solution to pedaling efficiency. From the previous chapters we should have a clear concept of where in the pedaling stroke to apply power, but that still leaves us with all the nuances of how to be most effective in applying that power in race conditions.

We All Have Limits

Think of it this way. At any given point in time, each of us, as athletes, has a maximum level of performance capability. This level is determined by a number of factors, both hereditary and voluntary. Muscular strength, aerobic capacity, injuries, rest, nutrition and a host of other variables all add up to 100% of what you can possibly do on a given day.

But that doesn't mean you will get 100% of your potential out of a given performance. Your skill in pedaling the bike, your pedaling efficiency, will determine whether you maximize your capabilities or whether you fall far short of your potential.

The requisite skills cover everything you will encounter from the moment you first mount the bike until your ride comes to an end, whether that end is marked by a triumphant raising of both arms as you cross the line victoriously or a speedy transition to the run in a triathlon.

The range of skills is considerably more complex than it might appear. At its simplest, a bike leg might be nothing more than a 25–mile straight line on a level surface with no wind and no other distractions such as fellow competitors, cars, dogs, etc. Even in this unrealistically simplistic example, it's not an easy matter to know what gears to select and what cadence to turn the pedals with, and then follow through by maintaining perfect concentration and perfect aerodynamic position for the entire duration of the time trial.

In fact, the mental and physical challenge in getting 100% of your potential in these perfect conditions is enormous. That's why the World One Hour Record on the velodrome remains one of the ultimate tests of human athletic performance.

Now, transition from the test–tube conditions of the 25–mile straight line to the real world, where there is far more to pedaling efficiency than maintaining a constant speed ad infinitum. Changes in terrain, road conditions, race conditions, cornering, tactics, wind and weather all must be taken into consideration as you constantly modify your pedaling to maintain peak efficiency. On top of all that, you've still got to think about what you'll have left in the tank to transition to the run in a triathlon to be able complete that leg just as efficiently as you did the bike.

How and Why to Use Gears/Cadence Ratio

Although it seems fairly obvious, it is worth mentioning that the gears and wheels on your bike present a mechanical advantage that amplifies your physical efforts and translates into a faster ground speed than you could ever obtain unaided. After all, the bike didn't get the unofficial title of the "world's most efficient form of human transportation" by accident.

Like any other useful tool, however, the bicycle must be used properly in order to gain the best results. The bottom line is that the more you understand about selecting the proper gear/cadence combination for any given situation, the closer you will come to achieving 100% of your potential.

As we discussed earlier in the book, your maximum power on the bike would come from pedaling your largest gear at the highest possible cadence. For most folks, the biggest gear they have is a combination of 53 teeth on the front chain ring and 12 teeth on the rear cog. This translates to 119.5 inches traveled for every rotation of

the pedal. In other words, this is one big gear.

The problem is that very few people currently residing on Planet Earth have the strength to pedal a gear that big long enough at a sufficiently high cadence to maintain the super fast speeds that such a gear would allow.

At the other end of the spectrum, a typical smallest gear on a racing bike would have 39 teeth on the front and 25 on the back, which would yield 42 inches of forward travel for every pedal stroke. Just about anyone can pedal a 39/25 gear at ridiculously high cadences, but again not for a very long time. The aerobic cost is just too high for the resultant speeds.

The answer lies in balancing your physical force with your aerobic capacity to find the gear/cadence combination that yields your maximum possible performance at any given point in a race and also over the course of the race in total.

The variables that come into play include not only gears and cadence but your competitors, speed, wind, heat, humidity, heart rate, muscular effort, body position, road surface, hills, corners — basically an infinite list. With all these variables in play, it is clear that changing any one parameter inevitably impacts the factors over which you have the most control: gear selection and pedaling rate.

The Logic of the Trade

It all comes down to the simple logic of a trade. If the road goes up, we have to choose to either ride a smaller gear at a higher cadence or put greater muscular effort into the current gear. Either way, we're likely to sacrifice speed, but the question is which choice will allow us to lose the least amount of speed AND still have the resources to continue a maximum effort performance after the hill.

The defining point of the trade is how we pay for each change. We could memorize a gear inch chart and make swift mental calculations as to what gear/cadence combination will yield the desired speed for a given situation, but, realistically, that's never going to happen.

Instead, the keys are perception and experience. While your mental calculator might tell you to maintain 100 rpm in a 53/15 gear to hold a certain speed, you're going to get conflicting information from the feeling of muscular tension in your legs or the suddenly overtaxed breathing and heart pumping of your cardiovascular system.

In essence, your mind is saying "ride like Lance," but your body is saying "hate to break it to you, dude, but you're not Lance." We can try to follow the mind's instructions, but inevitably we run into our limits. This boundary is the threshold of the optimal functioning of our body's separate systems as well as our body as a whole. Push beyond this boundary and we can go very quickly from maximum performance to complete shutdown.

In a nutshell, this highlights the difference between training and racing. In training, the objective is to increase our maximum potential, either by building greater physical strength or a higher level of aerobic capacity. In racing, conversely, the idea is to recognize your current potential and work as efficiently as possible to see how close to 100% of your maximum possible performance you can achieve. Get close to your boundary, but don't step past it and 'blow–up'.

Finding your boundaries is actually pretty easy. If you're struggling to turn over a big gear at the speed you want to maintain, you don't currently have the leg strength you need and you should shift to an easier gear. If you're pedaling so fast that your heart rate is at its maximum and your breathing is labored, you're in too small a gear.

You should know your own boundaries from your personal experience and training, and you should always be aware of how close you are to the perilous edge of your capabilities. If you've ever heard an elite athlete describe a race or a game as being a break from the daily practice sessions, it's precisely because the elite athlete recognizes that training is where you push to expand your boundaries and racing is where you control your efforts to remain within them.

The Tension Standard

The standard for judging your efforts is actually very simple and lies in the muscular tension you feel in your legs as you ride the bike. The standard for muscular tension is the perception of tension you feel in your leg muscles when you stand and bounce lightly on the pedals with your feet in the three and nine o'clock positions. You can perform this simple test either with your bike mounted in a trainer or while coasting down the road.

While this is the right amount of tension for flat riding, you may think that climbing requires a greater level of muscular power or tension. Well, let's look at what happens when you climb in too big a gear. You try to 'mash' the gear by applying more muscular force (tension) but instead of going faster you just rise up off the saddle. The 'push–back' created by the combined effect of the gear and gravity forces your weight off the saddle. This attempt to use excess muscular power leads to cramping and fatigue, not better performance.

Now, let's see how this plays out in race conditions and effects your overall performance. You're feeling great, zooming along in a 53/15 gear, pedaling about 90 rpm, holding 25 miles per hour. Ahead looms a short hill, not too steep, less than half a mile.

"I'll just power through it," you think to yourself, so you blast into the hill — same speed, same gear, same cadence. For the first couple of hundred yards, things are great, but you're forgetting one thing — you always slow down going uphill.

As the pain builds in your legs, both your cadence and speed drop rapidly. With gravity acting on your body weight, the gear that you were turning so easily now is more than you can handle. You're faced with a dilemma: shift to a smaller gear or try to come out of the saddle and soldier through it.

Neither choice is good. Come out of the saddle and your cadence will drop even more. Shift to the smaller gear and it's going to be very tough to spin it up to a higher cadence, so your speed will drop even if there is some relief for your overloaded legs.

By the top of what seemed to be an insignificant hill, your competitors are flying by, but the worst isn't over yet. Your gear is still too big, your breathing and heart rate are maxed out, your legs are painfully loaded with lactic acid and worst of all, your positive mental framework is shot and flooded with doubt.

Instead of accelerating across the false flat at the top, you're desperately trying to recover, waiting for the descent to offer you much needed relief. But when you get to the descent, your bike is moving so slowly that it takes forever to accelerate. More time is lost. More self–doubt creeps in. You begin to accept that this just isn't your day and lower your expectations accordingly. Your day is done, and all because of errors in perception and judgment on one simple hill.

Ever hear somebody say "that hills kicks my butt every time?" Well, you just became that person. But it wasn't the hill; it was you.

The Common Sense Approach

There is a better approach. Common sense and experience tell you that if you're riding 25 miles per hour on the flat, you won't be able to maintain that pace going uphill. Rather than let the hill 'kick your butt' the plan is to anticipate the increased difficulty of the climb and manage the hill to get the most out of your abilities.

Before you even get to the climb, drop your rear cog from the 15 to the 19 or even the 21. Depending on the climb's severity, you may even go to the small ring up front. Switching to the smaller gear will allow you to increase your cadence as your momentum carries you into the climb with good speed.

You're now able to relax and spin easily as you approach the spot where your legs normally begin to overload. The idea is to stay out of discomfort and ride within yourself. Nearing the last 10–15% of the hill, you may even choose to shift back to a slightly *larger* gear and use your higher cadence to accelerate across the top and take full advantage of the first part of the descent to get back easily to full speed. NOW you can rest, recover and get mentally set for the rest of the race.

This same type of perception–aided judgment may present itself many times throughout the course of a triathlon or time trial. These disciplines often have 180° degree turnarounds on open roads. The key here is to shift to a much smaller gear before the cone marking the turn, maybe even take advantage of the opportunity to rest as you coast through the turn, and then spin quickly out of the 180° to recover your cadence before working back up to your bigger gears.

Bear in mind that the 180° degree turnaround may also involve a quick switch from a tailwind to a headwind, another good reason to be in a smaller gear as you come out of the turn. You want to be able to efficiently accelerate out of the turn, not find yourself struggling to get back up–to–speed in a gear that is way too big.

While external conditions, be they wind, terrain, road surface, heat or speed dictate the need for a trade in efforts, internal indicators of muscular tension and aerobic activity are the bargaining chips and the gear ratio and pedaling cadence determine how the trade is made.

Pedal too fast in too small a gear and you're wasting energy, just flailing away at the pedals without developing enough speed. You're simply not efficiently applying your body weight to the pedals. Hammer away at too large a gear, conversely, and you build the muscular tension that will ultimately lead to fatigue and cramping. Again, you're not being efficient in the way you apply your body weight to the pedals.

Choosing Your Gears

The simplified chart at the end of chapter 33 shows the gear inch values for the two most common front chain ring combinations. While the predominant combination has been 53 teeth on the big ring and 39 on the small ring up front and a cassette that has 12 teeth on its smallest cog, lately many cyclists have switched to the so-called compact configuration, with 50 teeth on the big ring and 34 on the small ring.

While at first blush it might seem that there is a great difference between the two, all you have to do is switch to a rear cassette with 11 teeth on the smallest cog and you see that the gear inches offered by the two configurations are not all that dissimilar.

A further benefit of the chart is that it allows you to pinpoint the so–called crossover points, the gear combinations where you can achieve the same gear inch value from the small or big ring up front. For example, a 34/12 gear choice develops 76.5 inches per pedal rotation, not all that different from a 50/18 at 75 inches. In this case, you might be better off in the big ring, because you're closer to the center of the rear cassette and have more latitude to switch quickly to bigger or larger gears just by changing the rear cassette.

A closer look at gear selection sheds more light on the trades you have to make to achieve optimum performance. Let's say that you are relatively comfortable pedaling a giant gear like 53/11 at the low cadence rate of 60 rpm. That demonstrates that your muscular strength is quite good, but you're not really going fast enough. However, if you can't push that gear up to 70 or 75 rpm, it's clear that you lack the ability to efficiently transfer your weight from one pedal to the next. So you're investing maximum muscular effort, but not achieving your best results in terms of road speed.

If you are incapable of increasing the cadence in that gear, the obvious trade is to shift to a smaller gear that reduces muscular effort (tension) but allows you to spin the pedals at a substantially higher cadence. While your muscular effort decreases, the higher cadence will make greater demands on your aerobic capacity and heart rate. Go to too small a gear and eventually the price paid in terms of aerobic capacity and heart rate will be too high, just as it was with your muscular tension in the massive gear.

Faced with the choice between the rock (the big gear) and the hard place (the higher cadences) the objective is to find the right balance for any condition the road presents to you. In triathlon and time trialing, what you would *like* to do, for example, is hold exactly 24.8 miles per hour for exactly one hour thus allowing you to knock off a 40–kilometer course in the 'magic' one hour.

The Need For Acceleration

But real life (and racing) is not like that. Hills, corners, turnarounds, road surfaces and other variables dictate that you will have to constantly change your speed in order to wind up with that 24.8 mile per average – and that means you will often have to accelerate your bike rather than ride in the same gear at the same cadence for that full hour.

When we think of acceleration, the image that most often comes to mind is that of the cyclist out of the saddle, pumping hard and blazing past the competition. It's an exciting and compelling image, but is that really the right thing to do in an event that may require dozens, if not hundreds, of accelerations over a course that may range from twelve to one hundred twelve miles?

Is it really necessary, or even desirable, to pound away so hard, literally jolting the body weight against the pedals, redlining the muscular tension and pushing the heart rate to the ceiling, just to get back up to speed? Actually — no. In most cases it is exactly the wrong thing to do.

The negatives to out–of–the–saddle acceleration are just too profound. To begin, standing acceleration puts excessive loading forces on your muscles at the low cadences typical at the beginning of an acceleration.

The protocol for efficient acceleration is to always begin with higher cadences and smaller gears. This not only avoids excessive muscular tension, but is also actually the faster way to get up to speed. Try to accelerate in too large a gear and you will

simply bog down, whether or not you're out of the saddle.

And because you want to begin your acceleration with higher cadences, it's better to be on the saddle, not off it. It's just easier to pedal fast when you're on the saddle. As you begin to accelerate, your increased momentum will allow you to start working into bigger gears, still maintaining the high cadence and staying below the threshold of muscular tension.

At the start of an acceleration, for example, you might shift down to a 53/23 or, on the small ring, the similarly sized 39/17 (62.2 gear inches versus 61.9), regain your high cadence quickly and then work your way right through the gears to 53/17 or even 53/14, depending on your skill and ability to maintain this level of cruise speed.

In virtually all cases, the protocol is the same. Stay in the saddle, use smaller gears to ramp up cadence and speed, then work your way back to bigger gears. Only rarely should the need for instant speed arise so quickly that you need to apply more body weight to the pedals by standing up.

This same logic of using gear selection to control muscular fatigue and heart rate during acceleration can also be applied to the challenge of maintaining a constant speed. While a certain combination of gear and cadence may feel ideal for long stretches, as fatigue sets in you may experience increased muscular tension. It can help to play around with your gears and cadence to freshen up the legs. To reduce the tension, you can shift to a slightly smaller gear, increase your cadence and, keeping an eye on your bike computer, maintain the same speed. This can be particularly useful when grinding away into a relentless head wind.

As previously discussed, riding uphill is where gear selection has the most impact.

While your ego may say to mash a big gear and power through a climb, the best choice is to choose a gear that allows you to apply your body weight to the pedals more often with less cost in terms of muscular tension. The phrase you may have heard in Tour de France coverage is "dancing on the pedals" and it refers to someone who climbs so beautifully by maintaining a high cadence with seemingly no effort.

The speeds are slower when climbing, but the same logic of trading gears for cadence applies. The objective is still to ride at the highest sustainable speed without putting undue stress on the legs. This is particularly important in triathlon when you don't want to appear at the transition to the run with 'dead' legs.

The cost of climbing at high cadences comes in the form of high aerobic output, so you have to prepare for this with focused training. If you want to "climb like Lance" then you're going to have to put in the training and develop your aerobic system to the point where you can maintain this level of high heart rate and oxygen consumption for long periods.

Going down the other side of the hill is a much easier matter, but, depending on the gradient of the descent, you may still have some choices to make. On relatively shallow descents, you still have to pedal and the temptation is generally to put the bike in your biggest gear and let 'er rip. That's okay, but don't hesitate to shift to a slightly smaller gear to keep the cadence up if you feel the tension building in your legs.

As the grade gets steeper, eventually you'll come to the point where pedaling just doesn't make sense. If you're pedaling at super-high cadences and 'chasing' the pedals in an effort to squeeze out one more mile per hour, just relax, get in your aerodynamic tuck and enjoy the ride.

Try Hard, But Don't Look Like You're Trying

The most critical consideration in the whole gears/cadence trade-off is determining the boundary between the two and the answer is always shifting depending on both the race conditions and your own conditioning. If you are lacking in leg strength, then even the easiest gears will tense your legs in relatively short order. If you've put in time in the weight room, but haven't put in the miles, you may be able to move a huge gear, but lack the fitness to sustain your effort.

While your perception will guide you, there are external manifestations of your limitations that would be clearly visible to anyone. If your cadence is slow and non-rhythmic, that's what they call 'pedaling squares'. This labored pedaling is usually accompanied by shoulder rolling, your body moving exaggeratedly from side to side or even bouncing up and down.

While this may look like you're really trying hard, what it means is that you lack the strength and ability to channel your weight to the pedals through your legs and you're trying to recruit assistance from other areas of your body. This excessive body movement is just a waste of energy. When you are properly trained and pedaling skillfully, none of these movements will be visible. The best cyclists are always the ones who look 'quiet' on the bike, with no extraneous movement what-so-ever.

If you find yourself struggling on the bike like that, it's a clear indication that you lack the strength to sustain your level of effort. Even worse, if you try to hold your speed through this movement, you will overload the tendons and ligaments you've recruited and that could lead to debilitating injuries down the road.

The other side of the coin is the fatigue you run into from riding at cadences higher than those to which you have been accustomed. The energy cost is very low at cadences in the 55–65 rpm range, but unfortunately so are your speeds. There is generally a curvilinear relationship between energy expenditure and the increase in cadence, but it's fairly difficult to pinpoint the exact spot where the cost exceeds the gains in speed. While the existing scientific data can shed some light on this magic cadence number where efficiency is maximized (2), the real world answer is that the perfect cadence is a shifting target and depends not only on conditions but on your strength, skill and training. And that depends on your perceptions of your effort at any given moment.

Getting Ready To Run

From a triathlon standpoint, there is one last topic to cover as regards the gear/cadence choice and that is the end of the ride. Where a cyclist may be headed to the shower, a hot meal and massage after the ride ends, the triathlete still has to deal with the matter of the run.

Just as you shift to a lower gear when approaching a hill, you should do the same as you near the end of the ride. The reason is that you want to release as much leg tension as possible before starting out on the run. If you keep riding a huge gear right until the end of the ride, you'll arrive at transition with legs that are fatigued, tense and quite possibly cramping, the classic definition of dead legs. Hammer in, stumble out!

Equally important is to get your legs moving at a higher cadence before you start running. If you do stumble out of the transition area with dead legs, it will take you forever to get to a good running speed, just like it does if you enter a 180° degree turnaround in too large a gear and then find yourself facing a headwind.

You want your legs to feel fresh, light and fast when you head out on the run course. You should aim for a running rhythm of at least 180 footfalls per minute, which is equivalent to a cadence of 90 rpm's on the bike.

How far out from the transition area you begin working the smaller gear/higher cadence recovery phase depends largely on the length and difficulty of the course. In a short, flat sprint triathlon, possibly only the last quarter mile is needed to freshen the legs and get ready to run. In an Ironman–length race on a difficult course, you may want to begin your run preparations several miles from transition. Your perceptions and experience will be your guide, but generally speaking the harder and longer your legs work on the bike, the more time you will need to loosen them up before the run.

References:

1. Horning, D. and Couzens, G. *Triathlon Lifestyle of Fitness*, A Wallaby Book, New York, 1985, p. 62.

2. Marsh, A.P. and Martin, P.E. *Effect of cycling experience, aerobic power, and power output on preferred and most economical cycling cadences*. Medicine and Science in Sports and Exercise Vol. 29, 1997, pp. 1225–1232.

CHAPTER 35
PEDALING DRILLS

Excellence is to do a common thing in an uncommon way.

— *Booker T. Washington*

Once you learn to ride a bike, you never forget how, right? True, and in this case, unfortunately true. The process by which we learn a skill involving identical repetitive motions can be called *overlearning.* After the appropriate balance and steering skills are acquired, the simple motion of pedaling a bicycle, repeated 70, 80, 90 times a minute, basically buries itself into your DNA. Ride a bicycle enough and you couldn't forget how even if you wanted to... which constitutes a bit of a problem as you seek to relearn and refine your pedaling skills to improve your performance.

The sequence of drills that follows has been designed to heighten your awareness of what actually happens as your legs rotate through the 360° degrees of the pedaling stroke. By working through these drills, you will begin to unlearn your previous pedaling style and develop a subtly–different technique that will vastly increase your cycling efficiency and performance.

Having read the preceding chapters on the science of pedaling, you probably have an intellectual idea of the essential elements of proper pedaling. Now the challenge is to translate that grasp of theory into changes in your pedaling mechanics that will even-

tually rewrite your "hard drive," replacing your old pedaling style with a new one that will over time become second nature to you.

The key to this process — and these drills — is to open yourself up to the feelings of your muscles, tendons and joints as you rotate the pedals. To brand these feelings with an appropriately serious name, call it your proprioceptive awareness. Instead of thinking about how hard you are working, how fast your cadence is or how long you've been at it, concentrate on your balance, the effect of gravity on your actions and your overall control of your body.

As an endurance athlete, you most likely relate to training as an outlet of effort designed to make you stronger. In this case, the pedaling drills are designed to train you to be more efficient, so don't expect these drills to wear you out or put your heart rate into the stratosphere. That said, you still want to be fresh and particularly focused each time you do them, because while these drills won't wear you out, they can be very tricky to master. In fact, you can expect to feel a little foolish the first couple of times you try them as you learn how little you really knew about your balance on the bicycle.

For safety's sake, the first set of drills is designed to be performed on a stationary trainer. Once you've got the hang of it, most of the drills can then be repeated on the road as well. In the beginning, try to do the drills two or three times a week. Once you've got the feeling, you can cut back to a once–a–week schedule, just to maintain the feel of proper pedaling.

It's a good idea to practice the drills for 15–20 minutes before you head out on a ride, so that you can immediately transfer your heightened proprioceptive awareness to actual on–the–road performance.

The main goal of the drills is to learn how — and when — to apply your body weight to the pedals, and, just as importantly how and when to remove that body weight from those pedals. The key is to transfer the body weight to each pedal from the one o'clock through the three o'clock position in the pedal rotation.

The starting point for all drills is with the pedals at the three o'clock and nine o'clock positions, the point where the body weight is equally distributed between the two pedals. As previously discussed in the book, this is the static point from which movement can only take place by removing the body weight from the rear pedal and transferring it to the front pedal. There is no push or pull involved in this movement — it is a simple unweighing of the foot from the rear pedal with a resultant transfer of the weight to the front pedal, which makes it automatically drop toward the ground.

When the foot drops, it rapidly reaches the six o'clock position, otherwise known as the dead zone, the point where no power can be applied to the pedals. To understand the implications of the dead zone, before you undertake these drills, you should set a cadence benchmark for yourself. Set your trainer to no resistance and put your bike in the easiest gear, say a 39–23. After warming up, see how high a cadence you can reach before you begin bouncing in the saddle and experiencing excessive hips movement. Whatever cadence you reach will be your cadence benchmark, a number you can expect to dramatically increase as you refine your pedaling mechanics.

It helps to understand why you started bouncing in the saddle at cadences as low as 120 or 130 rpm. Well, our old friend Isaac Newton answered that question several centuries ago, with his Third Law. As you continue to apply force to the pedal, it becomes a ground reaction force (GRF) and bounces back, pushing your body up. Anytime you apply "force" faster than the pedals are moving, you create a lack of synchronization and create bounce. The more tension in your muscles, the greater the bounce.

Off the trainer, you can easily experience the bounce by trying to outpedal the force of gravity on a modestly steep downhill. As gravity pulls the bike downhill, the pedals are "empty." Trying to wildly pedal at high rates by continually applying force just doesn't work and you end up comically bouncing for a couple of moments before you abandon the effort and enjoy the ride. Later, as your skill develops, you can use downhills of varying inclinations in concert with different gear ratios to further increase your ability to pedal at higher cadences.

Getting Started

The sequence of pedaling drills has been designed to start at the most elemental level and progress to more sophisticated and difficult drills. Similarly, your progression will go from low to high cadences and from a stationary trainer to on–road riding. The good news is that this isn't a process that will take months and months. In fact, in your very first session, you will begin to "get it" and will see rapid increase in your cadence as you control your efforts and learn to transfer your body weight from one pedal to the other.

In these progressive drills, you will start with low resistance and increase it either from your trainer or from bigger gears on your bike, while continuing to maintain the same cadence and heart rate. This ability to hold cadence and heart rate, something you would normally attribute to more and harder training, will instead come from better and more efficient pedaling, a dramatic demonstration of the effectiveness of proper technique. With practice, these drills will help you develop the precise ability to place your body weight over the pedals effectively, synchronized in space and time to develop the highest torque output. Over time, as you progress to higher cadences and bigger gears, this will give you a substantially higher power in your cycling.

Your goal in these drills is to transform your abilities from pedaling easy gears to pedaling harder gears, from pedaling low cadences to pedaling high cadences with an increased awareness of your body weight application and point of support on the pedals.

Please note as you perform these drills that at any time your muscular tension goes up, you must try to relax. If you can't relax, stop the drill, rest, re–focus and start over. As long as your muscles are tense, you can't change support from one pedal to the next. You'll end up clanking the pedals in the six o'clock/twelve o'clock dead zone. Similarly, if your heart rate starts to jump quickly, rest, relax and start over.

Indoor Drills on the Trainer

The following drills are designed to be practiced on your own bike, with a magnetic or friction trainer on the rear wheel. It is best to put a book or small piece of wood under the front wheel to level out the bike to simulate a realistic riding position. Only the very advanced rider should attempt these drills on rollers, where the bike is not stabilized.

Start out doing the drills with the easiest gears, such as 53/23, in order to develop the precise perception of body weight application to the pedals. The lower gears require the least body weight application and muscular effort allowing you to focus solely on perception. Try to become comfortable with the spatial perception of your foot on the pedal at the 3 o'clock position.

Why does your perception matter, if you're clipped in to the pedals anyway? It's important because accurate application of force is both economical and efficient. The 3 o'clock pedal position is the point of maximum torque, which is the basis of pedaling power. However, it gets even simpler — this is the optimal pedal position, where we can apply maximum body weight. With the progression of drills, as your perception improves, gears will get harder and consequently the level of muscular efforts as well.

In order to simplify your drill routine, please note the following classifications of body positions on the bike.

All drills should be performed in four basic body positions on the bike:

I. Pedals at 3 and 9 o'clock. Hands on the aero–bars. Hips on the saddle. The cycling "Pose."
II. Pedals at 3 and 9 o'clock. Hands off the bars. Hips on the saddle.
III. Pedals at 3 and 9 o'clock. Hands on the bars. Hips off the saddle.
IV. Pedals at 3 and 9 o'clock. Hands off the bars. Hips off the saddle. Body weight balanced on the pedals.

There are four basic drills for learning the perception of pedaling:

1. Balance on the pedals.
2. With pedals at 3/9 o'clock position, move the front (3 o'clock) pedal to the 1 o'clock position and then back to the 3 o'clock position where it should pause for an instant before you repeat the drill again. The front pedal moves about of 1/6 or 60° of the full circle of pedaling.
3. With pedals at 3/9 o'clock position, move the front (3 o'clock) pedal to the 9 o'clock position and the rear pedal to the 3 o'clock position, stop for an instant, reverse the pedals back to starting position and perform the drill again with the same leg. Pedals are moving about 1/2 or 180° of the full circle of pedaling.
4. With pedals at 3/9 o'clock position, move the front (3 o'clock) pedal a full circle to 3 o'clock position, stop for an instant, and begin the cycle again with the same leg. The front pedal completes a full circle or 360° of the full circle of pedaling.

In addition to the four main drills, there are pedaling drills for one leg with the rear foot off the pedal and placed on the rear axel or the trainer. For one leg drills we use the basic body positions #I and #II on the bike, and basic pedaling drills #2 and #4. All together there are a total of 4 basic pedaling drills that should be performed with one leg.

As we've done in running, the pedaling drills are structured in the form of lessons in order to make your progression more comfortable and efficient.

Drill Set One: Balance — the basic sequence.

Introductory "balance" drills

Learning objectives: develop perception of balance on the pedals from every body position on the bike.

1a) *The Starting Pose* (Fig.35.1) Position #I Pedals at 3/9 o'clock, body in riding position with hips on the saddle and arms on aerobars (alternatively, hands on drops.)

Fig.35.1 Start in the cycling Pose on
your trainer.

Fig.35.2 Hips off the saddle, maintain
your balance.

The Drill (basic cycling drill #1)

While maintaining riding position, raise hips slightly so that hips are barely in contact with the saddle. Hold position for 10 seconds, repeat 5–10 times.

The Point

The objective here is to develop a kinesthetic awareness of what your body weight feels like balanced on the pedals, not planted on the saddle. Since efficient pedaling depends on weight transfer to the pedals, the more of your weight over the pedals, the greater potential you have for fast cycling.

1b) *The Starting Pose* (Fig.35.2) Position #III

Pedals at 3/9 o'clock, hips completely off the saddle, hands touching handlebars for balance only, with no weight on bars.

The Drill (basic cycling drill #1)

Balance with all your weight on the pedals, making every effort not to lean forward and put your weight on the bars or to rock back and sit on the saddle. Repeat until you feel like you've "got it."

The Point

Building on your awareness of what your body weight feels like on the pedals, you want to work on relaxing your body and minimizing muscular tension while staying balanced on the pedals. Unnecessary tension minimizes the fluidity that will make you a better pedaler.

1c) *The Starting Pose* (Fig.35.3) Position #IV

Pedals at 3/9 o'clock, hips off the saddle, hands off bars, weight distributed evenly on the two pedals.

The Drill (basic cycling drill #1)

The obvious next step from drill 1b, you try to remain balanced and relaxed on the pedals, while not lurching side to side or fore and aft.

The Point

As above, with even more body control. By now, you should have a good sense for what all of your weight feels like on the pedals, instead of a large percentage of that weight resting on the saddle and the bars.

Fig.35.3 Hips and hands off of support, maintain your balance.

Drill Set Two: Balance — the 3 O'clock, 1 O'clock sequence

Introductory "body weight application" to the pedals perception drills

Learning objectives: develop perception of the application of body weight to the pedals by executing the drills within a narrow range of the pedaling stroke. Keep your body weight supported on the BOF.

2a) *The Starting Pose* (Fig.35.4) Position #I
Pedals at 3/9 o'clock, hips on the saddle, hands touching bar tops for balance, with no weight on the bars.
The Drill (basic cycling drill #2)
Move the front foot from the 3 o'clock position up to 1 o'clock and back down to 3 o'clock without stopping. Start slowly and increase the speed of the drill as you get

comfortable. Do 20–30 repeats with one leg and then rotate the other leg to the front and repeat. Increase gear as you progress in this drill. The keys to the drill are to unweigh the rear pedal, when the front pedal gets to 1 o'clock and to not apply force to the front pedal, when it goes down.

Fig.35.4 Start in the cycling Pose on your trainer.

The Point
A lot is going on in this drill. If you unwittingly apply force on the downstroke, you will bounce on the pedals while going past the 3 o'clock point. You'll also sense how the leg works as a unit to transmit the body weight, with no dorsi or plantar flexion.
Immediately After the Drill
Assume an aero position and pedal the bike in a small gear, pedaling as fast as possible without making a huge physical effort. Note how your cadence is increased as you pedal without tension in your legs. Your legs should feel light on the pedals, even as your cadence increases.

2b) *The Starting Pose* (Fig.35.5) Position #II
Pedals at 3/9 o'clock, hips on the saddle, hands off bars.

Fig.35.6 Hips off the saddle, hands on bars, repeat 1 – 3 o'clock cycle.

Fig.35.5 Hips on the saddle, hands off bars, repeat 1 – 3 o'clock cycle.

The Point
Now you begin to develop a more acute awareness of where the work is performed in the pedaling rotation and how precise control and lack of muscular tension help you progress from wild flailing on the pedals to a much smoother, controlled and efficient pedal stroke.

Immediately After the Drill
As above, return to the aero position and pedal rapidly in an easy gear. Note how you feel more and more fluid as you control your efforts and minimize muscular tension.

The Drill (basic cycling drill #2)
Exactly like drill (2a), repeating the 3 o'clock/1 o'clock/3 o'clock cycle 20–30 times with one leg, then the other.

The Point
This drill provides you with the necessary awareness of the pedaling rotation and precise body weight application should be in order to preserve an efficient stroke.

2c) *The Starting Pose* (Fig.35.6) Position #III
Pedals at 3/9 o'clock, hips off the saddle, hands touching bar tops for balance only.

The Drill (basic cycling drill #2)
Exactly like drill (2a), repeating the cycle 20–30 times with one leg, then the other.

2d) *The Starting Pose* (Fig.35.7) Position #IV
Pedals at 3/9 o'clock, hips off the saddle, hands completely off bars.

The Drill (basic cycling drill #2)
Obviously, things are getting a little trickier here, as you repeat the 3 o'clock/1 o'clock/3 o'clock cycle in the "Look Ma, No Hands!" position.

Fig.35.7 *Hips off the saddle, hands off bars, repeat 1 – 3 o'clock cycle.*

The Point

Once again, it's not the muscular effort, it's the balance and weight transfer that propel the bike. Here you concentrate on keeping your weight over the pedals while your legs stay in the most efficient zone for pedaling.

Immediately After the Drill

As above, return to the aero position and pedal rapidly in an easy gear. By now, you should experience dramatic increases in pedal speed and fluidity.

Drill Set Three: Unweighing — the 180° sequence

Introductory "unweighing" perception drills

Learning objectives: develop perception of unweighing the back pedal as you apply your body weight to the front pedal. Given that the pedals are 180° degrees apart, it makes no sense to "push down" and "pull up" simultaneously. Focus on applying your body weight to the front pedal and unweighing the back pedal. Applying the body weight with the front and pulling up with the back foot doesn't make sense because you'd be canceling out your efforts. Thus our focus should be on transferring our body weight from one pedal stroke to the next. This and only this is the most critical aspect of cycling.

3a) *The Starting Pose* (Fig.35.8) Position #I Pedals at 3/9 o'clock, hips on the saddle, hands just touching bars for balance.

Fig.35.8 *Hips on the saddle, hands on bars, 3 – 9 o'clock (180°) cycle. Stop. Repeat.*

The Drill (basic cycling drill #3)

Rotate pedals exactly 180° degrees and come to a full stop, then perform another 180° degree rotation and stop. Start the drill in easy gears, using only your body weight to control the movement of your legs. Repeat the cycle 10–20 times per leg.

The Point

This drill teaches you precise control of your body weight on the pedals.

3b) *The Starting Pose* (Fig.35.9) Position #II Same as drill (3a), but now the hands are completely off the bars.

Fig.35.9 Hips on the saddle, hands off bars, 3 – 9 o'clock (180°) cycle. Stop. Repeat.

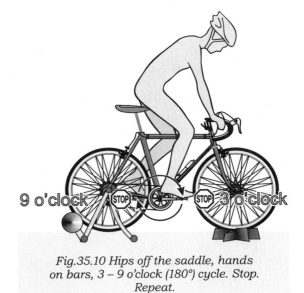

Fig.35.10 Hips off the saddle, hands on bars, 3 – 9 o'clock (180°) cycle. Stop. Repeat.

The Drill (basic cycling drill #3)

You need to perform the same 180° degree pedal rotations, with brief controlled stops at the 3 o'clock position every time, 10–20 repeats per leg.

The Point

It takes some mental efforts to keep precise performance with almost no support and absence of any feedback from muscular tension during pedaling.

3c) *The Starting Pose* (Fig.35.10) Position #III

Same as drill (3a) but now the hips come off the saddle.

The Drill (basic cycling drill #3)

Also like drill (3a), perform 180° degree pedal rotations, with brief controlled stops at the 3 o'clock position every time, 10–20 repeats per leg.

The Point

By now the point is this: you really can do this. With virtually no support and no 'muscling' of the pedals, you can control the application of your body weight to the pedals with tremendous precision.

3d) *Starting Pose* (Fig.35.11) Position #IV

Pedals at 3/9 o'clock, hips off the saddle, hands completelly off bars.

Fig.35.11 Hips off the saddle, hands off bars, 3 – 9 o'clock (180°) cycle. Stop. Repeat.

The Drill (basic cycling drill #3)
The same 180° degree pedal rotations, with brief controlled stops at the 3 o'clock position, 10–20 repeats per leg.
The Point
At this condition of balance perception of the body weight on pedals is the most important thing you can operate with.

Drill Set Four: Shifting the body weight/ unweighing — the double leg 360° sequence

Introductory "body weight shifting" drills

Learning objectives: develop the perception of shifting your body weight from one foot to the next within a full pedal stroke.

4a) *The Starting Pose* (Fig.35.12) Position #III
Pedals at 3/9 o'clock position, hips off the saddle, hands just touching bars with no weight on bars.

Fig.35.12 Hips off the saddle, hands on bars, 3 – 9 o'clock (360°) cycle. Stop. Repeat.

The Drill (basic cycling drill #4)
Focus on unweighing the rear foot to initiate the drill as you rotate the pedals 360° degrees, stopping exactly where you started. Repeat 20–30 times, then switch to other foot on 3 o'clock pedal and repeat 20–30 times.
The Point
You continue to hone your perception of body weight on the pedals as you get ever closer to reworked pedaling mechanics.

4b) *The Starting Pose* (Fig.35.13) Position #IV
Same as drill, (4a) only hands no longer contact the bars.

Fig.35.13 Hips off the saddle, hands off bars, 3 – 9 o'clock (360°) cycle. Stop. Repeat.

The Drill (basic cycling drill #4)
Same as above, only hold repeats on each lead leg to 10–20 times.

The Point

Once you've got it, you will contrast the stillness of your well–balanced upper body with the ease with which your legs spin the pedals. There is no up–and–down vertical oscillation of your body and the pedals appear to virtually spin on their own.

Immediately After this Drill

Get into the aero position, take a quick spin, and then continue with the next phase of the drill set.

4c) *The Starting Pose* (Fig.35.14) Position #III
Pedals at 3/9 o'clock position, hands balanced on bars, hips off the saddle.

The Drill (basic cycling drill #4)

Again, begin the drill by unweighing the rear pedal, but this time continue pedaling 20–30 rotations non–stop.

The Point

This should be the 'a–ha' moment, when all the fine–tuning of the previous drills manifests in a fluid, fast pedal stroke.

Fig.35.14 Hips off the saddle, hands on bars, 3 – 9 o'clock (360°) cycle 20–30 reps.

Immediately After this Drill

Get into the aero position, take a quick spin, and then continue with the next phase of the drill set.

4d) *The Starting Pose* (Fig.35.15) Position #IV
Pedals at 3/9 o'clock position, hips off the saddle, arms off bars.

Fig.35.15 Hips off the saddle, hands off bars, 3 – 9 o'clock (360°) cycle 20–30 reps.

The Drill (basic cycling drill #4)

Begin the drill by unweighing the rear pedal, but this time continue pedaling 20–30 rotations non–stop.

The Point

Reality check: you don't want to lose your sense of weight shifting and balance just because you're now pedaling complete strokes.

Immediately After this Drill

Get into the aero position, take a quick spin, and then continue with the next phase of the drill set. If you have a cadence counter on your cycle computer, you should see numbers well in excess of where you were when you first started these drills, numbers you might expect to see from a track sprinter, not a hard–core roadie or triathlete.

Drill Set Five: Advanced balance — the single leg sequence

Advanced level "balance" drills

Learning objectives: develop the perception of applying your body weight one foot at a time. This dramatic contrast should give you a heightened sense of support on the balls of your feet (Note: you will need cycling shoes that clip to the pedals to perform this drill with one leg).

5a) *The Starting Pose* (Fig.35.16) Position #I
The rear foot is released from the pedal and rests on the rear axle (or on conveniently placed stool next to the trainer), hips on the saddle, hands on bars, the front foot in the 3 o'clock position.

The Drill (basic cycling drill #2)
Repeat the 3 o'clock/1 o'clock/3 o'clock cycle with the drill foot, while maintaining balance. Then switch feet and repeat.

The Point
Isolating the key movement of the pedaling stroke, you learn how to precisely apply your body weight in a compact pedaling zone.

5b) *The Starting Pose* (Fig.35.17) Position #II
Same as drill (5a), except that now the hands come off the bars.

Fig.35.17 Hips on the saddle, hands off bars, repeat 1 – 3 o'clock cycle with one leg.

Fig.35.16 Hips on the saddle, hands on bars, repeat 1 – 3 o'clock cycle with one leg.

The Drill (basic cycling drill #2)
Repeat the 3 o'clock/1 o'clock/3 o'clock cycle with the drill foot, while maintaining balance. Then switch feet and repeat.

The Point

With unassisted balance, you learn the necessity of complete body control, with a "quiet" body and fluid leg movement channeling your body weight to the pedals.

Immediately After the Drill Set

As before, return to the aero position and pedal rapidly. You should continue to note a progression in your pedaling speed and efficiency.

Drill Set Six: Weight shifting/unweighing — the single leg 360° sequence

Advanced level "body weight shifting" drills

Learning objectives: develop the perception of the full stroke. That is — both the application of body weight as well as the unweighing of the foot. Focus on shifting your body weight towards your idle foot while in the latter part of your stroke.

6a) *The Starting Pose* (Fig.35.18) Position #I

Fig.35.18 Hips on the saddle, hands on bars, 3 o'clock (360°) cycle. Stop. Repeat with one leg.

Drill foot in the 3 o'clock position, the rear foot on the axel (or stool), hands barely touching the bars, hips on the saddle.

The Drill (basic cycling drill #4)

Rotate the drill foot exactly 360° degrees and come to a complete stop. Repeat 10–20 times and then switch legs. As much as possible, use only your body weight to achieve the pedal rotation.

The Point

Further fine-tuning of your perception of body weight on (and off) the pedal.

6b) *The Starting Pose* (Fig.35.19)

Same as drill (6a), except that the drill pedal is in the 1 o'clock position.

Fig.35.19 Hips on the saddle, hands on bars, 1 o'clock (360°) cycle. Stop. Repeat with one leg.

The Drill

Rotate the drill foot exactly 360° degrees and come to a complete stop. Repeat 10–20 times and then switch legs. As much as possible, use only your body weight to achieve the pedal rotation.

The Point

1 o'clock is where the weight transfer takes place; 3 o'clock is where you begin to unweigh from the drill pedal. Failure to begin the unweighing process will find you lurching forward, completely out of balance.

6c) *The Starting Pose* (Fig.35.20) Position #II Drill pedal at 3 o'clock, rear foot on the axel (or stool), hands completely off bars.

Fig.35.20 Hips on the saddle, hands off bars, 3 o'clock (360°) cycle. Stop. Repeat with one leg.

The Drill (basic cycling drill #4)

Rotate the drill pedal 360° degrees, coming to a complete stop in the original starting position. Repeat 10–20 times, and then switch legs.

The Point

It's all about maintaining balance, while focusing on shifting the body weight to rotate the pedal.

6d) *The Starting Pose* (Fig.35.21)

Same as above (4c), but with the drill pedal at 1 o'clock.

The Drill

Fig.35.21 Hips on the saddle, hands off bars, 1 o'clock (360°) cycle. Stop. Repeat with one leg.

Rotate the drill pedal 360° degrees, coming to a complete stop in the original starting position. Repeat 10–20 times, and then switch legs.

The Point

It's all about maintaining balance, while focusing on shifting the body weight to rotate the pedal.

Immediately After the Drill Set

Once again, resume the aero position and pedal at a high cadence without excess effort. Continue to focus on how easy it is to achieve and maintain high pedaling speed, while keeping your legs tension free.

Drill Set Seven: Full pedaling from multiple positions

Learning objectives: this is where we put it all together. At this point your perception should be finely tuned to the minute feedback of the pedals from different cycling positions.

The Starting Pose
Start from the Pose cycling position.
The Drill
Begin by bringing pedals up to a sufficiently high cadence (110–120 rpm) and begin changing positions without affecting cadence. Bring your hands off the bars and put them back. Come off of the saddle and back down. Experiment, but always stay focused on maintaining balance and pedaling speed.
The Point
By simulating actual riding and racing conditions, where you may frequently switch positions in reaction to terrain changes or race situations, you learn to stay focused on keeping your body weight on the pedals and maintaining your pedaling mechanics, no matter what is going on in the race.

In total there are seven sets of indoor drills, please view the table below.

Simple combinations of these sets can be broken into lessons as follows (Please note that every lesson should start with set 1 of the drills to reinforce your perception of balance on the pedals at the beginning of every lesson):

Lesson # 1 – set 1, set 2.
Lesson # 2 – set 1, set 3.
Lesson # 3 – set 1, set 4.
Lesson # 4 – set 1, set 5, set 6.
Lesson # 5 – set 1, set 7.

Given these lesson outlines, it does not mean that there cannot be other possible combinations of sets during your progression of skill development in pedaling. Combinations of sets could be used in any order

Sets of Cycling Drills
Set one — sequences of balance drills (1a, 1b and 1c).
Set two — sequences of pedaling drills from the 3 o'clock to the 1 o'clock positions (2a, 2b, 2c, 2d).
Set three — sequences of pedaling drills from the 3 to 9 o'clock positions 180° (3a, 3b, 3c, 3d).
Set four — sequences of pedaling drills from the 3 to 3 o'clock position 360° (4a, 4b, 4c, 4d).
Set five — sequences of one leg pedaling drills from the 3 to 1 o'clock positions (5a, 5b).
Set six — sequences of one leg pedaling drills from the 3 to 3 o'clock position 360° (6a, 6b, 6c, 6d).
Set seven — sequences of different cycling positions (7a) — integration.

you feel comfortable with, after which you should begin to develop your perception to help you decide for yourself, which drills you need go over in order to reacquaint yourself with a particular perception. As you get better and better at performing the drills, the natural progression would be to use harder gears for each of the drill sets. Another point you can continuously perfect while performing these drills is to constantly push the envelope and try to perform the drills as quickly as you can without loosing control of the action. There is plenty of room for improvement, take your time!

One thing I like to do when introducing the "Pose" technique to cyclists is to recommend that you perform these drills in regular running shoes, not cycling shoes. However, lets be clear on our definition of running shoes. Please do not wear anything with a sole thicker than 1 – 1.5 cm. In other words, wear racing flats or something comparable; thick padded shoes will not only hold your foot at an incorrect position, they will hinder your perception of support due to the layers upon layers of cushioning. Using lightweight racing flats allows us to avoid common incorrect cycling habits such as pulling the pedal up while the opposite foot is on the down stroke, the so called 360° degree stroke. When these bad habits or desires are eliminated, then it will be appropriate to use cycling shoes in order to move towards a higher quality and consistency of pedaling technique.

Outdoor drills come later in your skill development, when you've mastered the stationary pedaling drills so that their outdoor execution can be relatively safe. Nevertheless, I still recommend that you perform the major portion of your drill work on a stationary bike.

Outdoor Drills on the Bicycle

As you transfer these drills from the safe confines of your rec room or garage to the open road, you should continue to focus on the subtleties of balance and control. It's a good idea to start off every ride with a quick five–ten minute run–through of the drills as a part of your warm–up. This will reinforce your awareness of weight–shifting and the precise application of your body weight to the pedals. If you consciously bring these sensations to your mind at the outset of every ride, they will stay with your subconscious, as you focus on road conditions, tactics and physical effort.

A few things to bear in mind when you move outdoors with these drills...

Do the 1 o'clock/3 o'clock drills, while rolling along at a slow speed. Do the 180° degree drills while standing out of the saddle, with hands only touching bars for balance. To do the single leg drills, try resting the non–working foot on the rear skewer. If this doesn't feel comfortable, leave the foot attached to the pedal but let it remain passive while you concentrate on the drill foot. And, finally, don't get so absorbed in the drills that you forget you are on the open road, with real cars, motorcycles, pedestrians, dogs, cats and other cyclists all posing potential hazards. Stay safe!

Outdoor Drill Set One: Balance — the 3 O'clock, 1 O'clock sequence

1a) *The Starting Pose (Fig.35.22)*
Pedals at 3/9 o'clock, hips on the saddle, hands touching bar tops for balance, with no weight on the bars.
The Drill
Move the front foot from the 3 o'clock position up to 1 o'clock and back down to 3 o'clock without stopping. Do 20–30 repeats with one leg and then rotate the other leg to the front and repeat.

1b) *The Starting Pose (Fig.35.23)*
Pedals at 3/9 o'clock, hips off the saddle, hands touching bar tops for balance only.

Fig.35.22 Start from the cycling Pose.

Fig.35.23 Hips off the saddle, hands on bars, repeat 1 – 3 o'clock cycle.

The Drill

Exactly as above (1a), repeating the 3 o'clock/1 o'clock/3 o'clock cycle 20–30 times, first with one leg, then the other.

Outdoor Drill Set Two: Advanced balance — the single leg sequence

2) *The Starting Pose (Fig.35.24)*

The rear foot is released from the pedal and rests on the rear axle (or remains passive on the pedal), hips on the saddle, hands lightly on bars for balance, the front foot in the 3 o'clock position.

Fig.35.24 Hips on the saddle, hands on bars, repeat 1 – 3 o'clock cycle with one leg.

The Drill

Repeat the 3 o'clock/1 o'clock/3 o'clock cycle with the drill foot while maintaining balance. Then switch feet and repeat.

Outdoor Drill Set Three: Unweighing — the 180° sequence

3a) *The Starting Pose (Fig.35.25)*
Pedals at 3/9 o'clock, hips on the saddle, hands just touching bars for balance.

Fig.35.25 Hips on the saddle, hands on bars, 3 – 9 o'clock (180°) cycle. Stop. Repeat.

The Drill
Rotate pedals exactly 180° degrees and come to a full stop, then perform another 180° degree rotation and stop. Start the drill in easy gears, using only your body weight to control the movement of your legs. Repeat the cycle 10–20 times per leg.

3b) *The Starting Pose*
Same as above (3a), but now the hips come off the saddle.
The Drill
Also as above, perform 180° degree pedal rotations, with brief controlled stops at the 3 o'clock position every time, 10–20 repeats per leg.

Outdoor Drill Set Four: Weight shifting/unweighing — the single leg 360° sequence

Fig.35.26 Hips off the saddle, hands on bars, 3 – 9 o'clock (180°) cycle. Stop. Repeat.

4a) *The Starting Pose*
Drill foot in the 3 o'clock position, the rear foot on axle (or passive), hands barely touching bars, hips on the saddle.

Fig.35.27 Hips on the saddle, hands on bars, 3 o'clock (360°) cycle. Stop. Repeat with one leg.

The Drill

Rotate the drill foot exactly 360° degrees and come to a complete stop. Repeat 10–20 times and then switch legs. As much as possible, use only your body weight to achieve the pedal rotation.

4b) *The Starting Pose*

Same as above (4a), except that the drill pedal is in the 1 o'clock position.

Fig.35.28 Hips on the saddle, hands on bars, 1 o'clock (360°) cycle. Stop. Repeat with one leg.

The Drill

Rotate the drill foot exactly 360° degrees and come to a complete stop. Repeat 10–20 times and then switch legs. As much as possible, use only your body weight to achieve the pedal rotation.

Outdoor Drill Set Five: Weight shifting/unweighing — the double leg 360° sequence

5a) *The Starting Pose*

Pedals at 3/9 o'clock position, hips off the saddle, hands just touching bars with no weight on bars.

Fig.35.29 Hips off the saddle, hands on bars, 3 – 9 o'clock (360°) cycle. Stop. Repeat.

The Drill

Focus on unweighing the rear foot to initiate the drill, as you rotate the pedals 360° degrees, stopping exactly where you started. Repeat 20–30 times, then switch to other foot on 3 o'clock pedal and repeat 20–30 times.

Outdoor Drill Set Six: Weight shifting/balance — full rotation pedaling

6a) *The Starting Pose*

Hands balanced on bars, pedals at 3/9 o'clock position, hips off saddle.

The Drill

Start in your easiest gear on the big chain ring (i.e. 53/23). Begin the drill by unweighing on the 9 o'clock pedal and pedal for 10 seconds at a cadence of 80 rpm. Without stopping, click through the gears, maintaining the same cadence for 10 seconds in each gearing, until you get to the 53/15 or until you can't maintain the same cadence without your heart rate jumping. Go back to the 53/21 and start over, working through the progression again. If you can get through all the gears without substantial heart rate increase, then try the sequence with a cadence of 90 rpm. Over time, you should work your way up to 110 or even 120 rpm as you adapt to your new pedaling mechanics.

After the drill
Sit down on the saddle, resume the aero position, put the bike in an easy gear and go as fast as possible without making a huge effort. Once again, note how your cadence increases as your release tension from your legs. Now you're ready to ride!

Fig.35.30 Hips off the saddle, hands on bars, 3 – 9 o'clock (360°) cycle 20–30 reps non–stop.

The Point
This little drill represents the application of all that you have learned in your adaptation to a new pedaling style. As you work your way through bigger gears and higher cadences, you'll see that precise application of body weight trumps brute force every time.

CHAPTER 36
PEDALING THE BICYCLE

*Somebody showed it to me
and I found it by myself.*

— *Lew Welch*

Having now progressed through the pedaling drills in the preceding chapter, it's time to return to the central issue: how do you determine the optimum gear/cadence combination for the best possible performance? That's really what you want to know, right? Surprisingly, the answer derives not from a complex calculation, but from a simple test.

This test requires that you put on your bike shoes, put your bike on the trainer and clip in. Cycling clothes are not necessary. Spin the pedals a few times, just to get comfortable and then come out of the saddle with your weight evenly distributed on the pedals in the three and nine o'clock positions (Fig.36.1). Gently bounce up and down a few times, flexing your knees but staying off the saddle.

As you do this, focus on the tension you feel in your legs as you stop bouncing and maintain a 'ready' position just off the saddle — hands on the drops, knees flexed, body weight balanced. Do it again and really feel the level of muscular tension. Developing an awareness of that level of tension is the key to knowing what gears and cadence to ride, because that is the level of

muscular tension you want to maintain as you pedal the bike.

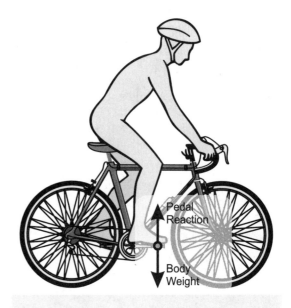

Fig.36.1 Body weight on the pedals.

With this proprioceptive fix on what it should feel like to pedal with optimum muscular tension, you can begin to hone in on the gear/cadence combinations that work for you in each cycling situation. The keys to this process are pretty basic. From any given riding situation, increasing your cadence will draw more on your cardiovascular fitness, while increasing the gear will tax your muscular strength.

In both racing and training, there are short and long–term implications to your choices. Further, even your specific event may greatly affect your pedaling strategy. For example, a mass start road racer riding in a large peloton may elect one gear/cadence strategy for a given course, while a triathlete riding the same course may employ a completely different strategy... and both may be right. The difference, of course, is that the road racer knows his event is over at the finish of the ride, while the triathlete still needs his legs for the run that follows.

A telling example of this came at the Men's Triathlon at the Athens Olympics in 2004. While the 40–km distance of the triathlon cycling leg is relatively minor, the surprisingly hilly (Fig.36.2) and tough route made great demands on the triathletes who were basically in sprint mode for the entire ride. Many were the talented runners who rode

Fig.36.2 Athens's Olympic Triathlon cycling leg.

too large gears at lower cadences, particularly on the challenging climbs. Once on the run, instead of charging to the front, they found their legs were trashed from pushing the big gears and their performances suffered accordingly. Had these talented racers trained themselves to pedal higher cadences in smaller gears, it's likely that they would have been fresher for the run.

In general, it's safe to say, riders at all levels pedal at cadences that are too low. With the evolution of gearing to the point where 10–speed rear cassettes are all but standard, we have come to equate pushing big gears with going fast. Obviously, in the theoretical world, that is the case. Pushing the biggest gear with the fastest cadence delivers the highest speed. But, just as obviously, limitations due to human and environmental factors require that each rider develop his own pedaling profile. A cyclist with the heart/lung capacity of a hummingbird and the leg strength of overcooked pasta will gravitate to small gears and high cadences while the rider with tower of power legs and underdeveloped cardiovascular system will grind it out on the bigger gears.

And this brings us back to the previously mentioned choices in training and racing. Human nature being what it is, the hummingbird will probably do off–season training at high cadences and dance up as many climbs as possible, while the tower of power will sail along the flats at high speeds and low cadences.

Of course, both should follow the adage 'train your weakness and race your strength'. The hummingbird should focus on gaining leg strength, whether it's in the gym or on the open road, while the tower of power should deliberately spend time polishing his pedaling skills at vastly higher cadences, perhaps even putting in time on a velodrome.

If both pursue this strategy, they will be more complete and competitive racers, but the advantage will go to the tower of power. Why? Because there's more opportunity for improvement in the cardiovascular system than there is in strength development. Power is more of an innate quality, the result of genes and bone structure, while fitness is more trainable.

That being the reality, it's time to take a look at the case for higher cadences. First, as just indicated, there is more room for improvement in the speed and technique of pedaling than there is in the development of pure strength. Second, pedaling smaller gears at higher cadences creates less muscular tension and hence can be continued for longer distances. And third, maintaining higher cadences in smaller gears makes it easier to react to race situations, no matter whether the race at hand is pure cycling or triathlon.

The classic illustration of the latter point is the superb cyclist, Jan Ullrich. A champion many times over, Ullrich is the classic tower of power cyclist. Give him a road to the Moon and he could likely climb there, maintaining the same metronomic pace. Unfortunately for him, that metronomic pace is on the slow side, as he is known for pushing giant gears.

That may have won him an Olympic time trial gold medal, but in the Tour de France he has never been able to react to the attacks of faster pedaling riders on the highest climbs. He'll be in the final selection, riding with the elite riders, but when the rapid bursts of acceleration come from his competitors, he's never able to hold their wheels. In his huge gears, he keeps soldiering up the mountain — and often catches the over-ambitious attackers — but he's never able to spring a winning move.

But the downside of over-gearing can be an equal plague to the most talented tri-athletes. While most tri-riders consider the cycling leg to be a steady-state maximum effort, most triathlon courses are full of situations where the ability to react and accelerate is crucial.

Every corner, every climb, every change of wind direction can create a situation where time is lost due to the athlete being caught in too large a gear. Any time the muscular tension exceeds that level illustrated at the beginning of this chapter — that feeling you get when you're out of the saddle and balanced on the pedals — is a moment when valuable time is lost. Get caught in a gear bigger than you can 'spin up' quickly and you might as well have the brakes on. Furthering the problem is the inevitable sprint to gain back the lost time. This increases the muscular tension, draws down your energy reserve and only makes things worse.

Going back to road racing sharpens the focus of this effect. In a four-corner criterium of only 25 laps, there may be 100 acceleration opportunities. A racer who rides in too large a gear will continually bog down coming out of every one of those corners and then be forced to sprint to get back onto the back of the group. After several repeats of these efforts, the inevitable happens and the racer is dropped.

The irony is that instead of learning to ride smaller gears at higher cadences, the rider will think "I've just got to get stronger," and continue to train on those huge gears instead of adopting a style that is more suited to quick acceleration.

The same thought process is only magnified with triathletes. Absent the obvious growing gap that a criterium rider sees between him — or herself coming out of every corner, the triathlete may not even be aware of where time is being lost and even more readily reach the same conclusion: "I've just got to get stronger."

CHAPTER 37
PEDALING FASTER

We think in generalities, but we live in detail.
— Alfred North Whitehead

Learning to ride at higher cadences requires self–discipline and focus, but the rewards can be substantial. As with any new technique, the off–season is the ideal time to start, but you can start the gradual shift toward faster pedaling at any time. Bear in mind that the idea isn't just to pedal faster, but to pedal more precisely and focus your efforts on making the most of the force moment.

It may help at the start to separate yourself from your regular training group and do some solo rides where you can rid yourself of the competitive urges that inevitably arise when training with a group. It's even better if you can find a flat road with minimal traffic. Finally, as you begin your work to transition to higher cadences, adopt a mental framework consistent with learning, not training. Don't concern yourself with mileage or speed, just concentrate on pedaling technique.

In the best of all worlds, your bike will be equipped with a computer that measures both cadence and heart rate. If not, at least try to get something on the handlebars so you can easily count your pedal strokes in 15–second increments and multiply by four to get a reliable cadence count.

Begin the process by pedaling in the small ring on a gear like 39–21. With your hands on the drops, start out at a relatively slow cadence and gradually increase your pedaling speed until you're in the 110–120 range and hold it there while you thoroughly analyze your form. Are you bouncing on the saddle? Are you 'chasing' the pedals? Do you feel a lot of muscular tension or a little? Can you feel the force of your downstroke right through your shoe on the ball of your foot? Is your upper body relaxed or tense?

These same few questions will be your guide throughout your entire adaptation to a new pedaling style and will continue to be with you throughout your cycling career.

For many cyclists used to pedaling in the 80–90 cadence range, saddle bounce can be the hardest problem to overcome. Assuming proper bike positioning, the problem can be very annoying and the usual fix — moving into a bigger gear to smooth out the stroke — is the wrong one. Why? It's really pretty simple. The bounce is caused by ground reaction force, meaning that the cyclist continues to apply downward pressure to the pedal past the four o'clock position all the way down to six o'clock. Continuing that pressure to the bottom of the stroke forces your body weight to bounce away from the ground, hence the hop off the saddle.

So, if the bigger gear helps smooth out the ride, why not go with it? What happens with the bigger gear is that the rider is not strong enough to persist with downward force past four o'clock, the ground reaction force disappears and the bounce goes away. The problem is that the cadence also slows and you're right back where you started, pedaling too big a gear at too slow a cadence.

The way to handle saddle bounce is to stop pedaling, relax and review what you were doing when the bounce started. While continuing the forceful downstroke past the four o'clock point in the pedal arc is no doubt the cause of the bounce, there are likely to be other contributing factors. Cause number one is usually just trying too hard. Neophytes naturally believe that pedaling fast requires great effort and they often 'tense up' their entire bodies, making a great show of physical effort.

Along with this, many riders will straighten their arms against the drops, thus transmitting every last bit of bounce into the front wheel and making the situation worse.

Fast pedaling actually is facilitated by great fluidity, the opposite of muscular tension. The arms should be slightly bent, with hands resting lightly on the drops. The upper body should be very relaxed, almost completely cut off from the legs, which are free to transmit the subtly shifting body weight to the pedals without a visible show of force.

Having taken the time to ponder the bounce, start pedaling again and gradually increase the cadence. As you approach the cadence rates where you generally start feeling the bounce, take special care to feel the force being applied to the pedal through the ball of your foot. As you hone in on that feeling, it's helpful to think of the analogy of the hammer.

Earlier, we had mentioned of cyclists who just go out and 'hammer', but when you think of the precision with which a master carpenter drives a nail, the analogy makes sense. Most of us just bang away at a nail until we get the job done, but a professional carpenter usually uses one or two light taps to set the nail and a then a single strike to drive it in. When the carpenter makes initial contact with the nail head, the hammer is just slightly above parallel to the ground, placing the hammerhead roughly in the two o'clock position. Maximum power is applied at three o'clock, the greatest force moment, and by four o'clock, the nail is driven and the hammerhead is already moving back away from the surface. Continuing the downstroke would just cause the hammerhead to bang into — and damage — the wood surface. You can call that a very visible manifestation of ground reaction force.

So now, as you approach 'bouncing' speed, concentrate on unweighing from the pedal at the three o'clock position. Don't drive the nail further into the wood than it needs to go. Just apply the necessary force and move onto the next pedal. It may take a while and the process can be frustrating at times, but soon you'll experience that transcendent moment when you truly comprehend that pedal speed and force application are two independent concepts. Once you get past that hurdle, you'll be able to pedal at astonishingly high cadences without bouncing all over the place. At that point, you will be ready to go from learning to pedal at higher cadences to training at higher cadences, the next step on your way to becoming a more effective cyclist.

While there is a variety of training intervals effective in increasing the size of the gear you can pedal at higher cadences, you first have to find your current base, the gear/cadence combination that your present fitness and strength supports. The key indicators are the level of muscular tension and your exercise heart rate.

Over the course of several training rides, work through this progression: start with a gear that you can pedal at 115–120 cadence without pushing your heart rate anywhere near the red zone. After three to five minutes, with your heart rate settled in, drop your rear chain sprocket down one ring and continue pedaling at the same cadence. If you can continue at the same cadence without your heart rate 'blowing up' repeat the process and drop down another ring.

Conversely, if you drop down a gear and can't hold your cadence above 110, then retrench and go back to the last gear that you could maintain. That's your base gear. From there you can start working intervals into slightly bigger gears until your strength and cardiovascular system can handle the greater workload. Now you're on the road to assimilating your new style of riding.

One of the most basic interval sets for training at higher cadences is a version of the exercise you used to discover your base gear. Similar to a treadmill step test, this exercise lasts about 20 minutes, depending on your fitness level. After a suitable warm–up, start out in a gear you can easily pedal between 110 & 120 rpm. Ride that gear for two minutes and shift to the next hardest gear. Ride another two minutes and drop it down again.

Keep progressing gears until you hit the gear where you simply can't hold above 110 cadence — but don't stop there. Simply shift back to the previous gear and pedal for two minutes and then try the harder gear again, focusing on maintaining a cadence over 110 as long as you can. This quickly becomes a very difficult challenge, as you are training at the intersection of the limits of your physical strength and

your cardiovascular capabilities. When you reach the point where you back of a gear and still can't maintain 110+, back way off and pedal easily until you recover.

While you do this, keep a close eye on your heart rate. If you don't recover to under 120 beats per minute in less than 1:30, you're done for the day. Just pedal easily home and mark it down as a good session. If you do recover in less than 1:30, give it another go. You can do up to three of these sets without overdoing it as long as you recover in the allotted 1:30.

Hill intervals are a special treat and should be a weekly feature of your training regimen. They are particularly useful when you are first learning the higher cadence style of pedaling because they will quickly expose any flaws that could be disguised on the flats. To begin, select a nice incline of 3%–6% where you can pedal for one to two minutes without topping out the climb.

Select a gear that you think you can pedal between 110 and 120 rpm up the climb and start back on the flats so that it takes you about 30 seconds to hit the base of the climb. When you hit the climb, don't change a thing. Don't tense up. Don't try harder. Just keep pedaling fluidly. Watch your cadence carefully. If you drop below 110, drop down a gear and keep going. Make your first couple of intervals 60 seconds, including the run–up on the flats. Before you progress to longer intervals, work your way up a couple of gears. When you find your limit in gear size, start working on the length of the interval. Over the weeks, you'll gradually increase both your strength and the ability to sustain the pace over longer hills. As with the previous interval set, always monitor your recovery heart rate. Any time you can't recover to under 120 beats in less than 1:30, you're done with the day's hard work.

Whether you are a sprinter, a climber or a triathlete, everyone can benefit from some excruciatingly hard sprint intervals. The idea here is to do a set of hard efforts ranging from 15 to 30 seconds. Select a suitable gear (in the big ring), get the bike moving easily and then jump hard, winding it up to a cadence of between 110 and 120. If you find you're going way over 120 or you're able to hold the cadence for more than 30 seconds, you're not in a big enough gear. Keep working your way up in gears until you find one where you have to summon every bit of strength to wind up the cadence and every bit of cardiovascular power (not to mention willpower) to sustain the tempo for the full 30 seconds.

These three types of intervals — endurance, hills and sprints — can form the basis of your training. Feel free to develop your own variations that fit the terrain and conditions of your ride. One great twist on the endurance theme is to trade two–minute pulls with a training partner. This allows you to never drop off the cadence or the gear size, but still recover on the wheel of your partner. You can even adapt this set for riders of different fitness levels — one rider does a two–minute pull, the other stays in front for only a minute, but both benefit.

After you've thoroughly adapted to your new pedaling style, return to your local peloton and see how you fit in. Be vigilant not to revert to your old ways and just stick it in a huge gear when the pace gets fast. Instead, play around a little bit. Let a gap open up and notice how quickly you can close it. Sit near the back on the approach to a climb and see how many riders you pass, particularly near the top when overgearing will slow many of the pack down. See how quickly you can come out of corners and how easy it is to stay at the front instead of having to suffer just to stay attached.

On corners and turnarounds you just need to drop gears to the easiest one before the turn and start with high cadence after turning around with softly shifting gears back to the harder one while gaining the speed. Doing so you are saving your leg's muscles from extensive tension and overwork.

In all situations, you should become a quicker, more responsive rider. And you will find your post–ride recovery much easier. Not only will you be more fit, but you'll find that you're not as 'trashed' after a long hard ride.

The final test, of course, will be competition. Again, whether your event is a road race, a criterium, a time trial or a triathlon, you'll need to concentrate until your new pedaling style is truly second nature. Road racers will find that sitting in the group and crossing gaps to attacks is easier and their ability to figure in the final sprint is much improved. Time trialists will pick up time in all the rights places — turnarounds, corners, and hills — and reach new personal bests. Triathletes will record better times and have more left for the run... and that's what it's all about.

CHAPTER 38
ERRORS IN PEDALING AND THEIR CORRECTION

To lose is to learn.

— *Anonymous*

What's the best way to learn something?

That's an easy one: just make mistakes — and correct them. It might be trite to say it, but we learn best when we learn from our mistakes. The key of course, is to recognize the mistake so that you can, in fact, correct it.

This is a particularly vexing challenge when you're trying to learn a new skill from a book or a video. Without a second set of eyes in the form of a coach or a training partner, it takes tremendous focus and understanding to recognize errors and take the appropriate corrective action to perfect your technique.

The first requirement in refining your cycling technique is to have a standard to which your performance can be compared. This standard is the Pose Method and it's vital to understand the breadth of errors that can be corrected against the Pose standard. There are errors in time, space and effort; errors in comprehension and perception; errors of body position and application of body weight.

In a sense it can be a comfort to know that there is a standard against which to measure your efforts. If you were trying to learn a complex sport like pole vaulting, for example, without the aid of either a teacher or a textbook, you could flounder around forever, always saying to yourself, "I don't know what I'm doing wrong." And without being able to understand your errors, your learning curve would be steep and slow.

By having a standard, you immediately have a priority list you can use to identify and rectify your mistakes. The first step is to identify the cause of the error: is it created by a lack of understanding, undeveloped perception, insufficient muscular strength or physical ability, or perhaps by wasted physical effort?

In Pose cycling, the first measure by which errors are identified is the degree to which your body weight is applied to the pedals. This absolutely defines everything in your pedaling technique. All errors in cycling technique can be traced to inefficient application of body weight to the pedals. It's a two–way street: errors reduce the degree to which your weight is applied to the pedals and rob you of power; correcting the errors increases the weight applied to the pedals and adds power.

Your technique in pedaling a single stroke is the basis of the production of power, cadence, a smooth stroke, the expenditure of energy and so on... any other mistakes or errors arise out of your pedaling technique and can be corrected through it.

So the main errors in cycling are (in order of priority): mental, psycho–emotional, anatomo–physiological and mechanical; but all of them are related in one way or another with the application of your body weight to the pedal through:

- lack of muscular strength;
- wrong body position;
- incorrect application of body weight to the pedal in relation to space and time;
- misunderstanding of the muscular effort in weight application;
- wrong perception of efforts and body weight application;
- wrong focus and attention; and,
- wrong action.

To simplify matters, we can classify these errors into the following groups:

Strength Errors

Muscular strength is obviously an important part of developing an efficient pedaling stroke; there's no argument there. But there is a limit to how it should be used. Essentially, we only use our muscular abilities when we are able to apply our body weight to the pedals.

This can be difficult to comprehend, and if so, it is necessary to review Chapter Three and the discussion on the Gravity–mass–body weight–muscular efforts relationship. Essentially it can be summarized as this: we are only as strong as we are skilled in using our body weight, because our mus-

cles act as transmitters of this body weight in any movement.

Positional Errors

Body position is constantly influencing your ability to apply your body weight to the pedal and the amount of drag created through your aerodynamics. So if your position on the bike is limiting both your ability to apply your body weight to the pedal as well as your aerodynamics, you are creating problems for yourself on two fronts — committing a double sin, if you like.

To eliminate any excessive air resistance or drag, the body position you adopt should not include overly rotated elbows (inward or outward) or an open upper body, but should be as compact as possible. Particular attention should be paid to the position of the saddle (vertically, as well as fore and aft) as well as the handlebar and the cleat positions. Any errors in the positioning of these elements can be corrected by checking the proper bike set up in Chapter 39.

All this talk about body weight and the correct position to apply it to the pedals might have left you confused about where exactly to *place* your body weight. As you sit on your bike you can probably feel some weight on your saddle, some on your pedals and a little on your handlebars. But where should you direct it? More to the saddle where it feels it wants to go? More to the handlebars to take some of the effort off your legs? You could be excused for not getting this exactly right first off.

In everyday cycling or touring, people take the comfort option of putting most of their weight on the saddle. Unfortunately, this "comfort" doesn't equal performance; the more weight you have on the saddle, the less you can apply to the pedals, where you really need it. Unless you can apply your body weight to the pedal, and effectively change support from one pedal to the other, then all your muscular efforts will be in vain.

Another common deviation from the Pose standard in cycling is to put your body weight on the handlebars, loading up your arms and shoulders. You know the habit — your lungs are burning, your thighs are throbbing, so to take a little load off them you lean forward onto the bars in an effort to give your legs a "rest." It's a self–preservation reaction of the body, but one that comes at a high price — a dramatic reduction in your pedaling power. At the same time you start loading up the upper body — creating a new basis for fatigue.

Your clips are in the wrong position if they don't allow you to apply your optimal body weight to the pedal. Any position which prohibits the optimal application of body weight is considered an error. When people start talking about "X legs" and "O legs" or other shapes, ask them: "What's the difference?" Gravity doesn't make that distinction and will act on you in exactly the same way — no matter how you hold your legs. You can point your clips overly inward or outward, but either way you still have to put you body weight on the pedal at the right time and remove it just the same. The configuration of your clips simply needs to allow you to do this on time, every time.

Pedaling Errors

Pedaling should be your main focus — getting your technique down pat and correcting any mistakes. As mentioned in previous chapters, your body weight needs to be applied (thinking of a clockwise face) on the front pedal from one to four o'clock during each 360° degree stroke. Depending on cadence of pedaling, gears used, mental, psycho–emotional, and physical stress (fatigue), it is very easy to miss applying your weight to the pedal in this narrow zone, which is only a quarter of the space/time of one pedaling rotation.

Considering how small this "target" becomes with higher cadence and increasing fatigue, it's clear just how difficult it is to put your body weight on the pedal on time. Gears and cadence, as mechanical factors, are power production mechanisms related with the degree of the body weight used in each pedaling stroke. Gears are a reflection of how much body weight is being applied and cadence is a measure of how often this portion of the body weight is used. So any corrections to your pedaling technique need to include developing a much higher perception of how to apply your body weight to the pedal during this "target" zone.

At this point you're probably wondering how — or even where — to start developing this perception. Bear with us, it's not too difficult.

The most obvious indicator of this application of your body weight comes from the pressure you feel on the ball of your foot during this brief part of the pedaling cycle. You should feel your body weight on the pedal between one and four o'clock, but only during this brief period. If you notice pressure on the ball of your foot before or after this zone, for example at 12 o'clock or 6 o'clock, then it's a sign that you're missing the right application time. Take a look at your gears and cadence; with the pressure on the ball of the foot through the 12 to 6 o'clock zone, it's a sign of using too hard a gear and too slow a cadence. Check your quads — if there's undue tension in these muscles then, there's no doubt about it.

The right cadence and gearing will result in no tension in your quadriceps and will be evidenced in quick pressure appearing and disappearing on the balls of your feet during the pedaling stroke. This kind of perception or feeling should be present no matter what the terrain — yes, even climbing the toughest mountains!

Perception Errors

One of the main errors in this area is that we have an **uncertain perception** of what it should feel like to apply our body weight at the right time and we therefore miss it. How do you correct this error? All your focus needs to hone in on getting a feel for applying your body weight to the pedal in this zone. You should have no doubts as to what this feels like. Review your pedaling drills which help you to develop a feeling of the pressure on the ball of your foot at the specific zone and then immediately release this feeling by unweighing the pedal.

For most cyclists this is a weird feeling — and goes against all the conventional theory of pedaling, where a lot of effort is applied to the pedal. But you have to remember that improvement can only come through change, and this change is about developing the elements of good technique, which will lead to higher levels of performance. This is a conscious choice you are making to become a better cyclist and not following the same method you have always used, which might feel comfortable, but leads to inferior results.

Errors in Effort

Another major error is to apply **muscular effort,** instead of your *body weight* to the pedal. This relates to a common misunderstanding of the role of your muscles. It's very important to be clear here: you do not produce a rotation of your pedal by applying muscular effort. You can apply effort to this task, but that's not what produces the rotation. It is — and can only ever be — rotated through the application of body weight to the pedal. Your muscles are merely *transmitters* of that body weight — they are the postmen that deliver the message to the pedal, not the message (weight) itself.

Any effort you feel in your muscles is only there to support the application of your body weight to the pedal. Many people attempt to apply extra effort by extending their knee — and it looks like this should be done — but it's an illusion. You can't use that extra effort, because the pedal is moving away from you and you are going nowhere in relation to it. It would be like trying to kick a passing car — you can't apply any force to it and all muscular effort would be empty, wasted. As our friend Newton explains through his Third Law of Motion: if two masses of different magnitude interact, they must have either different speed to equalize each other or similar masses have to have similar speed. Effectively, the pedal is canceling out any efforts you attempt to apply to it.

The first thing you need to be clear on is just how much effort you need in order to transmit your body weight to the pedals perfectly. Too much, and you create "empty" pedaling, just as you might in steep downhill riding. Too little, and you end up with too much tension. The standard for the development of this perception is the amount of tension it requires to hold your body weight on the pedals at three and nine o'clock, while off the saddle. The feeling that you have in the balls of your feet and your muscles at this point is the feeling of one body weight — your own *one body weight*. This is the standard for how much muscular effort you need. No more than this! No matter how fast you are going, this is the amount of tension that you need to apply to transmit your weight to the pedal.

There are two exceptions to this rule, when you can apply more than one body weight to the pedal. In both cases, you are pedaling 'off the saddle', either during uphill climbing or sprinting/accelerating. At these times, your body is moving up and down and thus can deliver more than one body weight to the pedals.

And remember — it's your body weight which does the work on the pedal. Any extra efforts will show themselves up — particularly during hard pedaling — as tension and fatigue and ultimately, soreness. It's not easy to develop this perception, but remember that you are working to develop a *skill* and it is through becoming a more skillful technician that you will become a better cyclist.

Mental Errors

So it should be clear by now that it would be the **wrong focus and attention** to think about how to apply more muscle to your cycling — because your muscles can only transmit whatever body weight is available. It's a common mistake among triathletes and cyclists, who mistakenly think that improvement comes through strength. It's a seductive illusion, because it looks like the right approach. But if you go back to Chapter 3, you'll remember how muscles are only servants of body weight and without body weight, there is no muscular involvement. End of illusion.

Which only leaves **mental errors** — those mistakes related with the wrong understanding of the mechanical and biomechanical laws of force production and application. Thinking that we can produce "additional" efforts above or beyond our body weight is quite a common approach. The popular idea, for example, that you could improve your pedaling stroke by pulling the pedal backward and upward ("scraping") has no scientific support or foundation even in basic mechanics. Any such concepts need to be dropped from your mental repertoire entirely.

Mental errors are also a result of our focus and psycho–emotional condition. The variety of factors that go into making up our condition create a diverse and complex range of mental errors. So in looking at these issues, it is important to keep in mind all of these diversities and complexities in order to understand the logical sequences of them and their input into the error we want to address. You must identify which mental factor, belief or misperception is the biggest contributor to your error, because correction of this error will be largely dependent on correction of this factor. So the final point of correction of errors and beginning point of identifying them is to find the point at which the deviation from the standard occurs.

Just the Action

It is this point, which brings us back to the correction of **wrong actions**. It is about which action to do and not to do. Do we need to push the pedal or not? In Pose, the answer is not to do, which goes against conventional pedaling theory, with all this scraping and pulling up movement to create the illusion of improving the pedaling stroke and increasing power, etc.

The first and last thing you must understand is that all of these "actions" are impossible to do. The second thing is that all this excess doing has no positive effect on your pedaling stroke. If you accept the leading role of gravity, which we have been at pains to point out, then you also must accept that these actions are futile. And it is this understanding that will form the basis of correcting all your errors in cycling.

CHAPTER 39
BIKE SET–UP

*Before anything else, preparation
is the key to success.*

— *Alexander Graham Bell*

Do you remember what happened the first time you were 'fitted' for a bicycle? If your experience is typical, once you picked out the color of bike you wanted, you were instructed to straddle the top tube with both feet on the ground. If the clearance was sufficient, the bike was deemed to be your size. With females, the absence of a top tube in most 'girl's bikes' made the fitting process a little more problematic, but a quick eyeball measurement by the salesmen was all it took to verify the correct size.

We've come a long way since those days, but the matter of bike fit and set up remains very much subject to the whims or closely held beliefs of the personnel in the shop where you do business. You may fall under the spell of an 'old school' mechanic who does everything by eyeball, intuition and experience or you may enter the realm of a shop that has invested heavily in a high–tech fit system. In either case, you may wind up being perfectly situated on your bicycle... or you may find yourself in a position that is just enough 'off' that it will cause loss of power or — even worse — severe problems in the knees, the back, the hips, the neck or the ankles.

The one certainty is that proper bike fit and set–up is vital to your performance on the bike. Evidence of this can be found in the top Tour de France contenders who make annual pilgrimages to do wind–tunnel testing and refine their positions on both time trial frames, as well as regular road frames.

While you may not have the means to go to such extremes, you still want to make sure that you are properly situated on your bike... and you want to do it sooner rather than later. The reason the pros do it off–season is so that they have loads of time to adapt to their new position on the bike. The last thing they want to do is make a significant change to their positions when the real racing season looms.

What's The Objective?

While it's obvious that you want the correct set–up, you first have to determine the most important factors that have to be satisfied to achieve that perfect set–up. The obvious first step is to determine the proper frame size with a somewhat more sophisticated approach than the old top tube straddle.

On this topic there is no shortage of advice. By visiting the website at http://www.

cyclemetrics.com/Pages/FitLinks/bike fit_links.htm you can find an exhaustive list of links to bicycle set-up advice by a wide range of cycling authorities ranging from great cyclists like three-time Tour de France winner, Greg Lemond, to bike designers like Keith Bontrager and a 'master bike fitter' like Serotta Cycles' Paul Levine.

Virtually all of these experts are immensely qualified and have dedicated years or even decades to all aspects of the cycling experience. In general, all these experts agree that the correct bicycle set-up will maximize a cyclist's energy efficiency, comfort and performance potential.

The variables to be adjusted to achieve these objectives include:

1) Frame size
2) Saddle height
3) Fore & aft seat position
4) Stem length
5) Upper body position
6) Cleat position

As you scan through the various philosophies and guidelines for proper bike set-up, you will come across different schools of thought. Though all have in common the above-mentioned objective of "maximizing a cyclist's energy efficiency, comfort and performance potential," you find plenty of disagreement about how that is to be accomplished.

While there is a wealth of information from coaches, riders, scientists and specialists, what seems to be missing is a unifying guidance according to which informed decisions about bike set-up could be made. In scientific jargon, this would be a system of reference that would render much more useful all the various bits of information.

According to the principles of the Pose Method of cycling, this system of reference begins with the effective application of body weight to the pedals. The rider's position on the bike should facilitate application of body weight at any cadence in any gear and satisfy specific biomechanical requirements (see chapter 29).

In the Pose methodology, after the critical positioning of the body weight the next priorities are the aerodynamic positioning and positioning to ensure that the muscles can work efficiently. The final considerations are the positioning of the body itself, defined by the location of the saddle, the handlebars and the cleats along with the rider's overall comfort.

In the Pose approach, the body size itself is secondary to the primary consideration of keeping the body weight on a pedal with the ability to easily shift the body weight from one pedal to the other, no matter what the circumstances of the ride may be. The placement of the saddle (height, fore-aft, incline), the handlebars, and the cleats, as well as the aerodynamic orientation must be subject to the overall goal of body weight placement on the pedals. This single requirement of the bike set-up condition is crucial for cycling success.

Dialing It In

As you begin the process of dialing in your bike position, you should mount it on a stationary trainer so that adjustments can be easily made and evaluated.

Frame Size

The most important thing about the size of the frame is how it fits the requirement of the body weight application, i.e. how well your body will be situated with the main support being on the pedals... not on the saddle or handlebars. Beyond that, a correctly sized frame will give you a balance between height and length, as well as between responsiveness and comfort.

The frame size of the bike obviously depends on leg length and height, but inside these parameters the main thing again is how the frame fits the body weight placement on the pedals. If the size of the frame is such that your upper body is stretched between the saddle and the handlebars then your body weight is spread between them as well and the frame is too large. You'll have to use a smaller size frame to put your body in a more compact position.

As the supplementary support points, the saddle and handlebars shouldn't be so far apart that they make it difficult to shift the body weight in any direction, especially side–to–side.

Saddle Height

Overall seat height is one of the most significant parameters determining correct positioning on the bike. Correct saddle height by the Pose Method philosophy follows the same system of reference — the ability of the cyclist to apply his body weight to the pedals from 1 to 4 o'clock during the pedaling stroke. If the saddle is either too high or too low, the result will be inefficient pedaling action and body weight application.

The first objective in the setting the saddle height is to comfortably place the body weight on the pedals positioned at 3 and 9 o'clock with the knees bent to the angle allowing the leg muscles to produce maximum efforts. This means they have the ability to transmit the largest possible percentage of the body weight to the pedals. If the knee angle is too small relative to the cyclist's muscular strength, then the seat should be moved higher to reduce muscular stress. Conversely, if the knee angle is too big, then the cyclist won't be able to apply his body weight effectively to the pedal during 1 to 4 o'clock phase, no matter how strong his or her legs are. In this case, the saddle should be lowered.

The second requirement concerns the knee angle and foot position at the six o'clock position in the pedaling stroke. Here, the knee should still be bent with the heel of the foot higher than the pedal. This allows the pedal and foot to pass through the bottom of the stroke much faster, because of the shortened radius of rotation of the leg. Additionally, this allows the body weight to shift efficiently to the other side.

If the saddle is too low, the cyclist will have difficulty shifting the body weight quickly from one pedal to the other and applying body weight to the pedal during 1 to 4 o'clock phase of the pedaling stroke. In turn, this lead to inefficient overuse of the leg muscles in the subconscious effort to compensate for the incorrect saddle position.

In order to correct saddle height we use two positions as reference points. The first position is the Cycling Pose, where the pedals are at three and nine o'clock. In the Cycling Pose it is important for the muscles of the front leg to feel comfortable with full body weight placed on the pedals. To assess the comfort level, raise the hips just slightly off the saddle and bounce easily on the pedals. If the legs feel comfortable and there is no excess tension, nor are the legs 'reaching' for the pedals, the height is in the right ballpark.

Then move to the second position, with the pedals at six and twelve o'clock. Here, the leg position on the six o'clock pedal is the most important. First, check the heel position relative to the pedal by coming off the saddle and straightening the knee completely. If the seat height is correct the heel will be below the ball of the foot and possibly the pedal as well. Setting the saddle height by this method allows you to keep the knees bent with heels higher than the pedals during the entire pedaling stroke. This makes it possible to effectively apply body weight to the pedals, shift the body weight quickly from one pedal to the other and maintain a high pedaling speed throughout the stroke.

Fore & Aft Saddle Position

Not surprisingly, the same concerns about applying body weight to the pedals and shifting the body weight from side–to–side determine the saddle's fore and aft positioning. It's important to understand that the saddle is the transitional support point and can be used to regulate the percentage of body weight applied to the pedals. When riding at slow speeds, where the gearing and cadence don't require a high percentage of the body weight, then the "unused" portion of the body weight will rest on the saddle and not the pedals. But as the speed increases, it is necessary to shift more of your body weight to the pedals. Thus, the saddle position should permit quick shifting of the body weight from the saddle to the pedals in order to make the body weight "available," as soon as it is needed.

To set the fore/aft position of the saddle, balance your body weight on the pedals at the three and nine o'clock position with your hips off the saddle. Then lower your hips down to the saddle, while keeping your weight on the pedals. When the hips rest lightly on the saddle, carefully check the orientation of the hips to the saddle. If the hips hang past the end of the saddle, then slide the saddle back. If the saddle protrudes past the hips, then slide the saddle forward to line up with the vertical line of the rear part of the hips.

Handlebar and Upper Body Position

Here we go again. Before addressing aerodynamic considerations, the first consideration remains the application of body weight to the pedals. The height and distance from the saddle to the handlebars should be set so that the cyclist can't either consciously or subconsciously put most of the body weight on the bars. At the same time, the positioning shouldn't lead to either an inefficient aerodynamic position or an uncomfortable position for muscles of the upper and low back, shoulders and arms. Nothing should be unnecessarily stretched or strained, or reaching for the bars. While these may seem to be irreconcilable requirements, there is a way to get everything just right.

Generally speaking, you can use the combination of the stem length and positioning of the aero bars and aero bar pads that allows you to place your elbows directly under the shoulders at a 90° degree or slightly larger angle. This will keep the upper body and shoulders on a stable support with no stress to the muscles of the arms and shoulders and with no unnecessary stretching of back muscles.

Fore Arm Positions

Generally speaking, it is likely that you will end up with your aero bar extensions on a flatter plane that had been the style for many years. When the bars are tilted up too high, you lose the aerodynamic properties for which the bars were designed, while at the same time compressing your head, neck, shoulders and arm into too tight a space, which can lead to cramping and other discomfort.

Cleat Position for Clipless Pedals

Position the cleat so that the pedal axle lines up directly underneath the ball of the foot. This is the point where you will get the greatest transfer of body weight to the pedal. Provided you don't have any structural/alignment problems with your feet, they should point directly forward when in the pedals (parallel to the crank arms). This is called the "ZERO" position.

Should you have structural/alignment problems with your feet, DO NOT attempt to straighten this out. Set the cleats to accommodate this characteristic rather than correct it.

The matter of whether or not to use a clipless pedal with float is one of personal preference. Many cycling experts believe that the locked–in position of a clipless pedal can lead to overuse injuries in the knee, ankle and hips. Others find that the movement in the foot that results from float can be annoying and compromise the application of power to the pedal. In all likelihood, if you have no structural/alignment problems with your feet and ankles and you have otherwise set up your bike position properly, you should do fine in the locked–in setting. If you do have alignment problems, then float may minimize the chance that you will suffer overuse injuries.

SECTION VI
SWIMMING TECHNIQUE

Dr. Romanov teaches Pose swimming in Australia.

CHAPTER 40
SWIMMING INTRO

Nothing in life is to be feared.
It is only to be understood.

— *Marie Curie*

And now, we end at the beginning.

The vast majority of triathlons get underway with an open water swim, which to beginners and spectators alike can appear to be a frightening bit of mayhem. In a mass start open water swim, competitors typically dash from a beach or shoreline into the water, execute a modified racing dive, dolphin their way through the shallows, and then attempt to set a course for the first buoy. This is all accomplished while trying to keep goggles fixed in place and bodies free from inadvertent scratches inflicted by the windmilling hands of hundreds of other swimmers with exactly the same first target in mind.

It's the greatest — and arguably the only — 'spectacle' in triathlon. Was there a more compelling image from the 2000 Olympics than triathlon's Olympic debut in Sydney Harbor with the famed Opera House serving as a dramatic backdrop? The only thing missing was another thousand or so competitors as the very select Olympic field was abnormally small by triathlon standards.

Turning docile laps in the local 'Y' where lane lines, the side of the pool and an attentive lifeguard all yield a sense of security is one thing, but venturing from 'here' on the safe shore to 'way out there' and waging a battle with bashing waves, thrashing competitors and potentially–slashing sharks is a whole different deal altogether.

How hectic can a swim start get? Let's put it this way. Say you happen to be a not very strong swimmer, yet you find yourself near the front of the pack after the initial dash into the water. Just behind you, however, is a good swimmer intent on taking advantage of the considerable draft generated by the lead swimmers. Hemmed in by competitors on both sides and unable to swim past you, your trailing swimmer has but one choice — to go directly over you. Think we're kidding? It's actually very easy.

In the mayhem, the swimmer takes a normal stroke that happens to land on the waistband of your swimsuit. Firmly grasping said waistband, he (or she) uses the leverage to lift his chest over your rear end. With the next stroke planted firmly on your shoulder (or even your head) your trailer is now your leader... and if you're smart, you'll do everything you can to keep up.

Understand — this wasn't a malicious move; the swimmer involved was simply doing what he had to do to remain competitive. You, on the other hand, were in the wrong place by getting in the way of stronger competitors. But not to worry; getting momentarily dunked is no big deal as long as you don't lose your composure. It's all a part of the fun in a triathlon swim start.

The swimming leg of a triathlon can be great fun, if you happen to be an experienced swimmer familiar with the barely-controlled chaos that is the first minute or so of a mass–start swim. However, for most newcomers to the sport, the swim stage is the most intimidating aspect of triathlon. It isn't by chance that the comparatively unimaginative sport of duathlon has emerged as a popular alternative to the tri–sport. Lots of people are just flat–out scared of jumping into the watery fray.

It's a shame that so many people are put off from triathlon by the swimming leg, because swimming truly is a lifetime sport with much to recommend it. As a non–impact sport that involves the whole body, swimming is a great overall conditioner — good for the heart, the lungs and the entire musculo–skeletal system. Moreover, it requires virtually no equipment and can be practiced just about anywhere there's a navigable body of water, from microscopic backyard pools with resistance currents to the world's great oceans.

Swimming welcomes very young practitioners and is a favorite with those of advanced years. It appeals equally to buff lifeguard types as well as those who suffer limited mobility due to disease or injury. Whether you're aiming for Olympian achievement or just trying to recover from a serious workout, putting time in the water always yields return on investment.

And here's the best part — it's really pretty easy to learn to swim well. While many folks carry the fear–induced baggage of well–intended parents who warned them to stay out of the deep end or to not go in the water after eating, swimming is a safe pastime with an easily mastered set of fundamentals.

Throughout the next few chapters, we'll do everything we can to help you overcome any trepidation you may have, get you swimming with perfect form and clue you in on anxiety–easing strategies to take the fear out of those nasty looking open water starts. This is going to be fun — trust us.

CHAPTER 41
TRUTH AND MYTHS ABOUT THE ESSENCE OF SWIMMING

I am still in the dark, I am not sure.

— *Dr. Ernie Maglischo*

With all we know about the world today — from aviation and rocket science to big–bang theories and brain surgery, it may come as a surprise to hear that there is no scientific consensus about how human bodies move through water. We may know a considerable amount about the shapes of hulls for everything from ocean liners to surfboards and we may have studied the movements of fish for centuries, but on the exact topic of what causes the propulsive force that moves a fish — or a human — through water, the debate still lingers.

Before we dive into the deep end and begin working our way through the drills that will serve as the basis for your transition to the Pose Method of Swimming, we first want to take a look at some of the long held misunderstandings concerning propulsive movement in water.

Conventional academic swimming instruction varies and different theories abound as to what makes for good swimming technique. The swim coaching community can always work up a good debate on the matter of proper technique, as summarized by Brent Rushall who concluded that the debate over propulsion still simmers (1).

The Role of Natural Selection

In the absence of any consensus, it can be argued that the best swimmers rise to the top not because of great coaching, but because of natural selection. When you think about the chain of development in young swimmers, this makes a lot of sense. It is widely considered an element of good parenting to 'drown–proof' children at a very young age, so most kids get their introduction to the water from parents or elementary learn–to–swim classes.

The emphasis is not on technique as much as it is keeping the head above water. Once the child is considered safe in the water that may be the end of training for a lifetime. However, those who show an unusual aptitude may be asked to join a local club team, sometimes as early as six years of age. Here, the coaching may be done by the pool lifeguard, typically a high school or college swimmer, and the emphasis is more than likely on workouts and not instruction.

As the most talented swimmers work their way up through the ranks, they may never run into a coach who actually makes substantive technique adjustments based on superior knowledge of propulsive forces and mechanics in swimming.

How far can a swimmer go on natural talent? Consider the case of Mark Spitz, who racked up an amazing nine Olympic swimming gold medals. Spitz came up through some of the best swimming programs in the country, culminating in a college career at the then–dominant Indiana University where he came under the tutelage of the legendary coach, Dr. James Counsilman.

Counsilman (2) once asked Spitz to describe exactly what he did when he swam the freestyle stroke. Spitz responded with a detailed description of how he pulled with a straight arm in a straight path from the point where his hand entered the water until it went behind him. It was a fascinating description — and utterly wrong. In fact, he pulled not with a straight arm, but with a 90° degree bend in the arm and the path that his arm took was not straight, but a marked S–curve. Despite having access to the best programs and the best coaches, Mark Spitz was in every sense a natural talent who swam based on feel and not by the precise molding of his technique.

But just because natural selection wasn't on your side when it came to the swimming gene doesn't mean you can't become an excellent swimmer — if you understand the basics of human movement in water and use that understanding to improve your technique.

The Lift and Drag Theories

The hand movement through water is traditionally referred to as 'sculling' and most basic explanations for this action have revolved around two competing theories: Lift and Drag (3). The Lift theory holds that "good swimmers use sculling actions with their hands pitched to utilize lift forces as a dominant means of propulsion."

Similar to the aviation principles that permit aircraft heavier than air to fly, the Lift theory holds that, in accordance with Bernoulli's Principle, there is a relative difference in the pressure created by water flowing across the more or less curved surfaces of the body (4, 5). When it was developed, the Lift theory described a specific curved path of the hand during the pull phase, with the hand held at a slight angle between the plane of the hand and its line of motion. This so called "sweep" of the hand created pressure on the underside of the hand, creating the lift that propelled the swimmer forward. This theory, which quickly became universally accepted among coaches and scientists, concluded that there was less energy "waste" when force was generated by lift than by drag (6).

While the Lift theory was given credence in the 1970's, subsequent research supported reverting back to drag as the dominant propulsive force in freestyle swimming (1, 7, 8). Simply put, drag is the force created by pulling the arm straight back through the water, much as Mark Spitz described his own stroke. Other studies (1, 8) demonstrated that the hand path of swimmers was not as curved as it was thought, a conclusion that supported drag over lift as the dominant propulsive force.

According to these studies, the path taken by the hands of elite swimmers "is not deliberate and swimmers are actually reducing the curve and this is another strong indirect evidence that swimmers rely on drag forces rather than lift forces" (3).

When you think about it, that may be the case with Mark Spitz who, in a subconscious effort to favor drag over lift, may have perceived that he was pulling straight back, because he was more successful than other swimmers in minimizing the natural curved path taken by a swimmer's hand when pulling back through the water. Even though the reality was that his hand was in fact describing a curved path, to him it felt straight because his muscular efforts had a straightening effect on his hand path.

But of course, the debate over the source of propulsion doesn't stop there. As soon as research was published holding "that drag made a larger contribution than lift throughout the propulsive part of the pull" and came to the conclusion that the "commonly held belief that it is dominated by lift may be ill–founded and incorrect" (3), new theories were offered.

The Vortex Theory

"Instead of belabouring the lift versus drag argument," a new theorist maintained, "we need to move on and learn more about the way water reacts when we swim" (10). Efficient swimmers were observed to leave mini–tornadoes of circulating water (vortices) in their wake with axes of rotation perpendicular to the direction of travel. Cecil Colwin (11) explained that "a vortex forms as a reaction to the propulsive impulses generated by the swimmer." Here we might add that it is a simple matter to observe the same vortices by efficiently paddling a canoe or kayak and watching the spiraling funnels of water trail off the paddle at the end of the stroke.

Raul Arellano (12) then added that these flow formations carry a certain amount of momentum that is transferred from the swimmer's body to the water. The vortex theory came to be seen as a means of explaining how lift forces can play a major role in swimming propulsion. The next observation came from Carla McCabe and Ross Sanders (13) who noted that much of the knowledge about vortices had come from research of marine animals shedding vortices in their wake as they swim.

The vortices are continually created and shed in pulses as a fish travels through the water, specifically as the fish changes its direction, the angle of its tail, or its body alignment. Further research determined (14) that the backward momentum of the vortex rings corresponds to the forward momentum gained by the fish.

Interestingly, according to the vortex theory the stroke of the swimmer "is complete when the vortex is shed, as this event indicates the end of each propulsive impulse, within a swimming stroke in a particular direction" (11). Thus "the swimmer's actions move water, thereby transferring kinetic energy to it. As a reaction, the swimmer recaptures this energy from their own vortex, which is essentially their propulsive force that thrusts them forwards in the water. In other words, the movements made by the swimmer are directly connected to the movements of the water. Thus when the swimmer moves their limbs in the water, it will directly act back upon the swimmer almost instantaneously" (13).

So, was vortex theory the final answer? If so, what did it tell us about *how to move in the water* to be an efficient swimmer? Nothing really.

The problem is that it is difficult to craft a perfect swimming stroke based solely on the vortex theory. There are challenges related to correct timing in changing direction of the stroke, in holding the hand too rigidly, and in excessive acceleration and application of force (11, 12). The recommendation was not to push vortex in a paddle action, but use it to "control the energy, not spending it… and not to execute the movements too forcefully" (15). Nevertheless "the main problem with the vortex theory is that it has never really been tested to show that these vortices in the water are associated with propulsive impulses and should thus be treated with caution" (13).

And all of these cautionary notes ignore the obvious: a swimmer can't see his or her own vortices as they are created, making it rather difficult to fine–tune their creation. You can almost hear a coach try to explain it to an exasperated swimmer, "You looked pretty good on that last repeat, but I think the flow of your vortex from the left hand is a little bit off." Yeah, that would be a little tough to coach.

Axial Flow

Of course, in one of the same studies (13) reviewing swimming propulsion, yet another mechanism of propulsion was put forward. This propulsion from axial flow was proposed by H. Toussaint (16) who called it "pumped up propulsion." Toussaint's original concept was based on the idea that the rotation of the arm around the shoulder creates a fluid velocity gradient along the arm with higher velocity near the hand than near the elbow.

Briefly summarized, Toussaint's theory "illustrates that a rotating arm during the outsweep acts as a pump, driving water along the trailing side of the arm toward the hand, increasing the pressure difference and consequently propulsion" (13). But of course (and you knew this was coming) the same summary concludes "the implications of the pumped up propulsion concept for teaching and performance development are somewhat unclear at the present time" (13).

So, despite all the research, study and theories, it's really not possible to make a definitive conclusion as to which is the dominant force of propulsion in swimming. In fact, it is conceptually possible to conclude that the various forces are all in play and they work together in a cohesive system that yields the best results for the best swimmers... which somewhat brings us back to the natural selection theory.

The fact is that swimmers swim and most of them do so with no real knowledge about how they do it. To return to the Mark Spitz paradox, his coach, the legendary Dr. Counsilman, simply ventured that Spitz had an innate talent in movement absent from most "normal" people, who themselves would have to learn that which came naturally to Spitz.

While that's nice for the Mark Spitzes of the world, of whom there are obviously very few, but that yields no enlightenment for the rest of us who are not privileged or gifted by nature. Which leaves us with the central question of how we are supposed to do the swimming stroke still unanswered. Lots of theories, lots of inspired science, but still a paucity of practical advice.

Back to Square One

So we're still at square one. How are we supposed to take all this sophisticated knowledge of hydrodynamic science with theoretically optimum hand angles of the arm relative to the body and the fluid medium, the theories of lift and drag, of vortex and axial flow and translate them to improved swimming? Will we really ever be able to control all these angles, curves, vortices ... and execute them during an exercise where there is virtually no feedback and no ability to even see where the arm is moving or the resultant flows and vortices? How can we "normal" people do all this if even supremely–talented athletes like Mark Spitz have very little knowledge about how they themselves do it?

Taking the long view of the evolution of swimming, we have to admit that the development of the swimming stroke happened despite specific knowledge of exactly what constituted a perfect stroke. The best swimmers swim with ideas about what is the best stroke, but without an ironclad, proven formula to follow. So the question is this: what guides the best swimmers that eludes the rest?

One school of thought recommends, "Swimmers should be encouraged to feel pressure and differential pressure through the pressure sensitive cells and kinesthetic proprioceptive system. By doing so, the swimmer becomes better at controlling the direction of resultant force as their ability to feel difference between pushing water and applying effective force is increased" (13).

While there is much wisdom in that concept, again we have to consider the practicality of a coach on the deck exhorting his or her charges, "on this next set, I really want you to engage your kinesthetic proprioceptive system to gauge and optimize the differential pressure on your hands."

Feeling, Another Way of Saying 'Perception'

Okay, so that's pushing it a little bit, but it really comes back to the age–old tactic of coaches telling their swimmers to develop a 'feel' for the water. So we have a very complex objective that of propelling a human body through water and that boils down to a very simple instruction: feel the water.

The tool we bring to this task is our perception of movement. A perception is clearly higher in talented individuals (i.e. Mark Spitz et al) and lower in average people. Just as important as having innate perceptive ability is the knowledge of what it is that we are supposed to be feeling.

It's a little bit farfetched to go to the advanced physics level and tell a swimmer to try and control differential pressures on the surface of the hand, but it is relatively simple to instruct the swimmer to develop a feel for... SUPPORT.

In previous chapters of this book (The Perception Concept, The Support Concept) we

discussed our perception of body weight, its relation to support, and how it all relates to the involvement of our muscles in movement. Exactly the same logic is applied to the swimming.

To dive into this discussion, let's start with a couple of seemingly silly questions. First, how do fish swim without knowing anything about science of hydrodynamics? Too much for you? Okay, what about children who start to swim before they have learned to walk and talk? Do either fish or children study swimming technique? While they seem to be silly questions, they serve to stress a most important point. And what about elite swimmers? What are the factors that determine who remains merely a good swimmer and who rises to the elite level? If the best swimmers don't even know how they do it, there can only be one answer — PERCEPTION! Perception of the support, perception of body weight and perception of alternating support. The laws of hydrodynamic forces manifest themselves to us as our perceptions. Those athletes who recognize, react to and use their heightened perceptions are the ones who will be the most successful.

Whether we're talking about unschooled children trying to stay afloat or highly trained elite swimmers trying to achieve a perfect swimming stroke, everyone uses perception on a subconscious level no matter what they are thinking about as they swim. 'Doing' by perception and 'thinking' about swimming theories are just two different, unrelated activities until we create a platform that allows us to successfully apply perception to theory and achieve a technique of skillful movement.

What The Theories Ignore

No matter how you study all the various theories of propulsion, drag, lift, vortices or axial flow, you see that all ignore the concepts of **BODY WEIGHT, SUPPORT and**

CHANGE of SUPPORT, the basic principles that permit our bodies to move. Learning to move as efficiently as possible — whether on land or in the water — requires a sound understanding and perception of the concept of Support. Support and its perception is what allow us to apply our body weight and muscular efforts to movement. In the context of swimming, perhaps the most important factor to consider is this: where is the support and how do we feel it?

Because water is by definition more fluid than land, the essence of support there, is more elusive or even deceptive. Very often it is unclear what is moving relative to what, and this has tremendous relevance in terms of propulsion. For example, it is very important to keep in mind that in the water, the hand acts as support for the body. We should focus on the concept that the "body" (shoulders, trunk, legs, etc.) moves relative to the hand.

This goes against traditional swimming instruction, where you are taught to 'pull' the hand past the body down to the hips. This creates a mental image of the hand moving relative to the body instead of the body moving relative to the hand. If the hand is moving, it cannot function as support for the body but the opposite, which is the body being a support for the hand, immediately making all movement dramatically different.

To complicate things even further, even when we have support with our hand for the body, and are moving the body with the hand, the important thing is where the body is moving. Conventional thinking says that it is moving "forward," but in reality — having our hand in front of us — we actually have two components (vertical and horizontal) of the vector moving the body both forward and up.

As we develop our swimming technique, we have to follow this logic of moving in two directions and keep it foremost in our muscular efforts, thoughts and focus. Realizing that our forward progress as measured in the horizontal plane is a by–product of these two vectors of movement.

This is a classic vector relationship. While providing support, the hand never stays in the same place — it goes under the body as the body moves upward and forward according to the resultant vector and its components, which themselves are constantly changing.

Additionally, the water provides the support for the whole body, while the body slides through the water, rising up and falling down and actually going from one side to the other falling down from one support to the other. This complex movement ultimately manifests as forward movement of the body. Learning how to apply your perception of your movements in the water as you apply your body weight to support will be the key to improving your swimming.

References:

1. Rushall, B.S., Sprigings, E.J., Holt, L.E. and Cappaert, J.M. *A re–evaluation of forces in swimming.* Journal of Swimming Research. Vol. 10, 1994, pp. 6–30.

2. Counsilman, James E. *Competitive Swimming Manual for Coaches and Swimmers.* Counsilman CO., Inc. Bloomington, IN, 1977.

3. Sanders, Ross. *Lift or Drag? Let's Get Skeptical About Freestyle Propulsion.* <http://sportsci.org/news/biomech/skeptic.html> May 1998.

4. Brown, R.M. and Counsilman, J.E. *The role of lift in propelling swimmers.* In Biomechanics, Editor Cooper, J.M. Chicago, IL: Athletic Institute. 1971 pp. 179–188.

5. Counsilman, J.E. *The application of Bernoulliis principle to Human Propulsion in Water.* In First International Symposium on

Biomechanics of Swimming. Editor Lewillie, L. and Clarys, J. Universite Libre de Bruxelles, Brussels, Belgium, 1971, pp. 59–71.

6. Toussaint, H.M. and Beek, P.J. *Biomechanics of competitive front crawl swimming.* Sports Medicine, Vol. 13, 1992, pp. 8–24.

7. Holt, L.E. and Holt, J.B. *Swimming velocity with and without lift forces.* Unpublished paper, Sports Science Laboratory, Dalhousie University, Canada, 1989.

8. Valiant, G.A., Holt, L.E. and Alexander, A.B. *The contributions of lift and drag components of the arm/forearm to a swimmer's propulsion.* In Biomechanics in Sports: Proceedings of the International Symposium of Biomechanics in Sports. Terauds, J. Editor. Research Center for Sports, Del Mar, CA. 1982.

9. Cappaert, J. *1992 Olympic Report. Limited circulation communication to all FINA Federations.* United States Swimming, Colorado Springs, CO. 1993.

10. Sanders, R.H. *Extending the "Schleihauf" model for estimating forces produced by a swimmers hand.* In Eriksson, B.O. and Gullstrand, L. Proceedings of the XII FINA World Congress on Sports Medicine. Goteborg, Sweden, Apr. 1997, pp. 421–428.

11. Colwin, C.M. Breakthrough Swimming. Human Kinetics. 2002.

12. Arellano, R., Pardillo, S. and Gavilán. *Underwater undulatory swimming: kinematic characteristics, vortex generation and application during the start, turn and swimming strokes.* Universidad de Granada: ISBS 2002.

13. McCabe, C. and Sanders, R. *Propulsion in Swimming.* <http://www.coachesinfo.com/category/swimming/323> July 2005.

14. Müller, U.K., Van Den Heuvel, B.L.E., Stamhuis, E.J. and Videler, J.J. *Fish foot prints: morphology and energetics of the wake behind a continuously swimming mullet (Chelo labrosus risso).* The Journal of Experimental Biology, Vol. 200, 1997, pp. 2893–2906).

15. Ungerechts, B.E., Persyn, U. and Colman, V. *Application of vortex flow formation to self–propulsion in water.* In Biomechanics and Medicine in Swimming. Editors Keskinen, K.L., Komi, P. and Hollander, A.P. Vol. 8. Jyvaskla: Gummerus Printing House. 1999, pp. 95–100

16. Toussaint, H.M., Berg Van den, C. and Beek, W.J. *"Pumped–Up Propulsion" during front crawl swimming.* Medicine and Science in Sports and Exercise, 34(2), 2002, pp. 314–319.

CHAPTER 42
IT'S ALL ABOUT CHANGING SUPPORT

*So we have designed certain type of
drills that will increase their feel of
the water, the amount of pressure that
can be generated with the hand.*

— *Marty Knight*

Support? Support? Again with support?

At this time you're probably asking yourself "what support has to do with swimming?" Isn't swimming the anti–gravity sport, where you just float and pull yourself along? Running? Sure, support is really obvious there. Cycling? Okay, the concept was a little tougher, but body weight does end up being supported on the pedals (as well as the saddle and handlebars). But swimming, what do support and gravity have to do with stroking your way across a pool.

Only this — everything.

The very reason that water gives you the feeling of being free from gravity is the generous support that it provides to your body. Where relatively thin air permits gravity to do its thing relatively unfettered, the high viscosity of water cushions your body somewhat against gravity's relentless pull. Yet, as we all know intuitively, gravity will eventually pull your body to the bottom of whatever body of water in which you find

yourself — unless you take corrective measures.

If you happen to be shipwrecked at sea, the first corrective measure would be to scan the surrounding water for something floating that would be able to support your body weight and keep you from sinking. In the absence of a readily available life raft or door plank, the next alternative is to turn your body itself into a float by adopting the position so inappropriately known as the "Dead Man's Float" (Fig.42.1). To do this, you float face down with your body as spread out as possible, legs and arms mostly extended but 'hanging' loosely in the water — arms at roughly 10:30 and 1:30, legs at 4:30 and 7:30.

This position allows the body to relax and use minimal energy while it presents as much surface area as possible to the water. In effect, you turn your body into a parachute, hoping to delay your descent into the depths. By breathing slowly and fully when you come up for air, you hope to generate enough buoyancy to allow you to indefinitely maintain your position on the surface.

Fig.42.2 Moving support on the hand.

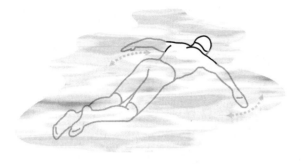

Fig.42.1 "Dead Man's Float."

This is floating support. A simple test will demonstrate the dynamics of floating support. Jump in a pool where the water depth is just overhead. Put your body in a vertical position with toes pointed toward the bottom and hands extended overhead. You'll find that you sink rather rapidly. Now, assume the previously described Dead Man's Float position. By using the surface area of your body to its maximum potential, you've increased the amount of support that the water affords you. Instead of sinking rapidly, you should be able to sustain that survival float for quite some time.

In general, we can describe floating support as a passive support. To optimize floating support, we do as little as possible, relax and let nature's law control the situation. However, to actually swim, we have to switch from passive (floating) support, to active or (moving) support. Just as there is passive support on the bicycle, found at the handlebars and saddle, and the active support on the pedals, the same dynamic is at work in the pool. Here, the body provides the passive support on the water's surface and the moving support is found — 10 points if you guess this correctly — on the hands (Fig.42.2).

This is where the Pose Method of Swimming gets very cool. Once you 'get' the notion of providing moving support through your hands, you can take just about everything anyone ever taught you about swimming technique and throw it all away. "Long, strong strokes?" Forget about it. "Hip rotation?" Don't even think about it. "Pressing against the water with your chest?" Huh?

Rethinking your approach to swimming in terms of alternating support while establishing and destroying balance will be key in the relatively simple process of becoming a very effective swimmer. As with running and cycling, there is both an intellectual and a proprioceptive component to swimming with the principles of Pose.

To drive home the concept of Pose swimming, we'll first run through the science behind the application of the Pose technique, then prescribe a series of drills that will give you the feeling of a very precise application of your body weight to your hands to generate forward momentum in the water. Finally, as somewhat of a bonus, we'll cover specific tactics and other methods of coping with the peculiar demands of swimming in close proximity to hundreds of other athletes in the open water environment. Take a big breath and jump in — it's time to really learn how to swim.

CHAPTER 43
BALANCED SUPPORT

The demonstration of floating support (Fig.43.1) in the previous chapter reflected the two extremes of support offered by water, neither one of which happen to be quite suitable for actual swimming. However, they are useful in addressing the issue of balance in the water.

To demonstrate the rather dramatic effects of balance on swimming, it's now time to jump back in the pool and reassume the Dead Man's Float position.

Once you get all comfortable floating there, slowly lift your right hand out of the water.

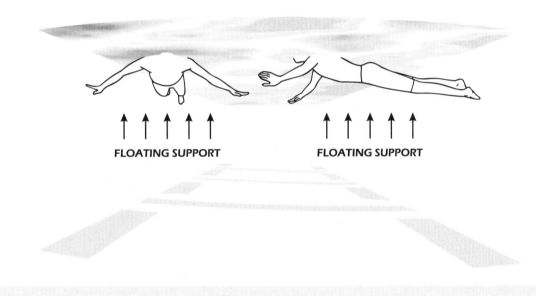

FLOATING SUPPORT   **FLOATING SUPPORT**

Fig.43.1 Floating support in the water.

In the first example, where you maintained a vertical stance in the water, you were perfectly balanced but nonetheless sank rather rapidly. In the Dead Man's Float position, you again held perfect balance as you forestalled sinking as long as possible.

By unweighing the right hand, you automatically transfer more of your body weight to your left side, so your body begins listing rather awkwardly to the left. Now, get back in the Dead Man's Float and this time bring your legs together on the surface and extend your arms out to the side at 90° degree angles before lifting the right hand. This time you will roll to the left precisely along the centerline of your body.

Clearly you will feel your balance along the centerline being achieved and destroyed as you lower and raise your hand. Even a minute movement of your hand can upset your balance in the water. Now, change your position so that your arms are extended out in front of you and your feet are straight behind you, fingers and toes pointed (Fig.43.2). It's the same position you had when you sank rapidly, except that you are now horizontal on the surface of the water instead of penetrating it vertically.

So, as long as we use only floating support to maintain position, we have a good idea of what it takes to remain balanced. Nice to know, but how do we translate that knowledge into swimming?

We'll get to that in a second, but first it's time to let you in on a little secret: when you swim efficiently, your hand enters the water and exits the water AT VIRTUALLY THE SAME PLACE (Fig.43.3). Think about this for a minute. It feels like your hand is sweeping past your body, but in reality your body is speeding past your hand. Once you put your hand in the water it makes a slight sculling action to find still water and presses down — but it never pushes back.

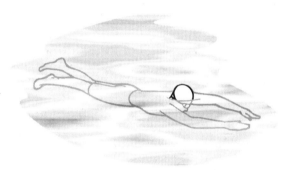

Fig.43.2 Position with your arms extended out in front and your feet kicking.

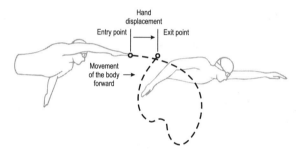

Fig.43.3 The hand enters and exits the water at virtually the same place.

Now, lift your head and shoulders. As you do this, your legs will begin to sink. The tipping point will be at your hips, the general center of mass of your body. What this shows us that we are in fact delicately balanced along two axes in the water when we get ourselves in position to swim. It also shows that relatively small movements of the arm or head can upset balance rather quickly.

To get a mental picture of this, think of the monkey bars found in a playground swing set. To make your way across monkey bars, you reach out, grab a bar and swing until your free hand can reach the next bar ahead (Fig.43.4). Your hand on the bar provides support for your body weight and you alternate support from hand to hand as you make your way down the line. But once your hand grabs a bar, it doesn't move anywhere until you are ready to transfer your body weight to the next hand. If you fail to release one hand as the next grabs the bar in front, you'll swing back and forth for a couple of seconds until your momentum dissipates and you hang suspended between the two bars, each supporting half your body weight. You are now balanced on support, but not moving anywhere.

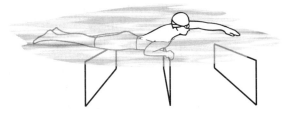

Fig.43.4 The dynamic support of the water is constantly changing, yet dense enough to resemble our movement through the water as if it were on imaginary monkey bars.

Now imagine taking that monkey bar and placing it on the surface of the water and then letting it sink to roughly a foot below the surface. Place yourself (mentally) above the submerged monkey bar and reach out to grab the one in front of you. As the lead hand reaches forward and down, the trailing hand is lifted out of the water. As we know from our balance tests, that rolls the body on the center axis of the body and now places the displaced body weight on the support of the monkey bar.

At this point, the lead arm acts as the transmitter of the energy supplied by the displaced body weight as you lift your chest over the bar. By the time the body weight is centered over the lead hand, the previously trailing hand has recovered and is now reaching for the next bar forward. It is time to alternate support — and balance — from one hand to the next and continue the forward momentum.

Let's analyze what happened in this scenario. First, the balance of the body was destroyed as one hand reached for the bar and the other lifted out of the water. That in turn transferred the body weight onto moving support, i.e. the hand that grasped the bar. That hand, in turn, did not pull. Instead, it maintained a fixed position and supported the body as the chest was lifted over it. And when the general center of the body's mass was directly over the support hand, that hand released its grasp on the bar and began the process of unweighing so as to transfer the body weight to the new support hand.

Where have we seen this process before? Of course, in the introduction to the swimming section where you, as the out of place beginner, were 'overswum' by someone from behind. Remember the tugs, first on the waistband of your trunks, then on your shoulder as someone swiftly went right over you?

That someone found support, first at your waist, then at your shoulder, and used that support to lift his body right over yours. It would have been virtually impossible for the trailing swimmer to pull you backwards and even if he did, that would have resulted in no net gain in position. Instead, he found support, pressed down and lifted himself up and over you. Neat trick — totally made possible by the physics of weight transfer and balanced support.

And we were able to piece all this together by recognizing just one little fact — the hand enters and comes out of the water in exactly the same place. In the next chapter we'll learn how to apply all these lessons in the Pose Method of Swimming.

CHAPTER 44
ALTERNATING SUPPORT AND FALLING FORWARD

*Doubt, of whatever kind, can be
ended by action alone.*

— *Thomas Carlyle*

The last chapter should have given you a new mental image of what swimming is, and, just as importantly, what it isn't. To deal with the latter first, we know that swimming isn't accomplished by pulling the hand backwards past the body... and, boy, that's a tough image to get out of your head, isn't it?

For those of us who grew up swimming it was a phrase repeated endlessly — pull all the way until your thumb grazes your thigh. Swimming was pulling... and kicking for that matter. And that's another thing swimming is not — kicking. Notice how in all that description of submerged monkey bars or submerging other swimmers, there wasn't the slightest mention of what the legs do when you swim? Well, they do have a role to play, but it has nothing to do with forward propulsion, but we'll get to it later.

So if swimming isn't pulling and kicking, what is it? Would you believe it's all about alternating support and falling forward? You're probably ready to accept the alternating support bit, given that we've spent a couple of chapters talking about it, but

you've got to be wondering how on Earth you can fall forward in the water.

Perhaps a little review is in order: in the first section of this book, you learned that running is basically a controlled fall, with the alternating support of your feet keeping you from going SPLAT! on the tarmac or trail. As gravity pulls your leaning body toward the ground, the timely placement of your feet under your body controls the fall, reestablishes momentary balance and allows your to speedily proceed toward the finish line.

In cycling, things are a little subtler. As you unweigh one side of your body, your weight shifts to the other side, and (assisted by gravity) falls toward the ground. In this instance, your leg transmits the energy of that fall through the pedals and generates the force that propels the bike forward.

In swimming, things become more subtle still. If you look back on the descriptions of the submerged monkey bar or the swimmer (you) being submerged, you'll note the references to lifting the chest over the bar or over the swimmer. The hand maintains a fixed position on support in the water as the chest and body move up and over the hand.

As the transition from one hand to the next begins, the body weight naturally begins to fall forward, driving the next hand downward in search of support. When support is located, the process begins again and the chest is lifted past the new support hand. In the same way that the running foot arrests a fall, the finding of support in the water stops the fall and begins lifting the chest once again.

Let's emphasize again that this is a very subtle effect. Just as on onlooker wouldn't watch you running and think you were about to fall flat on your face, neither will you appear to be an undulating dolphin to the casual viewer. But there are benefits to the chest riding high, so to speak. The most obvious is that air presents less resistance to your forward progress than water, so the higher your body mass rides, the less resistance it has to overcome. Equally important, the rise — and subsequent fall — of your chest permits the maximum transfer of your body weight to your support hand.

In our discussions of both running and cycling, the matter of precise timing of the support phase was fundamental to success. So it is in swimming, though the periods of time involved are quite different. In cycling, which, because of mechanical assistance involves the fastest speeds of the three; you remain on active support from one o'clock until four o'clock with each foot. With each foot making 110 or so complete revolutions per minute that works out to a foot working on support for a little over a tenth of a second per pedal stroke.

In the middle comes running, where you overcome the same air resistance as you do on a bike, but without the mechanical assistance. Count on each foot remaining on the ground for about a quarter of a second or so if you're moving right along.

In swimming, things are a little different. Swimming speeds are the slowest because of the greater resistance of water versus air and because the power of your moving body weight is transferred through your arms instead of your legs. The effect of this increases both the time spent on active support and the transitional time spent on floating support.

These factors combine to put a premium on perfect swimming mechanics. This leaves us with a couple of questions: what are perfect swimming mechanics and how do we achieve them?

CHAPTER 45
POSE PERFECT SWIMMING

*They always say time changes things, but
you actually have to change them yourself.*
— Andy Warhol

Now that we've adopted a new world view of what swimming isn't — namely, kicking and pulling — we have to hone in on the mechanics of what swimming really is — transferring body weight through the arms to propel the body as it falls forward through the water. Good thing that it's easier than it sounds.

First, let's run though a few things that we've already learned. First, in the water, the body benefits from both floating and active support. Second, the body is balanced along two axes in the water. Third, the hand enters and exits the water at the same point; it doesn't pull backwards to drive you forwards. Finally, and obviously, as a medium through which we must pass, water presents greater resistance than air.

This last little nugget will guide our mechanics in two ways. In both running and cycling, the speed of the 'work' phase and the 'recovery' phase are the same. This is illustrated most clearly in cycling, where the fixed element of the cranks ensures that the foot recovering on the upward arc must move at the same speed as the foot working on the downstroke.

In swimming, however, this is not the case; since the active support phase takes place in a medium of greater viscosity (water) than the recovery phase (air). This allows the recovery hand to play catch–up while the other hand is working. This will play a key role as we delve into proper swimming mechanics.

The other effect of water's greater density is that there is a premium on hydrodynamics. With the adoption of aero bars, aero helmets, disc wheels and 'slippery' fabrics, most cyclists are well aware of the benefits of presenting as little resistance as possible to the wind. In swimming, any mechanical inefficiency that presents additional surface area to the water will be penalized severely because of that additional drag. Essentially, you want to be as sleek as a seal, as slippery as a dolphin.

Let's begin with the stroke mechanics and then polish up everything with the hydrodynamic details.

As we know, a stationary body in the water rests on floating support; a swimming body enjoys both floating support and moving support. The degree to which each is employed at any given moment goes a long way toward determining the speed with which we swim.

To wit, the greater ratio of time spent on efficient moving support versus time spent on moving support, the faster we will swim. This little pearl of wisdom effectively debunks the 'long, strong strokes' theory of swimming. Think about it. Once the center of the body has moved past the active hand, that hand has lost its ability to transfer the body's weight and generate power. It is literally dead in the water. Yet, by waiting for the body to work its way past that hand all the way to the hips, the swimmer has delayed the transfer of weight and power to the other hand, which is waiting to take over its duty. During this 'wait time', the swimmer's body is decelerating, slowly down as it waits for the next pulse of power.

So the key becomes finding a quicker, more efficient way, of transferring body weight from one hand to the next. This is where the benefit of two different viscosities comes in handy. As the active hand is completing its work directly under the body's general center of mass, the recovering hand has had time to work its way all the way around and is now ready to enter the water.

Thus the hand that was working has to be unweighed quickly to start the process of transferring the weight to the next hand. As the hand is lifted toward the surface, the hips automatically roll toward the other side. This unweighing of the hips continues the process of weight transfer. This is vital to understand: the rotation of the hips does not initiate the power of the stroke; it continues a weight transfer initiated by the arm.

The hips are the primary source of floating support and an anchor against which the active arm applies the force of the transferred body weight; they are not the source of power in the stroke.

The source of that power comes from applying body weight to the hand as it first enters the water and then finds sufficiently still water to facilitate the application of that power.

It is at this point that we should take a look at the various relationships in play as the swim stroke is initiated. The object of swimming, of course, is to move the body relative to the water. In that equation, however, you also have the movement of the body relative to the hand. While we time swimming by the former, it is our ability to perform the latter that determines our efficiency and success as swimmers. Simply said, it is the ability to move the body relative to the hand that makes for fast and efficient swimming.

The interaction between using the hand as support to move the body, and using the body as support to anchor the movement of the hand, is the true demonstration of the skill of swimming.

CHAPTER 46
THE FORCE MOMENT IN SWIMMING

*We can figure out how it's done, we just
don't know exactly why it's done yet.*
— *Dr. Ernie Maglischo*

In the previous chapter we redefined the concept of swimming and recast it as the interaction between the body and the hand, with each playing a role in supporting the other. If we go way back into the book, we'll recall the great quote from the Greek thinker, Archimedes, who, when talking about the power of levers, said: *"Give me a place to stand and I will move the Earth."*

In swimming, that *place to stand* is your hand in the water and what it allows you to *move* is your body. To create a mental image of this, it can be helpful to think of an environment that is truly free of gravity — a spaceship. We've all seen video of astronauts or cosmonauts, flailing about the bay of their ship, only able to move in a given direction by pushing off a fixed object, generally the wall of the cabin.

The reason they can't move without the assistance of a fixed object is that in a truly gravity free environment, there is no support. Without a reliable source of support, there is simply nothing against which we can apply the energy of our body mass, no way to generate forward momentum.

While we tend to think of water as being almost like outer space in regard to its ability to diminish the effects of gravity, we have already demonstrated that gravity is in fact hard at work, when we're in the pool or the ocean. But it is this phenomenon of reduced effects of gravity that makes it vital that we are as efficient as humanly possible in establishing — and working against — support in the water.

What Your Hips Really Do In Swimming

This is where the hips come in. It is a common misperception that the hips are the source of power in swimming. The thinking holds that the drive of the hips as they rotate from side to side generates the power that pulls the arm backward and move the body forward. There most certainly is a vital interrelationship between the arms and the hips, but that's not it.

As we discussed in the last chapter, when the moving support hand finishes its work under the general center of mass of the body, it begins to unweigh and lift out of the water. This causes the weight to come off the moving support hand and transfer to the opposite hand by passing through the floating support of the hips. The quicker this weight transfer takes place, the sooner the next hand can begin its work.

The key is that the hips must be in position to apply the body weight to the moving support (hand). Once the hip is in position, the hand can then establish its own support in the water to apply the weight of the body. This establishes a relationship between the floating support of the hips and the active/moving support of the hand, onto which the body weight is being transferred (Fig.46.1). It is in this relationship where our ability to swim fast and efficiently is developed.

Fig.46.1 Floating–Moving support.

As it is with all other sports, in swimming we are only as strong as our ability to use our body weight. The hand enters the water and exits the water at virtually the same point (Fig.46.2, Chapter 43, Fig.43.3), **but it is the ability to move the body relative to the hand that makes for fast and efficient swimming.** The interaction between the use of the hand as support to move the body, and the use of the body as support to move the hand, is the true demonstration of the skill of swimming.

The skill of any movement is the skill of shifting the body weight from one support to the other. What we **feel** is the pull of the hand toward the body and the shift of our weight to the other side. But what really happens is that — balanced on the support of the hand — we lift the body past the hand. The hand/arm serves as a support for the body and the body as a support for the hand/arm in order to change support.

It is a mutual relationship — neither one can do its work without the other, but the primary aim is to move the body relatively to the hand on support.

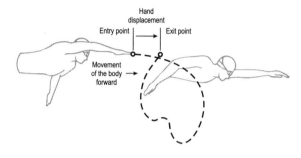

Fig.46.2 A swimmer's hand entry and exit points, into and out of the water, are virtually in the same place.

The Force Moment

This mutual relationship leads to the force moment in swimming, **the instant when you apply the maximum force possible in your stroke.** With the hip and the hand locked into support, the weight of the upper torso begins its pass over the support hand. As it passes, the energy of that weight is pushed down on the hand, driving the swimmer forward. It is exactly the same phenomenon as in cycling, when the foot passes through the 3 o'clock position (Fig.46.3).

To get a clear picture of how closely the swimming stroke resembles the cycling stroke, visualize the 'clock' of the cycling stroke, where the foot at the top of the stroke is said to be in the 12 o'clock position. In swimming, the point where the active hand first makes contact with the water correlates exactly — that is the 12 o'clock position for the swimming stroke. As the hand presses down and the weight of the upper torso is transferred onto the support of that hand, the hand passes from two o'clock through four o'clock, with the position of force moment peaking at three o'clock.

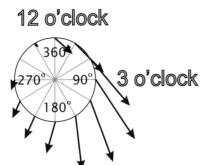

Fig.46.3 The pedal position at 3 o'clock.

By the time the hand is at six o'clock, the weight of the body has passed the hand, which can then no longer provide support. The hand is no longer 'loaded' and it is important to quickly transfer the body weight to the next hand... again, just like in cycling. At this point, **any effort to push back toward the hip is wasted effort and only serves to delay the transfer of support to the other hand.**

Channeling Body Weight

So the strength of our swimming comes not from the strength of an independently 'pulling' arm, but instead from the swimmer's ability to channel the body weight through the arm and hand, transmitting that potential energy as completely as possible. Without the strength and the skill to channel the energy, the swimmer will use a smaller percentage of body weight as a power source and consequently swim slower.

The power source boils down to the communicative abilities of the arm and the body, which must work together as a single unit to achieve the best results. It is not a case of strong arms dragging the body along, but instead a case of a strong framework being established between the body and the arms that allows the body to pass most quickly through the water. Paramount in this is the swimmer's own perception of what is happening, as the weight is transferred to the hand and his concentration to make the most of that relationship with every single stroke at the peak force moment.

This relationship and the ability to maintain it, is the key to an efficient and powerful swim stroke. The extent to which the arm is able to move the body weight or become a spring for the body (Fig.46.4), determines the efficiency of the stroke. The better you can channel your body weight and its power through the arm, the more efficient your swim stroke will be.

Fig.46.4 The arm in the spring position.

How much of your own body weight do you think you are channeling through the connection between your arm and your body? Most of us don't have the skill to perceive this. In Pose Swimming we learn how to manage our own body weight by heightening our perception of feeling it and then transferring it to the next support.

CHAPTER 47
LEARNING POSE SWIMMING

*Telling is not teaching and
listening is not learning.*

— *Bill Boomer*

There are probably as many theories about how to teach swimming as there are coaches and parents. From parents who play 'motorboat' with their kids or back away from the pool edge as they yell "1–2–3 Jump!" to coaches who use super slow–motion underwater video analysis, everybody has his or her own approach to the task. Teaching someone to swim is a very rewarding task, particularly if the student is "water–averse."

In the case of adults, the fear of water — particularly the open water of lakes, rivers or oceans — can be deeply ingrained and undoubtedly has kept many wannabe tri-athletes on the sidelines. While it is quite possible for complete non–swimmers of any age to be taught very quickly how to swim effectively, the focus of this section will be on athletes who already know how to swim but want to significantly improve their performance.

As with the 're–learning' of running and cycling, the process of substantially altering an athlete's swimming style presents its own set of challenges. The most obvious is overcoming the virtually instinctive body movements that have been overlearned through countless repetitions.

While an on–site coach can offer virtually real–time feedback to a runner or cyclist with corrections being made on the fly, a swimmer has to stop, remove the goggles and then recover normal breathing before being able to listen to coaching instruction. Then the coach has to wait for the student to implement the changes before starting the teaching process all over again. And, generally speaking, it is simply more difficult for a coach to see exactly what the swimmer is doing (or not doing) and offer the correct adjustments.

This makes it even more important for the swimmer to have a clear mental picture of what is supposed to happen in Pose Swimming. The set of drills to teach Pose Swimming will follow in the next chapter, but first let's take a look at the role of each of our body parts in the physical act of Pose Swimming.

What the Arms Do and When They Do It

We've already discussed in some detail the fact that the arms and hands provide the active support that channels the weight of the body and drives it forward. The sequence of drills that follow will make it possible for you to truly feel that support and internalize how the alternation of support is the essence of fast swimming.

In terms of timing, the number one thing to remember is that the swing (recovery) arm only enters when the support (active) arm has finished its work. As we discussed in the last chapter, this happens when the support arm approaches the six o'clock position directly under the body.

If the swing arm enters the water too soon, it will interrupt the stroke of the support arm and diminish its effective power to propel the body forward. This interruption is duly bad as it not only diverts the effective movement of the support arm, but it also throws off the delicate balance of floating support. The result is that the swimmer flounders in the water without propulsive movement and is also thrown out of the proper frame for setting up his next stroke.

While it is important that the recovery arm does not enter the water too soon, it is even more critical that it is not too late in its entry into the water. This late arrival is a typical result of the "long, strong strokes" theory of swimming where the swimmer is taught to exaggerate the push of the hand all the way back until it brushes past the hip. Since we have already learned that there is no effective power to the support arm once it passes six o'clock, what happens here is a gradual, but perceptible, deceleration as the recovery arm delays its entry into the water while it waits for the support arm to finish its 'pull'.

The question of time and space is a simple one: the recovery arm must enter the water just as the support arm finishes its work, not before and not after.

As you work your way through the drills, keep your focus on placing the weight of your body on your hands and emphasizing the force moment. Think about supporting your weight, not on "pulling back" and you will have the correct mental framework for Pose Swimming.

The Role of the Hips

While the hips are popularly considered to be the source of power in the swimming stroke, their actual role is quite different. As floating support for the moving arm, the hips facilitate the application of body weight to the hand and only move as a result of the support arm reaching the end of support as it approaches the six o'clock position. At this point, with floating support no longer needed on that side, the hip unweighs rapidly so that support can be transferred to the other side. Each hip unweighs as a result of the arm finishing its work and briefly acts as floating support until the next moving support is established.

The hips don't start the generation of power; they facilitate the body weight application to the moving support. Without the stability of floating support provided by the hips, the arm would not have the intermittent support from which to apply the body weight; the true power of the swimming stroke.

The hips **do not** initiate the movement. If the movement were to be initiated by the hips, you would no longer have stability from the hips to use for your moving support. In effect, you would be robbing your arm of its power by removing the application of body weight before it has completed its working cycle. Once the arm reaches the hips, the support of the hips and the whole body shifts and a new support phase begins on the other side. The hips merely "un–weigh" to allow the shift to the next support. When the active arm finishes its moving support and approaches the hips, it is no longer a necessity to stay on this side — that is why the hips rotate.

The stroke is done, the GCM has moved forward and a new support arm is ready to work, but it can only work with a stable hip. It is the hip of the support side that moves away when the arm reaches the six o'clock position, not the opposite hip beginning a propulsive movement (as is commonly believed) before the new cycle begins.

The hip on that side is now ready to engage the new support arm as a facilitator of body weight application to the support. If the hips were to move and swivel without providing a solid connection to the support arm this would cause the floating support to dissipate, leaving no base for the moving support — or the body moving forward. Therefore the role of the hips is not to actively produce rotation, but rather to facilitate application of body weight to the moving support.

What the Legs Really Do

Most people think that the legs are there for kicking. With the possible — and arguable — exception of the 50–meter freestyle sprint, there is actually no reason to actively 'kick' the legs as a source of forward propulsion while swimming freestyle. However, that doesn't mean that the legs don't play an essential role in swimming. They're not there just to be dragged around behind you; they actually fulfill three critical functions: balance, hydrodynamic efficiency and floating support.

The first of these is balance, which, as we know, is a key factor in the transfer of body weight and is vital in the development of power. Thus, even though the legs themselves do not provide propulsive power, they must be carefully controlled to maintain balance and permit the easy fluid weight transfer from one hip to the next. What might appear to be a classic 'two–beat' kick is really nothing more than the rise and fall of the feet caused by the slight body roll as the hips weigh and unweigh in turn. The legs aren't kicking, but by their carefully controlled, limited movement they promote rapid efficient weight transfer. The lesson here is to keep the legs in a tight circumference with very slight movements and to not consciously kick.

Equally important — and closely related to the balance function of the legs — is their role in maintaining hydrodynamic 'slipperiness'. Just as the well–known aerodynamic features of bicycles like aerobars, disc wheels and 'aero' tubing permit higher speeds, a swimmer can increase his or her speed by presenting a more narrow profile to the water.

While you may have never thought about being aero in the water, it only stands to reason. Being much denser than air, water provides a tougher barrier against forward progress. Swim suit companies have recognized this fact and have developed special fabrics that permit faster flow of water past the body, thus gaining microseconds of speed at the Olympic level. But while tiny gains can be made with fabrics, huge gains are possible with body control.

To return to cycling for a moment, it is well known that while the aforementioned aerobars, wheels and tubesets all are important, the biggest factor in aerodynamics is the rider. Starting with America's first Tour de France champion, Greg LeMond, all top–level riders have made annual pilgrimages to wind tunnels to refine their time trial position on the bicycle. Nothing contributes more to aerodynamic efficiency than a proper position that enables efficient weight transfer while streamlining the body.

In the water, a swimmer that flails about and makes big, deep kicks is working against himself by trying to bore a bigger hole through the water than is necessary. That alone is reason enough to minimize kicking. The deeper and harder you kick, the more energy you waste and the harder you make it for yourself to move quickly through the water. So, you should always concentrate on keeping your feet in a very tight 'circle' as they roll with the movement of your hips.

Moreover, you really have to focus on keeping your toes pointed behind you. The trailing edge of any object provides the greatest resistance to forward progress, which means that the greatest speeds result from slippery back ends. When a raindrop falls, its front end is rounded but its back end tapers to a point. So should your toes, plain and simple. If you get lazy and let your feet and toes point down or drift in a wide circle as your hips rotate, you will rob yourself of substantial speed.

Finally, the legs function as an extension of the trunk in providing floating support. This makes it important to keep the legs right at the water surface and not relax and let them drop down in the water. Besides ruining hydrodynamic efficiency, this would also rob you of power by placing less of your body weight over your hands as they push down in the power phase of the swim stroke.

In short, the legs don't 'do' much. You could almost say that what they don't do they have to do very well. Failure to concentrate on your leg position and movement could result in deterioration of your form and subsequent substantial loss of speed.

How — and how often — should I breathe?

The mechanics of breathing have provided a stumbling block for many a young or fearful swimmer. The fear of placing the face in the water is by no means limited to the very young; it keeps an astonishing amount of adults from ever experiencing the joys of swimming — and by extension a wide range of water sports from snorkeling and SCUBA to surfing, kiteboarding, and water skiing.

Among those who do overcome the instinctual reluctance to put the mouth and nose where the ready availability of air is compromised, there is still a lot hand–wringing and debate about breathing technique. Questions abound. Do I breathe every stroke or every other stroke? On the right or on the left? Or both on the right and on the left, in what is known as alternate side breathing?

For something so important, the basics are really simple: exhale under water and inhale out of the water. Don't laugh. While that may seem obvious, it is not unusual for fearful swimmers to keep their lips frozen tight under water and then try to both exhale and inhale before plunging back in again. Obviously, this would destroy any semblance of proper timing in the execution of the swim stroke, but it also underscores how vital the timing of breathing is.

In a way, breathing is somewhat of annoyance in the execution of proper swimming mechanics. Since it fulfills no mechanical function in the matter of forward propulsion, we would be better off if we didn't have to breathe while swimming — backstroke anyone? But try as we might, we can't seem to swim backstroke as fast as freestyle, and since backstroke presents its own open water problems in terms of navigation, we have to accept the fact that we will have to breathe on a very regular basis while swimming freestyle.

To do this, we have to integrate the mechanics of the breath into the intricate timing pattern established by the alternation of support. There is simply no time to add a beat that is reserved for breathing alone; each breath must be taken without interrupting or slowing the quick movements that lead to the highest swimming speeds.

Following that logic, we can answer a couple of the basic questions from above. If the breathing function takes place within the time frame of the swimming strokes, there is simply no reason to limit the number of breaths taken. Therefore, there is no compelling reason to breathe every other stroke on the same side (or one breath for every four arm strokes) or on alternate sides (one breath for every three strokes).

Further, since the air we breathe contains the oxygen that fuels our efforts and since triathlon swims tend to be longer than most pool races, it makes perfect sense to breathe every stroke on the same side, thus keeping the oxygen flowing and anaerobic effort at bay.

Which leaves one question: which side? For most of us, this will be a natural selection and generally follows handedness. If you are right handed, it is most likely that you will breath on the right; lefties will breathe on the left. Simple as that... and not worth complicating any further.

This brings us to the central objective of integrating that breathing pattern into the swimming stroke pattern without a hitch in the latter. There are a few keys to this that will take the mystery out of breathing in the water and make it as natural as breathing on the land. The first hint is found in yoga, where practitioners learn that the exhalation period is longer and less forceful than inhalation. To apply this to breathing while swimming, you want to continually exhale the entire time your face is in the water. This exhalation is measured and steady and comes from both the mouth and the nose.

Then, when your weight shifts to support on the hand where you breathe, you want to time the slight turn of your head to the force moment. As your head, chest and shoulders rise slightly due to your weight being placed on support, this is the time when you will have to exert the least effort to turn the head and breathe in air and not water.

The head turn is in the direction of the shoulder, which creates a little pocket where air can be taken in without trying to lift the head. There is a distinct difference between the rise of the head due to your weight being on support and trying to lift your head by bending it upwards to breathe. The former should be automatic; the latter should never happen.

With the slightest turn of the head, you begin your inhalation. This is where breathing for swimming differs from yogic breathing. In yoga, the inhalation comes through the nose, but in rapid swimming there simply isn't time for the smaller 'pipes' of the nose to take in enough air to fill the lungs. Instead, you inhale forcefully through the mouth, and then turn your head back toward the bottom as your support hand approaches six o'clock.

That's it: continuous underwater exhalation, slight head turn toward the shoulder, forceful inhalation and repeat every stroke on the same side. Easily said and easily done.

Putting it All Together

As we head into the drills, we should now have a mental picture of the components of Pose Swimming: the alternation of support, the role of the hips as anchors, the balance, support and streamlining of the legs and the rapid, effective breathing that fuels the whole enterprise.

While pondering the individual role of the arms, the hips, the legs and the head, always bear in mind that we swim as a unit. The arms don't 'pull'; they work in concert with the back and shoulders to support your body weight. Similarly, if you ignore your legs and let them drift in a wide circle as you turn to breathe, then you increase drag and slow the transfer of weight during the hip turn, thus slowing your stroke cadence and your overall swimming speed. Everything matters. Focusing on your form as you grow increasingly fatigued is the single most effective means of swimming faster from start to finish in every training session and every race.

The good news is that the point of the drills that follow is not to show you how to put the components together as much as it is to show you how automatically they come together once you embrace the concept of alternating support. By working step–by–step through the drills and taking the time to understand how they relate to the concept of alternating support, you'll quickly become a much more effective swimmer. You're going to like the way you swim once you put it all together.

CHAPTER 48
POSE SWIMMING — THE DRILLS

Success is not an accident.

— *Bill Boomer*

The concept of 'doing drills' is one of the biggest turn–offs there is. Nobody likes to 'do drills'. Figure skaters don't want to spend countless hours tracing perfect circles, one–foot spins, or figure eights; they want to soar through the air and execute dazzling triple axels. Young basketball players raised on watching their NBA heroes throw down slam dunks and launch threes from beyond the arc are almost impossible to reign in for mundane exercises like perfect lay–ups and free throws. And time–pressed triathletes are universally more interested in getting their two thousand yards in the pool over and done with so they can move on to the next appointment in their overscheduled Type–A lives.

Is it a waste of time doing drills when you can rack up some big yardage? Who has time for that? Only the people who want to improve. After all, no figure skater who doesn't have the precise edge control that comes from what they used to call 'school figures' will ever pull off a triple axel, much less dazzle you with it. And basketball players who never bother to learn the fundamentals will be exposed every time they go against skilled opposition.

The same goes for swimming — in spades. The high viscosity of water as the medium, the fear factor that affects many people in open water and the variables like currents, waves, hidden obstacles and thrashing competitors all combine to make it imperative that you are as skilled as possible in the basics of swimming. Every little flaw is exposed and magnified, when you enter the competitive realm of open water triathlon swimming.

And yet so many triathletes seem content to accept the fact that they just aren't talented swimmers. "I suck at swimming, so I just hammer the bike" is a phrase so common that it's probably uttered in some variation at every triathlon on the face of the Earth. That's kind of crazy, isn't it? Earnest athletes, who try so hard to improve their triathlon times, yet are so willing to write off the first phase of every event as something to get behind them before the real racing actually starts.

Here's a little hint: triathlons are much easier when you're among the leaders in and out of the water. After the first hundred yards or so, you're free and clear in the water, no banging shoulders and arms with dozens of competitors. Transition areas are still in good order and free of traffic. On the bike, the road is wide open, not clogged with clusters of riders through whom you have to weave to establish any kind of smooth tempo. And by the time you get to the run, you'll realize that instead of racing 500 or a thousand competitors, you've probably been involved with 100 or less — those who know how to swim and have the cycling and running skills to hold their positions at the front ranks of the race.

Life is good at the front of a triathlon, so it makes sense to take the time to hone your swimming skills and move closer to the front ranks, doesn't it?

With that in mind, let's take just a minute to consider what it is we're trying to accomplish as we work through these drills. Over the past few chapters, we've consistently talked about swimming as an exercise in changing support.

At first, this probably sounded like a crazy concept to you and, admittedly, it is a tough concept to visualize. That's why the Pose Swimming drills start off just demonstrating what support in the water feels like.

From there, we move on to the key concept: *the relationship during support is where we harness the transformation of energy.*

In order to shift weight, we must finish support. Support is the place where the energy or body weight is applied in order to change direction. We are manipulating all of the variables to channel energy in the desired direction — this is what movement is all about. The body would lurch forward chaotically without understanding this relationship. *The support moves toward where the energy transformation goes. For energy transformation, we need support, so support follows the vector of energy. Support should pair with the transformation vector. The hip "unweighs" at the pivotal point of support transformation. Something is moving us. What is it? — It is our body weight when applied to support, which in turn recruits our muscular system to perform the action of swimming through the water.*

Activating the opposing hip, is to move it without a support system. We need to work with the hip that is on the same side as the pulling arm, for support of that arm. The hip we are concerned with, is the hip on the working side — not the other one. In order to incorporate these rules, we should understand certain elements of swimming technique:

A. Floating Support
B. Moving Support
C. Change of Moving Support

Just as we did in running and cycling, we will use specific movement pattern exercises in the following drill sets to expand the scope of your perception and develop the ability to execute correct movement in the water for efficient and faster swimming.

Dry Land Swimming Drills

Drill Set One: Getting the initial perception of support on the hands in specific body positions out of the water.

1a) *The Starting Pose* (Fig.48.1)

Hands on a bench or an elevated platform with arms and the body stretched almost horizontally with both feet on the floor.

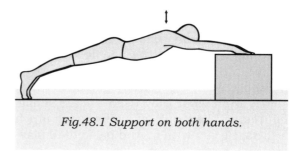

Fig.48.1 Support on both hands.

The Drill
Bounce up and down from the shoulders.

The Point
This is the first and obvious perception of support on your hands in order to keep your body in that position.

1b) *The Starting Pose* (Fig.48.2)

This time, use only one hand for support. The other arm is in the recovery position along the hip.

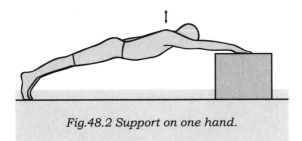

Fig.48.2 Support on one hand.

The Drill
Bounce up and down from the shoulder.
The Point
Sense perception of support on one hand. You'll notice that your body naturally shifts your body weight in the direction of support in order to keep balance. The same occurs in the water, as your body shifts from one support, to the other.

1c) *The Starting Pose* (Fig.48.3)

Start in the same position as drill 1b.

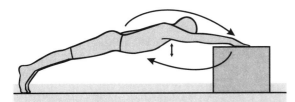

Fig.48.3 Support on one hand. Alternate support by pulling the hand from the bench and quickly replacing support with the other hand.

The Drill
Alternate arms from support by pulling your support hand from the bench (exercises 48.1–48.3 may be performed on the knees if your strength conditioning is not developed enough).
The Point
The recovery hand does not move to the bench until the support hand is removed. This exercise provides you with the perception of changing support in the water.

1d) *The Starting Pose* (Fig.48.4)

Start from the leaning position supporting your body weight in your partner's arms.

Fig.48.4 Support on both hands.

The Drill
Bounce up and down from the shoulders, but not below your hands. Remember to concentrate your support on the hands.
The Point
This drill further develops the perception of support in the water by providing you with the sensation of a less stable point of support.

1e) *The Starting Pose* (Fig.48.5)

Start in the same position as drill 1d), but with one hand on support.

Fig.48.5 Support on one hand, the other hand is kept alongside the hip.

The Drill
Bounce up and down with one shoulder.
The Point
You are getting the perception of support on one hand in addition to a higher demand of muscular efforts to stay balanced.

1f) *The Starting Pose* (Fig.48.6)

Start with one hand on your partner's hand; keep the other arm outstretched forward.

Fig.48.6 Support on one hand, the other hand is kept out in front.

The Drill
Change support by pulling the support hand from your partner's, while simultaneously switching support to the opposite hand.
The Point
This exercise provides you with a very subtle perception of changing support and calls for a tremendous amount of muscular strength.

1g) *The Starting Pose* (Fig.48.7)

Start with the support on one hand, while the other hand rests in a recovery position along the hip.

Fig.48.7 Support on one hand. The other hand is kept alongside the hip.

The Drill
Change support by pulling your hand from your partner's, while simultaneously switching support to the opposite hand.
The Point
This drill sharpens your perception of support and timing.

1h) *The Starting Pose* (Fig.48.8)

Start with one hand on your partner's hand; keep the other arm outstretched forward.

Fig.48.8 Support on one hand.

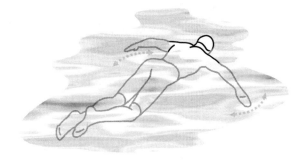

Fig.48.9 Scull with your hands.

just to keep your stationary body level in the water.

The Drill

The change of support is initiated by your partner's removal of support (#1) which should signal you to quickly find support with your outstretched arm (#2).

The Point

This is the ultimate tool required for the development of perception and strength for changing support in the water.

Drills For Floating Support

Drill Set Two: Sculling — getting the feel of support in the water.

2a) *The Starting Pose* (Fig.48.9)

Lie face down on the surface of the pool with your hands at your side.

The Drill

Scull the water (make quick back–and–forth movements) with both hands to maintain horizontal position, then use only one hand at a time to maintain the same position.

The Point

This is the first step in developing a higher awareness of floating support. While the body almost floats by itself, you'll notice that it takes the support of your moving hands, doing a surprising amount of work

2b) *The Starting Pose* (Fig.48.10)

From the previous pose, drop your feet down until you are vertical in the water with your head just above the surface, and your hands down by your side at waist level.

The Drill

Scull first with both hands, then one at a time, making sure to notice the effort necessary to keep your head above water.

The Point

With floating support diminished because of the reduced surface area of your body on the water's surface, it takes even more effort to keep your head above water, which forces you to support your body weight on your hands.

Fig.48.10 Scull with both hands at about waist level. Experiment with shifting your body weight in the water by sculling with one hand at a time.

2c) *The Starting Pose* (Fig.48.11)

Now lie on your back on the water's surface, again with your hands at your sides.

Fig.48.11 Scull for support while lying on your back.

The Drill
As before, scull the water first with both hands then with one at a time.

The Point
Many people are more comfortable and float better on their backs, yet there is still effort from the hands required to maintain a stable position. Also, because of the natural bend of the knees, there is a tendency for the feet to hang lower in the water. Emphasizing the point that the body has to work as a unit in the water, you'll notice that you may have to contract your abdominal muscles to keep your feet on the surface.

2d) *The Starting Pose* (Fig.48.12)

Return to the first position, on your stomach, but this time extend your hands out in front of you (and don't forget to keep your toes pointed).
The Drill
Scull with both hands, but stay in place — don't let your body move forward.
The Point
With your hands in the position where they will enter the water during every stroke, you can sense the displacement of support from floating support to moving support.

Fig.48.12 Scull with both hands out in front of you. Experiment with shifting your body weight in the water by sculling with one hand at a time.

Go back to the sentence just before the drill started: *"The relationship during support is where we harness the transformation of energy."* When support changes, this is where energy is channeled into forward movement.

2e) *The Starting Pose* (Fig.48.13)

Face down, extend your hands out in front of you.

The Drill
Now scull with both hands while lightly kicking; allow your body to move forward.

The Point
This exercise actually looks and feels a little like the 'dog paddle', but you'll notice some very important things. As your hands go deeper, you'll feel your head, neck and shoulders rising slightly out of the water in a subconscious effort to bring your weight over your hands. You should also sense that instead of your forearms and hands doing all the work, your shoulders and trunk are very much involved.

Fig.48.13 Scull with both hands while moving forward.

2f) *The Starting Pose* (Fig.48.14)

Same position as drill 2(e), but now only one hand is extended, the other is back by your side.

The Drill
Scull for several seconds with the extended hand, then alternate to the other hand.

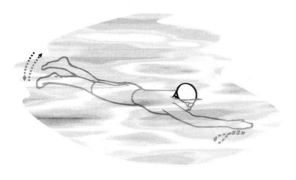

Fig.48.14 Scull with one hand while lightly kicking with your feet.

The Point

For a seemingly simple little exercise, this is starting to get hard, isn't it? Here's what you should be feeling: The hip and shoulder opposite the extended hand automatically begin to unweigh as a result of the support being placed on the extended hand. This concentrates more weight onto the hand, which you will clearly feel being supported. Even though you might have thought of water as being relatively gravity–free, you get a clear sense of gravity attracting your body weight, which is now centered increasingly on just the one hand. As you alternate to the next hand, you'll feel the hip and shoulder, opposite again, unweigh automatically.

Drills For Moving Support

Moving on to the drills for moving support, we have to clearly understand the meaning of support in swimming in order to develop our perception of moving support in the water. What we observe as stretching out our hand in front of us and pulling back is actually the application of our body weight to the hand; which is our support relative to the body's movement. So our hands are our support, and the water is the support for our hands, albeit fluid and dynamic support, which does not provide the consis-

tency and reliability like the ground — but support nonetheless.

Indeed, there exists a chain of supports to provide support for the body weight from the hand to the trunk. This chain consists of the hand, forearm, arm and shoulder — all connected by joints, ligaments, tendons and muscles. They transfer the body weight to the support hand efficiently by applying some specific rules of movement.

The first *rule* is that support is the least moved part, or relatively unmoved part in contrast with the moving parts. In swimming, the least moved parts are the hands while on support, despite our quick judgement and observation of a large oval the of hands' trajectory. The fact is that the hand's entry and exit points are located almost in the same place, telling us that the hand is not moving in a horizontal direction. The body, however, is substantially transferred, providing irrefutable evidence that the body is indeed the moving part.

The hand's trajectory in the water is necessary to maintain support, which is constantly moving under the hand's pressure. So the hand moves to find unmoved water and support in order to apply our body weight to the support and move us forward in the water.

The secret to making the arm a good transmitter of body weight to the support is to never allow your hand, relative to the horizontal plane (during entry and stroke) to reach above your elbow and shoulders —a typical mistake in swimming. In order to make the hand and arm perform in unison and efficiently transmit the body weight during entry and stroke (moving through the water as a support), the hand in the water should stay lower than the forearm and your elbow should remain lower than the shoulder to provide support for the body. This intricate relationship between your hand, elbow, and shoulder should be maintained consistently as the "Pose" position in swimming so that you are able to effectively and efficiently apply your body weight to the hand.

Drill Set Three: Body weight perception on support.

3a) *The Starting Pose* (Fig.48.15)

Both hands on the pool deck, arms are extended and locked and the body vertical in the water with your head just above the surface.

The Point
Notice how different the perception of the body weight is when we move support to a solid foundation such as a pool deck.

3b) *The Starting Pose* (Fig.48.16)

Both hands on the pool deck, arms are extended and fixed, the body is horizontal in the water with your head just above the surface.
The Drill
Move your body weight (trunk) up on both hands, with the arms extended and fixed,

Fig.48.15 Raise up on your hands on the edge of a pool deck. It's important to raise from the shoulders, not the elbows, keeping the arms relatively fixed and extended.

The Drill
Move your body weight (trunk) up on both hands, with arms extended and locked, out of the water, lifting your upper body on to the pool deck. Then move to the original position and start the drill again. Your feet and legs are slightly kicking to maintain the balance of the body. Take your perception to the next level by performing this drill with one hand.

out of the water, lifting your upper body onto the pool deck. Then move to the original position and start the drill again. Your legs and feet are slightly kicking to maintain balance. Take your perception to the next level by performing this drill with one hand.
The Point
This is the same perception development as in drill 3a), but with the body floating in the water, simulating swimming conditions more closely.

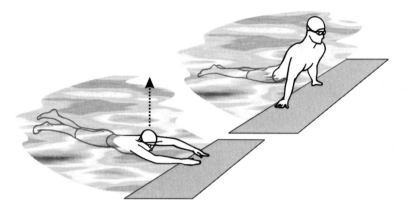

Fig.48.16 Raise up on your hands on the edge of a pool deck while floating horizontally.

3c) *The Starting Pose* (Fig.48.17)

Both hands rest on the hands of a partner who is standing on the bottom of the pool, your arms are extended and fixed; the body is horizontal in the water, with your head just above the surface.

The Drill

Move your body weight (trunk) up on both hands, with arms extended and fixed, out of the water, applying your full body weight on the hands of your partner. Then move to the original position and start the drill again. Your legs and feet lightly kick to maintain balance. Take your perception to

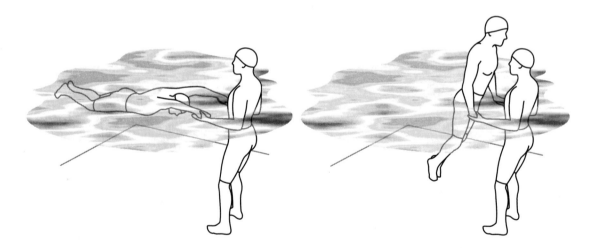

Fig.48.17 Raise up on your hands from floating horizontally while being supported by your partner in the pool.

the next level by performing this drill with one hand.

The Point

The same perception development as in drills 3a) and 3b), but with a more dynamic point of support which resembles water more closely than a pool deck.

Drill Set Four: Perception of support in place or basic sculling.

4a) *The Starting Pose* (Fig.48.18)

Stand on the bottom of the pool, with the water about chest height.

4b) *The Starting Pose* (Fig.48.19)

Start in the same position as drill 4a), standing on the pool bottom.

The Drill

Create support with your hand by sculling back and forth in circles.

The Point

When you swim, all your body weight is supported on one hand... pretty tough!

4c) *The Starting Pose* (Fig.48.20)

Move to water that is slightly overhead in

Fig.48.18 Scull with both hands just below the surface.

The Drill

Create support with your hands by sculling back and forth in circles. Once you feel the support on your hands, lift your legs from the bottom and try to maintain your body position on the support created by your hands.

The Point

This reinforces on a very physical level the concept of supporting your body weight on your hands.

depth, but assume the same starting pose as in the previous drills.

The Drill

Start out by suspending your body as in drill 4a) with the use of your sculling hands. When you are stabilized, increase your effort and thrust your body up and further out of the water. Maintain this elevated position for a few seconds, then relax and let yourself back down and resume supporting yourself as in the starting pose.

Fig.48.19 Scull with one hand at a time, notice the body weight transfer sideways.

Fig.48.20 Raise up out of the water and hold the position by sculling with your hands.

The Point

Notice how your entire upper torso works as a unit to support the effort directed towards your hands.

4d) *The Starting Pose* (Fig.48.21)

The body is horizontal in the water, with both arms outstretched in front and head just above the surface.

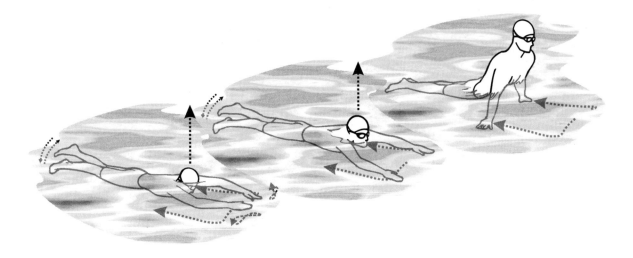

Fig.48.21 Raise up out of the water and maintain the position by sculling with your hands.

The Drill

While sculling with both hands in a circular motion move your upper body up out of the water. Then move to the starting pose and start the drill again. Your feet are slightly kicking to maintain the balance of the body and floating support. Keep the body in the same place.

The Point

The perception of support on your hands in addition to the development and prioritizing the vertical movement of the body.

4e) *The Starting Pose* (Fig.48.22)

The body, horizontal in the water with both arms outstretched in front and head just above the surface.

The Drill

While sculling with one hand in a circular motion move your upper body up out of the water. Then move to the starting pose and start the drill again. Your feet are slightly kicking to maintain the balance of the body and floating support. Keep the body in the same place. Alternate the sculling hand when your support arm gets fatigued.

The Point

Develop the perception of support on one hand and prioritize the vertical movement of the body.

4f) *The Starting Pose* (Fig.48.23)

The body, horizontal in the water, with one arm outstretched in front and the other arm held alongside of the body with your head just above the surface.

The Drill

While sculling with one hand in a circular motion move your upper body up out of the water. Then move to the starting pose and start drill again. Your feet are slightly kicking to maintain the balance of the body and floating support. Keep your body in the same place. Alternate the sculling hand when your support arm is fatigued.

The Point

In this drill there is a greater requirement for a more precise support of the body weight on your hand; muscular efforts follow suit in order to produce a vertical movement of the body.

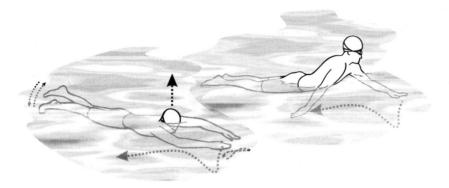

Fig.48.22 Raise up out of the water by sculling with your hand, keep your other arm extended.

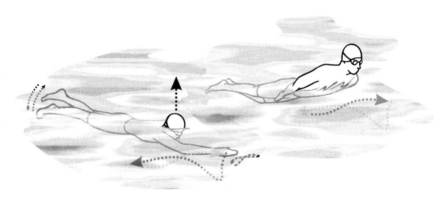

Fig.48.23 Raise up out of the water by sculling with your hand, keep your other arm by the hip.

Drill Set Five: Perception of support while swimming forward.

5a) *The Starting Pose* (Fig.48.24)

The body, horizontal in the water, with both arms outstretched in front and your head just above the surface.
The Drill
While sculling with both hands in a circular motion move your upper body up out of the water and allow the body to move forward while kicking with the feet to maintain the balance and floating support. Then move to the starting pose and start the drill again.
The Point
This drill helps you develop the perception of support on your hands while the body is moving forward.

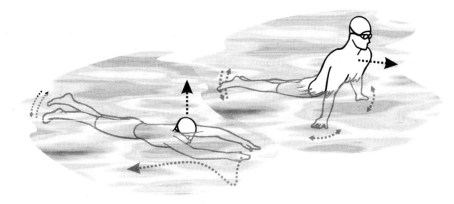

Fig.48.24 Raise up out of the water by sculling with your hands, while moving forward.

5b) *The Starting Pose* (Fig.48.25)

The body horizontal in the water with both arms outstretched in front and your head just above the surface.

The Drill

While sculling with one hand in a circular motion and keeping the other arm in front, move your upper body up out of the water while moving forward. Then move back to the starting pose and start the drill again. Your feet are slightly kicking to maintain the balance of the body moving forward. Alternate the sculling hand when your support arm gets fatigued.

The Point

This drill demands a deliberate increase in perception of support for your hand.

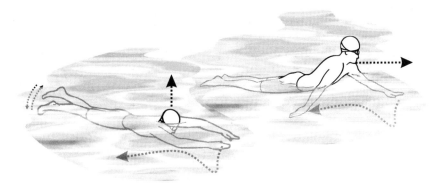

Fig.48.25 Keep one arm extended. Raise up out of the water by sculling with your hand, while moving forward.

5c) *The Starting Pose* (Fig.48.26)

The body, horizontal in the water, with one arm outstretched in front and the other arm held alongside the body with your head just above the surface.

The Drill

While sculling with two hands in a circular motion, move your upper body up out of the water and maintain this position by swimming forward. Your feet are slightly kicking to maintain the balance of the body and floating support. When fatigue

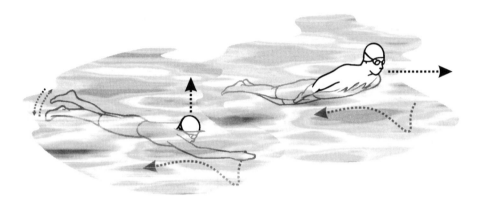

Fig.48.26 Raise up out of the water by sculling with your hand while moving forward.

The Drill

While sculling with one hand in a circular motion, move your upper body up out of the water while moving forward. Then move to the starting pose and start the drill again. Your feet are slightly kicking to maintain the balance of the body moving forward. Alternate the sculling hand when your support arm gets fatigued.

The Point

This drill requires the highest perception of body weight support on your hand; muscular efforts follow suit in order to produce vertical movement of the body.

5d) *The Starting Pose* (Fig.48.27)

The body, horizontal in the water, with both arms outstretched in front and your head just above the surface.

Fig.48.27 Raise up on your hands and maintain the position while moving forward by sculling with your hands.

prevents you from being able to maintain your position, revert back to the starting position, rest, then start again.

The Point

This drill will stress all muscles involved in holding the body in this position. This drill's purpose is to integrate all movement and to develop strength.

5e) *The Starting Pose* (Fig.48.28)

The body is horizontal in the water, with both arms outstretched in front and your head just above the surface.

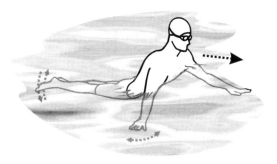

Fig.48.28 Raise up on your hand and maintain this position while moving forward by sculling with your hand.

The Drill

While sculling with one hand in a circular motion move your upper body up out of the water and hold this position by sculling forward. Feet are kicking in order to maintain the balance and floating support.

The Point

This drill incorporates all previous perceptions and takes your awareness in the water to the next level; this drill also works as superior exercise for specific strength development.

5f) *The Starting Pose* (Fig.48.29)

The body, horizontal in the water, with one arm outstretched in front and the other arm held alongside the body, with your head just above the surface.

The Drill

While sculling with one hand in a circular motion move your upper body up out of the water and hold this position by sculling forward. Feet are kicking in order to maintain the balance and floating support.

The Point

To hold body in this position is almost impossible at first. The requirement of balance and muscular efforts may be beyond your current condition. It will take time to build it up, but it will greatly increase your perception of support and specific strength.

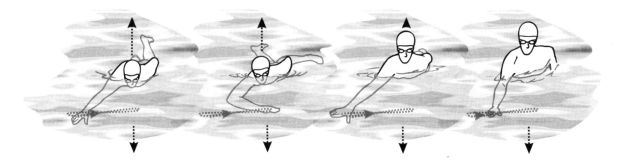

Fig.48.29 Raise up out of the water by sculling with your hand, while moving forward.

Drill Set Six: Water Polo Drills.

6a) *The Starting Pose* (Fig.48.30)

The body, horizontal in the water, with both arms outstretched in front with the head raised out of the water as in a lifesaving or water polo style.

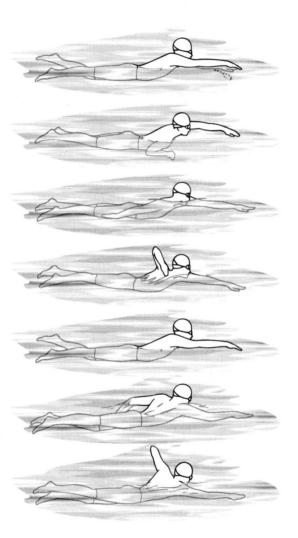

Fig.48.30 Swim in water polo style, scull your hand for support, then shift your body weight to your next support.

The Drill

Make the initial circular sculling motion with one hand until you establish support on it and then pull that hand through the water allowing your body to stay high in the water. Just as you feel the support is lost, move the other hand in the same manner maintaining the upper body above the water.

The Point

Here, you really feel what it is like to focus all your weight and force on the support of the active hand. As you gain the perception for what it feels like to have the shoulder/arm/hand chain accept and transmit the body weight, you will then understand what it is like to shift that weight to the support of the other hand.

6b) *The Starting Pose* (Fig.48.31)

The body, horizontal in the water, with both arms outstretched in front with the

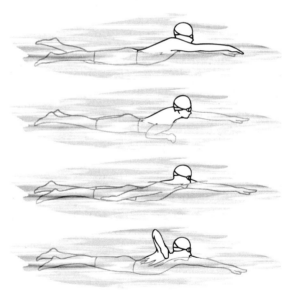

Fig.48.31 Swim in water polo style, scull with your hand for support.

head raised out of the water as in a lifesaving or water polo style.

The Drill

Perform the same action as in drill 6a), but this time with one sculling, the other arm/hand in front for the balance. Repeat with this hand several times before switching, when that arm is so fatigued you think it might fall off.

The Point

Here you gain a greater sense of the transfer of weight as it occurs in real swimming.

6c) *The Starting Pose* (Fig.48.32)

The body, horizontal in the water, with one arm outstretched in front and the other alongside the body with the head raised out of the water as in a lifesaving or water polo style.

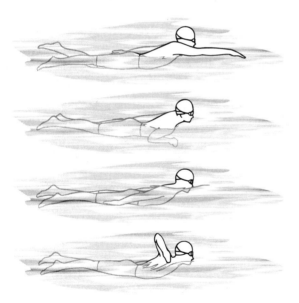

Fig.48.32 Swim in water polo style, scull with your hand for support. Keep your other arm alongside the hip.

The Drill

Perform the same action as in drill 6a). Repeat with this hand several times before switching.

The Point

Here you gain a greater sense of the balance and support on your hand.

Drill Set Seven: Perception of moving support.

7a) *The Starting Pose* (Fig.48.33)

In normal swimming position with your head in the water and the arms extended in front of your body.

The Drill

Put your body weight on one hand and lift your upper body up out of the water. When you feel that the vertical displacement of the body is done, quickly release this hand from support (unweigh) and pull through (recover) as in normal swimming to place it in front, for another support and next vertical lifting of the body.

The Point

This drill closely relates to freestyle swimming, allowing you to transfer the perception from the previous drills to full coordination swimming.

7b) *The Starting Pose* (Fig.48.34)

In normal swimming position with your head in the water, one arm extended in front and the other held alongside of the body.

The Drill

Put your body weight on one hand and lift your upper body up out of the water. When you feel that the vertical displacement of the body is done, quickly release this hand from support (unweigh) and pull through (recover) as in normal swimming to place it in front for another support and next vertical lifting of the body.

The Point

Maintain support under more demanding conditions to enhance the depth of your perception of support, because it is more subtle during freestyle swimming.

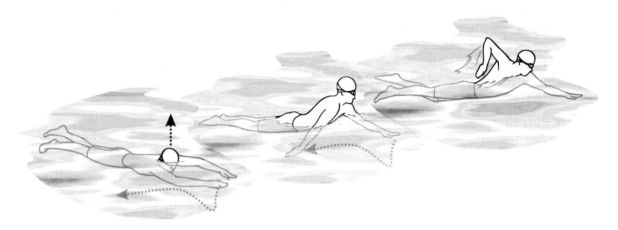

Fig.48.33 Raise up out of the water by finding support for your hand with the other arm extended in front, while pulling through.

Fig.48.34 Raise up out of the water by finding support for your hand with the other arm held alongside the hip, while pulling through.

7c) *The Starting Pose* (Fig.48.35)

In normal swimming position with your head in the water, one arm extended in front of your body and the other held alongside the body.

The Drill "Hesitation"

After all these other drills, this is what we actually call the "Pose Drill." Pull with

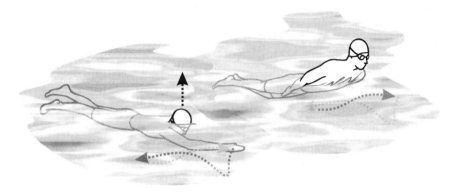

Fig.48.35 Perform one stroke at a time, "hesitating" to perform the next stroke.

the downside hand until it reaches the hip and unweigh the hip just as before. This is the Pose position. Keep the first arm by the hip and begin the same movement with the second hand. Do not allow the arm next to the hip to begin the recovery stroke until the working arm has reached the opposite hip. When the second arm reaches the hip, the first arm then recovers — out of the water — to the original starting position. Alternate from this pose on one side to the other. Do not bring a new working arm into the equation until the work is done with the current working arm.

The Point

The "hesitation" of the arm recovery is needed to re–enforce the other hand's perception of seeking for support and maintaining it, while holding the body weight on this support (hand).

Drill Set Eight: "Diving" drills.

No, you're not headed for the three–meter springboard. This collection of drills emphasizes the subtle lift of the upper body while on support of the working hand and the subsequent fall forward as support alternates.

8a) *The Starting Pose* (Fig.48.36)

Regular swimming position with both hands extended in front of the body.

The Drill

"Look" for support on both hands by pressing down and sensing pressure on your hands, as you would at the beginning of a breaststroke. As you press down, feel your head, shoulders and chest rise up out of the water. As soon as you have reached maximum height, thrust your hands to the front and "dive" forward with your head and upper body.

The Point

If you've ever watched Olympic caliber breaststrokers, you will have noticed this diving motion. The same thing happens in freestyle, but not nearly as obviously.

8b) *The Starting Pose* (Fig.48.37)

Regular swimming position with both hands extended in front of the body.

The Drill

Press down with one hand and bring your head and upper body out of the water as in water polo or lifeguard swimming. When

Fig.48.36 Raise up out of the water while trying to look for support with both hands.

the active support hand finishes its work, recover out of the water with that same hand and dive forward.

The Point

The diving motion allows you to develop a more acute perception of support on the hand, which you need to achieve in normal Pose Swimming. This drill continues to develop the hand/arm/shoulder connection.

8c) *The Starting Pose* (Fig.48.38)

Regular swimming position with one hand extended out in front, the other back by the hip.

The Drill

Press down with the front hand and bring your head and upper body out of the water as in water polo or lifeguard swimming. When the active support hand fin-

One Arm at a Time

Fig.48.37 Raise up out of the water by performing one stroke at a time.

Fig.48.38 Raise up out of the water by performing one stroke at a time. Keep the other arm along the hip.

ishes its work, recover out of the water with that same hand and dive forward. Change "working" hand when it becomes difficult to continue the drill.

The Point

This overemphasis of the diving motion is not only a good strength builder but it ingrains the motion that you will achieve in normal Pose Swimming. As before, it continues to emphasize the hand/arm/shoulder chain connection.

8d) *The Starting Pose* (Fig.48.39)

Regular swimming position with both hands extended in front of the body.

The Drill

This time, keep both hands out in front, but press down with only one hand at a time and repeat the diving motion. Alternate hands as you get a feel for the lifting effect of support on one hand.

Fig.48.39 Raise up out of the water by performing one stroke, then alternating to the other arm.

The Point

As you focus all your weight on just one hand, you will feel the importance of maintaining a solid connection from the hand through the arms and into the shoulders. Everything works together as a unit.

Drill Set Nine: Elastic Tubing Drills.

The basic set–up for these drills is to anchor six foot lengths of elastic tubing at the end of the pool and attach them to your ankles by using a Velcro cuff or simply tying loops at the end of the tubes and slipping them over you feet. The objective is to develop a greater awareness of how to establish and maintain support throughout the swimming stroke. As you move through these drills, any weakness in the connection between the hand, elbow and shoulder will result in the tubes pulling you back toward the wall.

9a) *The Starting Pose* (Fig.48.40)

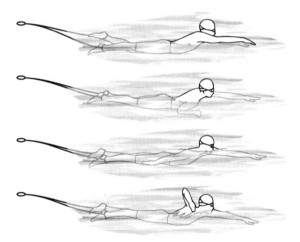

Fig.48.40 Swim with one hand; the other hand extended in front with stretch cords attached to the ankles.

Normal swimming position with hands extended out in front.

The Drill

Start by pulling through a normal swimming stroke with only one hand, while the opposite hand remains outstretched, helping to maintain balance. Do this one–armed swimming for a few strokes with one hand, then switch to the other hand. Finally, swim normally, alternating hands.

The Point

Any flaw in your "power chain" will be exposed with the use of elastic tubes. You will feel the floating support of the water and develop an awareness of the proper body position. If you drop your elbows and lose the connection from the hand, through the elbow to the shoulders, you will feel your body begin to sink as your power development and support decrease.

9b) *The Starting Pose* (Fig.48.41)

Normal swimming position with tubes attached to the ankles.

Fig.48.41 Swim in water polo style; stretch cords attached to the ankles.

The Drill

This time, keep your head out of the water and swim in water polo fashion.

The Point

Even greater emphasis is placed on maintaining a high elbow position.

9c) *The Starting Pose* (Fig.48.42)

Normal swimming position with tubes attached to the ankles.

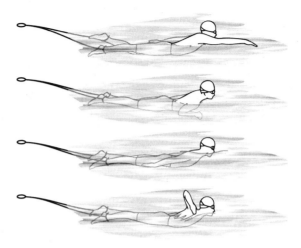

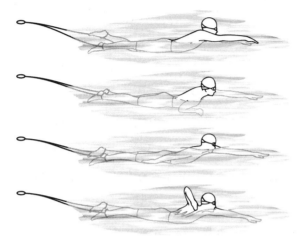

Fig.48.42 Swim in water polo style with one hand; the other hand extended in front with stretch cords attached to the ankles.

Fig.48.43 Swim in water polo style with one hand, the other hand held alongside the hip; stretch cords attached to the ankles.

The Drill
The same swim in water polo fashion, but with one hand only. The other hand is in front to keep balance. Feet are lightly kicking just to maintain balance. Switch the hand when fatigue becomes intolerable.
The Point
The hand has to return back to support much faster in order to counteract the tubes' pulling effect.

9d) *The Starting Pose* (Fig.48.43)

Normal swimming position with tubes attached to the ankles. One hand extended, and the other at rest by the hip.

The Drill
The same swim in water polo fashion, but with one hand only. The other hand is held near the hip. Feet are kicking just to maintain the balance. Switch the hand when fatigue becomes intolerable.
The Point
There is a much greater demand for balance and change of support when performing this drill with one hand. Your coordination and timing will improve dramatically.

9e) *The Starting Pose* (Fig.48.44)

Normal swimming position with tubes attached to the ankles. One hand extended and the other at rest by the hip.
The Drill
Call this one the 'one–arm elastic tubing diving drill'. Find support with your lead hand and then explode as much of your body as you can out of the water. At the apex of your 'flight', dive back in with the same hand leading the way. Do several repetitions with one hand and then switch to

Fig.48.44 Raise up out of the water by performing one stroke at a time; stretch cords attached to the ankles.

the other hand. Finally, alternate between the two hands.

The Point

This is where you really feel the complete hand/arm/shoulder chain supporting your body weight. Besides helping to develop your proprioceptive sense of support, this drill is a heck of a good strength builder and should remain in your regular training plan long after you've completed the transition to Pose Swimming.

Contrast Drills

To further develop your sense of support, you can perform any or all of the above drills by using paddles on your hands or by repeating them with your hands balled into fists. Then, to further heighten the contrast, try the drills with a paddle on one hand while you make a fist with the other. By changing the surface area of your hand, you gain a greater feel for the water and the necessity of supporting your weight precisely on the hand.

Although there is a section for elastic tubing drills, all of the Pose Swimming drills can be performed with the tubing. If you can't find a satisfactory spot to anchor the tubes, a partner can hold them for you. This is a good idea, since your partner would be able to offer immediate feedback as you work through the drills, In this case, it can be a good idea to trade places with your training partner, since observing someone else work through the drills can sometimes be as helpful as doing them yourself.

It's also a good idea to swim a lap of 'real' swimming after you complete each drill. This gives you an immediate sense of how the progression of the drills impacts your swimming efficiency.

Virtually all of the drills can be performed on dry land on benches like the VASA® swim trainer or standard weight room benches, where cable pulls are available. Failing that, you can make your own training device, using a bench and elastic cords on your hands.

The bottom line is simple: do whatever you can to develop a strong connection between your hand and the body, and learn to focus all your weight on the hands. Once you get the feeling, your swimming will improve remarkably and you'll no longer be at a disadvantage from the very first moments of the race.

CHAPTER 49
FROM DRILLS TO SWIMMING: THE SWIMMING POSE

When the subject faces the dilemma how to solve the motor task, he needs to distinguish from the flow of behavior activity which includes many images of movement, the main group of movement and poses.

— Edward Reed

Having worked your way through the sometimes tedious, sometimes challenging set of drills in the previous chapter, you are no doubt eager to "just swim." Whether you are a virtual beginner or are just trying to rebuild your technique for greater performance, the desire to start training and see real progress is certainly understandable.

As you make this transition, though, don't be too eager to start piling up yardage, just for yardage's sake. Keep some of the drills as a part of your swimming routine and don't be in too much of a hurry to swim faster. Stay focused on technique and form and let the speed come.

The Importance of Poses

It will help if you constantly remind yourself that movement in any sport is comprised of a series of poses through which the athlete moves... over and over and over again. Like running and cycling, swimming is a classic example of this. These three sports are all about pure physical movement and involve neither balls nor direct contact with an opponent. Move perfectly and your potential is limitless. Conversely, the high number of repetitions in each sport serves only to magnify the slightest flaw.

Imagine a high–speed film of your movements through a complete cycle in any of these sports and take a look at each individual frame. Though you'll see clearly every position through which your body passes during every stride, rotation or stroke, for each sport there is one — and only one — "Pose" that affects the creation and flow of movement.

Knowing the location of this position or "Pose" is the crucial element for understanding and performing efficient movements. The Pose position for each sport has distinctive and specific features that lead to more skillful and efficient performance. Perfect the Pose for your sport and you're well on your way to faster times and higher places in your races.

The distinguishing characteristic of the Pose in a given sport is that it is the position from which it is easiest to destroy balance and then change support. This basic rule holds for skillful and efficient movement in all sports. The Pose is a balanced position loaded with the potential energy of your own body weight. Your goal is to become skilled in getting into the Pose position in every cycle of your sport.

The Swimming Pose

In swimming, the hand position, the arm position and the chain of connections from the hand through to the hip, are the key factors in achieving the correct point of balance or Pose. This is the point where one hand is extended in front of the body, just below the surface and is providing active support for your weight. Simultaneously, the same side hip is 'cocked', pointing downward and providing floating support for your body weight. With support on both your hand and your hip, you are balanced, but in perfect position to destroy balance.

In this 'loaded' position, you have created a chain of connections from the hand through a strong elbow into the shoulder and down to the hip. Operating as a whole that moves as one, this chain operates as a spring on which you first catch your body weight, and then apply it to generate force. The better and more efficient you become at shifting your weight onto this support and the stronger you can keep the chain of connection, the better stroke you will have and the faster you will swim.

Developing Swimming Perception

To get to that point, however, you must first awaken your perception of these connections, establish them and then strengthen them. That's why the drills of the previous chapter emphasized different elements of the swim stroke, all with the goal of developing your perception of what it is like to

create a strong chain of connections as you place your weight on your hand.

The swim stroke itself is a specific arm/body function that you can neuro–muscularly train to perform accurately and precisely every time, whether you're fresh in the water or nearing the end of an Ironman–length 2.4 mile swim. The Pose Swimming drills are deigned to help you develop the correct hand–arm–body position to maximize efficiency on both floating support and moving support. The drills will also promote the development of the strong connections needed to shift your body weight onto the "hand to hip spring."

As your physical development takes place, the drills' equally important function is to aid in the development and strengthening of your powers of perception, which in turn will enhance your ability to continue building stronger connections. The two work together: strengthen your perception to strengthen connections and strengthen connections to strengthen perception. You will go through many layers of this as you become a more skilled and finely–tuned swimmer.

Making Poses Automatic

You may have noticed that during the drills there was almost no specific mention of the traditional elements of a proper swim stroke. However, if you perform the drills as instructed, those elements will come into play automatically. For example, the classic high elbow position during recovery that all elite swimmers seem to share is not an objective in and of itself. Further, if you attempt to pull all the way past the six o'clock position until your thumb grazes your hip, you will find it difficult to emulate the high elbow position.

However, if you end support when your hand approaches six o'clock, shift your weight and begin your arm recovery, you'll find that your elbow is the first part of your arm out of the water and automatically goes straight up into the desired position. From there, it takes only a slight pendulum action for your hand to re–enter the water and assume support in the Pose position. In short, the drills are designed to make perfect positions become automatic.

Even though swimming by definition takes place in the water, the same definition of movement for land–based sports is the common thread that we will use as a guide for developing swimming technique.

Movement, Balance and Alternating Support

As with all other sports, the best method for learning technique in swimming is guided by a single unifying principle: *All movement is the result of falling from balance or support into the destruction of that balance. To continue movement after destroying balance, we simply continue changing support in sequences.*

If you recall, back in the Trilogy of Concepts chapter, the following sentence was used to describe running: *Running really is nothing more than the rapid, controlled alternation of support. Whenever this finely–calibrated cycle of support is interrupted, running form immediately deteriorates.*

Swimming works exactly the same way. It is a rapid, controlled alternation of support, from the hand and hip on one side of your body, to your hand and hip on the opposite side of your body. And, as with the finely calibrated cycle of support required by running, swimming is even more demanding of precision.

One example of the need for precision in swimming is the previously discussed integration of proper breathing technique into the cycle of your arm movement. Another is the elimination of any deep or slow kicking

movements that would delay the transfer of weight from one side to the next. As soon as the active support hand finishes its work on one side, your ultimate swimming performance will be determined by how quickly and efficiently you transfer your weight to the next support hand so that work can be continued with a minimum of interruption.

Applying Movement Principles to Swimming

Since the goal in swimming is forward movement, it's worth it to review the underlying principles common to all movement:

- All movement exists in the field of gravity, and interacts with this environment.
- All movement is the result of the force or group of forces acting upon a body.
- All movement involves changing the position of the body in space and time, or changing of support.
- All movement is the result of destruction and recovery of balance.

The next question is a simple one: how do we apply these principles to effective swimming technique?

We have previously discussed that gravity is still hard at work in water, which remains the constant force acting on your body. Obviously, forward movement will require changing the position of the body in space and time, which leaves support as well as the destruction and recovery of balance as the objectives of your swimming technique.

When you are in the Swimming Pose, as described above, with your body weight caught on the active support of your lead hand and floating support on the same side hip, you are balanced and full of potential energy. As you transfer your weight to the active hand, your upper body rises slightly in the water, thus positioning you to 'fall' forward. Balance is ready to be destroyed as the weight of your body passes the point where you can remain balanced on the support hand.

In the same way that your opposite foot moving forward arrests your fall when you run, the entry of your recovery hand serves the same purpose in swimming. No, failing to get your recovery hand in place just in time won't result in the same dramatic face–plant you would have if your foot didn't provide just–in–time support when running, but the effect is the same. Your recovery hand is timed to catch your fall and accept the weight of your body just in time to perpetuate the cycle of your forward progress through the water.

Strength in the chain of connections from hand to hip is important to accept as much of your weight as possible on the support hand. Timing and quickness in the transfer of support are equally critical: the hip must unweigh as the active support hand finishes its cycle so that as much of your body weight as possible is ready to be transferred to both active and floating support on the opposite side.

And there it is. Just like running, swimming is a simple matter of Balance — Unbalance — Alternate Support — Balance.

It may be initially hard to accept, but as you embark on your swim training, it is far more important to concentrate on how well you transfer and apply your weight than on how fast your 100 repeats are or how hard you think you are working.

If you focus on keeping a strong chain of connections from the hand, through to the hip, transferring weight quickly and eliminating any extraneous activity while maintaining a streamlined body, the 100 times will come down and you will soon swim faster and more efficiently than you ever imagined.

CHAPTER 50
TIPS FOR TRIATHLON SWIMMING

There is no way to know before experiencing.
— Dr. Robert Anthony

Pools are wonderful places, full of the kind of features that make swimming with perfect technique quite easy. The water is almost always crystal clear, the temperature (despite our many complaints) is most often just right, there are lines on the bottom and at regular intervals a nice wall to push off from... or hang onto. But as venues for triathlons, pools just don't cut it.

Oh, sure, there's an occasional beginner style event that kicks off in a pool, but for the most part, if you're going to do a triathlon, you're going to have to deal with open water — big scary open water.

Where pools are clinically tested to be safe for human habitation, open water can present all kinds of challenges that can take your concentration off maintaining perfect form and switch it to more pressing concerns, like survival for example.

Rivers, lakes, canals, bays, anchorages and the king of all, open ocean, have all hosted triathlons and all offer unique obstacles that can turn a well prepared swimmer into a quivering jellyfish in about ten seconds flat.

While many triathletes truly thrive in open water and gambol about in the surf like young dolphins, there are plenty who stand frozen at the water's edge and put off entering the abyss until the very last second. Many will even forgo a proper warm-up just to forestall the inevitable moment of immersion. Bad plan.

As with anything else, familiarity breeds confidence and success. If you are at all hesitant about the prospect of open water swimming, you should prepare for it just as enthusiastically as you run, ride and swim in your favorite pool. The better you know the setting for a particular swim, the better you'll feel about jumping in there with hundreds of other amped–up tri–people, all racing for the same first buoy.

Nothing Beats Local Knowledge

If the venue in question is conveniently located, plan a couple of visits well in advance of the race to do a full reconnaissance. The best place to start is with the local lifeguard, who can give you a quick rundown on potential water hazards, near shore water depths and current direction. And, yes, if you happen to be going open ocean, they can tell you the current mood of our friends the men in the grey suits (aka sharks).

While it helps to get this local input, bear in mind that in open water almost all conditions are subject to change. A gentle north–south current on recon day can morph into a raging south–north by race day. Piers and rock groins can radically change current patterns. A tidal change can take the four–foot depth of a sand bar and make it something you'll have to run over on race day. And, happily, the school of man–o–war that has been menacing local swimmers may be blown out to sea before the race takes place.

Still, there's a lot to learn in your site visit. If the organizers have been kind enough to post the course online, print it out and try to guess where the start and finish lines will be and where the buoys will be placed. Spend a little time just going in and out of the water at the start and finish areas, noting any sudden drop–offs as well as any slimy disgusting mud flats you'd rather swim over than run though.

Once you feel confident in your ability to get in and out of the water cleanly, swim out to where you think the buoys will be. As you swim out, check routinely to see if currents are having substantial effect on your heading. If the course affords the opportunity, aim for a fixed object such as a tower or building or line up on a navigational buoy in the water to gauge your directional accuracy. Even though conditions may change by race day, you'll benefit from your ability to 'read' the current.

In a recon session such as this, resist the urge to hammer through the swim to see how fast you can do it. Just take your time and get a true feel for the course itself. Consider whether you think you'll want to wear a wet suit or just go bareback. If you are confident of where the finish area will be, look for a tall fixed object that will be a reliable sighting device on race day.

If at all possible, visit the course at the same time as the event will be held. This will give you insight into such things as possible early morning fog, air and water temperatures and, most importantly, sun angles. Many times a noon visit to a venue will reveal the finish area or first buoy to be clearly visible. However, in the early morning, that same target may be blotted out by the blinding light of the rising sun. It helps to know what you'll be looking at when your quiet recon swim becomes the maelstrom of hundreds of swimmers.

But the main point of your pre–race visits is to ratchet up your confidence and ease your anxieties. If you can turn the swim into one less thing to worry about, you'll do that much better in the race, whether your goal is an age group win or just a successful completion of the race.

If You Can't Go There...

...Don't despair. Fortunately, in our ever–shrinking world, a few quick e–mails should turn up someone who knows the local swimming hole. While it won't be a match for an actual visit, pump them for info on things like water temperature, water hazards and that kind of thing.

If you're lucky, you may wind up contacting someone who will be happy to give you a guided tour of the course the day before or on the morning of the event. Just knowing someone who knows the course should be a big help.

Things Change on Race Day

No matter how many visits you make to a race site, you can be sure things will be different when you show up for the race. A finish area that was a lonely stretch of beach may now be a three–ring circus of finish chute, ropes strung up to guide you to the transition area, spectators and even specially installed ramps for entry and exit to the water.

Even though you will have approximately seven million things to check and re-check before the start of the race, make sure you build time into your schedule for a thorough once-over of the swim course.

Treat your warm-up just like you did your recon visits. Check entry and exit points. Familiarize yourself with the route from the swim finish to the transition area. Pay particular attention to any current that may be in the water. Check the sight lines to and from the buoys.

Once you have the course nailed down, plot your starting strategy. If the start is from the shore and you've noticed a particularly strong current, you may want to start off to the side of the pack and let the current push you toward the first buoy rather than get stuck in the middle of a crowd fighting against the current just to make it around the marker.

If you're confronted with choppy surf, plan on dolphining your way out past the breakers. Just run into the water until it gets a little over knee deep then take a shallow dive under an oncoming wave. As you slow, put both feet on the bottom and launch yourself on another dive. If you've practiced this move, you can blast your way to the front of the group while many of your competitors are choking on white water.

Know Where You're Going

One of the toughest challenges in an open water swim is maintaining the shortest distance between two points. Even when you're alone in swimming the course, sighting can be a difficult chore.

CHAPTER 51
ERRORS IN SWIMMING AND THEIR CORRECTION

I'm not in the dark, I'm sure.

— Dr. Nicholas Romanov

No matter what the action is, it is important to perceive whether you are performing it correctly or incorrectly. This brings us back, as it did in running and cycling, to the necessity of having a standard against which our athletic actions can be compared. In swimming, this can be a challenge, particularly for new swimmers who may not feel comfortable in the water.

The very fact that the Pose standard exists should go a long way to ease the anxiety of nervous swimmers, because it reduces the number of things you have to think about and simplifies effective swimming. Still, being in the water does complicate communication and can make the teaching/learning process difficult.

The Pose Method is very specific about what is required to swim correctly. The major premise is that you use gravity to apply your body weight to support on your hands and that provides force for forward propulsion. If you follow the guidelines to do this, almost all of the other elements in swimming will fall into place automatically. Conversely, anything that you do that doesn't fit the process of applying body weight to support is an error and must be corrected.

There are three categories of errors: conceptual, visual, and muscular efforts in space and time; all are related to body position and the application of body weight to support and the incorrect muscular efforts that result.

On the conceptual side, most errors come from the unclear catch phrases coaches traditionally use with their swimmers. Phrases like "catch the water with your hand," "feel the water" or the slightly more helpful "feel the pressure on your hand" (1) are just too imprecise to be useful.

And in none of these oft-repeated phrases is there any reference to body weight or support. It's safe to say very few swim coaches have ever thought of their sport in that way. So the major component of every human movement on Earth is totally left out of the equation when most people learn to swim.

It may actually be easier to adapt to the Pose Method of Swimming if you've never been coached in swimming before. At least you won't have to actively 'unlearn' concepts that have been drilled into veteran swimmers for years. It's easier to start fresh than to switch paradigms and the paradigm shifts required in swimming are significant.

What Moves?

Case in point is the vital question, "what moves in the water — the hand or the body?" Almost every bit of swimming instruction you've ever heard is based on detailing the way the hand moves through the water on each stroke. If you watch a swimmer as a neutral observer, what you see — the visual component — appears to be the movement of the hand through the water.

This in turn leads to the swimmer devoting tremendous concentration and energy to replicating the S–shaped sweep that the hand appears to make through the water on each stroke. It seems to make sense; why not copy that which you see being done by better swimmers?

The problem is that it is the wrong paradigm in thinking, in perception and in muscular effort. Thinking about the S–curve switches your focus from moving your body to moving your hand. Since one has to provide support for the other to move, this reverses roles and you find that you are using your body to support the movement of your hand rather than using your hand to support the movement of your body. Even if that's not what you want to happen, as soon as you start thinking about the path of your hand, that's where your mental focus goes.

The deceptive nature of being in the water makes it easy to confuse the thing that causes the movement and the thing that is being moved. It just seems more 'natural' to think of the hand as a device used to push water in the opposite direction of the moving body. Along that same line, it also seems that this is a natural fit with Newton's Third Law: the hand pushes back,

therefore the body moves forward. What's wrong with this picture?

Empty Hands

Just this: when we move our hand, it carries with it only the force of its own mass or 'hand weight' and the water pressure against the hand. Without the body weight of the swimmer being applied to it, the hand is essentially 'empty' and generates almost no force or acceleration. This is clearly demonstrated when you watch unskilled swimmers flailing away with their hands but going nowhere fast.

From a philosophical standpoint, you could compare this to the adage, "we don't live to eat, but we eat to live," meaning the point of eating is merely to support life and not the opposite. In swimming, running or cycling or any other movement this happens all the time as athletes confuse the part of the body providing support and the body itself being the moving part. When we try to move the support, we are in the wrong paradigm.

Thus, if you try to move your hand when you swim, you then have to try and push the water, which means you will of necessity apply muscular effort to the hand. But to swim correctly, your muscular efforts should not focus on the hand, but on transferring the body weight to the hand.

This is critical. Muscular efforts to move the hand amount to nothing. **Muscles should only be used as transmitters to apply the body weight to support on the hand.** Most swimmers find this very confusing, but trying to swim with the hands is like a boxer trying to throw a punch using only the hand and arm, without the force of the body weight behind the punch.

In boxing, the muscles transmit the body weight through the hand to the opponent. In swimming, the muscles transmit the body weight through the hand to support on the hand. In cycling, the legs transmit the body weight through the legs to the pedals. It's all the same thing.

Determining Correct Body Position

Following this logic, the correct **body position in swimming** is the one that streamlines the most efficient application of body weight to the hand. Body position per se is not important in and of itself; it is only important from the perspective of the body weight application to support. If you correctly apply body weight to the support, your body position will be perfect. Consideration of balance and drag follow the main question: did you apply your body weight optimally on support or not?

Again, this is just like running or cycling by using gravity to the greatest possible extent. To teach Pose swimming, you do not start with body position, you start with support. The only concern is to search for the means to apply body weight to support and then change support.

Just as the search for support dictates the body position, the same holds true for the positioning of the support arm as well. Maintaining a high elbow with a 90° degree bend is necessary to provide the most effective support for the body weight. If your elbow is not at 90° degrees your application of the body weight to support is not ideal.

The reverse is also true: if you do not apply your body weight to support, your elbow will not be in a high position at 90° degrees. Interestingly, young swimmers who have never received any instruction intuitively search for support and swim relatively well while remaining clueless about the underlying concepts.

Support Determines Everything

The correct elbow position of the arm performing the stroke in the water is the result of the proper application of body weight to support. If it is one degree more-or-less than 90° degrees then transmission of the body weight is reduced. An Olympic swimmer doesn't care about the angle of the elbow, but he or she does care about perception of support. Scientists and coaches should know the specifics of elbow position, but this by itself is not a primary thing that we need to teach the swimmers.

The pitch of the hand is another example. The pitch is the angle of the hand towards the angle of direction of movement. From the scientific point of view this is important, but what swimmer cares about this? It simply isn't possible to precisely control this because the angle of the hand in relation to the movement is basically imperceptible and certainly can't be checked while your body is moving up and down and side–to–side. Trying to tell a swimmer to hold a certain pitch during a stroke is basically absurd. Just tell them to keep support on the hand.

Attempting to move the hips as a major propulsive force for power production (2) is a complete error. To move the hips is to shift body weight from one support to another. Before you move your hips somewhere you have to have support there. If you move your hips to a place where there is no support you are essentially dropping your hips to nowhere and claims of resulting power production make no sense.

If you move to non–existent support, where can you apply your body weight? Nowhere is the answer. If you move your hips, your hands are empty and there is no power production. To avoid this error you must develop an acute perception of support. Otherwise you will continue to be an inefficient swimmer.

It is the hips themselves that provide the floating support. Moving the hips does not add propulsive force. They must be set in place before each stroke so that the force can be applied.

Errors in arm and hand action occur when you try to pull water with the hands and arms or with the lower arm by pulling from the front to the back. From an observer's viewpoint it looks exactly like you move water by pulling your arm and hand from front to back. However, this is a very misleading interpretation and trying to pull this way leads to subtle difference inside your muscles' connections and basically causes you to activate your muscles the wrong way.

There is a huge difference in muscular connections between pulling your hand to the body versus pulling your body to the hand, even if from an anatomical perspective it looks to be the same movement. Think of it this way: muscles are attached to body weight (not your bones), so they constantly work according to the logic of transferring the body weight in the desired direction.

If you try to pull your arm, you will inevitably drop your elbow down and sacrifice the strength of connections that hold your body weight on support. Novice swimmers often drop the elbow down in an effort to move the arm and hand and push the water. Next, the shoulder drops as well and support is further compromised.

Rotational activity of the hips and body is another common error in swimming. If we focus on rotating the body and give it priority in our swimming movement, that rotational effort forces the shoulder down. As the shoulder drops lower than the hand, support on the hand is lost completely. Instead of the hand supporting the body weight, it winds up out in front of the body 'empty', without any body weight on it at

all. The body loses the support required to make forward and upward propulsion. Later in the stroke, the swimmer may regain support but by that time most of propulsive force has vanished. The most powerful moment of the stroke is lost, resulting in much slower swimming speed.

Putting pressure on the chest is another error of shifting priority from the support on the hand for the body weight to the chest. Clearly, if you put the body weight on the chest by pressing it down on the water, you don't have support on the hand. Your chest is not capable of providing support for your body to move forward. You have to keep your body weight on support, both the floating support on the hip and the active support on the hand. This facilitates the rapid shift of body weight from one support to the next.

When the hand is positioned in front of your body you can put more and more of your body weight on it. The entire body weight should be somewhere above your hand when the change of support takes place. While from the outside vantage point it appears as if the swim stroke is a process of pulling the hand under the body, what actually takes place is the transfer of body weight on support. It is exactly like landing in running, when your body weight gradually is transferred to support starting at first touch down through mid–stance where the transfer is complete and unweighing begins.

Your muscles tense and become increasingly loaded as more and more body weight arrives on full support in the Pose position. As soon as your body weight is fully loaded on support, be it on your foot while running, or on your hand while swimming, you immediately have to start falling from support again.

Of course, your muscular efforts are vital in this process, serving to brace your body on support and transfer the maximum amount of energy to allow you take full advantage of gravity's force. So, in swimming, you put your body weight on your hand in front of your body and transfer more and more body weight onto your hand until you have to fall from this support to support on the other hand.

The biggest error with the legs is moving them too much. The primary function of the legs in swimming is to provide balance in the water. Therefore, particularly in triathlon swimming, the best plan is to minimize active kicking of the legs and focus on their main function role of providing balance. This keeps the legs fresh for cycling and running.

Observing the best swimmers in triathlon confirms this strategy. In sprint competitions in the pool, the legs move faster because you have to maintain the balance in more sophisticated way, and kicking can add some marginal additional propulsive force that may be critical in events where winning margins may be less than a hundredth of a second. However the scant gains that might be realized by forceful kicking are not energy cost effective in the longer swims of triathlon.

While the legs don't contribute significantly to forward propulsion, they still have a job to do. The body consists of multiple parts and it is the job of the legs to maintain connections throughout the body as it moves horizontally through the water. As the hand and arm supports the body when it moves up and over support and then falls forward, the legs push themselves forward and hold the posture of the body together as a unified whole. If the body is not held together in proper alignment as an integrated system, then the inertia of the body will effectively separate the upper body from the lower body and the legs will drag behind slowing forward propulsion tremendously.

The position of the head directly impacts your body position. Novice swimmers, particularly in open water pack–swimming situations, may tend to want to bring their heads out of the water more often than is necessary for navigation. The mere lifting of your head throws the entire body out of alignment and shifts body weight from support on your hand.

This is a major error that not only robs you of power but also creates drag because if the head goes up the legs will go down and ruin your hydrodynamic efficiency. Other problems arising from the 'turtle move' with the head include greater difficulty in shifting support and greater tension in your muscles as the upper body is forced to work harder. And though it is a much more rare error, holding your head too low in the water creates a whole host of problems as well.

Correcting Errors

In general, every error you can make in swimming ultimately impacts your ability to apply maximum body weight to support. Correcting these errors begins with a clear vision and understanding of the relationship between support and body weight and the necessity of changing support to move the body forward.

Correction of support errors begins with a more acute perception of support in the water. Frustrated swimmers continually get hung up on questions of hand entry, hand path, elbow position and numerous similar considerations. Instead of worrying about those things, focus on feeling the pressure of the body weight on the hand. To do this, make sure you include the drills related to developing perception of pressure as a part of your regular in–water routine. These drills include:

- moving support in place
- support for the body in a vertical position
- support for the body in a horizontal position
- maintaining support with two hands
- maintaining support with one hand
- doing all of the above, while moving forward

As you continue to correct your swimming errors, you will have to fine–tune your perception of support at any hand position. As you do these drills on a regular basis, you'll understand exactly how much muscular effort you need to expend. Your muscles should only work as hard as is necessary to keep your body weight on support — and not a bit more. As you work your way up from lower speeds and approach your top speed, you should never work any harder than is required to establish you weight on support and then change support.

In the Pose methodology it is very important to understand that no matter what sport you're doing, the efforts to establish and change support are not separated by space and time but by your perception. In running, at the same moment that you fully load your body weight on support, you begin removing it from support by pulling up your foot. In pedaling your bicycle, your mind may tell you that push and pull are separate actions but in reality and in perception both actions are integrated at three 3 o'clock position. As soon as your body weight is established on the pedal, you have to release the weight from the pedal. In swimming it is the same way. The very moment you find support on the hand is the exact moment of losing it as well.

Feeling support and losing it is not a matter of space and time but of highly developed and controlled perception. The more you work to develop this perception the better you will perform in all three sports.

References:

1. Knight, M. *Teaching Freestyle Fundamentals. Modern History of Articles in Freestyle From Past ASCA World Clinic's and Related Sources.* American Swimming Coaches Association Advanced Freestyle School. Ft. Lauderdale, FL, 1995, p. 7.

2. Prichard, Bob. *Being Hip in the Water.* Metro Sports Magazine, Mar. 1994, pp. 40–41.

SECTION VII
RACING PERFORMANCE AND TECHNIQUES IN TRIATHLON

CHAPTER 52
RACING PERFORMANCE AND TECHNIQUES IN TRIATHLON

Activate the mind without dwelling anywhere.
— *The Diamond Cutter Scripter*

So after all the work, after all of the time and commitment, you are ready to put yourself to the test. A race.

Race — the very word itself can conjure up all sorts of thoughts — anticipation, trepidation, a little fear, memories of past events... good or bad.

Even though it will be just another weekend morning to most people who'll get up, have breakfast and mow the lawn or do some shopping, the day already has a special meaning for you and as it nears it can bring up a strange mix of thoughts and emotions.

Maybe it's your first time out, maybe you're an experienced veteran; either way this art of racing can seem an elusive one. You only get one shot at it each time and before you know it, it's over.

Like all aspects of triathlon, there are more books offering advice on racing performance than you could fit in your kit bag. There's advice from "stay strong" and "maintain your focus" through to the opposite — "rid yourself of any focus on your performance," "listen to music," etc. The world of sports psychology is caught up in this debate between Association and Dissociation (1).

Table 1. Adopted from Lee Crust (1).

Techniques for dissociation
1. Music — This can generate positive thoughts, improve your mood state and distract you from the physical demands of your sport. But be careful not to get too distracted if you are running in a busy area;
2. Counting game — Count the number of blue cars you see, or the number of dogs, or post boxes. Be inventive;
3. Alphabet game — Work through from A to Z for a chosen category, such as women's names or countries;
4. Rainbow game — Try to notice as many colours as possible while you work out: aim for all the colours of the rainbow;
5. Active fantasy — Imagine yourself as a lottery winner and decide how to spend your winnings.

Avoid thoughts relating to your work, jobs you have to do and anything problematic, as this can increase tension. Try to be creative and have fun with dissociation. It can help you relax and enjoy your sport even more.

But what are you supposed to focus on? What's the seemingly–magical thought process which will lay the foundation for the fluid performance of the so–called "Zen condition" or the "Zone?" Are they real states of mind at all?

The answers are strikingly simple: in the Pose Method the major element of performance (in both training and racing), is your focus on the movement itself.

More exactly, it is only about what we operate with and how we can keep ourselves on this level of effortless, fluid movement. It keeps coming back to the same basic principle: the power of the perfect performance lies in maintaining and reproducing your skill of movement. Too simple? It might seem so, on the one hand; but on the other, it's impossibly complex!

The key to a perfect performance every time

So what's the key to unlocking that great performance for which you've been training so hard?

In order to answer this question we have to return to the major premises discussed in many of the previous chapters: the first being the Action Concept and the other being Perception. It's all about how we combine these two things to apply our minds to do this work as a means of focusing on the task at hand.

As you already know, in the modern paradigm of triathlon or endurance events the major focus in training and performance is devoted to such things as power system development or aerobic conditioning.

Movement by itself is something that is considered separately — almost as an aside and a subordinate contributor to performance. The generally held view is this: you are good as long as you can maintain your aerobic capacity.

Turn this view around 180° degrees and you have the Pose Method approach: your performance level lies in your ability to keep focused on producing and reproducing very specific actions which lead to the best utilization of your energy systems (aerobic capacity, anaerobic threshold, etc).

Just ask yourself: "What is the most difficult part of my racing performance in triathlon?" Your answer will be — most likely — difficulties in your breathing, high lactate levels, muscular weakness, soreness and so on. This is what your perceptions pick up on and your memory holds on to.

Your brain conceptualizes these thoughts into the idea that it is then necessary to combat these difficulties by developing a higher level of aerobic capacity and, as a consequence, pushing yourself through ever–more gruelling sessions and bigger training volumes.

So many triathletes feel they must almost punish themselves for what they perceive as this fundamental weakness.

The point they miss is that this approach does nothing to help their movement – the very (and only) thing which is getting them around the course. In taking this approach, you are abandoning your body, because it is your body that is moving — transporting your GCM through space. Your heart rate is not moving, your breathing is not moving, nor is your blood flow — these things only occur in response to one thing: the way in which your body is moving through time and space.

So while you might be struggling up a steep climb on the bike, frantically analyzing your HR and how best to bring it down before your start your run leg, there is only one answer — switch your attention to performing your movement perfectly. And you cannot concentrate on your action if you are too busy focusing on all the signals.

It's a bit like the following situation: you have driven into a major city for the first time and hit rush–hour traffic. There are horns, shouting, people switching lanes and cutting others off. You've got a map on your lap and are completely lost. As you start to panic, focusing on trying to read the map and worrying about how you'll get out of this mess — you lose focus on the actual task at hand: driving. So while you're desperately trying to work out which way to go, it's highly likely that you'll create a much bigger problem for yourself than being lost by hitting someone or something.

Racing performance is not really much different. It's all about keeping your mind on the action which allows you to move properly. This movement recruits your heart, lungs, blood, etc. — not your thoughts that you are taking part in an endurance event.

By allowing yourself to lose focus on the action and your mind to wander to interpreting the signals coming from your body, you allow fear to creep in and your brain will recruit a tremendous amount of tension and energy in order to stave–off this potentially life–threatening attack.

Let's illustrate this with another example: you are enjoying a nice evening stroll along a boardwalk, watching the sunset and chatting with your partner. All of a sudden someone rushes past, bumps into you and turns to start a confrontation. All of a sudden your body is flooded with adrenalin, your heart rate goes up and your muscles tense in readiness. What has recruited all of this tension and energy? Your thoughts and emotions. This is what happens to athletes at the Olympic Games and is why major international competition can be so difficult for some. As soon as they allow their emotions to become the energy recruitment system, they start to think negatively — comparing themselves to other competitors in front or passing them.

It really is all in the mind

So what's the conclusion we can draw from all of this? How do you formulate or design your racing performance strategy?

It starts from the very simple assumption that racing is a mental exercise.

After that, all you have to do is come to terms with how to use this piece of knowledge.

As we have mentioned already, perfecting the art of performance is about focusing on the action that you need to produce to create the performance. Which leads to the next point — in order to produce this action perfectly, you must have perfect perception.

In the swim, you must focus on your perception of support and changing support. On the bike too, all your attention must go to your support on the pedals — really developing your perception of the pressure on the pedals. Everything comes to this point — the application of body weight to support. The major mover, as you know, is Gravity. If you lose perception of your body weight on support then you revert to using something else in an attempt to create movement — unnecessary muscular effort. This is one of the major mistakes in racing. Without your perception of your body weight on support, you are guaranteed to have a below–par performance.

Out, out damn thought!

Your focus on your movement should almost be a "non–thinking" exercise. It is what is known in Zen as a no–mind state. Excess mental activity is as useful as excessive muscular activity — not at all.

As much as possible stay away from any estimation of your abilities. You don't know your abilities, You have to be free in your performance and leave behind any kind of estimations. Let your performance lead you to this — not your mental expectations. Just let go. If you were in love, you wouldn't follow any written plan to enjoy the relationship, you just follow your perception of the interaction. It is an unpredictable thing. When you run, it is exactly the same — you don't need to force the movement, the leading force is gravity, All you have to do is let yourself go there and use your perception of the proper action that follows. This is how you stay "in the zone."

So everything keeps coming to this same point: you have to precisely know the action and have perfect perception of this action in order to keep executing it properly. It has nothing to do with force, muscular effort or power production. It is movement free from muscular tension and muscular domination.

Another thought process to avoid is self–examination: judging yourself, evaluating your abilities, your aerobic capacity, your potential, etc. All of these thoughts will come back to haunt you during a race. Remember, all of these aspects are only by-products of your action. The process goes like this: you consume gravity in performing the action, gravity then consumes energy through your body and consequently your HR, breathing, etc. increases to allow

you to restore this energy to recover from, or maintain, the action.

Your brain interprets the signs arising from this consumption of energy — heavy breathing, increased HR, etc. — as warning signs and translates them into emotion: usually fear. This becomes the crucial point: if you allow yourself to focus on your feelings at this juncture then things start to cascade out of control. Not only do you lose focus on your action and become more inefficient (and subsequently require more energy to move), but the fear in your brain also triggers an increase in muscular tension and energy usage. So you find yourself spiralling downhill on two fronts.

Instead, as your brain receives these signals, you need to know that they are a normal part of the process and turn your mind back to the production of the action. You need to re–enforce your perception in order to maintain the proper and perfect action throughout the entire performance.

No excuses...

Stand around enough start lines of endurance events and it won't be long before you recognize the pattern — athletes playing down their performance even before taking a step. "I haven't been training that well," "I'm feeling a little off," "I think I'll just cruise and see how I feel," are all common variations of the same theme coming up again and again: the Philosophy of Failure.

The foundation for failure is to find excuses for your performance. It's one of the worst things you could do but millions of athletes do it. They might try to dress it up as a post–race review or poor racing tactics, but closer inspection usually reveals the same pattern — using an excuse to avoid addressing the things that really matter.

In the second that you start looking for excuses you have failed. Even though triathlons take place over a longer time–frame, they require the exact same discipline and focus as any other event. So just as it goes in high jumping — if you turn up with excuses, take off your shoes and go home. You are not ready to perform. So too, it goes in running.

Performance requires only focus, perception and action. These are the major contributors to your success and if you stick to the process, success will come.

References:

1. Crust, L. *Sports Psychology — Thought Control*. Peak Performance, <http://www.pponline.co.uk/encyc/0991.htm>

CHAPTER 53
HOW GRAVITY WORKS IN RUNNING

The important thing in science is not so much to obtain new facts as to discover new ways of thinking about them.

— *Sir William Bragg*

Nature doesn't adjust to our level of skill.

— *Lawrence Gonzalez*

As a coach, a sports scientist and a doctor of exercise physiology, I have devoted more than thirty years of my career to studying the human movement we know as running. While running has always been an essential element of human development and survival, I have always been captivated by a paradox: virtually all humans can run, but no one seems to know *how* to run.

By this I mean that there has never been a consensus on either the forces involved in running or on the best mechanics to use those forces to reach optimum running performance. In fact, quite the contrary seems to be the case. The only consensus is that there is no best way to run and that each and every human has his or her own unique running style.

As a scientist, I found this simply unacceptable. How could it possibly be that running was unique among all human endeavors, a skill that could not be taught, but was predetermined at birth? If we can

teach swimming, dance, gymnastics and an entire galaxy of movements, why can we not determine and teach the best way to run?

This became my quest: to study the skill of running, identify the forces and mechanics involved and design a curriculum that would let all people, regardless of age, gender, ethnicity or athletic background, learn the best way to run.

After many years of research and experimentation, I came to the inescapable conclusion that gravity was, is and always will be the primary force providing forward propulsion in running. Not surprisingly, when I first began presenting and publishing this concept, the response was not exactly universal acclaim.

My critics were merciless. Anyone with a modicum of knowledge and education in classical mechanics was quick to point out that gravity does not work for horizontal propulsion of the body. At best, gravity was considered a 'neutral' force in propulsion and there were many that held the opinion that gravity was the force against which we had to struggle in order to run.

Rather than be dissuaded by the arguments of these many critics, I am grateful for their thoughts and opinions. Proof is an essential component of the scientific process and the naysayers attempting to debunk my theories only drove me to work harder and widen the scope of my inquiries into the nature of human movement.

As I worked to gain a greater understanding of movement and fill in the blanks on what I had called the Pose Method of Running, I made two further discoveries. The first was that I wasn't standing alone with my theories about gravity and running. Instead, I was standing on the shoulders of giants.

Across the course of human history, numerous great thinkers had pondered and written about the fundamental nature of gravity and movement and all of their thoughts seemed to bolster my theories. From the ancient Greeks through geniuses like Sir Isaac Newton, Galileo and Leonardo da Vinci and into the 20th Century writing of the British scientist Thomas Graham Brown, I continually found support for my thoughts and work.

The second benefit spurred by my critics was the gradual realization of the role of gravity in all human movement, not just running. Once I had established a template for perfecting running technique, I saw that templates based on gravity's role in movement could be designed and taught for all propulsive sports. The Pose Method wasn't limited to running; it could be applied to everything from swimming, to golf, to the shot put; the applications are limitless.

While I am quite confident of the applications of gravity to movement, I also realize that many of those same critics that drove me to defend and expand my work remain to be convinced. While I have had the help of many esteemed colleagues in designing and conducting experiments to bear out my theories, work that is still ongoing, with this short paper I want to work through the basics of running as an endeavor powered by gravity.

The Inescapable Pull of Gravity

There is an enigma about the role gravity plays in running. Since we live, breathe, eat, sleep and run under the constant influence of a gravitational field, we interact with gravity every moment of every day. As the old axiom about never seeing the forest for the trees implies, we are so involved with gravity that we never really think about it. Even as we build relations with gravity and react to it, this activity and relationship building all take place on a subconscious level.

When we roll downhill on a bicycle, we don't question what moves us; we know it is gravity but we just call it descending or going downhill. It is the same thing with running. We know implicitly that it is easier to run downhill than it is to run uphill and leave it at that.

However when the grade levels out and is neither one degree downhill, nor one degree uphill, we pretty much discard the notion that gravity is in play. This is where we get the idea that gravity is a neutral force in running. For whatever reason, at that transitional point between uphill and downhill, we throw gravity out the window and start believing that it is our own muscular effort that propels us down the road. Can gravity's switch be turned off at that point or is there just a lack of understanding about the true role that gravity plays in propulsion?

One possible interpretation that easily could be accepted is the notion that muscular efforts are the dominant force in running and that gravity is simply a helper, adding a little momentum when we go downhill and taking it right back away when the road goes back up. Certainly, this is the paradigm that most runners believe.

If you accept that view, then a simplified hierarchy of the forces involved in running would place muscular effort at the top of the pyramid with gravity just below and a bottom rounded out by things including coriolis force, ground reaction force and even wind direction.

This general view of the forces involved in running has been so accepted that essentially no one involved in the biomechanical analysis of running even bothered to look at running from the opposing perspective, placing gravity as the primary propulsive and integrative force in running. As a result, virtually no experiments or theoretical modeling in physics, mathematics or biomechanics were done evaluating gravitational torque's role in horizontal propulsion.

Over the decades, among the thousands of scientific articles and books devoted to running, beginning with the classical work of the brilliant French scientist and chronophotographer Etienne–Jules Marey (1), no one attempted to define the hierarchy (in a system) of forces involved in running. This was particularly strange because in the science of General Systems Theory (2), hierarchy is one of the most important aspects of the system. To this day, science still has little to say about the impact of gravity on forward movement in running.

You could call this lack of inquiry the Flat Earth Syndrome. If everyone believes the same thing, then what is the point of testing a contradictory viewpoint?

In classical physics gravity has always been considered a neutral force in relation to horizontal movement. In this case 'neutral' is specifically defined as force acting perpendicularly to the direction of travel of the body. The implication of this is that gravity always pulls straight down and not forward.

Exceptional Thinkers

Historically there were virtually no significant attempts to explain running from any other point of view. The exceptions included the remarkable insights of Leonardo da Vinci in the 15th century and then, just a mere 400 years later, the follow–up work of Scotland's famed neurophysiologist and mountain climber, Thomas Graham–Brown in 1912.

Da Vinci weighed in with thoughts that left little doubt about his perspective on gravity's role in forward propulsion saying, "Therefore a man will always present more of his weight towards that point to which he desires to move than to any other place. The faster a man runs the more he leans towards the place to which he runs and gives more of his weight in front of his axis of balance than behind" (3).

So clearly did da Vinci make his point, and given his other monumental achievements, you might have thought that would have settled the issue right then and there. Perhaps it was those other achievements that overshadowed this little bit of wisdom, because his thoughts about propulsion attracted little attention.

Then, early in the 20th century, Graham Brown returned to the same theme, pointing out, "It seems to me that the act of progression itself — whether it be by flight through the air or by such movements as running over surface of the ground — consists essentially in a movement in which the center of gravity of the body is allowed to fall forwards and downwards under the action of gravity, and in which the momentum thus gained is used forward, so that from one point in the cycle to the corresponding point in the next, no work is done (theoretically), but the mass of the individual is, in effect, moved horizontally through the environment" (4).

But, as with da Vinci's earlier commentary, Graham Brown's work in this particular arena attracted little notice. Consequently, throughout the 20th century gravity's role in running was continually represented only as a neutral or downward force.

Is Gravity Truly a Propulsive Force?

This leads us back to the central question at hand: does gravity work in running as a propulsive force or not? While I have been quite confident that it does, I still find it necessary to be very careful about how I express my opinion in this regard since there remains a lot of uncertainty about exactly how it works.

The modern science of running began to accumulate data supporting gravity as a propulsive force, but it was not yet so obvious that we could precisely describe the working mechanism. It was very difficult just to get the cooperation of sports scientists to put the theory into research programs simply because of the strong establishment united behind the existing paradigm of running.

Nevertheless, the scientific community amassed more and more data that could be considered controversial and certainly was difficult to explain from the prevailing point of view, which held that gravity was a neutral force. Yet, even as the evidence started to mount, much of it was debated, debunked or discarded, simply because it is human nature to ignore or deny those things that we don't understand or that don't fit into our preconceived notion of the natural order of things,

Still, a substantial body of direct and mostly indirect facts began to grow, giving increasing support to the notion that gravity is in fact involved in horizontal propulsion during running. All it takes to accept the evidence is the willingness to view running from a new perspective, and the role of gravity quickly becomes quite clear.

The Prevailing Paradigm

Taking the currently accepted paradigm of running and placing it in a hierarchical model (Fig.53.1) yields something that begins with time and distance and then progresses to average speed and in the end comes to the forces exerted.

This logic is in conflict with classical mechanics' definition of movement as a product of force exertion upon a material body. Force must appear first to create a change in movement — acceleration. Time and distance cannot cause this change, therefore force, which is the origin of change of movement, has to be the starting point of the model. Among all forces in running the only one that is permanent and continually acts upon the body is gravity.

Despite the existing knowledge in the biomechanics of running, the role of gravity is not regarded as a dominant or leading force for propulsion (see Chapter 2 "Gravity"). The current hierarchical model (5) considers gravity to be a neutral force on stance, acting only during flight, and therefore not producing forward propulsion of the body.

Reexamining the Role of Gravity

Nevertheless, if you give strong consideration to facts and logical flow, it is difficult not to think of gravity as the leading force for forward propulsion in running. As we examine this proposition, there are two major questions to consider: 1) Where does gravity act as a propulsive force? 2) How does gravity do it?

To open this discussion and understand the real role of gravity in running, we return to fundamental physics and recall how force is defined in mechanics. First of all we need to state that gravity is a force and, as a force, has a very specific appearance and definition.

In physics, force is understood **not as** "the cause of movement, but a cause of change of movement. A single result of act of force on free material body, which doesn't in-

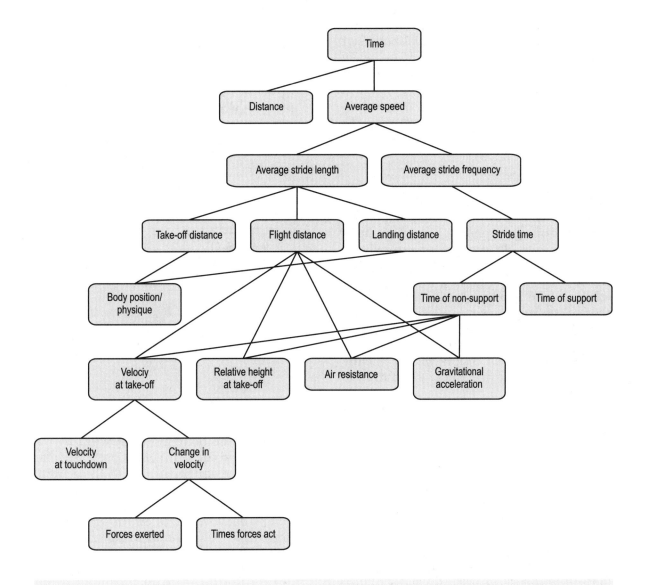

Fig.53.1 Traditional model of running (Hay and Reid, 1988; p. 282)

teract with a third body, is acceleration. In classical mechanics the term 'force' is understood as a quantitative characteristic of interaction between material bodies. No other meaning (sense) is included in the term 'force' in mechanics" (6).

Gravity is clearly a force, because it does change movement and accelerate bodies towards Earth. The one unique characteristic of gravity that could be considered a 'problem' is that it attracts all material bodies at the same rate no matter how big or heavy they are. As Galileo first demonstrated in the now clichéd experiment he performed at the Leaning Tower of Pisa, two objects of different mass are pulled toward Earth at the same rate of 9.81 meters per second squared.

This universal quality of gravity's attraction is an amazing thing with almost divine meaning, the depth and significance of which is difficult to comprehend. Gravity is a distant, invisible force with seemingly no direct interaction or application to another physical body. This gives gravity a hidden influence and impact on us, which we really notice only after we make a special effort. Therefore, gravity's role as a horizontal propulsive force is almost imperceptible, a role that goes unnoticed unless we specifically set out to examine and understand it.

To begin to understand gravity's role in horizontal propulsion, we can start with the assumption that there is a space and a time along with a specific condition of the runner's body in terms of position and stance that could permit gravity, in a cooperative effort with other forces, to produce a resultant horizontal force vector.

Theoretically (apriori) it is a simple matter to say that the ability of gravity to do its work as a forward propulsive force is limited to specific moments in space and time. Further, it is possible to predict that this could happen only during the stance phase

and, to be more exact, only from the precise moment when the body's general center of mass passes over mid–stance through the end of support (Fig.53.2).

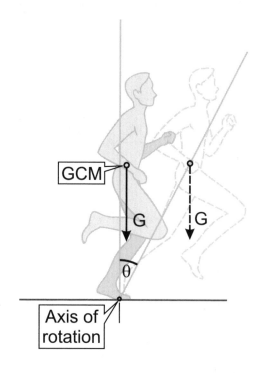

Fig.53.2 Forward rotation of the runner on support.

During this very short segment of the running cycle, the body moves forward by rotating around the point of support. Specifically, it is the runner's upper body (general center of mass) that moves forward relative to the foot fixed on the ground. Until the runner's body weight is on the ground, rotation, and therefore forward movement, of the body is possible. (The importance of body weight will be discussed shortly.)

During the time on support (i.e. when the foot is in contact with the ground), several different forces — gravity, ground reaction, muscle elasticity and muscular contraction — work together as a system (Fig.53.3).

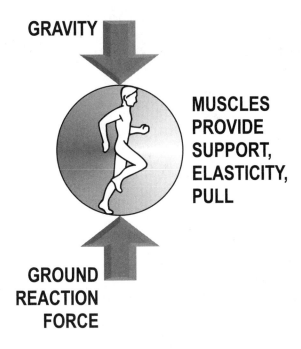

Fig.53.3 Forces in running as a system.

This system transforms gravity into energy through the body weight and support of muscles work. Body weight is an application of gravity through support. These forces could be represented by ground reaction force as a resultant vector and with directions and magnitudes in a geometrical form as a graphical model in order to visualize and understand their relationships. But this still lacks a clear explanation of how gravity directs these forces into the system that moves the body forward.

This requires several logical steps for us to understand how gravity interacts with the other forces during the second half of support and creates a resultant vector with a horizontal propulsive component. For this matter we'll consider some premises as well as visual and graphic images that would support this logic.

It Starts With A Ball Rolling Downhill

The first premise follows from a simple observation of the ball rolling on an inclined surface (Fig.53.4), compared with the falling forward movement in running. Basi-

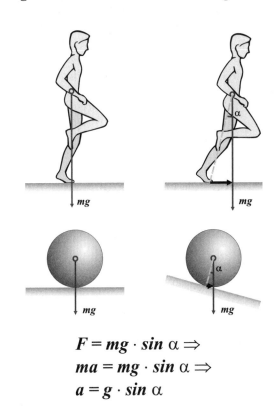

$$F = mg \cdot sin \, \alpha \Rightarrow$$
$$ma = mg \cdot sin \, \alpha \Rightarrow$$
$$a = g \cdot sin \, \alpha$$

Fig.53.4 Downhill/rolling ball model of running.

cally, the downhill velocity of the rolling body is a portion of the free falling body. This was an assumption in Galileo's study of the free falling body (7) where the acceleration of the body was related with the angle of the slope. As it was described by Isaac Asimov, "Galileo 'dilutes' the pull of gravity by having a brass ball roll down a groove in an inclined plane. Thus Galileo was able to study falling bodies in whatever degree of 'slow motion' he pleased" (7).

It is pretty clear that the ball could roll downhill only by gravitational force, which displaces the general center of mass of the ball relative to the point of support. The GCM of the ball on a flat surface can't be displaced horizontally from the stationary position, but on an inclined surface gravity, presented as body weight (mg), produces force (aka **gravitational torque**) that rotates the ball downhill, proportional to the angular deviation of GCM from the point of support equal to the angle of the slope. Magnitude of this force and acceleration produced by gravitational torque could be calculated from following equations:

$F = mg \cdot \sin\alpha$, **(1)** where F=ma, so equation (1) could be written as:

$ma = mg \cdot \sin\alpha$ **(2)** and then by extracting **m** from both parts:

$$a = g \cdot \sin\alpha$$

This model allows the assumption that from a certain body position we can use effect of gravity to perform work in a horizontal direction. Obviously the ball can't get GCM displacement on a flat surface — it needs a declining slope — but a runner can simulate a slope by leaning forward and putting his general center of mass in a falling position. This is the first step in understanding how gravity can work as a horizontal propulsive force.

Looking back at figure 53.4, you quickly notice that it represents exactly the situation described by da Vinci, "The faster a man runs, the more he leans towards the place to which he runs and gives more of

his weight in front of his axis of balance than behind" (3).

Another example supporting the same idea is the motion of a pendulum returning to the balanced position (after deviation) by gravitational force (Fig.53.5).

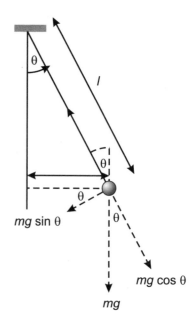

$mg \sin\theta$

$mg \cos\theta$

mg

Fig.53.5 Obtaining an expression for the period of a simple pendulum (8).

Gravitational force accelerates mass 'm' in a direction of the decreasing angle θ, so we can say that:

$$mg \sin\theta = -ma$$
$$g \sin\theta = -a$$
$$g\theta = -a$$

Therefore we can see that acceleration is proportional to the angular displacement θ (8). These two examples enable us to assume that this logic could be applied to the runner moving from mid–stance to the end of support.

The Importance of Leaning Forward

This assumption is the basis for the hypothesis that the forward displacement of the runner's body is determined by the geometry of the falling body on support. More precisely, by the angle of the body (from the general center of mass to the point of support) leaning forward from the vertical (what we call the Pose stance or Running Pose) until the end of support.

From this point of view the horizontal movement (acceleration) of the runner's body is a function of the angle of deviation of the body from its vertical position, and therefore is a function of the **gravitational torque** as well, which is formed by vectors of gravity and ground reaction force (Fig.53.6).

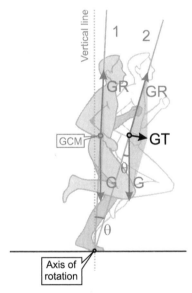

Gravitational Torque (GT) is a resultant force of Gravity (G) and Ground Reaction force (GR)
$GT = G \cdot \sin\theta = mg \cdot \sin\theta$, where
$G = mg = const.$

Fig.53.6 Gravitational Torque.

This analysis of the geometric relations of the vectors of forces in running confirms the hypothesis of the leading role of gravity in the forward movement of the runner. It further explains why support in running ceases at a certain angle of deviation of the body from its vertical position. Thus, while on support the muscles do not work after the mid–stance to push the body forward, but only serve to transfer the downward pull of gravity into horizontal movement.

It is necessary to show the arrows of horizontal and vertical components of ground reaction force.

In figure 53.7 below there are two systems of coordinates or systems of reference. The origin of the first one is the foot placement on the ground as the pivotal point of the body rotation, with the vertical (GRv) and horizontal (GRh) components of ground reaction force (GR). The origin of the sec-

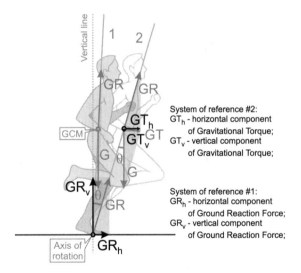

System of reference #2:
GT_h - horizontal component of Gravitational Torque;
GT_v - vertical component of Gravitational Torque;

System of reference #1:
GR_h - horizontal component of Ground Reaction Force;
GR_v - vertical component of Ground Reaction Force;

Fig.53.7 Ground reaction force and gravitational torque.

ond system of coordinates is at the GCM of the body, where Ground Reaction (GR) and gravity (G) have become the components of Gravitational Torque (R). From this system of coordinates, we can see how gravity — without changing its direction and magnitude (in accordance with classical mechanics) — creates a horizontal propulsive component.

By taking the position #2 of the body for vectors analysis (Fig.53.7, position #2,) it is possible to represent the gravitational torque as the result of the ground reaction and gravity vectors. The vector product (9) of any two vectors **A** x **B** is defined as the third vector **C, where A is a Ground Reaction (GR) force, B is Gravity (G) and C is the resultant vector (R),** the magnitude of which is AB $sin\theta$, where the angle θ is the angle between **A** and **B**. That is, if C is given by:

$$\mathbf{C} = |\mathbf{A}| \times |\mathbf{B}| \quad (1)$$

Then its magnitude is:

$$|\mathbf{C}| = |\mathbf{A}||\mathbf{B}| \, sin\theta \quad (2)$$
$$or$$
$$|\mathbf{R}| = |\mathbf{GR}||\mathbf{G}| \, sin\theta \quad (3)$$

From these equations we have one simple assumption: the resultant vector (R) is a derivative of two other vectors — gravity and ground reaction. While gravity pulls the body downward with a constant rate (g = 9.81 m/s²), ground reaction force pushes the body off the ground in nearly the opposite direction. The resultant vector (R) represents the moving body in rotational motion around the point of support, and during this motion the GCM of runner moves in the horizontal direction as well.

The nature of this motion can be understood better after analysis of the horizontal and vertical components of the resultant vector (Fig.53.8) during the leaning forward phase from the vertical (Pose stance) to the

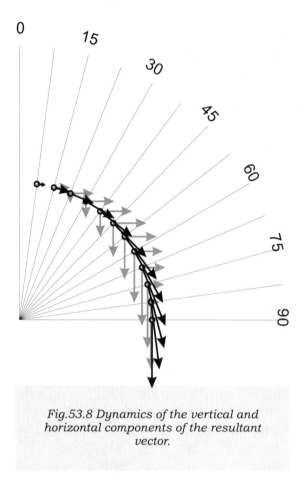

Fig.53.8 Dynamics of the vertical and horizontal components of the resultant vector.

end of support. We have to understand that the magnitudes of the components of the resultant vector change according to the change of the resultant vector angle, which in turn changes according to the angle of the runner's body leaning forward. Through the dynamics of falling forward to a certain angle, the horizontal component prevails over the vertical component. Past that certain angle, the relationship reverses with the vertical prevailing over the horizontal.

The complete dynamic of these parameters is evident on the graph (Fig.53.9) illustrating the falling rod model (10). We modeled the process of the rod falling from its vertical position on support with a graphic analysis of the dynamics of the vectors of the forces involved in this movement (body weight, ground reaction, resultant force) and their components.

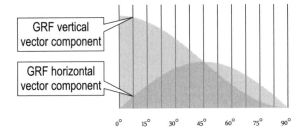

Fig.53.9 Dynamics of horizontal and vertical components of the ground reaction vector.

The falling rod model allowed us to see changes in the values of these forces depending on the changing angle of deviation of GCM from the vertical. Thus, when the angle of deviation of the rod changed from its vertical position to its complete fall, the values of horizontal components of ground reaction (Fig.53.9) and resultant vectors (Fig.53.10) changed in the form of a

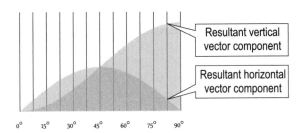

Fig.53.10 Dynamics of horizontal and vertical components of the resultant vector.

bell curve from zero at its vertical position to maximum at 45° angle and went back down to zero at 0° angle.

The dynamics of the vertical components of the same vectors of forces looked completely different, with a constant increase from minimum at the vertical position to maximum at 0° degrees for the resultant vector and the same mirror–like symmetrical increase of the vector of ground reaction.

22.5° is the Magic Number

Of the greatest interest were the dynamics of the interrelationship between the horizontal and vertical components of the resultant vector, shown as the difference between the components for every angle of deviation (Fig.53.11). As shown on this graph, the maximal prevalence of the horizontal component occurs at the 22.5° angle from the vertical or 67.5° from horizontal axis, after which the vertical component starts to dominate until the end of falling.

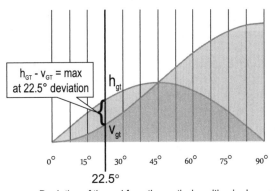

Fig.53.11 Dynamic of horizontal and vertical components of the resultant vector.

The end of dominance of the horizontal component at the 22.5° angle means that there is no need to stay on support any longer in order to have the maximum effect of this component and therefore support should be ended at this point. This theoretical conclusion was supported by research of R. Margaria (11), who found that "the minimal angle necessary to prevent the foot slipping back in compact soil" should have a value of 63.5° or 26.5° from the vertical.

This angle is close to our findings, even though our premises were built from an entirely different point-of-view. The main thing in our study was the angle at which the horizontal component of gravitational torque lost domination over the vertical component. Following this logic, the 22.5° angle fundamentally presents the maximum opportunity for gravity to do its work in a horizontal direction through vector relationships. This relationship between horizontal and vertical components defines the point when the body rotation on support should be ended, because after this point the body starts to move downward more than forward.

Theoretically, the 22.5° angle of deviation is a characteristic of the absolute maximal speed in sprinting. We are not discussing the unique case of acceleration from a resting condition where this same logic applies in another manner. At lower speeds the angles of deviation from the vertical position are commensurately lower as well. Figure 53.12 shows the maximal angle of deviation on support of Britain's 400-meter runner Lisa Miller to be approximately 16° degrees. At all distances, from longest to shortest, and at all speeds, from slowest to fastest, all running takes place inside the range of 22.5° between the 90° of the Pose stance and 67.5° relative to the horizontal.

For example, a recreational runner who runs ten kilometers in 50 minutes typically has 10° degrees of forward lean (deviation)** , whereas Ethiopia's former 5K and 10K World Record holder Haile Gebrselassie maintains roughly 16° degrees, depending on his speed. There is a corresponding cadence rate of running, related to the angle of deviation and speed, which we'll discuss shortly.

This brings up the question of why the end of support coincides with a certain speed and angle? Does the runner do it deliberately by knowing where the push-off is supposed to happen at a given speed and angle or is there another logical explanation?

Push Versus Pull

The first part of this question about the runner pushing off at a specific angle and speed can't be considered seriously. The current paradigm of running maintains that the "push-off" is a key component of forward propulsion, but it is difficult to even imagine, much less explain, how a runner could know when or where to push-off based on precise data like running speed and angle of inclination. There is no system of feedback that would give a runner that kind of information step after step. When and where the runner should push-off remains a completely blurry consideration, particularly in sprinting where the time on support is measured in the hundredths of seconds.

Seriously, is there a time to do the "action" of unbending the ankle, the knee, and the hip with precise timing and at the correct angle for each step while involving a number of muscles? Even if this could be done once, how could we explain doing that same action repetitively?

This is neither a rhetorical nor an easy question. It addresses a fundamental issue in running: do we need to "push-off" when we run? If so, how do we know when and how to push–off? This cuts right to the issue of how we move forward when we run.

In the Pose Method, the answer to these questions is very straightforward. Simply put, we can't regulate or even perform a "push–off" as it has traditionally been understood. The Pose concepts and the falling rod model help to explain the many uncertainties in running relating to the push–off.

To begin, Pose Method proposes the idea that the dominant force (in cooperation with other forces) moving us forward is gravity. As described above, the falling rod model explains the work of gravity. There is a limited range of space and time on support where our body falls forward during rotational motion around the support point from the vertical mid–stance (Running Pose), until the end of support. This falling forward range consists of *only* 22.5° degrees.

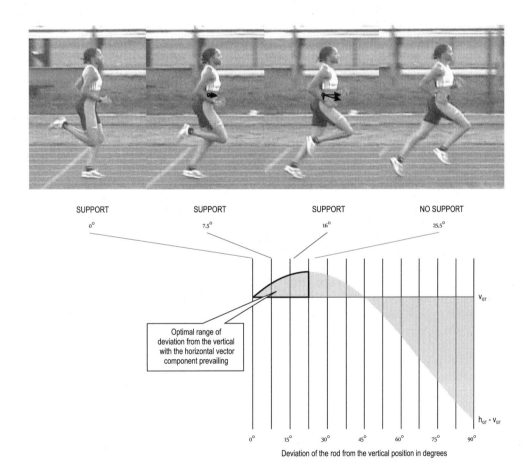

Fig.53.12 Maximum angle of deviation on support of Britain's 400–meter runner Lisa Miller appears to be approximately 16° degrees. All running takes place inside the range of 22.5° degrees, between the 90° of the Pose stance and 67.5° relative to the horizontal.

How does the runner determine where within this 22.5° degree range, support should be ended? Obviously, there are different distances and speeds in running all of which involve different time spent on support as well as varying efforts, cadence, and stride length. How do these variables relate to the end of support? Who or what defines the end of support?

It is convenient to say that this all relates to running speed and to a certain extent that would be the right answer. But according to Pose Method theory, running speed is a subordinated parameter, not the main one. Speed is a function of the body's angle of deviation from the vertical, which determines how much of gravity's force is used in the run. If the 22.5° angle of deviation is 100% of what we can utilize, then anything less than this angle will represent a certain percentage from the maximum attainable velocity.

One Body Weight — and Survival

The angle of deviation itself is not the reason to change support. No matter what the angle of deviation, and whatever speed of running that angle represents, our body's perception receives information more important and valuable than mere speed. This information is an undeniable sign of the necessity to end and change support — NOW!

This command comes from deep within our genetic code, on a cellular level, and is directly related to our survival instincts and the imperative to move, to change support. No living creature is free from this sign. It is not some mysterious sign from science fiction. It is the very real, very much from this Earth and very well known sign of **one body weight.**

Yes, it is all about the concept of one body weight. Not just a body weight, but one body weight. This is our boundary of sup-

port, our measure and our guide governing how we interact with support. This is the defining point telling us when to end and change support. No matter what distance and speed we are running, our perception of the support ends when the vertical ground reaction force drops below one body weight. Figure 53.13 illustrates this logic with the data of the ground reaction force of the runner with a body mass of 63 kilograms and a velocity of 9.5 m/s (12).

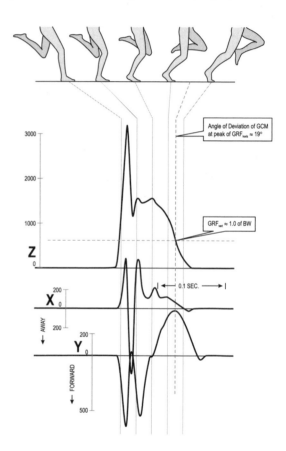

Force-time recording of a heel-toe runner (mass 63 kg, velocity 9.5 ms-1)
Payne, 1983; (p.748) Foot to ground contact forces in elite runners. In Biomechanics V111-B
(Edited by H. Matsui and K. Kobayashi), pp.19-41. Champaign, IL: Human Kinetics)

Fig.53.13. Ground reaction forces graphs. Adapted from Payne, 1983 (12).

This illustration allows us to compare the interesting interrelationships of five body positions with their corresponding vertical ground reaction forces (graph Z), and the propulsive parts of anterior–posterior ground reaction forces (graph Y). The peak of the propulsive horizontal component (the vertical dotted line) of ground reaction force coincides on the time line with one body weight (horizontal dotted line) on the graph of the vertical component of ground reaction force when the body is positioned on terminal stance on support. This means that one body weight is the absolute boundary of support. At this point, the runner's body stops its rotation around the point of support and stops falling forward in order to regain the vertical position during flight and prepare for the next forward fall.

There is an interesting combination of the body's angle of deviation during support and reaching the magnitude of one body weight in the vertical component of ground reaction force. The first parameter, the angle of deviation, potentially could be extended to the 22.5° angle. But this angle of deviation could be reached only if the vertical component of ground reaction force is greater than one body weight.

This is exactly what happens at any running speed from a slower pace to a full–out sprint. The perception of one body weight is the reason our body doesn't want to take full advantage of the 22.5° angle of deviation. Why? Because something critical and undeniable restricts the rotational acceleration of the body beyond this point. This restriction is the perception of the one body weight, which the brain not only recognizes, but also anticipates as a boundary in space and time of support. As the brain perceives the body approaching the boundary of one body weight, it feels the necessity to change the support in order to continue the forward movement of the body.

The **one body weight** is a standard of load or the pressure on the ground by the support foot while standing in a balanced position with no up or down movement (Fig.53.14). As living creatures, our perception of support, safety and reliability is precisely related to the body weight positioned on support. This perception is of **one body weight,** our internal standard that we have subconsciously developed and trained from the time of our births, and in all likelihood even before we were born.

ONE BODY WEIGHT
appears on support
when the body is at rest.

Fig.53.14 The running Pose, balance on one leg.

Knowledge of Physics Not Required

Without knowing any of the laws of physics we have an innate perception of gravity, body weight and support, all of which are associated indelibly with our physical safety and psychological and mental stability. **One body weight** has nothing to do with mass, kilograms, pounds or anything of the sort. It relates only to the perception of pressure by the feet. The brain perceives anything less than **one body weight** to be a deficiency of secure and safe support.

From day–to–day experience, we know how unpleasant and scary it is to experience an absence of support, which is related with having the one body weight securely on our feet. Any unexpected misstep that causes our body weight to lose support causes instant panic and forces our entire organism to desperately search for, and regain, the lost support.

So the body's deviation from the vertical is not the only form of deviation here, but instead it is interconnected with the body weight's deviation as well. In running, as the runner's body leans forward the magnitude of the vertical ground reaction force drops from two or three body weights to one, after which support is ended.

While the body could deviate further from the point of support, the perception of **one body weight** decreasing signals that support is over. It is a feeling very much like we experience when we descend rapidly in an elevator of a high–rise building and we feel like we are losing our weight and support. This same feeling governs our action to end support during — a "disappearance" of the body weight on support. Since **one body weight** is the boundary of support, when the present support is less than one body weight, the body feels that it must immediately find the next support. This is the main biological essence, sense, and meaning of **one body weight.**

Adapting to Our Environment

The material world in which we live, our environment, affects us through our senses and perceptions (13) giving form and definition to our thoughts, desires and actions (14). Without question, we are the products of the world that surrounds us. Like it or not, we live in a state of constant interaction with this world, never being free from

its influence at any point in our existence. The best we can do is to adapt to it by better understanding how to interact with our environment in the most efficient possible manner.

In running, this adaptation involves the mechanical and geometrical structure of movement and that structure's effects on our sensory system. As we run, the changes to our current position in time and space are constantly evaluated by our psychological and perceptive systems, which determine the necessity to change support.

Based on this continuous evaluation, the brain, as the main organ of perception, gives the command to "abort" support. But this rarely happens without a complication, the ongoing conflict between the conscious and subconscious mind. On the one hand, the subconscious mind is trying to end support because one body weight is no longer there and the next action of pulling the foot from the ground under the hip must be done in order to organize the body position (Pose) to alternate to the next support.

But while the subconscious is trying to do the right thing, the conscious mind has other ideas. Instead of working to lift the foot from support, the conscious mind is preoccupied with the other foot, the one about to hit the ground. Why? This conflict happens for exactly the same reason we discussed above — safety. This is because the conscious mind associates being on support with security.

This creates something of a missing link in the chain of action that should be pulling the lagging foot up under the hip before the next foot strike. The mind can do tricky things. When it should be concentrating on most essential task — ending support — it abandons the support foot and switches attention to the landing foot.

It's like switching from the past to the future without finishing the present action. Our physical presence is a body weight. When our body is on support all our mental, psychological, and physiological functions are attached to, and work to serve, the body weight. Our body weight makes "arrangements" for all these functions in space and time, coordinating their interaction.

The law of one body weight illuminates the "extensor paradox" (15). There is a logical and neurological link between the activity of extensor muscles and the magnitude of ground reaction force. At the instant the vertical component of ground reaction force reaches its peak, the runner's body starts falling forward. As soon as that happens, the need to use the extensor muscles to support the body isn't just reduced, it completely disappears.

Falling forward as a dominating movement of the body simply doesn't require any activity from the extensor muscles. Moreover, their activity, as muscles that extend the joints of the legs, actually compromises the ability of the body to fall forward.

Seen in this light, what we call the "extensor's paradox" is really the evolutionary means by which biological creatures (humans and animals) adapted to the gravitational environment on Earth. In layman's terms, gravity just commands deactivation of these muscles in order to take over the function of forward propulsion.

This also explains why astronauts on the Moon can't walk and run the same way they do on Earth (11). Since the Moon has only one sixth of the gravitational force of Earth, it also has a proportionally reduced horizontal component of gravitational torque. You would think that the strength of your muscles working against reduced gravitational pull would let you run faster, but just the opposite is the case. This alone is evidence that muscles are not playing the role that we have traditionally ascribed to them.

Cadence and Stride Length

Taking things a step further, the geometry of running lets us examine the relationship between cadence and stride length (16).

Cadence or stride frequency is a key parameter in sustaining the rate of falling in running. The faster the body falls forward, the higher the rate at which it loses balance and needs to change support, which in turn leads to the logical action of pulling the foot from the ground faster. The importance of the pulling action increases as the running speed gets faster, because the rates of falling and losing balance get faster as well.

In other words, you don't move your feet faster in order to run faster; you move your feet faster to avoid falling because your forward lean is making your body and your general center of mass move faster.

Of necessity, this logical sequence requires a well-developed muscular system to support these functions of falling, pulling and changing support. There are three major muscle groups related with efficiency of these functions: the hips muscles for falling, the hamstrings for pulling the foot from the ground and muscle–tendon elasticity (springiness) for moving body weight from support.

Our first assumption, subsequently confirmed by experiential data, is that stride length is directly proportional to the angle of falling with a correction for leg length, which is the radius of rotation of the falling body. Said more simply, stride length is a derivative of the angle of falling and leg length.

How exactly does this happen? Classical mechanics and geometry give us a very simple explanation. During the rotational movement of the body (Fig.53.15) on support, the angular velocity translates into the linear velocity of the general center of mass as expressed by the equation: v=rω where 'v' is linear velocity, 'r' is the radius of rotation (leg length) and ω is the angular velocity of a given rotation (ω= θ/t), where "θ" is the angle of deviation of the body from the vertical, and "t" is the time of passing through that angle.

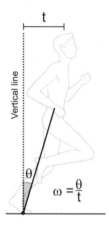

Fig.53.15. Translation of angular velocity of the GCM, into linear velocity.

From the falling rod model, it follows that the angular acceleration of the rod from vertical to horizontal is the function of the angle of deviation. This means that on support during the body's rotation from the vertical position (mid–stance or Running Pose) a runner can't do anything to increase this rotation; it is completely the prerogative of the gravitational torque.

From this equation, we can see that linear velocity defines the distance the general center of mass covers on the ground and in the air. (It's worth repeating at this point that in the traditional running paradigm,

the linear velocity of the general center of mass on support is the function of a push–off coming from ground reaction force and muscular efforts to extend the major joints of the leg from support.) The greater the angle of falling and length of the leg, the bigger the acceleration will be (a = g·sinθ) and therefore the linear velocity of the GCM will increase accordingly. Certainly this velocity developed on support during falling is extended on flight and landing time until the next Pose on the opposite leg. Therefore, increasing the angle of falling provides higher and higher linear velocity of the body.

This increase in the angle of deviation leads to the longer stride length, but it doesn't exceed the length related to the critical angle of 22.5° degrees. Again, the role of the muscles during falling is to provide support and rigidity of the body in order to fall better, quickly return the body to the vertical position in order to change support, and pull the foot from the ground. This latter function, as was mentioned above, is accomplished by muscle/tendon elasticity components and the voluntary contraction of the muscles responsible for removing the support foot from the ground.

And to put this in context, it's the same as with your cadence rate. You don't take longer strides in order to run faster; your strides are longer, because you are running faster. Higher cadence and longer strides are the result, not the cause, of faster forward movement.

Intelligent Design or Evolution — It's All The Same

No matter whether you believe in an omniscient creator or trust in Darwin's Theory of Evolution, it is clear that humans, like all living beings, are adaptive creatures. A good chunk of what separates humans from the other living beings on this planet is the hubris, the unyielding belief that mankind can improve on nature.

Give or take a few centuries, mankind has been walking erect for four million years and making some kind of shoes for anywhere from 26,000 to 40,000 years. Shoes specifically made for running have been manufactured since the 1890's, with 'jogging' shoes making their appearance about 40 years ago.

While it has certainly been clever of mankind to develop shoes that facilitated the migration to colder climates and there are few that would argue against the comfort of a fine sneaker or running shoe, the fact is that gravity holds about a four million years lead in molding mankind to the environment here on Earth.

In humanity's development, running was a key component of survival. With gravity operating as the unyielding force that it is, man's running style was molded, shaped and dictated by his interaction with gravity. That's something that simply can't be erased by a hundred years of building 'running' shoes.

Landing on your heel, rolling across the foot and pushing off from the toes just aren't how gravity molded man to run. And without a big fat cushion at the heel of your shoe, you wouldn't even try it. No matter how much we like our running shoes they have failed to improve on the design that nature — in the form of gravity — developed for running.

The answer to every question you have about running technique is found in man's relationship with gravity. Gravity built man into a running machine with a muscle, bone, connective tissue and cardiopulmonary structure designed to go fast or go for miles. Where to plant your foot, which muscles to use and how to use them, when to change support, when to work and when to let gravity take over — all the instructions to successful running have been engineered into your DNA.

To become the best runner you can be, all you have to do is to look to nature — and gravity — and heed the lessons that are found there. You'll run further, faster and injury free and enjoy it all a lot more.

References:

1. Marey, E.J. *Movement.* Arno Press & The New York Times. New York. 1972.

2. Ashby, W.R. *Systems and Their Informational Measures.* In. G.J.Klir (Ed.), *Trends in General Systems Theory.* New York: John Wiley & Sons, 1972, p. 95.

3. Keele, K.D. *Leonardo da Vinci's Elements of the Science of Man.* New York: Academic Press, 1983, p. 173.

4. Graham–Brown, T. *Note on some dynamic principles involved in progression.* British Medical Journal, 1912, pp. 875–876.

5. Hay, J.G. and Reid, J.G. *Anatomy, mechanics, and human motion.* Englewood Cliffs: Prentice–Hall, 1988, p. 282.

6. Gershenzon, E. and *Malov, N. Kurs obschei fisiki (General Physics Course).* Prosveschenie (Education). Moscow, 1987, p. 362.

7. Asimov, I. *The Intelligent Man's Guide to Science.* Vol. 2, Basics Books, Inc. New York, 1960, p. 748.

8. Dobson, K., Grace, D. and Lovett, D. *Physics.* Collins, 2001, p. 119.

9. Zatziorsky, V.M. *Kinematics of Human Motion.* Human Kinetics, 1998, pp. 9, 10.

10. Romanov, N. and Pianzin, A. *Geometry of running // Book of Abstracts of the 11th Annual Congress of the European College of Sport Science.* Lausanne, 2006, p. 582.

11. Margaria, R. *Biomechanics and Energetics of Muscular Exercise.* Oxford University Press, 1976, pp. 127–128.

12. Payne, A.H. *Foot to ground contact forces in elite runners. In Biomechanics.* Vol. 111–B, Human Kinetics, Champaign, IL, 1983, pp. 19–41.

13. Bateson, G. *The Mind and Nature. Necessary Unity.* Bantam New Age Books, 1980, p. 29.

14. Aristotle. *Movement of Animals. The Complete Works of Aristotle.* Jonathan Barnes, Editor. Vol. 1, Princeton University Press, Sixth Printing, 1995, p. 1087.

15. McClay, I.S., Lake, M.J. and Cavanagh, P.R. *The Extensor Paradox Experiment. In Biomechanics of Distance Running.* Cavanagh, Editor. Human Kinetics Books, 1990, pp. 179–186.

16. Hoffman, K. *Stature, Leg Length, and Stride Frequency, Track Technique.* Edition 46, Dec 1971, pp. 1463–69.

17. Alexander, R.M. *Principles of Animal Locomotion.* Princeton University Press, 2003, p. 59.

* Neutral force is the force perpendicular to the movement of the body.

** Forward lean is the angle between vertical line from the point of support and the line connecting this point of support with the GCM of the body.

Systems — are wholly composed of related parts, between which interaction occurs to a major degree.

ABOUT THE AUTHORS

Dr. Nicholas Romanov is a world class Olympic coach, author, educator and sport scientist with over 30 years of experience and hands–on work with athletes of all levels, specializing in sport biomechanics, kinesiology, sports training theory and physical education, exercise physiology and injury diagnosis, prevention and rehabilitation.

He started his science studies at the Central Scientific Research Institute of Physical Culture in Moscow in the laboratory of the renowned Soviet Union sport scientist and coach, Professor Vladimir Diachkov. After receiving his Ph.D. in Physical Education from the Russian Academy of Physical Culture and Sports in Moscow, Dr. Romanov advanced to become the Head of the Department of Sport Disciplines, Head Track and Field Coach, and senior lecturer of Sport Biomechanics, Theory and Practice of Physical Education and Sport Training, Theory and Practice of Track and Field.

In the mid–70's, long before coming to the United States, Dr. Romanov developed and successfully implemented the Pose Method® which proved that movement efficiency and athletic performance were dependent upon correct technique in running, jumping and throwing (track and field), swimming, cycling, gymnastics, speed skating, cross–country skiing and many other athletic events. It was during the 1990's that he came to America, becoming the first scientist to integrate this system of movement into his training work with runners.

Dr. Romanov has worked with members of several National Teams, including the United States, Great Britain, Russia and Mexico. He successfully coached the British Triathlon National Team to the 2000 Olympics in Sydney and 2004 Olympics in Athens. He also served as a member of the USA Triathlon Coaching Committee from 1996 to 2002. Scientific research supporting the Pose Method® has been conducted at the USA Olympic Training Center in Colorado Springs (G. Dallam, 1998), Florida Atlantic University (C. Sol, 2000), Cape Town University, South Africa (T. Noakes, 2002), Kubansky State University, Russia (A. Pianzin, 2003) and Sheffield Hallam University, UK (G. Fletcher, 2006).

In 1997 he released his first educational video "The Pose Method of Running," and in 2002 he published his first book "The Pose Method of Running," both international best–sellers. Dr. Romanov currently conducts clinics and seminars all over the world while continuing his extensive scientific research and work with world class athletes from different countries in Triathlon and Track and Field.

Dr. Romanov resides with his wife, Dr. Svetlana Romanov, and two sons, Severin and Nicholas Jr., in Miami, Florida. Their daughter, Svetlana Jr., and granddaughter, Sophia, reside in the same city.

Since the publication of the *Pose Method of Running*, co–author John Robson has relocated to a remote stretch of Central Florida beach near Sebastian Inlet, often called "America's Ultimate Surf Park." Living in a 'tree house' with a distant ocean view, Robson takes full advantage of not only the waves, but also the local network of trails alongside the Indian River Lagoon and Atlantic Ocean. As he worked to complete the final copy of the manuscript of the *Pose Method of Triathlon*, he ran and mountain biked the trails, swam in the open ocean and rode with the local road peloton, all the while field–testing the theories and concepts developed and articulated by Dr. Romanov.

Now 56, Robson travels regularly to a number of active sports Mecca's, making near–annual trips to the Tour de France; surfing locations in Costa Rica, Mexico, the Dominican Republic among others; and still carving out time to ride the road climbs in Georgia, Tennessee, the Carolinas and the Virginias or raft the occasional white water river. Many of these adventures, often shared with wife Gay and daughter Jane, wind up chronicled in the pages of *Competitor Southeast* magazine, for which he remains a frequent contributor. Against his better judgment, he also manages to squeeze in a few *Xterra* off road triathlons every year and fills in the odd open weekend with running or cycling events.

When not otherwise occupied, Robson is partnered in a New Jersey–based online marketing firm with clients in the cable television, music, publishing and consumer brands industries, making him a frequent flyer, both in the air and on the spectacular cycling routes along the New Jersey Palisades. All of which has made it increasingly difficult to launch his newest enterprise, *A Surfing Life*®, which is designed to be the next evolution of the traditional surf shop.